Perfect Pitch

Joe Price is a professor at Whittier College. I launched a professional baseball career from the same Whittier College. My career spanned through six decades. It took me to at least eighty of the stadiums where Joe sang the national anthem. In fact, I've heard him sing the song! Beyond the song, however, are the stories that go with his remarkable odyssey. They are stories I lived in part over my fifty years in major and minor league baseball. They are stories I never wrote about but stories my friends back home are always dying to hear over a round of beers. *Perfect Pitch* is a timeless piece of history and American culture, and it's fun to read!

— Jim Colborn, professional baseball player, coach, and scout—MLB, Japan, and Australia

Perfect Pitch is many things, but above all it's a celebration; a celebration of baseball, a celebration of America, and a celebration of song. Joe Price's anthemic account of his epic RV journey is by equal turns warm, funny, and educational. Rarely has the weird and wide-ranging world of minor league baseball been so well illuminated.

—Ben Hill, ballpark traveler and blogger (bensbiz.mlblogs.com)

Some of the most rewarding perks of playing professional baseball were traveling around to the different towns, meeting new people, and taking in all the history along the way. Joe Price captures in great detail the history and uniqueness of each ballpark where he sang the national anthem. He also brings to life the people he encountered along his journey. *Perfect Pitch* is sure to make you smile and bring out the patriotism in us all.

—Ila Borders, former minor league professional baseball player and author of *Making My Pitch*

A whale of a read! It's not often you can find a book that uses the word *omphalos* correctly, and also can catch the gap-toothed smile of a girl with her first foul ball. Joe Price takes us on a quintessentially American journey singing the national anthem in 109 ballparks across the country. But what makes it a great read are his observations of the players, fans, officials, family members, former students, and colleagues he meets along the way.

—Andy McCue, author of Seymour Medal-winning *Mover and Shaker: Walter O'Malley, the Dodgers, and Baseball's Westward Expansion.*

A perfect portrait of an America that still exists and thrives, and is the best of us. It's the ultimate American road trip—over 100 churches of baseball where all political partisanship is traded for rooting for the home team. *Perfect Pitch* is the perfect antidote to what ails us; a tour of baseball's minor leagues where the game is still fun, the dreams are still real, and the fans can touch the players while eating cheap popcorn in $8 box seats.

— Ron Shelton, writer/director of *Bull Durham*

MERCER UNIVERSITY

MERCER UNIVERSITY PRESS

Endowed by

TOM WATSON BROWN

and

THE WATSON-BROWN FOUNDATION, INC.

Perfect Pitch

The National Anthem for the National Pastime

Joseph L. Price

Mercer University Press | Macon, Georgia

2018

MUP/ P565

Published by Mercer University Press
1501 Mercer University Drive
Macon, Georgia 31207

9 8 7 6 5 4 3 2 1

Books published by Mercer University Press are printed on acid-free paper that meets the requirements of the American National Standard for Information Sciences—Permanence of Paper for Printed Library Materials.

Printed and bound in the United States.

This book is set in Adobe Caslon (text) and American Typewriter (display).

ISBN 978-0-88146-656-0
Cataloging-in-Publication Data is available from the Library of Congress

A Note to the Reader

While the reader can follow the route of my performances by reading the narrative in consecutive order, the alphabetical roster at the end of the book allows one to easily locate and read the sections about familiar teams, ballparks, and their communities.

The stories about each ballpark experience draw upon personal observations, information gleaned from ballpark signage and team publications distributed at the games, notes recorded about conversations, game reports and team histories posted on team websites (each clearly linked to www.milb.com), Internet searches for background material, and player data accessed on www.baseball-reference.com. When quoting from specific works or citing proprietary information, I have included attribution within the narrative itself. Supplemental sources related to teams, minor-league histories, and ballpark facts and lore are identified in a brief section at the end of the book.

To Bonnie—
whose support made the anthem tour possible,
whose voice enlivened the journey,
and whose love inspires me to sing.

Contents

Introduction

Warming Up

During a single summer season, I crossed America singing our song, our star-spangled anthem, our ballad about hard-earned rights, hard fought and hard argued. Wherever and everywhere, "The Star-Spangled Banner" signified liberty for me.

In all, I sang the national anthem to celebrate America's freedoms and baseball in more than 100 minor league ballparks in forty states stretching from Lake Elsinore's Storm in Southern California to New Hampshire's FisherCats in Manchester, and from Everett's AquaSox in the Pacific Northwest all the way to Jupiter, where the Hammerheads make their home in Florida. I sang it in urban settings in Memphis and Sacramento, in remote cities across Idaho and Iowa, and in tiny towns throughout Appalachia and along the mighty Mississippi.

Baseball Love and Anthem Passion

I love America: the personal freedoms that it affords, the incredible possibilities that it embraces, the energies and anxieties of its cities, the languages and lores of its citizens, the arts and activities of its diverse peoples, the varieties of its flora from the bluegrass hills of Kentucky to the hanging-moss avenues of Savannah, and the grandeur of its landscapes stretching from the Blue Ridge Mountains all the way to Chimney Rock.

Another of my greatest loves is America's game—baseball. I thrive on the game itself, whether played by kids on dirt fields in city parks or by grown men making millions in cathedral-esque structures often erected with public funds. Yet in both contrasting spaces—in fact, on all diamonds—players try to hit the same-size ball between foul lines that stretch farther than their dreams. I am fascinated by the momentary uncertainty of a dying bunt fading toward the chalk, the ballet of a second-baseman's leaping pirouette on a 6-4-3 double play, and the slide of a runner at home attempting to evade a sweeping tag.

While the dramatic elements of baseball's play attest the game's complex lure, its certain sounds also prove enthralling: the *crack* of the barrel of the bat squarely crushing a twisting, elusive round ball; the dejected curse of a batter following a called third strike; the *thwhop* of an infielder's fist repounding his glove, anticipating the ball being hit to him; the simple *splat* of a rosin bag thrown to the mound by a frustrated pitcher; and the tongue-speaking ebullience of teammates following a walk-off winner. I thrill to the sights and sounds of the game and to the anthem sung in its honor.

Even before learning to read, I loved to swing a bat and watch a baseball game. For my summer birthday before first grade, my mother sewed a baseball uniform that I proudly wore months later for the class photo with our teacher, Miss Prassel. My smile, broader than those of most of my classmates, displayed my deeper love for baseball than my heartfelt crush on Miss Prassel, to whom I proposed marriage before the year's end.

During schoolboy summers in Mississippi, I daily tuned the kitchen radio to afternoon broadcasts of Mutual Radio's "Game of the Day," and often on Saturdays I went to my friend Bubba's house to watch the "Game of the Week" since my family didn't own a television set. Frequently, I spent my entire weekly allowance on wax-packs of baseball cards. Hours after hours I feasted on the data displayed on their gray sides, or I traded multiples of Eli Grba with friends for a star player missing on my checklist, or I juxtaposed a Topps lineup with the players' probability cards in the Strat-o-Matic game. Seemingly by osmosis, I absorbed the history and hope that I held in each card the perfect size of a boy's hand.

Daily I pored over box scores to learn which players were hot, and on one April Fools' Day I cried when I read a sports-page hoax that Mickey Mantle had been traded for Ted Williams. (I had neglected to notice the story's byline: I. M. Lyon.) My love of the game extended beyond fascination with heroes far away and their ephemeral, statistical identities. With my earnings from mowing lawns, I attempted to elevate my own status by purchasing a catcher's mitt and face mask so that I could squat like Yogi and appear to be an unlikely baseball star.

As an early adolescent, I also keenly anticipated almost every chance to attend games, whether weekly church league softball contests or a rare major league game in St. Louis or Chicago whose schedule was coordinated with one of my family's summer vacation trips. During college years in Kentucky, my fraternity brothers and I pursued outings to see the Reds in old Crosley Field, and during grad school in Chicago, I often tuned to WGN to catch Cubs home games when I couldn't carve out a full afternoon to cheer among Wrigley Field's bleacher bums. When I began my professorial career in

Whittier, I enjoyed being equidistant from Dodger Stadium and the Big A in Anaheim. Each move provided new possibilities to follow nearby teams and attend their games.

Conveying my love of baseball to my two school-age sons, Jared and David, I spent countless summer evenings with them watching games and, as often as possible, going to ballparks. Routinely at Dodger Stadium the boys found different ways to heighten their fascination with the game. Jared cherished souvenirs, especially authentic ones like the batting-practice foul ball that we retrieved off the bat of Rick Dempsey and the bat handed to him by John Shelby following a Dodgers win. By contrast, David was drawn to every concession stand to try to sample each of its sweet snacks, and he was wowed by the chance to punch a Major League Baseball (MLB) All-Star ballot after each out, making sure to vote for Red Sox players, especially his favorite, Mike Greenwell. His early solidarity with Red Sox Nation surely signaled his independence from me, a devout Yankees fan almost since birth.

From our seats at Dodger Stadium, both boys became accustomed to hearing me sing the national anthem along with the featured performer, and occasionally they beamed when fans would turn to applaud and suggest that I should sing it on the field.

My foray into singing the national anthem for the national pastime had begun during grad school when Bill Veeck gave me the opportunity to sing for the White Sox at old Comiskey Park on Fan Appreciation Day in 1977. For the next decade I had thought that that on-field performance had been a once-in-a-lifetime experience, but in 1989 I got my first chance to sing on the field for a game at Dodger Stadium following a conversation with Hall of Famer Don Sutton.

Because Sutton, who had begun his career with the Dodgers, had taken courses at Whittier College during sessions between the World Series and spring training, he agreed to support a fundraising initiative for one of the college's programs by offering at silent auction the opportunity for a small group to join him for an on-campus lunch. Fortunately, Jared, David, and I joined a dozen other fans to spend the afternoon talking baseball with the strike-out artist. I'm not sure what prompted Jared to tell Sutton that occasionally I had embarrassed him by singing the anthem loudly from our seats in the stands, but he added that the one time that I had sung on the field for the White Sox, he had been a newborn at home with a babysitter. Sutton pursued a few questions with me and then offered specific encouragement by rattling off the Dodgers' phone number and urging me to call, indicate his personal recommendation, and request an opportunity to sing. Hurriedly I wrote the Dodger Stadium office number on a napkin.

First thing the following morning, I called the Dodgers, mentioned Sutton's suggestion with each transfer of the call, and finally reached an office assistant who politely indicated I would need to send a cassette recording to her boss. Undeterred, I hustled over to the college's music department, explained the situation to Danny Lozano (a faculty colleague and a Grammy Award-winning jazz flautist), and persuaded him to set up recording equipment in the college chapel, which enjoys resonant acoustics. Before the end of the day, I cut the audition tape and sent it to the Dodgers with a cover letter again pointing out Sutton's recommendation. Within days, the team offered me a chance to perform, and my unusual hobby started to take shape: singing "The Star-Spangled Banner" for baseball games.

During the next two decades, while I began to check off more than twenty major league ballparks on my national anthem bucket list, a number of my faculty colleagues accompanied me to games when I performed in various cities. Frequently they suggested ways for me to do more with my anthem avocation. So when Fred Bergerson, who had seen me sing at Camden Yards, read a blurb about a fervent fan crisscrossing the country to see a game in every professional ballpark in a single season, he quipped, "Joe, you should sing in all of them." I retorted simply that I needed to finish the major league circuit before taking a swing at such a ludicrous project.

But Fred's quick remark stuck in my mind.

Presented with the prospect for a sabbatical leave in the year following my wife Bonnie's retirement, I broached the idea to her of trying to sing my way across the nation's minor league ballparks. She thought that the idea was wacky, and a few close colleagues deemed it infeasible but fascinating. When I shared my dream of this great American road trip with two other friends in American studies, they excitedly offered to join me for parts of the journey. They recognized that little would be more distinctly American than making a summer road trip across country fueled by baseball passion and patriotic fervor.

"What could be more fun?" I wondered.

Not much. Except making the entire journey with my closest friend and catching up with scores and scores of friends along the way.

But there's the catch. My wife is my closest friend. While she had accepted my passion for baseball when I had proposed marriage to her decades before, seriously proposing this project to her involved a catch-22.

Bonnie isn't a baseball fan.

Thinking of my dream trip as a months-long nightmare, she envisioned spending her first free spring following retirement in Rome, Italy, at the Colosseum, not in Rome, Georgia, at the Braves ballpark. But when a group of her friends started to talk excitedly about the chance to see the country, sample local cultures, and visit with multiple friends and family in so many different places, she began to soften her attitude. When another friend offered to sell us her RV and tow car, the prospect took on an adventurous allure since an RV could relieve the daily chore of hotel check-ins, strange beds, and constant restaurant food. It also offered a chance to decorate and outfit a rolling condo.

Off-Season Prep

As the idea of the trip began to take shape, I surmised that I would need the backing of MLB in order to get the majority of minor league teams to approve my singing in a single season. To my surprise, Ruth B. Shannon—a friend and an Angels season ticket holder for forty years—put me in contact with Jackie Autry who, as former owner of the Angels and as honorary president of the American League, presented my appeal to the commissioner's office. Although Jackie struck out with MLB, which balked because it never sanctions such ventures, she encouraged me nonetheless to pursue the "worthwhile project."

With tentative confidence I warily began in mid-July 2010 to send each of the affiliated minor league teams an e-mail request and a link to my online video audition. In all cases I personalized the appeal, most often addressing the message to the general manager. It read:

> In anticipation of the 2011 baseball season, I write to you now with a bold proposal and invitation to participate—without cost—in a project on "The National Anthem for the National Pastime." During the spring and summer of 2011, I will be on a sabbatical leave, during which I will be researching and writing a book on the history and performance of "The Star Spangled Banner" at professional baseball games.
>
> At this time, I am requesting that you approve my audition to sing the anthem for one of your team's games next season that will fit

> into the complex travel schedule that will be required for me to complete a five-month road trip to many of the 140 Minor League ballparks. As part of the research for this project, I will draw upon my experience of singing the National Anthem at the Minor League ballparks, as well as more than half of the Major League stadiums—most recently, for the Nationals at their new ballpark in Washington, D.C.
>
> To verify my musicianship and my record, I am providing a link to a streaming video of me performing the anthem at a Reds game in Cincinnati a few years ago.
>
> If additional audition materials (such as a CD, DVD, or a complete list of my performances) are required, please let me know when it will be best to send them and to whom the materials should be addressed.
>
> If all works well, once the Minor League schedules are set for 2011, I will develop a travel schedule, and I will contact you with a target date for my singing the National Anthem for one of your team's games during the 2011 season.
>
> Patriotically and cheerfully yours,
> Joe Price

Initially, I targeted the teams in California, thinking that my position in Whittier might offer some regional appeal and jump-start the project. I really didn't know what to expect. Hours after sending my first query, I received an enthusiastic reply from the Visalia Rawhide. In the first three days following my blind requests to scores of teams throughout the country, eleven—including six on the East Coast—responded positively. Within a fortnight, almost forty others notified me that they had approved my audition and would be willing to participate.

While several respondents expressed excitement about my effort, none were more positive than the reply from Josh Donat of the San Antonio Missions:

> What you're doing sounds fantastic! I recommend you get in touch with Benjamin Hill about the effort...he's a blogger for MiLB.com [the official site for Minor League Baseball]. He tracks this kind of stuff, I'm sure he'd be interested.
>
> As for singing at our ballpark, we would love to have you. Our schedule will be set and published in October or November. Please

look it over and let us know when you'd like to sing and we'll schedule you for the event.

After thanking Josh for his affirmation, I immediately sent Ben a message explaining the project and its growing interest. Days later, Ben blogged a brief piece about the project, and his advocacy swelled the number of favorable responses. By the end of August, more than ninety teams had indicated their willingness to participate, and only one team had declined to join my national league, a decision that its front office would later reverse following one of my former students' appeal directly to the team's general manager, who was one of her friends.

With so many willing participants, I faced a new challenge: How could I design a schedule with enough flexibility to minimize the travel that would be required to maximize the number of actual game appearances?

After requesting and receiving season schedules from the leagues' offices, I set up a spreadsheet to include data about all of the possible participants: their leagues, their locations, their week-by-week home stands, and their contact information. As I started to think about where to begin the tour and how to reduce travel, I sorted the data by state, and I plotted teams' locations on a wall-size, highways map of the U.S. that I had picked up at the auto club. The arrangement revealed several significant clusters and components: the density of teams in California, Florida, North Carolina, and Texas; the long distance between teams' ballparks across the Great Plains; the fact that Midland, Texas (home of the RockHounds) seemed to be in the middle of nowhere and simply on the way to elsewhere; and the dearth of home dates in New England and the Northwest until late June when the Short Season A and Rookie Leagues would begin their play.

The problems about where to start and which direction to go began to resolve when close friends Don and Ruth Musser introduced a twist. They invited me to stay with them in DeLand, Florida, and to use their guest room as a hub while maneuvering among cities in the Florida State League. Years earlier, Don and I had met in grad school where we spent multiple afternoons at Wrigley Field and played more often on the Divinity School's intramural softball team. Since then, we had collaborated frequently on scholarly projects, writing and editing several books together and regularly hosting each other at our respective institutions for guest lectures.

Aligning the information from my database about clusters, distances, and possible Florida dates with the Mussers' invitation, I brainstormed the idea of starting there since major league spring training would have recently been completed and since, I figured, most anthem performers would likely have been queued up days earlier to sing for the games featuring major league players. By fixating on Florida's teams first, I also hoped to avoid summer's swelter there. If I accepted the Mussers' hospitality, I could rent a car and daily bungee back and forth from DeLand to nearby ballparks before returning to California to pick up Bonnie with the RV. Then we could traverse a southerly route across country in our mobile summer home, stopping in sequence at ballparks in Southern California, Nevada, New Mexico, Texas, and beyond—that is, if there is any place beyond Texas.

Hatching this general plan, I started to map out possible routes. Besides knowing that New England and the Northwest should be scheduled after late June, I considered several other factors in designing a feasible itinerary. Naïvely, I assumed that we could leave an RV park by nine o'clock each morning and drive for six hours, or about 300 miles, before anchoring at a new site. I also projected the need to include several significant stopping places that would appeal primarily to Bonnie, especially since she was—to say the least—less than enthusiastic about spending most weeknights at ballparks and watching the games. Attractive possibilities to her included connecting with her close friends in Houston and Charlotte, as well as in Vermont and Massachusetts; enjoying a baseball-free week for her to visit museums in Washington, D.C., while I might roam alone through Pennsylvania; and celebrating her birthday at the Art Institute in Chicago since we had grown to love its Impressionist collection when we had lived in Hyde Park.

Two other routing objectives contributed to my planning. One was specifically determined—coordinating my appearance for the Mississippi Braves with one of their few afternoon games so that my nonagenarian mother, who lived near Jackson in an assisted-living facility, could attend the game there if her health permitted. The other was more flexible—figuring out a few days when and where the RV could be serviced and, if necessary, repaired. When a gap of a few days without a potential performance within a 300-mile radius became apparent in June's schedule, I selected those dates for possible RV repair and personal respite, especially since the dates coincided with the chance to see relatives and friends in Kentucky. Considering the likely strain on an RV after a second month of intense travel, I forecast a similar rest period for its maintenance during the time that Bonnie would spend with friends in D.C., while I could continue in the car to venture through Pennsylvania on my own.

Finally, a manageable itinerary connecting 109 ballparks came together after weeks of appeals and repeated negotiations with anthem assigners; and my life's measure of baseball shifted from the norm of innings and games to the spatial dimension of miles.

Preseason Workouts

Before beginning our summer-long, thousands-mile venture, the cumulative experience that Bonnie and I had in RVs was three nights. Two decades earlier, we had borrowed a friend's Class-C coach to spend a night boon-docking near Palm Springs before taking a hot-air balloon ride at dawn the following day. Months later, I again borrowed the same RV for a couple of nights so that I could conduct some research on Super Bowl fans at Jack Murphy Stadium in San Diego. These brief trips had been our entire RV life until our purchase of a Class-A RV, a 1994 Fleetwood Flair.

Taking our inexperience into account, Bonnie and I went to RV driving school one weekend before we set out on a shakeout trip to road test the wheeled beast a month before opening day. Along the way, we playfully named the RV "Arbie"—a spelling of R.B., which was short for "Rattley Bang." That was the sound that the RV made when it bounced over dips in the road and hit potholes in our lane, or when our pots and pans shifted while we made sharp turns.

On our initial foray, we set Mendocino as our destination for a "shakeout" since it charmed us with memories about the place where Bonnie had spent vivid childhood Julys in the redwoods home of her grandmother. The distance from Whittier to Mendocino also allowed us to anticipate some of the rigors of the anthem tour by driving a few hundred miles on consecutive days through big cities, on clogged freeways, and across mountain roads. Although unexpected, strong winds along the 101 north of Santa Barbara and rain in the coastal range of mountains added to our learning experience.

As we drove north from Los Angeles, Bonnie began to read aloud Charles Kuralt's memoir, *A Life on the Road.* While I had expected to be inspired by Kuralt's reflections on travel, I was surprised to learn of his Southern roots, his prize-winning essay as an adolescent about a Charlotte Hornets third-baseman, and his subsequent coverage of junior-high sports for the Charlotte newspaper. Immediately, I connected with his Southern heritage and his reporting on junior-high basketball, which I had also done as an early teen for the Jackson (Mississippi) *Clarion-Ledger*. And the start of his journalistic career by writing an essay on a minor leaguer now resonated with my tour to minor league ballparks. I was charged up by his road life. I only hoped that his repeated troubles with RV mechanical systems would not be our experience.

When we reached Mendocino, we boon-docked Arbie on a private spot just off Highway 1, not far from Compche-Ukiah Road where Bonnie's grandparents had lived. Situated in forty acres of prime redwood forest sloping down to Laguna Creek, their house had burned several years after they had moved away; but the "Tom Thumb" playhouse, built in 1954 by Grandpa George for his grandchildren, had been the pilgrimage center for family trips ever since. The rainbow colors of remaining boards attested the durability of lead-based paint, even in the moist, coastal climate.

Our shakeout proved effective since Arbie had to overcome electrical difficulties when we started to leave the site. As we checked the turn signals and brake lights on Arbie and Toad (the towed 1996 Saturn that came with the RV purchase), we discovered no illumination. I hadn't wanted to identify so quickly and so closely with Kuralt's RV difficulties! Within a few hours, however, Steve and Jamie Shipman at the American Repair Service in nearby Fort Bragg were able to fix the problem and send us on our way to retrace the winding route through the Alexander River Valley, back toward Highway 101, and on to Los Angeles.

Spring Training

Because I had performed the national anthem for scores of major league games and numerous collegiate events, my invitation to sing for the 2011 season opener between the University of Georgia Bulldogs and Stetson University Hatters initially seemed somewhat routine, especially since an academic setting had been my professional home for three decades. To my surprise, however, I found my first anthem rendition of the year nerve-wracking.

Like crowds at the minor league games where I would sing throughout the season, most of the 2,200 fans paid to see the game, while students and faculty from the university were admitted free. It was the latter group—including colleagues at Stetson—that prompted my nervousness, because I find it more difficult to sing for friends and folks who know me than for strangers.

Usually when I sing for ballgames, I know the names of most of the players on the home team. But in a recognition reversal, this time the players knew me, not I them. Two nights before the game, I had presented a lecture on "Sports as Religion" to an overflow audience of Hatters student-athletes. Stetson Professor Don Musser, my good friend and co-author on several projects, introduced me by promoting my anthem tour by adding a few ballparks to the scheduled total of 109. Most of the Hatters hard-ballers in the dugout had attended the event with their coach Pete Dunn. Then ranked eighth in total wins among current NCAA coaches, Dunn later celebrated the success of Hatters baseball alumni Cory Kluber and Jacob deGrom, both of whom won MLB pitching awards in 2014.

At the ballpark during warm-ups and batting practice, I stood in the dugout chatting with Coach Dunn about fishing rather than the game's lineup, the season's promise, or ideas prompted by my presentation. As we scanned the stands behind home plate, I saw Larry Blakeslee, the fishing guide who had steered Don and me to big fish on multiple occasions, including the previous day. That morning with the first cast, I had landed an eight-pound largemouth bass.

A native Michigander and a lifelong Tigers fan, Larry frequently jokes and talks baseball with Don and me while we wait for the water to roil with striking bass. Most often, we tell stories about our favorite teams decades ago, intoning with affection and reverence the heroes of our childhoods: Norm Cash and Bill Freehan for Larry; Bill Mazeroski and Roberto Clemente for Don; Mickey Mantle and Yogi Berra for me. Larry now rarely has time to attend games, although he counts several current and former major league players among his frequent clients. In the dugout I looked at the players who had sat in front rows listening to me two nights earlier. Then, they had been individuals; now in uniform, they blended together as a team, jawing and jostling anxiously, wanting to get the game and season started.

Besides Larry and the student-athletes who had heard my lecture, I knew that seminary classmate Dixon Sutherland, Don, and Ruth stood nearby. Close friends, for sure: and that's the main reason why my Stetson performance was so unnerving. For once, I was singing the anthem because of their invitation, not my initiative. I wanted to make sure that I didn't let them down. In addition, the ballpark was almost within echo's reach of Christina Aguilera's mangling of "The Star-Spangled Banner" at the Super Bowl days earlier.

In most of my anthem performances, I am more concerned about dealing with feedback from the auditory system's speakers positioned in the outfield. But this time I was more nervous about remembering words than I had been on any occasion since my first baseball performance at Comiskey Park in 1977. Although the "Fan Appreciation Day" crowd approached 50,000 on that sunny Chicago Saturday, my greatest concern then was remembering the words, not how the fans would respond. Before beginning I confessed to the White Sox audio staffer that I had written the words on a note card that I kept within easy reach in the right-hand pocket of my denim blazer. Laughing, he said that if I forgot the words, I would join the good company of Nat King Cole, who had stumbled through the words before scatting half the anthem. But, I then protested, "I am not Nat King Cole and I can't scat!"

My restlessness about singing for the Stetson game was also intensified by the pregame ceremony. Throwing out the first pitch was Chipper Jones, third-baseman for the Atlanta Braves and future Hall of Famer. The godson of Coach Dunn and a native of nearby Pierson, Florida, Chipper is celebrated in DeLand as a hometown boy, with frequent reference being made to his having been the number-one draft choice in 1989. Sporting the tuft of a Van Dyke beard, he wore a fitted western-style shirt and fashionably frayed blue jeans. Coach Dunn introduced us, and Chipper extended his thick, calloused, right hand, which had gripped a bat on more than 400 successful home-run swings and had scooped up at least that many unsuccessful sacrifice-bunt attempts. I tried not to look awestruck as I shook his hand.

Despite a delay for the pregame ceremonies, the February evening proved splendid: mosquitoes and gnats had not yet begun to swarm, the humidity and temperature blended together at a comfortable level, and a rising orange moon appeared as full as championship hopes for the season. Chipper threw a knee-high strike with a fastball that rivaled that of most major league pitchers, and I sang the anthem traditionally and fervently. Although the microphone was inactive during the opening phrase, I proceeded without hesitation. Baseball season had started and my national anthem project had begun. And the home team won: Stetson Hatters 6, Georgia Bulldogs 3.

Opening Day

The 2011 opening day for Minor League Baseball was April 7, which was also my thirty-eighth wedding anniversary.

Throughout the previous month, Bonnie and I had celebrated our marriage while we decorated and outfitted Arbie for our four-month venture in it—an extended honeymoon. Even so, while I prepared to sing for the opening-night game, I dearly missed Bonnie, who had remained at home making final preparations for our RV journey. I could not think of a more loving anniversary gift from her than her enthusiastic support of my anthem project, freeing me to begin the pursuit of a nationwide ballpark dream.

Two days earlier I had begun the travel in a way that I had not anticipated: with a cold—hardly an auspicious beginning for a singer. Still sniffling, I had approached the check-in counter at American Airlines in Ontario, California, where I was pleasantly greeted by smiling Audrey Farrell. When I said that it was good to see her again, she recognized my voice and responded, "You're the anthem singer."

Incredible! A dozen years earlier I had flown out of that airport several times when traveling to sing for major league games. Always smiling, courteous, and efficient, Audrey would exchange pleasantries with me while I checked in with luggage. Since then, I had shaved my full beard and switched from Ontario to LAX for my regular airport departures. I was amazed that she immediately recognized me by voice even with the onset of a cold, perhaps a good omen for my anthem performances.

During the flights to Florida, I wrote postcards to friends throughout the country, inviting them to join me for my game in their hometown. Then arriving in Jacksonville, I found that my Hertz car rental was new, *really* new. It had four miles on the odometer as I turned on the ignition and began to navigate my way south on I-95 toward my weeks-long hosts Don and Ruth Musser in DeLand. Despite my continent-wide separation from Bonnie at that time, I felt a tethered connection with her as I crossed the eastern end of I-10, the freeway whose western end had directed us to Ontario hours earlier.

Typically when I visited Don, we would spend one of our first days with his friend and professional bass fishing guide Larry Blakeslee. And so we did on this visit, too. On our second morning we fed dozens of bream-size shiners to escaping largemouth bass, evil mud fish, and mean gar. We did, however, catch several big fish, including an eight-pounder that I managed to reel in. And we saw five manatees swimming calmly near the mouth of the Ichetucknee Springs as we idled through the current of the Santa Fe River. Although this was my first trip to the tranquil and remote Santa Fe, twenty-five years earlier I had tubed down the Ichetucknee with colleagues at the University of Florida, where I had spent the summer in a seminar sponsored by the National Endowment for the Humanities.

I was sure that seeing the protected manatees signaled a good start for my season opener for their namesake, the Brevard County Manatees.

1.

My Florida Foray

Opening Night: Game 1 in Brevard County

To minimize nightly wardrobe decisions and to encourage fans to inquire about the anthem tour, I had ordered several golf-style shirts in white, blue, and gray featuring the anthem tour logo. Anticipating that the season-opening ceremonies might be elaborate, I selected the least casual color to wear, but I also put a dress shirt and tie on the back seat of the car as I left DeLand, just in case more formal attire might be appropriate. Sure enough, the dress shirt came in handy, because I spilled coffee down the front of the anthem shirt when I bumped the steering wheel as I turned the car into the ballpark parking space. Lesson learned before the first night's first note: always keep a back-up shirt in the trunk of the car.

A short time later, the Brevard County team opened the ballpark gates—literally and fully. They offered a fee-free night by providing complimentary general admission to almost 5,000 fans. What a populist way to build enthusiasm for a team at the start of the season!

The pregame ceremonies featured a parachute specialist flying the American flag as he descended into centerfield, while an honor guard of Vietnam veterans presented the colors in front of the pitcher's mound. After the players on each team were introduced and took their places along the baselines, the strong wind stiffened the flags and whipped my tie as I started the anthem. Typically when I sing, I turn to face different sections in the stands, hoping to engage fans to sing along. But when I twisted toward a gust during the opening line of the anthem, the wind caused the pitch to slide without me making any changes in voice production. Years earlier, I had learned that while a singer holds a note, changing the shape of one's open mouth could alter the pitch. Now I quickly adjusted my posture as I heard the rebound of the opening phrase broadcast on the outfield speakers. I froze in one direction and completed the anthem facing the box seats behind home plate. After this glitch with pitch in the opening line, I enjoyed a triumphal finish.

As I walked past the dugout, Josh Prince, Manatees shortstop and leadoff hitter, expressed appreciation, patting me twice on the back. And pitching coach Fred Dabney smiled big and teased me: "Best anthem all year."

Prince played a stellar game, collecting one of the Manatees' hits, stealing a base, and fielding flawlessly. In the second inning he turned in a web gem ranging to the second base side of the bag on the outfield grass to stab the syncopated-hopper. Then pirouetting in Jeter-esque style, he made a leaping throw to first to nip the runner. Despite his hustle, the Manatees lost to the Daytona Cubs 3-2, who were led by their outfielders. Left fielder Michael Burgess hit a tape-measure home run to start the Cubs' scoring, and Jae-Hoon Ha and Nelson Perez cut down baserunners with laser throws from center and right.

From the Manatees ballpark, it is not possible to see the coastline, which lies about a dozen miles away. Yet its name—Space Coast Stadium—is fitting since it sits within blastoff-range of Cape Canaveral and since several of its features pay tribute to space exploration. A sculpture of the space shuttle stands at the main entry, and the field itself prominently displays foul-pole banners that honor the crews of the Challenger and Columbia shuttles.

One of the recurring joys of baseball and of my project was the chance to share games with friends. Accompanying me to this one was Greg Sapp, a colleague from Stetson and an enthusiastic fan of the minor leagues. A few years earlier, Greg had been a season ticket holder for the Braves' Class-A team in Macon, Georgia. Now living near Daytona, he had begun to follow its Cubs. Throughout the game, he provided background on several of the returning players from the previous year as we enjoyed the playful promotions presented by the Manatees staff between innings, especially the kids' run from the centerfield fence to the dugout.

While the evening had begun with my singing about "the rockets' red glare," it ended on a similar note—with a postgame fireworks display, which Greg and I observed in the car's rearview mirrors as we beat the traffic out of the parking lot and turned north toward DeLand.

As much as I enjoyed being able to share the start of the tour and my anthem performance with Greg, my closest friend, Bonnie, stood a continent away on the night of our anniversary. Although she had probably spent the evening watching a movie or reading a novel, I had no doubt that she would have preferred attending the Manatees home opener with me. Having been nationally recognized for her teaching as a Crista McAuliffe Fellow, Bonnie would have been thrilled to see the tribute to the Challenger displayed in the ballpark. And she would have glowed with appreciation as I sang the anthem. I missed her keenly as the dusky innings crept into the full darkness of the game's end.

More Than One Miracle: Game 2 in Fort Myers

For months, I had been dreaming this anthem project, plotting its possibilities, anticipating its encounters, cringing about its challenges, confirming its plans. Although I had sung three days earlier on opening day, Sunday afternoon's game was the first in a two-week stretch during which the tour really came to life. During this time I would have only one unscheduled day.

Before beginning the series of performances game after game, day after day, I had the uneasy sense that John Steinbeck confesses at the beginning of the second part of *Travels with Charley*: "In long-range planning for a trip, I think there is a private conviction that it won't happen."

Indeed. I had worried and wondered whether the wild idea of the anthem tour would actually be realized. Yet Sunday's performance for the Fort Myers Miracle suggested that my project was miraculously coming to life, thanks in large part to the enthusiastic cooperation of so many teams in accommodating my scheduling requests.

As I drove into the Miracles' parking lot, several vivid memories associated with their parent Twins (an oxymoronic relationship that would have been a biological miracle) rushed into mind. The first avenue that I passed was Puckett Circle. Immediately I flashed back to the morning in a Boston hotel in the late 1980s when my two young sons and I bumped into Kirby Puckett. While they jumped joyfully and asked for his autograph, he furtively looked around as I fumbled through my wallet searching for business cards. Telling them that he usually didn't sign in hotels, he took my cards and autographed the blank side. Of course, my sons and I still cherish the interaction and the autographs.

Driving nearer to the ballpark entry, I turned into a partially paved parking lane: Grant Circle. Ah, Mudcat, the Twins' winning World Series starter against Don Drysdale in 1965! During spring training fifteen years earlier, I had met Mudcat Grant on a flight from Los Angeles to Florida. When he learned of my position at Whittier College, he offered to coordinate a group of aging former Negro League players to share their oral histories during Black History Month. I leapt at the prospect, which proved so successful that he returned for three consecutive years, bringing to campus Sammie Haynes, Joe Scott, Luther Branham, Merle and Andy Porter, and others to spend an evening enriching the students' lives while recalling their own.

In these simple street signs leading to the ballpark, I was reminded of the miracle of baseball camaraderie.

Before the game, Gary Sharp, the Miracle's staffer with whom I had corresponded on several occasions, expressed excitement about the magnitude of my project and, as he put it, "its pure summer fun." Minutes later in his role as the P.A. announcer, he introduced me for the anthem, beginning with a description of the project, which prompted several stimulating conversations during the game.

The Miracle's game was one of a handful of their afternoon starts scheduled for the season—all on Sundays. After the previous night's sellout crowd of more than 8,000, this Sunday gathering of the faithful was less than a tithe of the night before. With the temperature beneath the blaring sun soaring octaves above the thermometer's official reading in the mid-90s, I was sweat-drenched by the time I began the anthem. While I sang for less than a minute and a half, the players would stand on the field for more than an hour, and the umpires would endure three hours of sun saturation without relief. The sun also bleached and burned the scouts behind home plate; but wearing shorts, wide-brimmed hats, and shrouding their necks and shoulders with towels, the scouts had come dressed for the heat. The sun also factored into the outcome of the game since the Hammerheads right fielder lost a two-out fly ball in the high sky, allowing the Miracle's winning run to score.

While singing, I had focused on several fans behind home plate, one of whom wore baseball pants and a jersey with "Naples" emblazoned across its front. Since he looked familiar, I approached him when I moved into the grandstands. "Are you Bill Virdon?" I asked, since I confidently recalled his likeness on Topps baseball cards when he had played centerfield for the Pittsburgh Pirates and, years later, served as their manager. "No," he responded, "but I get asked that question *down here* in Florida at least once a week. I am Mark Langemo."

He complimented my rendition and then inquired about the project, asking how I had conceived and planned it. The more we talked, the more we became fast friends. An emeritus professor of business at the University of North Dakota, he expected to return days later to his summer home in the town of Grand Forks where, he added, no one had ever asked him if he were Virdon.

Through three innings we shared our love of professorial work, our enthusiasm for seeing America, and our passion for baseball. Interested in the business aspects of the anthem tour, Mark asked about organizational details, especially when I had begun to set things up and the sequence of my tasks. Starting with my e-mails to general managers nine months earlier, I summarized the planning process:

> July—E-mail 140 affiliated minor league teams with an offer for them to participate, without cost, in my research for the national anthem as part of the national pastime. I requested that they preapprove me to sing the national anthem during the 2011 season based on the video of me singing at a Cincinnati Reds game a few years earlier.
>
> July through March—Continue biweekly vocal study with Mike Stevens, a member of the L.A. Opera who also served as chair of the voice faculty at the Colburn School for the Performing Arts.
>
> July and August—Respond to the 120 teams that prequalified me to perform.
>
> September—Contact the president of each minor league requesting assistance in early access to the entire league's 2011 schedule; all complied.
>
> October—Make a spreadsheet of the home stands of each of the 120 teams, devoting separate columns to each week and a separate entry for region so that sorting could be done. (I mounted the multiple sheets on a wall of my office devoted to the layout.)
>
> November—Map out possible routes, starting with the Florida State League, which I could complete by renting a car and staying with a friend in DeLand.
>
> November through January—Propose specific performance dates to teams, and confirm those dates.
>
> February—Purchase an RV and outfit it for the majority of the tour's schedule.
>
> March—Continue scheduling and confirming dates, and researching information about ballparks, cities, RV parks, RV repair shops, etc.
>
> April—Finally sing.

Mark had come to the ballpark fresh from his team's winning the division title in their "over-50" baseball league. Months short of seventy, he had caught the entire game; and now from his perch behind home plate, he could identify with the challenge and success of these Single-A catchers one-third his age.

If his own game hadn't worn him out, I think that my description of the project's planning did. His last question was about how many hours I had "put in" on the project: "More than 300 before I sang the first phrase for a minor league game three days ago!"

The afternoon affair between the Fort Myers Miracle and Jupiter Hammerheads featured a few near-miracles. Incredibly, the catchers and home plate umpire did not wilt in the heat. The game itself was set apart by a feat that major league teams rarely accomplish: players executed five successful bunts, two for base hits on successive pitches. But perhaps the most unusual display of the afternoon came from a six-year-old fan who sat in the few rows of shade in the upper section behind home plate. On each pitch she would peer to the mound and ready her glove in a horizontal position like a catcher. In the third inning a high pop foul caromed off a seat near her and then bounced like a pinball under empty rows. She ran toward it and reached for it, only to find that a strong male hand had seized it right before she could touch it. In frustration, she winced before immediately shrugging off her near-miss. When the man handed her the ball, her dejection reversed to joy as she acknowledged the gift with a huge, snaggle-toothed smile.

For several innings, she *thwapped* the ball into the pocket of her glove. In the eighth, another pop foul angled toward her ready position. This time, as the ball careened through vacant rows, she dashed toward the end of its path and won the race. Delighted by her success, she turned and handed the ball to the three-year-old boy who, like her earlier experience, had narrowly missed retrieving it and who, like she had earlier responded, erupted with the smile of baseball joy.

Where's the Pitch?: Game 3 in Bradenton

Since DeLand was near the Atlantic coast, I opted to stay in a hotel for a couple of nights near the Gulf Coast so that I could reduce the stress of travel while singing for consecutive games in Fort Myers, Bradenton, and Tampa.

With a morning free in the area, I turned to a different baseball project that examines how players are memorialized. Nearby in Sarasota was the gravesite of Hall of Fame knuckleballer Hoyt Wilhelm. To my surprise, when I checked with the office at the Palms Memorial Park, the records showed no listing of his gravesite even though the comprehensive resource *Baseball Necrology* identified the cemetery as the place of his burial. The records did show a location for James H. Wilhelm, and there I found a simple marker that identified his military service and rank, but nothing about his baffling prowess on the mound.

Hours later when I walked into the Bradenton Marauders ballpark, I asked Fred, one of the box-seat ushers, if he could direct me to Charlie, the staff member whom I was to meet for anthem assistance. Before pointing me in the right direction, Fred looked at the anthem tour logo on my shirt and asked, "Are you the guy who's going to all the ballparks and singing the anthem?" As I smiled and nodded "yes," he continued, "I heard about you this afternoon."

Enthusiastic about my performance and tour, Fred introduced me to a couple of his colleagues as I prepared for the pregame ceremonies. In Bradenton on this first Monday night of the season, the pregame ceremony varied from the routine of my previous performances. Since there were no corporate sponsors for the game and no groups in attendance—in fact, the game attendance was reported as 703—there was no typical first pitch. While I was reaching for my pitch pipe, the P.A. announcer introduced me simply by name and sooner than I had expected. With the wind blowing steadily, I recalled the pitch issues from gusts that I had experienced a few days earlier, and I made sure that I could hear the inverted F-sharp triad and started without difficulty. Following my performance, the P.A. announcer described the anthem tour, identifying Bradenton as the third ballpark.

When I returned to the stands, one of Fred's friends expressed appreciation for the pace and clarity of my singing. During spring training for the Pittsburgh Pirates, he said, several of the anthem performers had butchered the tune, changing keys, embellishing the melody, or simply screeching at the end. By contrast, he liked the way that I had kept the focus on the words.

Among the fans who commented on my performance, Mike Murphy was fascinated by the scheduling challenge that I had faced in finding teams in the same area at home on consecutive days, especially since he had been unable to set up a chain of games for his upcoming trip to the Midwest. In a couple of weeks, he and his wife would fly to Iowa for the Drake Relays in Des Moines. The promise of the meet had enticed him to return to his alma mater where he had played football and run track. Although frustrated by the fact that the Iowa Cubs would be "away" during the relays, Mike and his wife expected to catch minor league games in Cedar Rapids and Clinton.

Similar to David Lamb, who chronicled his re-immersion into Americana through the minor leagues in his engaging book *Stolen Season*, Mike enjoyed Minor League Baseball as a way of getting back in touch with the rhythms of America after having spent most of the previous decade abroad.

Unlike my two previous Florida ballparks, Bradenton's McKechnie Field is not positioned in open space surrounded by acres of grassy parking. Instead, one of its outer walls abuts an urban street, giving it neighborhood immediacy much like Wrigley Field. It also features spired garrets like Churchill Downs, and pillars that partially obstruct the view of a few seats in the higher grandstands. Built in 1923, the ballpark is named for former Bradenton resident Bill McKechnie, whose professional playing career was undistinguished but whose managerial career warranted enshrinement in Cooperstown. As an infielder in nine major league seasons primarily with Pittsburgh, his hometown, McKechnie batted under .250. But in his managerial career of more than twenty years, he won almost 2,000 games, including four National League pennants and two World Series titles with the Pirates in 1925 and the Reds in 1940.

After the Marauders repeatedly ran circles around Jupiter—hitting two home runs, stealing four bases, and building an 11-5 lead—the home crowd thinned in the eighth inning. But in the ninth, Bradenton almost fell out of orbit, needing to record four outs in ninth while holding on for an 11-8 win. As one of the last fans to leave the park around 10:30 that night, I appreciated not having to make the three-hour drive back to DeLand.

Mini-Yankees: Game 4 in Tampa

In a distinct way, singing for the Tampa Yankees echoed my experience of singing for major league teams. Like most major league ballparks, the Yankees scheduled a sound check for me before the stadium opened. I did not realize then what an unusual opportunity they afforded me. Throughout the remainder of the season and the tour, only a handful of teams would offer me a chance to run a sound check on the ballpark's audio system or even to rehearse in a secluded place.

Following the previous night's homey experience in the aged ballpark in Bradenton, capacious Steinbrenner Field in Tampa also looked "major-league" by comparison. In many respects it set the standard for minor league and spring-training facilities. Constructed in 1993, the stadium was modeled after Yankee Stadium with a mini façade suspended from the grandstand roof, a memorial park honoring retired Yankees, and field dimensions like those of the ballpark in the Bronx. But unlike the immediate surroundings of the stadium in New York, the exterior of the Tampa ballpark is landscaped with towering palm trees and partially surrounded by elevated walkways that peer out onto nearby Raymond James Stadium, home of the Tampa Bay Buccaneers. The ballpark also overlooks an artificial lagoon and one of the practice fields on the campus of more than thirty acres.

My early arrival at the ballpark gave me the time to roam through its recesses, where I watched players work out and take batting practice. After the visiting Manatees finished taking their swings in the batting cages beneath the grandstands, I spoke to shortstop Josh Prince. A few days earlier he had patted me on the back following my opening-night rendition in Brevard County. I congratulated him on his solid fielding, and he inquired about what had brought me to the bowels of the ballpark. When I identified myself as the professor undertaking the anthem tour, he brightened and asked if the New Orleans Zephyrs were on my schedule. Indeed. He had gone to Tulane, and he joshed that he'd like to ride along on my tour to return to his friends and haunts in New Orleans.

After practicing the anthem with the sound system, I saw one of the Yankees prospects in the dugout and remarked to him that, on the two occasions when I had sung for the parent Yankees, they had won. He seemed oblivious to my comment although he had smiled broadly while I had been rehearsing. Intervening, a staff member let me know that he had recently arrived from the Dominican Republic and understood very little English. His situation was not uncommon, and it showed the complex challenges that many of the minor leaguers face. Not only must they learn to adjust to the rigors of bus-league travel while they try to advance through their organization's system; they simultaneously must learn to swim in an alien culture and its foreign language.

Following my performance, Jessica Lack, the community relations coordinator for the team, presented me with an elegant Tampa Yankees souvenir shirt. I began to wonder about the various tokens other teams might offer, a dream that mostly went unrealized since few other teams recognized my singing with any souvenir.

While I moved toward my seat, I was greeted warmly by Myra and Ed Kryscnski from New Jersey. The P.A. announcer had briefly identified my anthem project and tour; and the Kryscnskis expressed interest in my itinerary. Devout fans of the minor leagues, they annually purchased partial season tickets to the Trenton Thunders games, where they hoped I would sing weeks later. "July 1," I replied. I had worked so often and long with the schedule that it was mired in the forefront of my mind. Myra said that although that date was not in their package of games, they would add it to their schedule. As we talked she also identified the possibility that they might join me for the IronPigs game in Lehigh Valley.

During the game, I chatted for several innings with Mike Lortz, a blogger for busleaguesbaseball.com. He let me know that a few days earlier he had met Tug Haines, a cranberry farmer and freelance writer from New Jersey who, like me, was summer trekking through minor league ballparks. Tug's goal was to see more than a hundred games in stadiums east of the Mississippi River. Mike also let me know that he had told Tug about my quest.

Needing to drive back to DeLand following the game, I left after the seventh-inning stretch, during which the P.A. system played a recording of Robert Merrill singing "Take Me Out to the Ballgame." Could I have more fun during the singing of baseball's song than to blend my voice with the rich baritone of the operatic Mr. Merrill? Although the crowd had dwindled far below the gate report of 841, I lustily sang the great, traditional melody, modulating along with the musical Met's star.

Although earlier I had claimed a perfect record when performing for the parent Yankees, these mini-Yankees lost 4-2 to Brevard County, which broke the Manatees season-opening, five-game skid.

Feedback: Game 5 in Dunedin

Since I had clustered several consecutive days singing for teams on the Gulf Coast, I had anchored in a hotel near Sarasota to allow for easy commutes to Fort Myers, Bradenton, and Tampa. However, rather than remaining in the area for the next game in nearby Dunedin, I returned to DeLand after the Tampa game so that I could pick up Don Musser to join me for the Blue Jays game the following night. I know that doesn't make geographical sense since it required more than 300 extra miles of driving. But it scores in baseball and personal terms because I shared a day-long road trip and another game with a close friend. In the forty years that we had known each other, not only had we written and edited five books together, we had also joined each other for major league games in Chicago, Denver, and Atlanta, and for Super Bowls in Miami and Pasadena.

Don and I left DeLand at noon, avoiding freeways and choosing blue highways as we headed across the state. We anticipated an intermediate stop near Wesley Chapel, an unincorporated community north of Tampa where Don wanted to pick up some unique hibiscus hybrids that he had ordered a few days earlier. Almost daily in DeLand, he delivered hibiscus blossoms to the staff at the nursing home where his then ninety-seven-year-old mother lived.

Driving along Route 44 as we approached Cassia, we crossed the headwaters of Black Water Creek. More than a decade earlier on a cold, rainy, blustery January morning, Bill Flowers, the senior naturalist of the St. John's River and its tributaries, had taken Don and me fishing in the creek near its mouth miles south at the Wekiva River.

We recalled how the boat ride with Bill that day had made the experience so memorable. For one thing, as Bill paddled us up the nearly impassible Black Water, we often had to crouch into the bottom of the boat to avoid low-hanging branches while we alternately had to rise and shove the hull away from submerged stumps. We didn't mind ducking since the hull of the small boat momentarily provided a baffle from the frigid wind. Even more distinct than our dodging obstacles in the swollen water was the incredible cold that we experienced as Bill had motored down the river to get to Black Water. I am not sure that I have ever been colder, even in the subzero temperatures intensified by gusting winds off Lake Michigan when I walked home from classes as a grad student. Despite the horrible conditions of that January day on the water, we managed to lure several keepers into the boat—thanks, I am sure, to Bill enticing the bass with promises of warmth. We were too cold to bait our hooks, making wiry Bill unglove his hands to hook the shiners. And truth be told, we were too cold even to care about taking photographs of our remarkable catch. Sharing these memories with Don made the drive to and from Dunedin worth the effort of tracking back to the Tampa area, where I had been hours earlier.

Miles later at the Dunedin ballpark, when I walked onto the field to sing the anthem, two fans in the front row behind the backstop greeted me. John Price and his brother-in-law Rick Miller had been at the Tampa game the previous night, and they expressed appreciation for my rendition as well as encouragement for the tour. Hearing them, Don immediately cackled that I had a groupie following. But John's wife Gail protested, joking that they really weren't stalking me, only pursuing genealogical research to find out if we were related. From Chattanooga, the Prices asked if they should be on the lookout for me singing weeks later in Tennessee. Regrettably, the Chattanooga Lookouts had been among the twenty minor league teams that never responded to any of my queries or appeals.

At Dunedin, the sound system suffered from about a half-second delay, one of the worst on the entire tour. Thankfully, Morgan Bell, the Dunedin Blue Jays Coordinator for Community Relations, had alerted me to the need for earplugs. Indeed they were helpful, although during the anthem as I heard the muffled rebound, I recalled the advice of the assistant at my first game in Chicago at Comiskey Park: "Whatever you do, don't listen. Keep going!" Try as I might, however, I couldn't suppress the sound of the feedback. When I finished and moved toward the stands, one of the visiting Tigers roving instructors standing near me commented, "How did you do that?" Then he saw me remove the earplugs and said, "Now I see!"

For the most part, the ballgame and the ballpark, Florida Auto Exchange Stadium, were almost as unremarkable as a used-car lot. Even though *Sports Illustrated* apparently had rated it near the top of Florida's spring-training ballparks, I wondered, "In what year? How recently?" One distinction of the small stadium was its commemoration of Tom Cheek among the former stars recognized in the old ballpark. Although he had never suited up in uniform for a game, Cheek had affectionately broadcast more than 4,300 consecutive, regular-season games during his twenty-seven years as the Toronto Blue Jays play-by-play announcer.

Several times during the game the lead vacillated between Dunedin and Clearwater, which squeezed ahead by a run in the eighth inning, only to give up three consecutive singles that tallied two in the bottom half of the frame. Since the Blue Jays prevailed 6-5 for their first victory of the season, Morgan gave me partial credit for inspiring the team. If only that were true!

Having enjoyed the memories of fishing together, the promise of bountiful hibiscus blossoms, and good old fun at the ballpark, Don and I spent much of the 150-mile ride back to DeLand in silence, the kind of silence that solid friends can enjoy: "The less said, the more," in the words of Duffy House, the retired sportswriter-detective in *Bleeding Dodger Blue.*

Sharing Anthem Honors: Game 6 in St. Lucie

An hour or so north of St. Lucie, I took an unanticipated anthem detour and added an unscheduled ballpark rendition to my roster of performances. Seeing a freeway exit to Vero Beach, where the Dodgers had trained in spring for more than sixty years, I spontaneously exited the freeway and gravitated toward the abandoned ballpark, which was difficult to locate since the GPS finder didn't know its current name. The ironwork on the locked gates to the complex featured the name "L.A. Dodgers," but an added panel identified the site as the Vero Beach Sports Village, operated by MiLB and restricted to authorized personnel. The corpse of the field reminded me of Ernest Green's description in *The Diamonds of Dixie*, his sociological examination of Minor League Baseball in the South. "Minor league baseball parks," he concluded, "die like paupers, lying there in unmarked graves."

Although I didn't qualify for admission to this Dodgers mortuary, I parked outside, walked around the gates, and found a groundskeeper mowing the abandoned ballfield. When I explained my project and asked him if I could sing the anthem on the field, he pointed me in the direction of a building where I could request official permission. Less than half an hour later, I returned and he turned off the mower so that I could record my rendition in the vacant ballpark while I stood atop Dodgertown's pitcher's mound.

A year after my serendipitous singing at Holman Park, the field would be saved by a venture involving former Dodgers owner Peter O'Malley in partnership with former Dodgers pitchers Chan Ho Park and Hideo Nomo. They purchased the site and established "Historic Dodgertown" as an athletic training and conference center.

Arriving an hour or so later in St. Lucie, where the New York Mets and their minor league affiliate Mets make their home, a twin-pillared sculpture made from remnant steel at Ground Zero graced the entry to the ballpark, paying tribute to the victims of the Twin Towers attack. Created by Patrick Cochrane, the piece had been donated by retired New York City firefighters who live in the St. Lucie area. The artistic relic reminded me of the consummate performance of the national anthem by Daniel Rodriguez, then a New York City policeman, at New York's memorial service for victims of the 9/11 tragedies.

While the crowd's response to my anthem rendition in St. Lucie was enthusiastic, the most expressive gestures and comments came from Mets players and a vendor. As I walked the gauntlet past the Mets dugout right after singing, manager Pedro Lopez gave me thumbs up and said, "Good job," followed by third baseman Richard Lucas reaching over the dugout railing to shake hands with me. A short time later, a vendor who was roasting pretzels over a charcoal fire near the backstop breezeway expressed great appreciation for the anthem itself. He offered that his wife Laura Mercado had auditioned a couple of days earlier to sing for the Mets and hoped to sing soon for one of their games later in the season.

Among the bits of advice and recommendations that I had received from friends while planning the anthem tour was the suggestion that I purchase a hat at each ballpark. I had countered: "Are you kidding? If I could get them for an average of twenty dollars apiece, I would be out more than two grand. And what would I do with 109 hats? Where would I put them?" No, thanks.

So before embarking on this wild venture, I had decided not to buy any souvenirs but to look for freebies—ticket stubs and folded schedules—that I might frame in a collage or some other artistic arrangement of a diamond, a baseball and bat, or a wall-size map tracing my route. Until my sixth game, I avoided all temptations to buy ballpark programs and souvenirs.

In St. Lucie, however, I couldn't resist paying for a Mets program for $1.50 because it included a raffle chance to win a New York Mets jersey, specifically #53: Mookie Wilson's jersey. And, oh, my goodness, a dollar fifty was surely worth the chance to win a Mookie jersey to give to my good friend Rick Censullo, who had made a weeklong road trip with me the previous summer. A lifelong, die-hard Boston fan, Rick had been a voting citizen in Red Sox Nation seemingly since it was founded. Of course, Rick had died hard in 1986 when the Mets had errantly prevailed over the Red Sox in the World Series.

With Boston leading New York three games to two, and ahead 5-3 with two outs in the tenth inning of Game 6 in the 1986 World Series, the Mets had no runners on base. Boston fans could taste the end of their seven decades of agony during which the World Series championship had eluded them. But a wild thing happened. The "Curse of the Bambino" started to shout. Twice down to their final strike, the Mets managed to string together three singles before a wild pitch brought home the tying run. Then Mookie Wilson hit a routine ground ball toward Red Sox first-baseman Bill Buckner. The ball asserted its own staccato rhythm, hip-hopping under Buckner's glove and allowing the winning run to score. Although Buckner's miscue on Mookie's roller has taken on mythic significance in years since, the misplays and missed opportunities earlier in the inning were really the errors that cost the Sox the series, which the Mets clinched the next night.

Nonetheless, the temptation offered by the chance to win a Mookie jersey for a patriot of Red Sox Nation dissolved my resolve to resist the purchase of a program for a souvenir.

For the St. Lucie Mets, two players distinguished their efforts: First baseman Travis Ozga collected two hits, raising his opening-week average to .600; and outfielder Cesar Puello also singled twice, but got picked off so far from first that he was caught stealing. St. Lucie improved its league-leading record to 7-1 by posting a 6-3 win over the Charlotte Stone Crabs, whose ballpark was the only one in the Florida State League in which I was unable to sing.

Extra Innings and Extraordinary Outcomes: Game 7 in Jupiter

Two teams in the Florida State League claim home dugouts in Roger Dean Stadium in Jupiter. Like the NBA's Lakers and Clippers who share the Staples Center as their home court in Los Angeles, the Jupiter Hammerheads and the Palm Beach Cardinals call the same ballpark "home." Fortunately for me, I got to sing for both of them in my one night at their ballpark while Jupiter claimed whatever home-field advantage there might be.

When I arrived in Jupiter shortly after noon, I located the ballpark and looked for a good meal that might satisfy me until after the game. Within eyesight of the ballpark I found Le Metro, where I enjoyed a delectable lunch, not only for the savory meal but also for the surprising conversation. Tiara, the waitress, recommended the broth-based mushroom soup and, as an entrée, grilled scallops, presented over tabbouleh, sliced tomatoes, and a fan of avocado slices dressed with an herbed, balsamic vinaigrette. When she asked what business had brought me to town, I indicated that I would be singing for the Hammerheads a few hours later. "Wow!" she exclaimed and then recounted how some years earlier, when she had been living in Newport Beach, California, her daughter Nicole Gero had sung the national anthem for the Freedom Bowl game.

It's quite simple: Anthem performances can unexpectedly bring people together.

An hour or so after lunch I approached Roger Dean Stadium and heard the P.A. announcer calling a game. Immediately, I feared that I had screwed up and missed a mid-afternoon start until I saw little activity occurring at the ticket booth and in the concession area. Then I heard the unfamiliar *ping* of an aluminum bat making contact with the ball, not the great wooden *crack* that distinguishes traditional and professional play. In the final week of the regular season of Florida's Class 2A High School baseball season, the Jupiter Christian Eagles were hosting the Benjamin Buccaneers. While their game progressed, I wandered around the ballpark's exterior and found tribute bricks to former players and fans in a patio area. Several caught my eye. Most vivid was one commemorating David Yolton, a "joyful anthem singer" who had died a few years earlier. Yolton, I later learned, was an accomplished musician who had guest conducted the Pittsburgh symphony while serving as a minister of music in Pennsylvania. After retiring to the Palm Beach area, he had enjoyed singing the national anthem for minor league games.

Another brick celebrated the appearance of Cody Palmer as a catcher in spring training one year with the St. Louis Cardinals. Before retiring from independent league teams, he had advanced as far as Class-A Advanced (Hi A) baseball in 2004 when he walked and struck out in his only plate appearances. Other messages promoted baseball enterprises (like the one for playattheplate.org, which sponsors adult baseball tournaments in professional and historic ballparks) as well as organizations (like the nearby Grace Immanuel Bible Church, whose simple name served as an invitation to prospective attendees).

After surveying the phrases inscribed in the bricks, I sat on a bench outside the ballpark reading yet another baseball book and listening to the P.A. announcer describe the action, while both teams scored an unbalanced number of runs in the final inning to even up the score. Then in extra innings I heard the typical sting of the high-school bats yield to a *clang*. Jupiter won on a walk-off home run.

Hours later, during the game between St. Lucie and Jupiter, I met Tug Haines, a blogger who was touring all of the minor league ballparks east of the Mississippi River. A cranberry farmer from New Jersey, Tug had fallen in love with minor league ball a few years earlier while his beloved Phillies had been on a long road trip. Six months before our meeting during this game, he had come up with the idea of hitting the road for a longer trip than the Phillies had taken that year. With his sister's assistance, then, he looked at team schedules and, like me, decided to begin his expedition in Florida. When he had checked my itinerary a few days after the season's start, he discovered that, although we would simultaneously crisscross the eastern U.S. throughout the next few months, the only place where we would land near the same dugout on the same night would be in Jupiter, coincidentally while the moon would be approaching its seventh house. Maybe baseball aligned us with "the dawning of the age of Aquarius," not merely part of the medley from *Hair*.

The evening game between the Hammerheads and the Cardinals featured two unusual plays, ones more extraordinary than the walk-off, bloop single that ended the game in the eleventh inning—the ballpark's second extra-inning game of the day.

In the first inning, Hammerheads clean-up hitter Kyle Jensen belted a home run off the "Moe's Southwest Grill" sign on the light stanchion beyond the 387 marker in left centerfield. He certainly cleaned up with his good aim, winning $100 in gift cards from the restaurant and generating coupons for a free taco for fans in one section of the grandstands. The promotion called to mind Abe Stark's scoreboard at Ebbets Field that read, "Hit sign, win suit." The trick there was to hit the low right-field sign on the fly. Cartoons often featured one of his clothing store employees standing as an extra outfielder in front of the ad, ready to catch any fly ball hit toward the target.

Two innings later the Cardinals mounted a rally with back-to-back singles, bringing Alan Ahmady to the plate with runners on first and second. He laced an apparent single past the second-baseman, but the baserunner from first, who had hesitated as the ball passed in front of him, was gunned down by the right fielder at second base, resulting in a force out.

Although not quite as unusual for baseball, another uncommon play spotlighted the umpires. With a runner on second, the Hammerheads batter topped the ball, sending a slow roller between the mound and first. Maikel Cleto, the Cardinals pitcher, scooped up the ball, crossed the foul line, and lunged after the runner—but missed making the tag. The base umpire, who had been positioned near second because of a runner on base, called the hitter safe as he crossed first base. Immediately, Luis Aguayo, the Cardinals manager, rushed to the field and argued the call. And within a couple of minutes of intense discussion with both umpires, the base umpire changed his ruling and called the runner out for having left the baseline.

By Jupiter, the second extra-inning game of the ballpark's day also ended on a walk-off, extra-base hit, this time a double by Dallas Poulk: Hammerheads 5, Cardinals 4.

Fireworks Seemed Secondary: Game 8 in Clearwater

The joy that I derive from watching baseball is intensified when I'm able to share a good game with friends. In Clearwater, that happened. The Stoub family from Orlando—Darren; his wife Sarah; and their two children Rachel and Tyler, ages eight and seven—joined me at the Threshers ballpark for an early evening game. Darren, then a chemistry professor at Rollins College, had been my colleague at Whittier several years earlier. And a week before the 9/11 terrorist attacks, Darren, who also has a pilot's license, had taken Bonnie and me for an airplane ride over Whittier, Disneyland, and other landmarks in the area. Now much of that airspace is more tightly controlled than the day on which he had given us the aerial tour.

After spending an afternoon at the beach, Rachel and Tyler continued their daylong adventure by attending their very first baseball game. The Threshers provided us with marvelous seats behind the Clearwater dugout, and we enjoyed ample space afforded by the empty rows in front of and behind us. In the bottom of the fifth inning, a foul ball bounced toward the dugout and was grabbed by left fielder D'Arby Myers, who tossed the ball to me so that I could give it to Tyler. At that point we almost could have forgotten the game on the field! Right away, Tyler got absorbed in tossing the ball a few steps up the aisle, watching its angle of rebound, and fielding it as it would roll back down the steps toward him.

That is, until the seventh-inning stretch, through which Tyler smiled while singing "Take Me Out to the Ballgame," and during which Rachel enjoyed the video projection of herself on the scoreboard screen. Up to that point Rachel had been most fascinated by the size of the women's restroom. After a mid-game visit there with her mother, Rachel returned to her seat and trumpeted the fact that she had counted "twenty stalls in the women's bathroom!"

Before the game ended, Rachel continued to enjoy a charmed evening. When Threshers staffers started to bazooka promotional tee-shirts into the stands, Darren caught one and handed it immediately to Rachel. Emblazoned with the logo of the Threshers on one side, the shirt also featured the sponsor Ozona's Southern-Style Barbecue on the other. And tucked into the tightly wadded shirt was a gift certificate. But Rachel's night was not yet done: After the top of the ninth inning, Threshers second-baseman Cesar Hernandez, who had caught the final out, tossed her the ball. Incredibly, both Tyler and Rachel received balls from the players.

During the game, the most distinct play had been a second-inning bunt that had rolled foul with its last breath. The Daytona batter had laid down what looked like an uncontested single, with the ball hugging the third-baseline in front of us. The Threshers fielder had escorted it down the chalk, waiting to tap it once it might cross the line. Yet it stayed fair, even while the batter stood watching and waiting on first base. As the ball's speed slowed, it held its course until its whisper reached the bag. Then, within a catch-breath of the base, the ball tilted across the line and died untouched in foul territory, a dime's distance from the base, while the third-baseman waited for the ump to call the dead ball foul.

Typically, postgame fireworks are the highlight of a young child's experience at a ballpark. Yet I'm not sure that even that colorful spray topped the delight Tyler and Rachel experienced eating ballpark concessions, getting game balls, catching a promotional tee-shirt, and being spotlighted on the scoreboard.

While the Stoubs stayed to see the fireworks following Clearwater's 3-1 loss to Daytona, I enjoyed a different celestial light display of the full moon rising over Tampa Bay as I headed back toward Orlando to catch an early-morning flight to Alabama for the Biscuits game in Montgomery the following night.

Beaten Biscuits: Game 9 in Montgomery

An old Southern food tradition is "beaten biscuits," so called because the dough was often whacked with a wooden tool to create air pockets, which would cause the biscuits to rise. Now that baking soda and baking powder can be added to the dough, simple kneading can achieve the same leavening effect.

Perhaps it's because of my love of biscuits that I desperately wanted to include the Montgomery Biscuits in my itinerary. When the most convenient dates that I proposed to the team's staff couldn't be accommodated, I went to extreme efforts to work out a date with them, the only team whose name is a food that is not an animal or plant. Of course, there were Stone Crabs in Charlotte (FL), Mudcats in Carolina, Kernels in Cedar Rapids, and Nuts in Modesto. But there were no Burgers in Burlington, no Fries in Fresno, nor Grits in Greensboro.

The only way to find a compatible date with the Montgomery Biscuits was for me to interrupt my crisscrossing through the Florida State League for a single-game junket into Alabama. In effect, the inclusion of the Biscuits in my menu required me to

> drive from Clearwater to Orlando after a Sunday-night game;
> sleep in an airport hotel and rise early;
> catch an early-morning direct flight to Birmingham;
> rent a car and then drive 110 miles south to Montgomery;
> sing for the game;
> retrace 110 miles to an airport hotel in Birmingham; and
> catch the only direct flight back to Orlando early the next morning, so that I could arrive in time to drive to Lakeland to sing for the Flying Tigers on the following evening.

But the extreme travel demands were worth it.

When I arrived at Riverwalk Stadium in Montgomery, I wondered about a possible dissonant distraction during the anthem performance. Beyond the left-field fence I saw a train rolling along and heard its shrill whistle, certainly not harmonious with the anthem's melody. I cringed at the possibility that another locomotive might belch its signal while I would be belting out, "...bombs bursting in air...!" Later as I talked with fans, I learned that occasionally anthem singers had been thrown off key by the coincidental serenade of the trains. Fortunately, I experienced no such difficulty.

The train tracks' juxtaposition to the field plays a more prominent role in Biscuits lore. A former Montgomery mayor apparently promoted the possible distraction as a distinction by offering a thousand dollars to the first hometown player who would hit a home run off a passing train. Eventually, the mayor supposedly paid up when one of the Biscuits belted one off a boxcar.

The pregame ceremonies featured two colonels from nearby Maxwell Air Force Base throwing out the first pitch. Neither was successful in commanding a hardball airstrike. Both tossed wildly, their throws landing fifteen feet short and wide of home plate. Other pregame participants included a local T-Ball team sponsored by a local pediatric dental clinic. Before the kindergarten and first-grade kids were introduced by name and position, they were instructed to run onto the field and sidle up to their respective Biscuits players, already in place. But as the announcer quickly read the T-

Ballers' names and positions, confusion arose. None went to right field or shortstop.

"Where are those positions?" the kids must have wondered. Instead of searching for their assigned places, a clump of them ambled happily over toward the easily identifiable second base and delightedly stood at attention while I sang the anthem. As they left the field, each of the kids received a ball that was autographed by his or her aligned Biscuits player. But the highlight of their evening seemed to be getting their picture taken with Big Mo, the Montgomery mascot whose costume featured a hula-hoop waist that created virtual biscuits for hips. The T-Ballers' joy was as delectable and true as beaten biscuits.

At the start of the game, the Biscuits had hoped to smother the Jackson Generals with record-breaking home runs, as they had accomplished the previous night when they had hit five. But this night, while the Generals ordered their own airstrikes, launching three home runs, I engaged James Anderson in lively conversation about the history of Minor League Baseball in Montgomery, the ballpark's construction, the naming of the team, and Alabama's support of AA teams (the state was then home to four of the thirty AA teams in the nation). A partner in a law firm whose offices across the street looked down on the field, Anderson and his legal team had occupied the same box seats behind home plate since the ballpark had opened.

He pointed out that a new state law prevented all public officials from being hosted at any ballgame. Since corporate sponsors had been able to share their seats with legislators and city magnates until the previous month, he conjectured that one consequence of the recent law would be that corporations might curtail their expenditures for luxury boxes. Coupled with this challenge, the recent downturn in the economy might reduce the number of games that ordinary fans would attend. Consequently, he feared for baseball's health in Montgomery.

Having seen his childhood Montgomery Rebels depart decades ago, leaving the city without a team for years and years, he expressed a desire to exercise influence to ensure that the Biscuits attendance would remain strong. Scanning the crowd on this Monday evening, he projected that the game's attendance would be challenged to break 500, despite having two youth teams featured as part of the pregame ceremonies. By the game's end, however, the official attendance was reported as 1,698. Maybe the concessions and in-game activities—which featured chicken biscuits, biscuits with gravy, and biscuits with butter and jelly—lured a hungry crowd on a school night! One of Montgomery's between-innings promotions also featured biscuits. Rather than hurling tee-shirts into the sections of the crowd cheering the loudest, the in-game staffers tossed foil-wrapped, warm biscuits to fans during mid-innings.

Although I had felt that I needed to include the Biscuits in my anthem tour, on Monday night they were simply beaten: Jackson Generals 6, Montgomery Biscuits 4. And so was I, even though I still had to return to a hotel near the Birmingham airport before rising for the "dawn's early 'flight'" back to Orlando.

Bingo Back in Florida: Game 10 in Lakeland

Bingo! I bounced back into Florida after my barnstorming jaunt to Alabama for the single game with the Biscuits.

In Lakeland, the Flying Tigers enjoyed the minor leagues' longest continuous relationship—forty-five years—with a single major league team. Although named for the city's longtime parks-and-recreation director, Joker Marchant, the ballpark and its surrounding area are unmistakably aligned with the Tigers of Detroit. Rather than displaying images related to the heroic World War II fighter squadrons who had trained in Lakeland, the art and architecture of the ballpark feature orange and black tiger stripes that reflect Detroit's major league team.

Near the home plate entrance to the ballpark, there are other obvious reminders of the team's connection to the Michigan metropolis. Adjacent streets are named for Hall of Famer Al Kaline and fan favorite Willie Horton, and beside the ticket booths inscribed tiles honor the success of popular players, team personnel, and devoted fans, like the ones devoted to Hall of Fame broadcaster Ernie Harwell and another to all-star shortstop Allan Trammell.

Before the game two players saw me preparing to sing and inquired about the anthem tour since they had heard me perform at Clearwater a couple of days earlier. One was reserve catcher Eric Roof. The name was distinct. Years earlier, I had tracked the career of Phil Roof, a catcher who had caught more than 800 games for eight teams during his fifteen-year major league career. So why would I follow a journeyman catcher? It's simple. He was from Paducah, Kentucky, where the Price family has a taproot into mid-nineteenth century.

I asked Eric if he were related to the Paducah Roofs—either Phil or his brother Gene, an outfielder who drank about fifty "cups of coffee" (the baseball cliché for a brief appearance in the majors) with St. Louis and Montreal. Eric said that both his uncle and father hail from the Paducah area. But I never learned which one was his father, although the catching gene would favor Phil as the likely sire.

Lakeland distinguished itself in other ways, too: Start with the osprey nest atop the outfield light standard, an attraction duplicated in Brevard County and later in Missoula. Also add the unusual timbre of voices that rang throughout the stands. The P.A. announcer was a woman, the only alto I heard in Florida. When she read the promo about the outfield egg hunt on the day before Easter, she noted that some of the 20,000 eggs would be dropped from a helicopter. Amazed and befuddled by that incredulous number, she reduced the number to 2,000, then checked the promo data again and restored the count to 20,000. I was familiar with the expression "raining cats and dogs," but never "hailing eggs." Since 2,053 fans were later counted as the game's attendance on the day of the hunt, it's possible that some quick kids with large baskets gathered as many as a hundred eggs. The curious question, then, would be whether they played egg toss during the game or, throwing harder, peg egg.

Another unique voice came from a leather-lunged fan, truly the loudest one all summer long, louder even than the chorus of women whom I would find weeks later in Lynchburg. With a particular rasp and pitch, he kept urging his Tigers to hit the ball, yelling for all to hear, perhaps even loud enough to puzzle youthful players at other ballparks miles away. "You're not in Little League anymore," he bellowed. "Swing the bat!"

On this weeknight before school began its summer recess, the sparse crowd of 448 was dominated by senior citizens. The in-game activities appealed primarily to them rather than to children and young adults, who typically were offered chances to outrun the mascot in a race from first to third, or to play water-balloon baseball. Lakeland involved scorekeeping fans throughout the early innings by playing a baseball bingo that correlated players by position with the results of their at-bats. Not quite like the older table-top baseball games of APBA or Strat-o-Matic, the bingo served as a blend of fantasy sports and familiar board games.

In Lakeland's 8-6 win over Dunedin, there seemed to be no single highlight, although Dunedin scored its first run in the first without a single hit (a walk, a stolen base, a sacrifice, and a fielder's choice) and Lakeland bunched together four singles in its five-run outburst in the third.

With lightning in the distance and miles to drive after the game, I left the ballpark following the fifth, with Lakeland leading shortly after the umpire called the batter out and a fan called out, "Bingo!"

Breaking Barriers in Florida: Game 11 in Daytona

Historic Jackie Robinson Ballpark in Daytona reflects the patriotic and embracing character of the Daytona Beach community.

In 1946, during the Dodgers spring-training tour of Florida cities, Jackie Robinson became the first African American to take the field in a professional baseball game featuring a major league team or one of its affiliates. In the first few days of their exhibition circuit, the Dodgers had been scheduled to play their Triple-A affiliate, Montreal, in a couple of central Florida cities. Yet complications and cancellations had developed in those communities, such as a supposed power failure that prevented stadium lights from illuminating the field.

Daytona, which already enjoyed a history of affirming civil rights, became the first place where Robinson actually took the field in integrated competition involving a major league team. While the number of African-American fans attending that game far exceeded the capacity in the special section that had been set aside for them, there were no racial incidents at the ballpark. And local newspaper reports the following day noted the positive reception that Robinson had received.

Later, in his autobiography *I Never Had It Made*, he recalled his own excitement: "When I got home, I felt as though I had won some kind of victory. I had a new opinion of the people in the town [Daytona Beach]. I knew, of course, that everyone wasn't pulling for me to make good, but I was sure that the whole world wasn't lined up against me. When I went to sleep, the applause was still ringing in my ears."

Now the ballpark houses a modest but interactive museum about the achievement and athleticism of Robinson, as well as other "barrier-breaking" athletes like Roberto Clemente and Althea Gibson. A basketball goal entices youngsters to jump to the height at which Robinson could touch the rim. A home-to-first-base path invites children to try their best to beat out an imaginary bunt. And, of course, there are displays about Robinson's baseball prowess.

While the ballpark is historic because of the significant games that have been played there, it also exudes an old-timey feel with its wooden stands behind home plate, obstructed views from some reserved seats, and a hand-operated scoreboard. Another distinction along the left-field fence was a sign that stated simply: "Front Row Joe's 1,069 Game Streak." And I thought that my project of 109 ballparks was impressive! "Front Row" Joe Rowe was a Daytona super-fan who had attended that many consecutive Daytona home games, a streak that had begun in 1995. After paying for his admission in the first few years, Joe then participated in a Daytona promotion that offered lifetime free admission for fans who would get the team name or logo tattooed on an observable part of their body. He did. And now before each game, Joe walked to the outfield and added that number of the game to the ongoing tally. Known for his boisterous, G-rated heckling of the Cubs' opponents, Joe usually sat with other Cubbie den-mates near the visitors' dugout.

At Daytona, my introduction included a brief description of my tour, as well as mention of the fact that Wrigley Field is among the major league ballparks where I had sung the anthem. A loud, good-humored beer vendor was effusive in his praise, greeting me before I could move into the stands, saying that my performance was the best he'd ever heard, and loudly inviting me back to sing the following night—or any and every other night during the summer. In Daytona, for the first time in my series of anthem performances, I saw fans singing along with me—at least a dozen or more seated in the wood-planked sections behind home plate. I love it when folks join me in singing *our* anthem.

Accompanying me to this final game in my swing through the Florida State League, Greg Sapp framed my Hi-A ballpark experience in the state since he had opened the season with me at Brevard County. While we sat in the picnic area in the third inning, a woman with close-cropped hair approached us and began to share her love of baseball and America.

"I'm so glad you didn't sing it like a dirge," Karen began.

She identified herself as a Navy vet who had come to the game to support breast-cancer awareness night. For this game, the Cubs had donned their jerseys with pink ribbon accents that would be auctioned off to support "Search for the Cure." Suffering from radiation treatments following her chemotherapy after a second radical mastectomy, Karen said that she found hope and joy in baseball, in humor, and in patriotic displays. She displayed great ease with her unintentional crewcut and joked about being flat-chested. She was simply glad to be alive and delighted to be at the ballpark.

One of the recurrent pleasures in the Florida ballparks was making contact with retirees who shared stories about their former favorite teams up

North, and with snowbirds who expressed a desire to see me sing again at one of the games in their hometowns, whether Trenton or Rochester. Daytona proved no exception to this phenomenon. Before the game, I was drawn to Bill and Carol Porter because Bill was wearing a University of Kentucky baseball cap. I mentioned to him that I had heard the report that three of Kentucky's players from their recent Final Four team had declared their eligibility for the NBA draft, although none had actually hired an agent. Waiting for the gates to open, we shared our passion for basketball in the Bluegrass and, of course, for baseball.

Inquiring about my travels, Bill indicated that he would attend the Lexington Legends game in late May when I was scheduled to sing there, and Carol expressed interest in the possibility of my singing for the Tennessee Smokies in Knoxville, where her daughter lived. Regrettably, I informed her, I had gotten "smoked"—or ignored—by the Knoxville team, which was one of the few minor league teams that never responded to any of my queries and proposals.

In the game, the Cubs jumped out to a four-run, first-inning lead thanks to two doubles followed by a single and a home run, the fifth in just fourteen games for outfielder Michael Burgess. With more than enough offense to hold off Lakeland, the Cubs pounded out nine more hits, but added only one run to their win, 5-2.

Following the game in Daytona, I returned to DeLand for a comfortable evening with my good friends and weeks-long hosts, Don and Ruth Musser. As I left the next morning for three games in South Carolina and Georgia, Don ribbed me a bit about my progress in the tour: "It's like you've just finished the first inning...and there's no relief pitcher in sight!"

So true.

Southern Style: Game 12 in Savannah

There's no question that Southerners love baseball and SEC football. While Georgians certainly love their Dawgs and long for autumn Saturday triumphs at home between the hedges, they are also among the most passionate Southerners in their devotion to baseball. They relish the epic brilliance of Ty Cobb, whose nickname embraced the state's identity: "the Georgia Peach." And for much of the 1990s, they celebrated the success of the Atlanta Braves, who, because of the promotional effectiveness of TBS sports, became known as "America's Team."

Given the character of Southern hospitality, it should have come as little surprise that, north of Jacksonville, I was greeted by official state signs welcoming travelers to Georgia. What did surprise me was a particular sign among the greetings. It identified the state as "The Home of the 1995 World Series Champions," its single major league championship. The victory had come a decade and a half earlier when Clinton had enjoyed his first term, gasoline prices had crested below two dollars a gallon nearby, and Hootie and the Blowfish had begun to climb to the top of the music charts. Still, Georgia spotlighted that passing moment of baseball supremacy as worth a mention when welcoming travelers to the state.

Pressing north on I-95, I was bemused by the idea that Georgia claimed to be a part of the Braves' new world.

The eastward approach to Savannah's ballpark along Victory Drive was an allée of moss-weeping trees, and historic Grayson Stadium, which had opened in 1926, radiated an aura of the past being present. The ballpark had felt the cleats of Hall of Famers Ruth, Mantle, and Aaron, and it was distinguished by wooden bench seats behind home plate, by a fully screened seating area between first and third, and by overhead fans that whirled as softly and slowly as a Southern drawl.

Prior to the game, I began my routine coursing through the ballpark. Because MiLB writer Ben Hill had alerted me to a unique Sand Gnats concession that had been featured on NBC as the best new ballpark food—chicken and waffles—I sought it out, even though I couldn't sample it since I'm allergic to sucrose. At the food window, however, I did delight in seeing two of the visiting Lexington Legends players wait for their delivery of the meal.

Often portrayed as a city where hanging moss is thicker than the humidity, Savannah exudes Southern manners, heritage, and cuisine. Yet the Class-A team that finds its home there didn't employ images of plantation life or Southern hospitality or soul food. Instead, it aptly adopted the name "Sand Gnats." Shortly before the game began, pitchers in the visiting bullpen sprayed themselves with insect repellant to stifle attacks by the persistent flying bugs. While the players bathed their necks and arms with Deet, I vividly recalled Joba Chamberlain's frustration in the eighth inning of the Yankees playoff game in Cleveland in 2007, when midges had attacked him on the mound, distracting his focus and allowing the Indians' resurgence.

As dusk enveloped the ballpark a short time later while I was singing about "the twilight's last gleaming," two of the gnats darted toward my nose, and I flashed on a story of an operatic tenor who had been pestered by a fly during a performance. While he had held a long high note with his mouth agape, the fly had helicoptered toward him and hovered momentarily in front of his mouth, wings waving so fast that the pitch of his voice changed. I sensed that the less violent wing movement of gnats probably wouldn't cause the same effect; yet I feared that I might inhale one of them with my next deep breath. Thankfully, the bugs proved simply to be a distraction.

Walking past the Lexington players following the anthem, I heard a couple of them offer congratulations, to which I responded that I would see them again in the Bluegrass in late May. Then taking my seat, I was greeted by Carol Turner, sister of my brother-in-law, California Appellate Justice Paul Turner. In ways that seemed to fit with Southern stereotypes about extended-family relationships, I found a kissing-kin-in-law to sit with in Charleston! How's that for making a Southern shirttail connection and trying to angle a good side with the law?

In the game, Lexington took a commanding four-run lead into the middle innings, only to see Charleston peck away and eventually score four in the ninth to win by a single run: 6-5. The game featured about as many hits by both teams—twenty-six, almost equally split—as there were gnat attacks before night's darkness settled in.

Good Friday and Bad Weather: Game 13 in Charleston

For more than an hour during the late afternoon on Good Friday, I sat stranded in the car in the parking lot adjacent to the Charleston RiverDogs ballpark, familiarly known as "The Joe." Raging thunderstorms had been pounding the area for more than an hour. I had no umbrella to use to enter the RiverDogs offices, and I had kept hoping that the storms would subside so that the game might proceed. I desperately wanted to perform for the RiverDogs since team president Mike Veeck had been instrumental in lining up my singing for them, and since, decades earlier, he had also played a formative role in setting up the first occasion for my singing the anthem for a professional ballgame.

On a Friday in late July 2010, I received a phone message from Mike in response to my e-mail request to sing for Charleston. Coincidentally, thirty-three years earlier on a July Friday evening in Chicago, Bonnie and I had been tending to our month-old, firstborn son in our Hyde Park apartment when the phone rang. When I answered it, the caller identified himself as Mike Veeck, a staff member in the front office of the White Sox, and he invited me to sing the National Anthem on Fan Appreciation Day at Comiskey Park a few weeks later.

Weeks earlier I had sent a letter to Bill Veeck, the owner of the White Sox and Mike's father. In it I had expressed hope that the senior Veeck could help me fulfill a dream of singing at a major league game. In those days before audio cassettes, I had no recording of my anthem performance. In my appeal, I simply had listed my singing credits in the Chicago area and had offered to audition at any time during the summer.

Hearing Mike's offer, I immediately responded, "When do you want me to audition?"

In those pre-Roseanne Barr performance days, he replied succinctly, "You're fool enough to ask. We're fool enough to let you do it."

When Mike called again while I was starting to set up the anthem tour project, he offered me support by RiverDogs staff in scheduling a date, and he indicated that I would be welcome to sing for the Fort Myers Miracle and the Hudson Valley Renegade, other teams owned by the Goldklang group with whom he was a partner. As we talked, I expressed appreciation for his role in getting me started in singing the anthem for ballgames, and he replied that he was glad that "good things persist"—that I still loved baseball and that I still enjoyed singing the national anthem.

These formative conversations played through my mind while the rain continued to crash against the roof of my car. Meanwhile, the charter bus ferrying the Greenville Drive players to the park pulled into the lot and opened its door. No one disembarked. After a few minutes the door closed and off the bus drove—or floated. As puddles deepened into mini-ponds, my single ray of hope was sustained simply by the fact that the lights on the field remained on. I figured that if and when the game would be cancelled, the lights would be turned out.

After ninety minutes, the deluge subsided and I went to look at the field—or wading pool. By comparison, the wet field in the playful scene when Crash Davis created a "rainout" in *Bull Durham* was merely a puddle. When the manager of the visiting Drive saw the expanse and depth of the water, he looked like he was awash in some of South Carolina's rice paddies. Even so, he directed his team to dress and prepare for play.

For two hours I watched the grounds crew shovel water into five-gallon buckets, empty the containers into fifty-gallon trash cans, and transport them time and again on a maintenance cart to dump beyond the outfield fence, creating a new tributary to the Ashley River about a hundred yards away.

While I photographed their efforts, one of the guys hollered up to me, "I hope we're on Sports Center tonight!" All told, Mike Williams, the head groundskeeper, and his staff shoveled more than 2,000 gallons of water off the left-field corner alone. At the same time, others swept the pools behind home plate, and another used a leaf-blower to blow-dry puddles behind shortstop. Meanwhile, as strange as it may seem, the hose crew turned on the spigot behind the mound and began to wet the infield dirt. The incredible effort by the entire crew enabled the game to begin merely a half-hour later than scheduled.

In keeping with the season-long custom of honoring American service men and women at their Friday-evening games, the RiverDogs introduced two Navy and Marine enlistees and described their tours of duty as part of the pregame ceremony. And for the second time in a dozen games, I faced the flag in the outfield rather than the fans in the stands behind home plate.

Walking back up to the concourse, I heard Tony "The Peanut Man" call out, "Man, that was good! That's the first time I understood every word." Having worked at the park since it had opened in the mid-1990s, Tony had heard hundreds and hundreds of anthem performances.

While his comment earmarked my performance and the rain removal had set a new standard for grounds-crew work, a couple of unusually placed signs distinguished the playing field and the grandstand. Unlike any other ballpark that I have ever seen, the distance from home plate to the backstop was measured and painted below the railing near the visiting team's dugout as "-57" feet. Somewhat similarly located in an odd position, a section of the upper grandstand was designated as "Doby's 3," recognizing Larry Doby, the former star in the Negro Leagues who, eleven weeks after the major league debut of Jackie Robinson, had become the first black player in the American League. A South Carolinian by birth, Doby lived throughout his adolescent and adult years in New Jersey, and he never played for a Charleston team. Yet as a tribute to Mike Veeck's father, who had signed Doby to his Cleveland Indians contract, the ballpark had named the section for Doby.

Some culinary delights also distinguished the fare at "The Joe." One was freshly boiled peanuts dipped from a vat large enough for hog scalding, and another was the ballpark's specialty sandwich—the "Monster Pimiento Pickle Burger." Of course, with a team name like the "RiverDogs," the "Dog World" concession featured a pack of dogs: the Yankee Dog, Dixie Dog,

Mexidog, and Mutt—create your own dog with any of the fifteen listed toppings, including pickled okra.

During the RiverDogs 6-5 win, Shane Greene and John Ryan Murphy combined as the battery for Charleston, a feat that they would accomplish during their rookie seasons with the Yankees a couple years later. Otherwise, the odd twist to the game was that Greenville held the RiverDogs to seven hits, all but one of which were clustered in their two run-scoring innings.

Despite the rain a few hours before game time, the Good Friday crowd in Charleston was the largest that I had seen since opening night. While they enjoyed the RiverDogs win and the postgame fireworks show, I appreciated the efforts of the two Mikes—Veeck and Williams—who had made it possible for me to be miked for the anthem in soggy Charleston.

Southern Style, Part II: Game 14 in Augusta

The shortest route from Charleston to Augusta, Georgia, took me through Denmark—a small, South Carolina town where I stopped for lunch at "The Diner," a historic eatery. Like a blue-tick hound tracking game, I was sniffing out prospects for authentic Southern vegetables, seasoned with bacon and simmered since sunrise. Regrettably, my arrival at The Diner was too early to take advantage of its "After 4 P.M. Special of the Day," an eight-ounce ribeye steak with baked potato and sides for only $6.99. Given my limited opportunities to find good vegetables at fast-food restaurants and ballpark booths, the "sides"—or accompanying vegetables—taunted my appetite.

Although The Diner's menu offered no collards or turnip greens, no limas or black-eyed peas, it did suggest fried chicken or a fried bologna sandwich as lunch-time features. As a child I had once eaten a fried bologna sandwich at a friend's house; now I felt no need to recapture that greasy experience. But when I tried to order the fried chicken, the waitress informed me, "We already run out 'cause folks bought up the breasts for their Easter fixin's tomorrow." Yes, Denmark showed its deep Southern roots in language, diet, and religion.

I settled for grilled chicken with mashed potatoes and green beans, none of which had been prepared Southern-style. I guess I really shouldn't have been disappointed since I had strangely thought that I might satisfy my Southern appetite in Denmark. Before stopping for lunch, I had paused in Branchville to photograph one of the more discouraging sites for a baseball fan: a public baseball field surrounded by high, chain-link fences topped by strands of barbed wire. A “NO TRESPASSING” sign hung on the chain-locked gates that prevented unauthorized play. The lockout of major league players during their salary strikes had been bad enough, but the lockout of kids from playing the game for fun seemed almost unconscionable.

By mid-afternoon I drove into the city and located the Augusta Museum of History, which featured an exhibit about a century of baseball from Cobb to Cal: Ty hailed from Augusta, and Ripken now owned the Augusta GreenJackets. The first professional baseball team in Augusta had taken the field in 1909, and through the years the Augusta teams had been known by various names. My favorites, even surpassing the inaugural “Tourists” and the current stylish designation as “GreenJackets,” were the “Dollies” of 1919 and, from 1922 to 1929, the “Tygers”—with the spelling variation a punning tribute to Ty Cobb, who was still starting and starring for the Detroit Tigers until 1927.

The GreenJackets ballpark also paid a simple tribute to Cobb. Rather than posting the fence distance in the power alleys or centerfield, the ballpark displayed a single distance in left field, more toward the foul line than in the power alley. It read, “.366,” the distance to that point corresponding to Cobb’s lifetime batting average.

Before I moved to the home-plate area to sing the anthem, GreenJackets pitching coach Steve Kline, a veteran major league pitcher known for his jovial nature, chatted with me about inconsequential matters until he learned that I was singing the anthem. Then he said simply, “Bring it home.”

Apparently, I did. He “high-fived” me as I left the field. After I took my seat, a fan in the row in front of me turned and offered a more surprising response, saying simply, “Nice singing.” Savannah was her name. Four years old, she later shared with me her drawing of a happy girl like herself, happy to be at the ballpark.

There’s really nothing quite like Southern graciousness and charm Georgia-style, especially in the expressions of a smiling preschool girl. Savannah was certainly the highlight of the evening in Augusta, far outshining the starting pitchers for the GreenJackets and the Delmarva Shorebirds: Each enjoyed a quality start, completing six innings, yielding three hits, and allowing two or fewer runs in the Shorebirds 6-1 win.

Hunting, Herding, and Singing: Game 15 in Jacksonville

On my way to the Will Call ticket window at Jacksonville, I stopped to talk with the chief of stadium security. When he learned that I would be singing the anthem, he quipped: "Do you know the last two words of the national anthem?" "Of course," I said: "the brave." Since the Jacksonville Suns were affiliated with the Florida Marlins and not Atlanta, I knew that his response would not be "the Braves." Instead, he countered: "Play ball."

He asked about the history of the national anthem and its performance at sporting events. Because ballgames are the only place where he routinely heard the anthem sung or played, he wondered aloud whether it had been written for baseball. I then surmised that he had not attended many PTA meetings.

Since I had made conference presentations about the performance of "The Star-Spangled Banner" at sporting events, I was primed to respond. I noted that the first verifiable performance of the song at a major league game occurred in Game 3 of the 1918 World Series, thirteen years before it would be officially adopted as the national anthem. Even so, the routine performance of the anthem at baseball games did not begin until the 1942 season, when Major League Baseball sought to bolster patriotism during the initial months of U.S. engagement in World War II.

At Jacksonville, two promotions took place on this Easter afternoon. One of the attractions to the holiday game was the annual Easter egg hunt, which began beyond the third base bag in foul territory and extended onto the outfield where the grass was divided into sectors for three age groups of children. The outfield was covered with colored eggs, some of which were plastic and contained gift certificates. In each of the three sectors, a single golden egg was hidden.

Along the left-field foul line, Brandon, age 4, carried an appropriate baseball-shaped basket for his eggs. Perhaps that was the good-luck charm he needed: He discovered the prized golden egg under an artificial grass rug beneath the bullpen bench. For his effort, he won a huge Easter basket filled with treats and Suns paraphernalia.

The other promotion was "Whiplash, the Cowboy Monkey," who performed before and after the game. A couple of weeks before my singing for the Suns, Tug Haines, the "casual fan" who was blogging about his trip to minor league parks east of the Mississippi River, had alerted me to this phenomenal act. Unlike Max Patkin's classic baseball antics, Whiplash's routine was not really related to baseball. It was a wild circus act or rodeo interlude that happened to be staged on a baseball diamond. Whiplash was a capuchin monkey that rode a border collie to wrangle sheep into a pen near the visitors' dugout. While the dog ran in patterns to herd the sheep, Whiplash jostled up and down as though riding a bucking bull or bronco.

By contrast to my traditional performance of the anthem, Whiplash's act was uncommon. Still, the Suns promoted my anthem project in two ways that no other team had done. For one, they featured my singing on their website along with the other promotions for the day. And in the introduction, not only did the P.A. announcer provide a brief description of the tour, but he also invited fans to check out the anthem tour website. Prompted by this publicity, several fans inquired about my venture and my work: How had I set up the tour? How could I take so much time off work? How would my voice hold up? Where had I been last week? Where would I sing the next day? While I emphasized the fun of the travel and the singing, I also let them know that the project really constituted work—a delightful, reassigned sort of work during my sabbatical from day-to-day teaching at Whittier College.

The game itself almost seemed to be the interlude between the two promotional acts of the Easter egg hunt and Whiplash's ride. The Jackson Generals commanded the Suns to submit to the offensive prowess of Ryan Flaherty and Rebel Ridling, who accounted for all of the visitors' runs. In the first inning, both players singled and scored before finishing the game with late-inning, solo home runs, leading the Generals to a 4-3 win.

Tracking the Hounds: Game 16 in Midland

The game in Midland, Texas, marked my final one alone before returning to California from my season-opening, month-long sojourn in Florida and nearby southern cities. Yet getting to Midland presented a more significant challenge than scheduling the fly-in game for Montgomery. When I first had examined the home-team schedule for the Midland RockHounds and pinpointed the remote location, I began to map out possible routes to and through Midland. None worked, especially since the week that I had tentatively mapped out for Texas teams proved incompatible with the RockHounds home schedule.

The distance of more than 325 miles from Midland to or from any of the other Texas minor league teams—in fact, it seemed, teams from anywhere—also appeared prohibitive. Midland certainly seemed to lie more at the edge of nowhere than in the middle of anywhere. Finally, I realized that I could most easily include the RockHounds in my itinerary by adding an overnight stop at the Midland-Odessa airport on my American Airlines return route from Jacksonville to Los Angeles, where I would pick up Bonnie, Arbie, and Toad to begin the major phase of the journey in the RV.

While the commuter jet from Dallas was buffeted by prairie gusts during its final approach into Midland-Odessa, I saw miles and miles of range scorched by wildfires weeks earlier. The landscape was covered with oil crickets routinely hunching crude from below. I perceived an incongruity—perhaps a prophecy—in the stark contrast between the blackened, surface sagebrush and the dark, steel arms that also depleted the deep crude.

After retrieving my rental car at the airport, I plotted a course from Midland to Odessa so that I could find and photograph Permian High School, the focal football program for *Friday Night Lights.* I'm not sure what I thought I would find there, simply having the chance to see the buildings and fields, but I had a sense that they were an omphalos for West Texas, a mythic center, a sacred space, an ironic cosmic mountain of hope in an otherwise unending, flat terrain of bleak economic and social repetition. The school's buildings looked unremarkable. Still, I took pictures of the front of the school before returning to Midland a half-hour away, locating the ballpark, and checking into my hotel, which proved to have few amenities, dingy rooms, and weak Wi-Fi—all for an exorbitant rate attributed to the oil exploration and extraction in the region.

Although the zephyrs across the plains seemed to push me away from the stadium while driving from the hotel to the ballpark, the entry to the parking lot cheerily greeted me with the likeness of Rocky, the popular RockHounds mascot. The sign also featured a mythic statistic identifying the ballpark's forty-year attendance total as its population: 6,552,953.

Like many of the minor league ballparks, a sculpture also welcomed fans to the main entry to the Citibank Ballpark. But unlike the creatively conceived and constructed sculptures at other stadiums, the piece in Midland was "found art." It was both natural and legendary. According to the plaque embedded on its brow, "Legend has it that this rock, excavated from below the playing field, guarantees fun and good times to all who touch it!" So it did. I touched it, and moments later I received a concessions gift card in appreciation for my singing the anthem.

Near this Texas blarney stone, a seating sculpture also provided a place to pay tribute to the team's success. A pentagonal bench in the shape of home included an inset home plate at its center as well as plaques noting team achievements and ballpark awards. Perhaps this design was baseball's version of Ezekiel's wheel within a wheel, a kind of plate within a plate.

The Midland ballpark crouched inconspicuously at the cusp of the city as though it was trying to duck below the path of blowing tumbleweed. Its low profile resulted from the fact that the field level of the ballpark was subterranean. Fans entered the concourse at parking-lot level and descended to their seats in an excavated bowl, unless they were among the few who rose to the VIP suites in the skyboxes. Even the hillocks beyond the outfield fences sloped downward from the surrounding plain to the level of the playing field.

The canyon-like floor of the field allowed prairie winds to howl above the rim of the ballpark, and its sunken site prevented "Baltimore chops" from gusting obliquely past a wary shortstop. But the submerged surface did not hamper winds from playing havoc with high fly balls, which routinely died in the alleys while gales blew in on most nights. For this game, the steady winds were clocked at thirty miles per hour and toward left field.

Although the slugfest between the RockHounds and the Corpus Christi Hooks produced eighteen runs, the wind did not play a jester's role in the game's twenty-six hits. In fact, to secure its victory, Midland utilized seven walks, two stolen bases, a balk, a wild pitch, and an error by the Hooks to achieve its two-run margin. I sensed that the game would be a wild one in the first inning when Midland's leadoff hitter, Jermaine Mitchell, struck out swinging, reached first on a passed ball, took second on an errant pick-off throw, stole third, and crossed the plate on a feeble grounder to the first-baseman. Innings later when he hit a home run, fans held up dollar bills for the ushers to retrieve and pass along to Mitchell as a slugger's bonus. I had not seen the hat passed in a game since a home-team home run in an independent minor league game some years before.

While the ballpark and game were enjoyable, what made my experience most pleasant was the affirming gesture by Hounds hitting coach Tim Garland and a conversation with Dan Jamierson, a Red Cross volunteer who appreciated the pace of my anthem rendition. Two nights earlier, Dan said, someone had mangled the anthem by "dragging it out for what seemed like the first inning." His comment reverberated the spirit of a newspaper cartoon earlier that morning. "In the Bleachers" had featured a singer standing near home plate with a word balloon providing the P.A. announcer's remark: "Now rise while another celebrity butchers the national anthem."

Dan also was the person who requested that I lead the crowd in singing "God Bless America" during the seventh-inning stretch. After he made the arrangements with the RockHounds staff about that possibility, I enjoyed my first two-hit game.

2.

Arbie's Anthem Debut

A Rare Night: Game 17 in Rancho Cucamonga

After spending three weeks in the storm-bedeviled Southeast, I was delighted to return to the sun-drenched Southwest, even if it placed me in the heart of California's earthquake country, where I hoped that my voice wouldn't crack while singing for the Quakes in Rancho Cucamonga. There the stadium is daringly known as the Epicenter—perhaps the ballpark whose name is most aptly aligned with its team—since the San Andreas Fault lies within view beyond the outfield fence. And the shaky theme is taken even further with the identity of the mascot, a dinosauric critter who instills the effect of his own name: Tremor.

In multiple ways the Quakes game was a rarity. For starters, it was the first game that Bonnie and our older son Jared were able to attend because we were able to commute to the game from our home in Whittier. In that respect, it also anticipated the final few games of the tour when I would again enjoy the postgame comfort of being greeted by Winston and Tucker (my two dogs), snacking from my full refrigerator and pantry, and sleeping in my own bed.

The game was rare in other ways, too. For one, it was the first game following Chris Erskine's witty column about my anthem project that had appeared in the sports section of the *Los Angeles Times* that morning. Right away, the effect of the article, which featured my opening weeks in Florida, was perceptible. As I left the home-plate area after singing, Quakes manager Juan Bustabad greeted me. "Great job," he said, adding, "I enjoyed the story in the morning paper. And when I saw you standing here, I said, 'Holy smoke! That's the guy. He gets around.'"

For this game, however, there were also other distinct features—especially the attendance of friends from different communities with whom I identify.

Because Rancho Cucamonga is just an hour's from drive Whittier—a relatively near distance for Southern California drivers—several of my colleagues from the college carpooled out to see the game. Deborah Norden, a professor of political science with whom I had collaborated in classes connecting Latin American politics and religion, brought her daughter Meghann, whose recent bat mitzvah I had missed during the Florida weeks of my trip. Then there were counterpoints to Larry, Moe, and Curly, otherwise known as Charles Adams, Warren Hanson, and Rich Scaffidi! Certainly the opposite of stooges, these three friends and I had participated in a Faculty Fantasy Baseball League for twenty-five years. Decades earlier, Rich had directed the college's production of *Bleacher Bums* and invited me to join the student cast by opening the play with a performance of the anthem. With typical slyness, he thereby secured a standing ovation for the production, even at its start! Warren, who had attended games in more major league ballparks than most major-leaguers, had made an effort to see me sing in several of them—including, most recently, the Nationals home field in Washington, D.C. And Charles and I had team-taught courses, traveled to conferences together, worked on common book projects, and enjoyed the deep friendship that is enhanced by the bond of baseball, even if he were devoted to the Mariners.

Another friend also had let me know that she would attend the game with her husband and young son. When she had entered Whittier College in 1992, Marcy Holmer had enrolled and excelled in my first-year writing seminar on "Humor and Faith in Recent Southern Literature." Now a middle-school science teacher, she was still laughing and smiling at the ballpark, even after spending a day with her adolescent students. To top things off, she brought me homemade treats, enough baseball-decorated cookies to provide Bonnie and me with snacks for a week of games.

While driving out to Rancho Cucamonga, I had thought about it being Thursday, the evening during which Bonnie and I would normally sing in choir rehearsal at Tustin Presbyterian Church. Throughout previous months, we had enjoyed anticipating our trip with fellow choir members, several of whom had informed relatives and friends throughout the country about our adventure. On this evening, I expected that they would begin choir practice twenty-five miles away about the time that I would sing the anthem. Imagine my surprise at the game, then, when I saw Russell Schmallenberger, a bass by whom I frequently stood, and Pam Roeth, an alto in the section with Bonnie! I was flattered by their effort to support me on a rare evening off in the choir's schedule: Coincidentally (or providentially?), my night of singing for the Quakes was timed for the first Thursday following Easter, a date for which the choir director annually canceled rehearsal.

Finally, the game itself proved rare, at least to me. It featured an inning unmatched in any game—whether major league or Little League—that I have ever attended. In the second frame, each batter in the Quakes' lineup reached base and scored before the JetHawks recorded an out: nine runs on five hits, several walks, and one error. While the Quakes pounded out fifteen hits during the game, Lancaster collected thirteen, with future American League All-Star Jose Altuve getting three of them and raising his first-month average to well over .400. Uncustomarily, however, the fleet-footed Altuve got caught stealing in a strike-out-throw-him-out double play to end the first inning.

In the end the Quakes enjoyed the rare good luck of "13," scoring that number of runs in their lopsided victory over Lancaster. But most of all the evening proved rare to me because I had shared it with family, good friends from the college and choir, and my new fan, Quakes manager Juan Bustabad.

Arbie's First Day: Game 18 in High Desert

On the first day of his participation in the journey, Arbie transported Bonnie and me to the High Desert ballpark where the Mavericks took the field in Adelanto. Somewhat surprisingly, in the first hour of our freeway driving Arbie showed enough "oomph" to pass two vehicles—one a sedan suffering homesickness for the junkyard from which it had apparently escaped, and the other an overly burdened truck. At the time, I didn't realize what an unusual feat Arbie's passing would be since we averaged passing about two cars a week during the next four months and thirteen thousand miles in the RV. But like his efforts and energy during most of our trekking, Arbie was content to stay in the right-hand lane, ably ambling along at about fifty-five miles per hour.

As we started up the Cajon Pass through the San Gabriel Mountains, Arbie geared down, valiantly climbing and toting Toad and the load of our stuff for four months. Only once—at 4,000 feet, less than a foul pole's distance from the summit—did Arbie request a brief rest when he thought he was about to break into a profuse sweat. But with his energy restored by the brief respite, during which Bonnie and I accessed e-mail through our iPhones, we eased back into the truck lane and made it past the freeway's crest.

When we checked into our first RV site, we were greeted by the manager, whose grandson Hayden Schmidt was a first-year student at Whittier

College, whose teams are known as the Poets. Although I didn't know Hayden at the time, a year later he excelled in one of my courses and, following graduation, entered a doctoral program in biology at Harvard. I love making such poetic connections like meeting Hayden's grandmother! One of the great delights throughout the tour was making connections with friends or family once removed, like this one.

In the High Desert we grabbed a quick, early supper, and easily arrived at the ballpark for a sound check an hour before the gates opened. That practice was a good thing. My earplugs merely muffled the distracting feedback from the centerfield speakers. In the rehearsal I made the mistake of listening to myself in instant replay. Ironically and momentarily, I lost the pitch on the word "perilous." Thank goodness wild pitches during warm-ups don't count!

In the pregame ceremonies, while an Air Force ROTC color guard presented the flag, I reminded myself of the anthem singer's feedback mantra: "Don't listen and keep going." All then went well, or at least as well as possible given the hiccup effect of the P.A. system, the gusty winds officially clocked at twenty miles per hour at game time, and the plunging temperature at desert's dusk.

Similar to the ballpark in Midland, at the one in Adelanto fans entered the concourse at ground level and descended to their seats. But unlike the excavated field on the Texas prairie, the grandstands in High Desert were contoured into the natural slope of the land, while the area beyond centerfield was at the same height as the surface of the playing field.

Not surprisingly, at dusk on the desert brisk winds ripped the American flag taut atop the centerfield pole. Recalling the pitch challenges prompted by the wind a month earlier in Brevard County, I asked a Mavericks staffer about the frequency and severity of the wind. "Usually, it's worse," he replied. "This is mild compared to the last two weeks."

Although the ballpark was only twenty years old, it featured a number of quaint designs that rendered an older feel. On the centerfield fence a hand-stenciled number—the distance from home plate—peered from its eyrie perch atop the high backdrop. Similarly, the columns supporting the grandstand canopy displayed the Mavericks opening-day lineups for each year in a homespun style.

Entered from the concourse level, the VIP boxes were simple cinderblock patios outfitted with plastic lawn chairs and bistro tables open to adjoining seats. The fan-assistance center appeared as though it was constructed by volunteers as a weekend project. And the Mavericks boosters' booth, a garden shed tucked to the side of the concourse, featured hand-lettered signs and blanket-wrapped fans sitting in folding chairs. The combination of these elements created a homey ambiance that lent itself to an unusually common experience by fans of all ages and backgrounds.

For the second night in a row, I watched Rancho Cucamonga win by scoring double-digit runs on twenty-four hits. Each Quakes batter collected at least one safety, eight enjoyed multi-hit games, and three had four-hit nights. Perhaps Quakes manager Juan Bustabad should have put me on retainer.

While the Mavericks yielded a two-run homer in the bottom of the ninth to spoil their shutout, Bonnie and I retreated to Arbie's warmth for our first night in our rolling summer home.

What Happens in Vegas…: Game 19 in Las Vegas

Heading toward Las Vegas, Arbie bucked all morning against gusting winds that caused even Joshua trees to bend away from their force. Beyond Barstow, scenery shifted while the winds persisted. Adjacent to the freeway nearing the turn-off to Death Valley, a series of roadside signs displayed the Ten Commandments. Their sequence made me think that there might be a twist at the end, an eleventh sign reminiscent of old Burma Shave conclusions. So I anticipated seeing a final post, warning: "I know what happens in Vegas—God." Alas, these commandment promoters showed no such sense of biting humor about divine judgment.

By noon Arbie was wind-weary and ready for a lunch break in Baker, where the World's Biggest Thermometer registered a reasonable, midday temperature in the high seventies. We happily settled for wrestling with the wind rather than suffering through the desert's typical swelter.

Following lunch, Bonnie and I re-boarded Arbie for the arduous climb toward Halloran Summit. Flexing his Toad-toughened muscles and exercising tortoise patience while watching eighteen-wheelers speed like hares past us, Arbie admirably made it up the fourteen-mile slope without a break.

Fittingly, Las Vegas was the destination for Game 19, which might have been a reasonable bet at one of its Blackjack tables. But rather than tempt Arbie with a casino's lure, we opted to park at the hospitable home of two Whittier alumni. Seven or eight years earlier, I had officiated at the wedding of Megan and Ben Hubble. Now parents of two lovely daughters, Adelaide and Allison, they hosted us for the evening and joined us for the game, where Allison enjoyed her first hot dog—bunless—and gobbled it like a banana.

My instructions about logistics for the ballgame started with directions for me to park in Lot C. Yet when I approached Cashman Field and turned into the series of parking lots, I was initially directed to exit, make several turns through a maze of streets, and enter a lot that was within sight only a shortstop's throw away. I must have looked like some of my students facing pop quizzes, because a chain of cordial parking-lot attendants moved cones and barriers to let me enter the wrong way once they learned that I was to sing the anthem.

After I found a space for Toad, the parking-security staffer who had moved the final barrier asked, "How long is the anthem?"

"Less than a minute and twenty seconds," I replied.

"How long for you?" he prodded. Looking puzzled, I didn't respond. Then he fessed up: "Some staffers have a nightly pool on how long the anthem takes."

"A minute fifteen or seventeen would be a good bet," I suggested, "depending on how much feedback there is from the speakers."

He'd have to wait through a long series of pregame presentations to find out. There were eight first pitches and testimonies from four Nevada organ donors and recipients. Two T-Ball teams accompanied the 51s starting players onto the field, and a color guard from Nellis Air Force Base presented the flags near the mound.

While I would encounter T-Ballers, health advocates, and color guards elsewhere in pregame ceremonies, Las Vegas was the only ballpark where several troops of Girl Scouts gathered on the third baseline to lead the fans in saying the Pledge of Allegiance. Several moments of silence followed their final phrase of "liberty and justice for all," while game-day staffers shuffled one of the two microphones from the scouts to me. After the series of presentations, I was hastily introduced by name only.

The game itself dragged on at a pace like that of my pregame predecessors. In more than three hours, seven pitchers combined for nineteen strikeouts and eleven walks while batters left seventeen runners on base. Despite the sluggish rhythm of play, there were a couple of individual highlights: Travis Snider went four for four for the 51s, and Josh Donaldson blasted a drive over the left-centerfield wall for Sacramento.

When we were leaving the ballpark, Bonnie paused at one of the commercial promotions that featured "free-play" slot machines. Given Major

League Baseball's caustic history in its dealing with players, coaches, and former stars involved in gambling (not only Pete Rose's excommunication for betting on games, but also Willie Mays's provisional penance of being barred from MLB appearances while he served as a greeter for an Atlantic City casino), it was a bit surprising to see the two slot machines on the concourse, even though they were rigged to make everyone a winner.

As we moved toward the car in Lot C, I looked for the attendant, figuring he had won the nightly pool with my insider info. Since Megan had videoed my rendition from her seat behind home plate, it was easy to determine its running time: 1:15! Ah, yes. It was Vegas, the place where even the anthem was subject to wager, as was the game itself, which the 51s lost to the RiverCats, 5-4.

Going Nuclear: Game 20 in Albuquerque

On May 2, my night for singing in Albuquerque, interest in the anthem was heightened throughout the nation, in part because of the spontaneous singing of "The Star-Spangled Banner" by a growing crowd at the White House gate the night before. The celebration followed President Obama's announcement of the success in the U.S. mission to terminate Osama bin Laden.

More locally, the front page of the morning's sports section in the *Albuquerque Journal* had reprinted Chris Erskine's story about my anthem tour, inserting a bit that indicated that I would be singing for the Isotopes that evening. The publicity prompted two afternoon phone calls from radio talk shows. Still en route to Albuquerque when the first interview call came in, I pulled Arbie off the freeway near the Laguna pueblo, and Bonnie and I picnicked while I talked with Peter Benson on his afternoon show on KNT, Christian talk radio in Albuquerque. Our conversation concluded with me reciting the fourth stanza of "The Star-Spangled Banner," which seemed appropriate for the day and Peter's radio audience. It celebrates the pursuit of peace and justice grounded in the concept of the nation's manifest destiny. Later I learned from a naval veteran that it had been the stanza that was sung aboard ship during World War II.

Oh, thus be it ever when free men shall stand
Between their loved homes and war's desolation;
Blest with vict'ry and peace, may the heav'n rescued land
Praise the Pow'r that had made and preserved us a nation!

Then conquer we must, when our cause it is just;
And this be our motto: "In God is our trust!"
And the Star-Spangled Banner in triumph shall wave
O'er the land of the free, and the home of the brave.

A few hours later, I entered the ballpark before the gates opened and identified myself as the anthem singer. Thomas, one of the ticket-takers, brightened: "You're the guy who's singing everywhere this summer. I read the story about you in the morning paper." There's nothing like ratcheting up expectations for a good performance.

My early arrival made it possible for me to talk with Erik Gee and his sidekicks, David Jubb and Brandon Vogt, on their pregame talk show on KNML, the sports radio station that anchored the Isotopes broadcasts. For half an hour we discussed the wild idea of a national anthem tour, the supposed difficult range of the anthem's music, the challenges of travel and singing almost every night, and my teaching, especially my course on "Sports and Religion." While they understood my lifelong love affair with baseball, they seemed amazed and envious of the love that I share with Bonnie—since she not only supported my anthem adventure but had joined in the traveling with me as my co-pilot. The media fascination with the anthem continued with the pregame ceremonies when the CBS and NBC TV affiliates interviewed me and taped my rendition for inclusion in their late-night newscasts.

And the P.A. announcer provided a thorough introduction, identifying me with Whittier College, briefly describing my tour, and noting my two books on religion and sports—a most affirming introduction following the previous game's slight in Las Vegas. Before beginning, I prefaced my singing by saying: "On this historic day in America, I invite you to join me in singing our national anthem." Because I was facing the flag in centerfield, I could not see whether folks in the crowd sang along. Bonnie reported that some did join me in singing, including Heidi Bailey, her children, and her mother and stepfather. Heidi and her husband James had been my students almost a decade earlier, and they were instrumental in securing the opportunity for me to sing for the Isotopes. Their advocacy for me with Albuquerque general manager John Traub proved persuasive since the 'Topes had initially expressed reticence about participating in my project.

For the anthem performance in most ballparks, I stood between home plate and the backstop, frequently facing the crowd and occasionally looking at the flag. The Isotopes had me stand between the pitcher's mound and home plate, facing the flag beyond the centerfield fence. Leaving the field, I walked toward the third-base dugout, where Isotopes designated hitter John Lindsey called out, "Good job. What's the title of your book?"

For four weeks I had been meeting with ballpark staffers and talking at length with fans. Yet the first person to inquire about my book was a ballplayer! Contravening *Bull Durham*'s stereotype that ballplayers don't read, I then switched the pattern of baseball-card exchange by handing him the promotional baseball card that Mercer University Press had designed for my book *Rounding the Bases.* The front of the card pictures Mickey Mantle rounding third base following a dramatic home run, and the reverse side provides a blurb about the book rather than featuring my publishing or teaching statistics. Alas, I failed to autograph the card for him!

The Isotopes ballpark is among the most elegant and elaborate of any of the stadiums in the country. The architectural design matches that of many of the newer and larger major league ballparks. All of the seats enjoy good sightlines, and two tiers of luxury boxes define the grandstand behind home plate. The landscaping on the berm in the outfield is artistically terraced and well groomed, and the scoreboard features two large screens, one for providing player information and the other for projecting replays and reports.

Several baseball sculptures enliven the park. An old, large baseball about four feet in diameter invites fans from the street corner where it was embedded in the sidewalk to the ballpark's main gate. When the former stadium had been razed to make room for the current one, the baseball sculpture was retained. Inside the new park, several dynamic baseball sculptures by Bill Arms animate the entry and the picnic area. Each of the works was comprised of multiple painted-steel silhouettes of players in action. The pieces' dynamic expression comes from their axial crisscrossing of multiple figures of pitchers and batters at different moments in their movement. Particularly energizing is "Batter II," which portrays a hitter's swing with six angles and elevations of the bat completing the hitter's revolution.

Other sculptures lining the concession concourse invite interaction in a different way: Fiberglass replicas of Homer and Lisa Simpson entice fans to sit beside them on benches with their backs to the diamond. The Simpsons play a major role for the team and ballpark, whose names fulfill Homer Simpson's desire to have Springfield, Ohio, build an Isotopes stadium. When Albuquerque's ballpark was completed in 2003, the name seemed to fit the physics of the region since New Mexico is well known for its history and industry related to nuclear energy, and since Albuquerque houses the Museum of Nuclear Science.

In the game itself, the Isotopes went nuclear, not with an explosive offense but with small particles igniting a win. Their tie-breaking, eighth-inning rally started with a bunt single, a stolen base, an intentional walk, and a wild pitch—not enough energy yet to score a run but enough to make the bases heavy with 'Topes, for sure, who eventually scored to secure Albuquerque's win, 5-3, over the Omaha Storm Chasers.

A Major League Evening: Game 21 in Frisco

I should have anticipated that the welcoming artwork outside the Dr Pepper Ballpark in Frisco, Texas, would signal a major theme for my experience at the evening's game: pitchers. Greeting fans outside the main entry to the stadium was a powerful bronze sculpture by Gail Slatter Folwell. Entitled simply "The Pitch," the life-size piece of a pitcher dramatically captured the tautness and movement of multiple muscles at the moment that the pitcher becomes the pitch. As part of the plate bearing the name of the piece, questions further engaged young viewers: "Why do you think the artist made the muscles so angular?" and "Was it a strike?!"

Inside the ballpark, I saw the pitcher motif come to life when two major league pitchers tossed the first few innings. No, make that three. The first two suited up for Frisco's RoughRiders, while the third—a Hall of Famer—evoked memories of my anthem renditions in a major league park.

The first two were players from the Texas Rangers on rehab assignment. In a reversal of timing to guarantee that his single-inning stint would begin with none on and the top of the order coming up, Rangers closer Neftali Feliz started the game. As usual, he completed a lone inning, regularly clocking fastballs in the upper nineties, with one cresting in triple digits. After surrendering a lead-off single to San Antonio Missions center fielder Blake Tekotte, who had entered the game hitting above .350, Feliz struck out the side.

In the second, his Texas teammate Tommy Hunter took over and threw four innings, allowing two runs, one on a homer by Vincent Belnome. From that point on, the RoughRiders relief corps shut down the Missions potent lineup, which lead the Texas League in scoring at that time, even having tallied at least twenty runs in a game three times in the first month of the season. Final score: Frisco 3, San Antonio 2.

As much fun as it was to see the two pitchers from the previous year's American League pennant winner, it was even more exciting to see Nolan Ryan, a former Ranger and then the team's principal owner, sitting behind home plate and scouting his recovering Rangers pitchers as well as prospects on both teams.

Regrettably, since Ryan had missed the pregame ceremonies, he hadn't scouted me on this evening. (I still list the Rangers among the ten major league teams on my bucket list of ballparks where I want to sing.) But he had heard me sing almost two decades earlier. In 1993, I had had the serendipitous fortune to be scheduled to sing the anthem in old Municipal Stadium in Cleveland on the day of Nolan Ryan's final appearance there. It also proved to be the final victory among his 324 major league wins.

While the pitchers held my interest in Frisco's game, the ballpark architecture proved even more fascinating. With typical Texas bravado, the Dr Pepper Ballpark replaced VIP suites and skyboxes with luxurious, two-story houses. In place of the small rooms and adjoining viewing decks that attract privileged fans and business clients to other ballparks, the Frisco facility expanded upon the idea of VIP hosting by providing multiple freestanding mansions, each with separate entries, air-conditioning systems, independent Wi-Fi networks, and huge balconies suitable for entertaining scores and scores of guests.

A second facet of the ballpark's configuration was its elevated pool zone beyond the right-field fence. Like the swimming pool popularized in Phoenix at the Diamondbacks stadium, the splash pool at Dr Pepper invited parties of hot fans to cool off. But unlike the pool in Arizona, the one in Frisco was integrated into the landscape of the hummock beyond the centerfield fence.

While various design elements of the ballpark distinguished it from other minor league facilities, the pregame ceremonies—or lack thereof—were unlike those at most minor league games. For this mid-week night contest, there were no series of first pitches, no children's team in uniform dancing onto the field with home-team starters, no young fans wooed from the stands to call out, "Play ball!" But home-plate umpire Seth Buckminster did dance "the hokey pokey" on the first baseline with the Frisco mascot between innings; and the RoughRiders provided me with a major league experience by presenting me with a DVD recording of my performance.

Throughout the afternoon and evening, Bonnie and I had enjoyed visiting with friends from the Whittier area, Bob and Cynthia Orpin. Their particular interests—Bob, an accomplished pianist, and Cynthia, a novelist—helped to shape our evening conversation about music and baseball, specifically how musical metaphors might enliven broadcasters' play-by-play descriptions. Duets and trios, we noted, had often been used to identify double-play combinations. Among those that we created, my favorites were:

an adagio to third—a slowly hit ground ball
the relay throw home suffered a retard
the home run soared like a descant
an arpeggio to short—a multiple-hop grounder
a glissando to left—a grass-hugging hit
a Boogie-Woogie snag by a middle infielder—the catch after reversing direction by an infielder moving to cover the bag on a ball hit behind him
a fermata fly—a pop fly that seemed to stay up forever
a deceptive cadence—turning the double play
a quartet or chorus of infielders gathering at the mound
an overthrow of first by two full octaves

Long after the game had ended, we finished our musical musing by wondering how we might orchestrate these suggestions.

Bridges: Game 22 in Corpus Christi

Ending the first week on the road with Bonnie and Arbie, I encountered the largest crowd that I had seen, many of whom had been attracted by the chance to enjoy postgame fireworks. And for the second time in a fortnight, I saw the Corpus Christi Hooks try to get un-snared from the Midland RockHounds. Although the outcome of the games was the same, with Midland scoring wins each time by two runs, the ballparks and my experiences were distinctly different.

In contrast to the sunken prairie site of the ballpark in Midland, the location of Whataburger Field in Corpus Christi was defined by its juxtaposition to the harbor and its orientation toward the Harbor Bridge. The architectural configurations of the Corpus Christi ballpark were similar to other sports venues designed by HKS, the Dallas-based architectural firm that conceived several minor league ballparks, including those at Frisco and Round Rock. Like the ballparks that resonate with their communities, the one in Corpus Christi reflected the heritage of its placement. Incorporated into the plan for the ballpark were structural elements that recalled the cotton industry and warehouses that formerly had stood on the site. The structures that framed the scoreboard looked like cotton gins, not merely because of their shape but also because of the rusty, corrugated-metal siding. The ballpark's fit with its landscape also echoed the spirit of Frank Lloyd Wright. The field's orientation made the Harbor Bridge appear as a kind of tiara for the grassy pate beyond the centerfield fence.

The layout of the ballpark complex also displayed the community's commitment to cultivate youth baseball. Beyond the centerfield fence and visually beneath the crown of the bridge was a youth ballpark—Stripes Diamond—where kids' games could be scheduled and where baseball activities could be held. The Hooks also contributed to the effort to nourish kids' love for the game by expanding their opportunities for on-field participation. Like a few other teams that scheduled children's mid-game sprints across the outfield, the Hooks sponsored a between-innings dash for kids, but unlike others, this one was roundtrip—from first base to centerfield and back to the baseline.

On many of the outfield fences at minor league ballparks, advertisements for auto parts, beverages, legal offices, educational institutions, health services, and scores of other businesses and operations stretched from one foul pole to the other. Yet for the first time in Corpus Christi, I observed an outfield billboard for a church. A long banner in front of the scoreboard promoted the Bay Area Fellowship, a megachurch founded in Corpus Christi by Bil Cornelius. Utilizing popular music styles of rock, country, and R&B in scores of weekly worship services conducted on its seven campuses, the church had experienced phenomenal growth using various marketing techniques. One of those, of course, was the large ad on the Hooks outfield wall. Another was the "game-show"-type giveaway on Easter Sunday a year earlier, which had been designed to attract folks who had never thought of going to church. For that occasion, more than $2 million in gifts were offered to attendees. Donated by church members and their businesses, the prizes included cars, flat-screen televisions, computers, bicycles, and gym memberships. That promotion exemplified the heart of the "prosperity gospel" as "cheap grace," Dietrich Bonhoeffer's scornful critique leveled at some Christians' tokenistic attempts at discipleship.

There were two metaphorical bridges—one in the stands and one on the field—that connected my experience in Corpus Christi with the earlier game in Midland, where the two teams had played several days earlier. Although there had been no mention of my tour during the anthem introduction, Mary Whitton, a Hooks fan, moved toward me quickly as I walked up the aisle following the pregame ceremonies. Expressing appreciation for my traditional rendition of the anthem, she asked if I had sung at Midland "last week." She had been there and remembered me. After I explained my anthem project to her, she indicated her delight in participating in the tour—by seeing me in two ballparks hundreds of miles apart. Then as I took my seat behind Midland's dugout, batting coach Tim Garland also reconnected with me, giving me "thumbs up" again when he moved to his position in the first base coach's box.

Similar to their offensive output in the game in Midland, the RockHounds used a big inning rally to prevail by two runs. This time, with none on and two out in the seventh, the Hounds ripped two singles before loading the bases on a walk. After fouling off five pitches with two strikes, third-baseman Stephen Parker hit his fifth home run of the season, a grand slam that propelled the RockHounds to their 7-5 victory.

Warming Up: Game 23 in Round Rock

Like players who need stretching exercises before games, or pitchers who gradually increase their speed from soft toss to hard throwing, singers also need to do vocal exercises before intoning their songs. From my voice coach Mike Stevens, I had learned multiple physical and vocal exercises for warming up, especially ways to focus the resonance in my naso-pharynx. And like players and pitchers whose initial movements might not look graceful, so, too, the sounds that singers make in warming up are not intended to be pleasing to the ears. Their purpose is to relax facial muscles and to reduce tension in the voice, thereby improving its sonorous quality.

Frequently at ballparks, it was difficult to find a place where, fairly discreetly, I could do these warm-up exercises and avoid the blare of hard rock and hip hop resounding over the P.A. system. Often when I had been able to find a family restroom, I had utilized its private, somewhat-muted space to do my vocal exercises. At other ballparks, I had sought far corners under the grandstands where I could secretly warm up, sometimes using earplugs to dull the distraction of the loud broadcast music. And at a few ballparks, I had resorted to the most remote men's restroom where I could stretch and vocalize. On those occasions, however, it almost never failed that while I would be making funny faces and voicing ugly sounds, someone would walk in and look at me in a bewildered way, wondering if I were crazy or asking if I were ill. So it was a surprise and delight that Kathy Wall, the fan-assistance coordinator for the Round Rock Express, warmly greeted me when I arrived at Dell Diamond and immediately offered to provide a warm-up room.

The evening featured the largest crowd (exceeding 10,000!) that I had ever seen at a minor league ballpark—in fact, one larger than the crowds at two of the major league games where I had sung in recent years. Attendance received a boost, I am sure, from multiple promotions related to youth teams (their reward was getting to walk the outfield warning track before the game), student achievement associated with the Georgetown Partners in Education (their reward was getting to stand in centerfield with a banner before the player introductions), and the fireworks fête following the game.

Like the other Texas ballparks where I had sung days before, Dell Diamond included several imaginative design elements: Greeting fans at the entry to the concourse was a painted, wooden bull labeled "The Express," the name of Round Rock's team and the nickname for Nolan Ryan, whose signature branded its side. The outfield stands featured a second deck that had some seats with partially obstructed views, like the historic ballparks in Boston and Chicago. The Round Rock stadium also creatively placed large advertisements. Billboards protruded above the grandstand roof, and images of a toothbrush appeared on the foul poles and screens, meaning that their brush of a ball would make it fair.

Between the foul poles and beyond the fence, blankets covered the berms where families sunned as though they were at the beach a few miles away. While many ballparks attracted children with bouncy rooms, the "Fan Zone" for kids at Round Rock presented a different challenge. A faux-rock climbing tower roped adventurous youngsters to practice belaying and rappelling while using fitted hand- and foot-holds. And a large trampoline enticed youngsters to bound and flip securely while anchored with bungees.

Before the pregame ceremonies had begun, Reid Ryan, one of Nolan Ryan's sons and the founder and CEO of the Round Rock team, stopped to chat with the participants. I enjoyed sharing with him the story of my having sung for his father's final victory, Texas's 4-2 win in Cleveland. Inquiring about the anthem tour, he seemed pleased that I had already sung in Frisco and Corpus Christi, teams also connected by the ownership group led by his family. While he winced at the loss that the Hooks had suffered in my previous game on a late-inning grand slam, he expressed hope that the Express would prevail this evening.

They did, thanks to the offensive output of Omar Quintanilla and Chad Tracy, the Express designated hitter. I was especially pleased to see Tracy do well since he had been on my fantasy-league team when he had played the corner infield positions at Arizona. In the sixth inning he hit a three-run home run, and in the ninth he kept the game-winning rally alive with a single that moved the winning run to third. The other hitting hero of the game was Quintanilla, the shortstop playing in his first game for Round Rock. In the eighth inning he singled and scored in the rally that tied the game, and in the ninth with two outs he hit a walk-off single for the win.

On a Mission: Game 24 in San Antonio

We knew it would finally happen—encountering travel difficulties in getting to a ballpark on time. The real surprise was that we hadn't imagined it would happen in quite this way.

We had left the Austin area in Toad in plenty of time to get to San Antonio for the late-morning game. As we approached the Alamo city, however, electronic road signs warned us about significant traffic delays on I-35 in the middle of the city. Since the route that we had mapped out would take us down I-35 to US 90 West, we thought it best to find an alternate approach. Quickly, Bonnie pulled out her iPad and typed in "San Antonio Missions." "Relief," we thought when the suggested route directed us to take upcoming I-410 toward I-37. The only sticking point in my mind was that the directions said to follow I-410 *East*. While I knew that the ballpark stood at the western edge of the city, I figured that I-410 must be a circumferential highway that would lead us more quickly to the ballpark, if not more directly.

When the green GPS locator of our position began to approach the red destination spot on Bonnie's screen, I noticed a historic marker for San Antonio Missions at the next exit. Indeed, what we found was one of the historic San Antonio missions, a relic of the religious life of old San Antonio, not the ballpark for the team by that name.

The time: 10:08. I was due to meet with the Missions staff for pregame instructions at 10:30, just a half-hour before their late-morning start.

Immediately adding "baseball" to the map search for San Antonio Missions, Bonnie relayed that the new routing from I-410 to I-37 North to US 90 West was estimated to take nineteen minutes. Thankfully, we enjoyed the speed of freeway freedom and made it to the ballpark's front gate to greet Bill Gerlt, Missions assistant general manager, at 10:29. Whew!

The close call of my arrival meant that I was not able to begin my customary warm-ups; and because of the pre-noon start, I had wanted to warm up a bit longer than usual in order to get all of the overnight cobwebs out of my throat. Instead, I breathed deeply while Bill and I talked about the wonders of Minor League Baseball and tried to avoid too much pregame sun. Already, the temperature before noon had reached the upper nineties.

While Bill and I talked, I noticed a "Storm" baseball shirt on a fan in the front row, and soon I asked if he had been to Lake Elsinore where the team is known as "The Storm." "Yes, but...," the father of Missions slugger Jaff Decker replied. He had seen the Padres' California League team play in Lake Elsinore, but his shirt referred to his own enterprise, a baseball academy named "Storm" in the Phoenix area. Jaff's dad had flown into San Antonio for a home-stand to see his son play. The previous night Jaff had poled his tenth homer of the season, a tape-measure shot over the top of the tree to which his father now pointed well behind the right-field fence.

Although there was no first pitch or other typical ceremony to precede the anthem, the P.A. announcer addressed the grade-school classes that filled the majority of the seats. He posed a math question to the upper-grade students: "In an average game, the Missions use eighteen dozen baseballs. Since there are twelve baseballs in a case, how many cases of baseballs do the Missions use in their seventy home games each season?" The spokes-child answered, "480!" When the announcer relayed the answer to the crowd of fifth-graders, he asked, "Is he right?" They resounded loudly, "Yes!"

I cringed, knowing that Bonnie, who had recently retired as a fifth-grade teacher, was standing behind them, wanting to take them through a series of steps to help them compute the correct answer: 1,260.

Although Jaff didn't homer in the 100+ heat that midday, he did collect two simple singles, raising his average to the .300 range, while the Missions collared Corpus Christi 5-2 with the benefit of only one home run. The little-ball approach to winning baseball was new to the Missions. During the first month of the season, they had slugged more home runs than any other Texas League team and had led all of the minor leagues in runs scored, topping twenty runs in three of those games.

The Expanse of Texas

Growing up, I understood that it was redundant to say that Texas is big. It's possible to spend one's entire life in the state yet still find new horizons every day.

So it also seemed at the end of our first week on the road with Arbie. We had entered the state near Amarillo in what appeared to be a bygone era. There we had seen saddled horses in parking spaces at a Dairy Queen where the riders were inside ordering soft-serve. Days later we futuristically left the state in another age when we learned about the approaching end of the world while we boogied past Beaumont. Our first notice of the predicted beginning of Final Judgment (on May 21, 2011) was posted on a billboard as the highway from Houston leveled off toward Louisiana. It certainly seemed like we had been driving in Texas for much of a lifetime, and I'm sure that most cross-state drivers wonder if the end of the world will indeed occur before they reach the state's opposite border.

In the expanse of Texas, we sampled its range of roads and spaces, from the farm-to-market county routes to the urban freeway interchanges in Dallas and Houston. While most of our nights were spent in cities, we had enjoyed our first Texas evening on the prairie, virtually alone. Because there are few RV parks between Amarillo and Fort Worth, we had targeted Copper Breaks State Park as a convenient point to split the long drive between Albuquerque and Frisco.

As we had entered the park at dusk, no rangers attended the check-in booth, although a live armadillo ardently greeted us from the shoulder of the road. We had our choice of campsites since none appeared occupied. But after docking Arbie and walking through the park, we did locate one pickup camper at the far end of the RV lot. Otherwise, we shared the evening with stars and critters, but thankfully not the rattlesnakes that are so plentiful in early spring. The crisp air and the absence of ambient noise made the evening eerily restful.

A couple of days later when we left Frisco, Arbie didn't particularly care for the freeway system through Dallas and points south. Moving rather cautiously in the mid-morning traffic, we headed south in the right-hand lane of the Dallas North Tollway. Nearing the core of downtown Dallas, we merged to the right and into the left fast lane of I-35 East. At least, I think those are the names of the two freeways that jolted my attention by the blind angle of their fusion. It was quite unsettling to be moving along at fifty-five miles per hour in Arbie and lugging Toad, while being abducted into the swifter flow of the left lane of another freeway. Even so, Arbie managed effectively, as did my nerves—barely.

Navigating our subsequent shifts through Dallas in the maze of mergers, we still faced the challenge of Texas freeway exits and re-entries involving the frontage roads—or feeders, as they are apparently called. The ramps connecting these parallel, one-way roads were short and often lacked the short-dash line markings that elsewhere routinely indicate lane disappearance. When we got to Austin after driving through the eternity of Texas south of Dallas, we were glad to anchor for three days, during which we could tether in Toad to Corpus Christi, San Antonio, and Round Rock for three consecutive games without having to uproot Arbie.

The extended stay in Austin also provided a chance for us to secure a house call—or an RV park visit—from a mechanic/repairman whose business card had been posted on the bulletin board near the park's office. Somewhere south of our lunch break in the Czechoslovakian town of West, Texas, Arbie's major air conditioner had failed because the generator would not kick on. Making matters worse, the heat of the freeways—exacerbated by the record summer heat of Texas—meant that we sweltered with windows open while trying to scurry on down to Austin.

Seeing an RV sales lot adjacent to the freeway just north of our destination near Austin, we exited and inquired about possible repair of Arbie's equipment, only to learn that a repair on our generator (a top-of-the-line, integrated Onan machine) could not be done by the mechanics; but the dealer did offer to sell us a more cumbersome, less-efficient, new portable generator that would have to be carted who-knows-where in Arbie's compartments. No, thanks.

After docking Arbie in his slot at the RV park, we scanned its notice board for nearby services and called an RV repairman who advertised that he would make "house calls." Shortly thereafter, Fred Summers came to our rescue and diagnosed the generator problem as a faulty regulator. Even though he did not have the part in stock, he identified its specifications and suggested that we order it for installation later on the tour. Bonnie did. After talking to an accommodating generator-repair manager near our next extended stay in Louisiana, she ordered the hundreds-dollar part on line, to be delivered to a repair shop with which she had begun a tech-facilitated relationship. In the end, all worked out well since Clinton Wilburn near Abita Springs was able to install the regulator in our generator on a Friday afternoon, before our departure the following morning for an evening game in Mobile.

But back to Texas: For our jaunt to Corpus Christi, we sought a change of pace, routing Toad along blue highways. That course took us through Lockhart, where the courthouse dominated the cityscape and where "Black's BarBQ," a block away from the town square, invitingly posted its hours as "Open 8 Days a Week."

From there, we meandered farther south to an anomalously named, seemingly anonymous Texas town—one called "Nixon."

Finally, I understood the size of Texas: It's big enough to embrace a Nixon, a Bush, and Lyndon B. Johnson.

During our stay in the Austin area, we spent Mother's Day afternoon at the LBJ Library. There we viewed exhibits about LBJ's early identification with and later advocacy for distressed Americans, whether they were of Mexican-American heritage (like most in the photographs and narratives on display), or whether they were Anglos (like Bonnie and me) who benefitted from the educational support that his administration instituted.

3.

Family and Friends

Mother's Day

Mother's Day—a rare day off from baseball, or so it might seem. Although I had no game scheduled for Mother's Day, a few intersections with baseball marked the day. For one, I called my ninety-four-year-old mother, who lived with assistance in an apartment in Mississippi. She expressed delight with the "beeYOOOOOtiful flowers"—as she described them in her elongated and melodious Southern accent—that she had received the day before. The inscription on the card had read that Bonnie and I hoped that the blooms would brighten her spirits until our arrival several days thereafter. Indeed, my schedule for singing with the Mississippi Braves had been constructed around the prospect of enjoying an evening visit with her. While baseball swung into my conversation with my mother, it also figured prominently in images that I hold dear about her, especially as I recalled them on Mother's Day.

Although my petite mother was by no means athletically inclined, I remember vividly how she spent some time one afternoon during my grade-school years playing ball with me in the front yard of the parsonage where we lived. She played ball with me when friends could not! And what a sight that must have been—a forty-year-old woman in a dress awkwardly wielding a wooden bat at a spot called home plate instead of swirling a spoon and serving up plates in the kitchen! Yet that certainly was my mother's love, feeding the passion of her son.

When I think about baseball and my mother and her appreciation for my love of baseball, I also recall the excursion that she took with my father and me from Paducah, Kentucky, where we annually vacationed at my grandmother's home, to St. Louis so that I could attend my first major league game. For the summer outing to see the Cardinals in 1960, I am sure that she endured the daylong and night-deep drives to and from St. Louis—in days before interstate highway ease—so that she could witness the delight that I experienced with the fulfillment of entering Sportsman's Park, cheering as Stan Musial homered off Bob Friend, shouting as Roberto Clemente threw a runner out at third, and simply slapping my small right hand into the black leather glove that I readied with each pitch.

While our flowers had been delivered to my mother's apartment before Mother's Day to signal our love for her, the deeper affection that I thought about throughout that day was the love that she had shown to me by embracing my passion for baseball.

Lagniappe: Game 25 in New Orleans

"Lagniappe," which was one of my mother's favorite words, describes our New Orleans experience at the Zephyrs game. A word of Creole origin, "lagniappe" means "a little extra, something unanticipated and good, often 'free.'" It was also the word used by Whittier alumna Jennifer Buddemeyer to describe the evening that we spent together at the Zephyrs ballpark.

For the second game in a row, I was praying like *My Fair Lady*'s Henry Higgins, "Just get me to the park on time...." Minutes before leaving Abita Springs to cross Lake Pontchartrain into New Orleans for the Zephyrs game, we learned that the causeway had been closed because of a big-rig fire that had shut down the long bridge's lanes in both directions. That meant we would need to follow the more circuitous route through Slidell, taking I-10 across the water and through much of New Orleans, as the rush-from-work traffic would likely swarm.

Off we went in Toad and made our way amazingly easily against the primary flow of traffic before exiting the freeway and continuing the last five miles on surface streets. No problems developed, and we managed to navigate our way through New Orleans and into the park early.

Some time later as I moved toward the place where I would check in with a staff member, I noticed Jennifer Buddemeyer walking toward me. She had been a residence hall advisor when Bonnie and I had lived on Whittier's campus as faculty masters almost two decades earlier. I wouldn't have recognized her by sight if she had not been wearing her purple and gold tee-shirt featuring the Whittier slogan, "Fear the Poet." A marvelous musician herself, she said that she would join me in singing the anthem from her seat adjacent to Bonnie. Knowing that she was singing along, I displayed a broad smile throughout the anthem. My joyful expression often meant as much to the crowd as the quality of my resonance or the clarity of my diction.

Walking past the Zephyrs dugout, I heard hitting coach Damon Minor offer a simple response to my rendition: "Thanks." His response was echoed moments later by one of the TV-camera operators, who became the first commenter to address me by name: "Good job, Joe. Thanks."

From our seats behind home plate, I had a grand time catching up with Jennifer during the game, learning about her progress on her literature dissertation at Tulane. Since she had attended quite a few games at Zephyr Field during pre-Katrina years, she was able to provide background on the ballpark and the city's support of the team. One of her most fascinating bits of information was that the hummocks beyond the outfield fence served a purpose other than providing a picnicking area for fans. They also functioned as a levee.

Jennifer's commentary must have calmed the Zephyrs, who collected only three singles until the ninth. By contrast, the Salt Lake Bees generated an offensive hive, scoring easily and often, putting up six runs in the first inning. About the only thing that the Zephyrs fans could cheer for until the final inning was the spectacular scoop of an errant throw and somersaulting tag by first baseman Mike Cervenak. Immediately, over the P.A. system came the unmistakable phrase and recorded voice of Harry Caray: "Holy cow!" Indeed!

As Bonnie and I left the ballpark while the Zephyrs were being blanked, a foul ball plummeted past our heads, bounced a few feet from us, and rolled into the bushes nearby. I picked it up and tossed it to a young boy who was leaving the game with his father. His bug-eyed delight more than compensated for giving up my first game ball on the tour. It provided a lagniappe to our early departure for dinner at MiLa's, an incredible restaurant where we had dined two years before and where, on this brief return to New Orleans, we had decided to eat our single meal in the city.

Lagniappe also ended up being the theme for the night for Jennifer. Following the game, she e-mailed me with a note that her original seat number had appeared on the scoreboard, indicating that she had been selected to win a free oil change! Indeed her seats were lucky that night. During the seventh-inning stretch when Zephyrs staff members had tossed promotional baseball caps into the stands, one had landed in her lap while she was sitting in one of the complimentary seats provided for me and my guests. And following the game there were fireworks. "You gotta love minor league ball," she wrote.

She also let me know that although the Zephyrs lost 7-1, their lone run was, in her description, "poetry." (You gotta love English majors who are alumni of the Poets, Whittier's mascot!) With two outs in the bottom of the ninth, Vinny Rottino lined a triple into the right-field corner. The next hitter roped a single to right, scoring Rottino. His hit was followed by another and a walk to load the bases before a grounder ended the game on a force play. Jennifer concluded her note with the observation that "the Zephyrs went down playing all the way to the end—and that's something, ain't it?!? I wished you'd been there to see it! That kind of baseball, which doesn't happen at every game, was lagniappe, too."

Memorable Mobile: Game 26 in Mobile

To minimize the difficulty in making the transition from a night game in Mobile to an early-afternoon game the following day in Jackson, Mississippi, we decided to dock Arbie in Hattiesburg. From there we could use the better speed, maneuverability, and efficiency of Toad to cover more than half of the route from Alabama's Gulf Coast to Jackson. That plan allowed us to situate Arbie in the early afternoon, slip into Toad to hop down to Mobile for the evening game, and then return to Arbie before midnight so that we could leave early the next morning in Arbie for the Trustmark Ballpark, a hundred miles north, in time for the scheduled noon preparation for the game.

The triangulated plan worked well. After leaving Abita Springs, where we had settled Arbie for a couple of days, even getting the repair of his generator completed nearby, we angled northeast on state highways through Southern Mississippi. To our surprise and delight, the roads were unusually smooth, much better than the surfaces that we encountered elsewhere. Only later did we realize that their good condition resulted from their reconstruction as part of the recovery projects following Hurricane Katrina.

North of Hattiesburg shortly before noon, we moored Arbie at the Okatoma RV Park, several miles off Highway 49, the artery that we would take the following morning to make our way on up to Jackson. During the restoration work following Katrina, the RV park had served as one of the camps for FEMA crews that had been working daily on the coastal area, about seventy-five miles away.

Shifting from Arbie into Toad for the afternoon, we dipped back down to the Gulf Coast, stopping briefly for boiled peanuts at a roadside stand shortly before getting to Mobile. Our approach along Satchel Paige Drive to "The Hank," whose address was 755 Bolling Brothers Drive, animated memories of childhood baseball heroes and foes. Paige, of course, had been the seemingly immortal pitcher for the Kansas City Monarchs before getting his first chance to hurl in the major leagues at age forty-one—or whatever age might be identified with him that year since he played with conflicting reports of his birth year. The number of the ballpark's street address paid homage to Hank Aaron's career home-run total. And the Bolling Brothers—both Milt and Frank—had played in the major leagues. All had been Mobile residents.

Adjacent to the entry to the ballpark, a marker paid tribute to Mobile's extraordinary baseball history: Five Hall of Famers—Aaron, Paige, Billy Williams, Willie McCovey, Ozzie Smith—had been born in the city, the third highest total of any municipality in the nation. The childhood home of Hank Aaron had been moved to the ballpark's adjoining site a few years earlier, and then it had been restored and outfitted with multiple artifacts from and tributes to "The Hammer." Regrettably, because of my tight pregame schedule and because of our need to return to Hattiesburg even before the game ended, I was unable to tour the facility. It's not clear whether I might have been able to do so since there had been conflicting information about whether the museum was open only on weekdays, or also during games. Missing the chance to walk through the structure where Aaron's early life had been spent was one of my keenest regrets of the entire summer. Incredibly, Aaron's father had built the entire structure during World War II with scrap lumber that he and Aaron's mother had scrounged from refuse piles. Over the years, Hank's father had added various rooms and additions to the small home, but even in refurbished condition for public tours, the modesty of the house gave testimony to the difficulties of African Americans in the South during the mid-twentieth century.

Although I never saw Aaron play in person, I admired the purity of his play, his gracefulness in swinging, running, throwing: swift on the bases, efficient in the field, and powerful at the plate, with a controlled swing that made explosive contact because of his quick wrists. When the Milwaukee Brewers held their closing ceremony for the old County Park, where he had played so many games and won the 1957 World Series, I had interviewed him briefly for a different baseball project. I was so awestruck by standing adjacent to him—talking to him and listening to his stories about the ballpark—that I could hardly write legible notes about our conversation.

In a different way, the tributes to Paige reminded me of his six rules for living, which I first encountered as a teenager when I was inspired by his autobiography, *Maybe I'll Pitch Forever.*

> Avoid fried meats which angry up the blood.
> If your stomach disputes you, lie down and pacify it with cool thoughts.
> Keep the juices flowing by jangling around gently as you move.
> Go very light on the vices such as carrying on in society. The social ramble ain't restful.
> Avoid running at all times.
> Don't look back. Something might be gaining on you.

On several occasions when I have been invited to deliver sermons in recent years, I have been tempted to use his simple, sage rules as the focal text for the homily.

Another of Mobile's native baseball sons was Billy Williams. During his final year with the Chicago Cubs, he had helped me adjust to Chicago in my first September in the city. Via the afternoon Cubs telecasts on WGN, he daily provided respite and relief from my entrance-exam studies, and he converted me to Cubs fandom, at least among National League teams.

In addition to its tributes to the Hall of Famers and Mobile players who made it to the major leagues, the ballpark also had distinctive architectural elements. Unlike the luxury boxes that sit atop most grandstands, the VIP seats at The Hank were at field level between first and third. The private spaces featured enclosed suites that opened onto a couple of rows of covered, dugout-level seats. The unique design certainly provided welcome relief from the sun on summer days.

While I waited to participate in the pregame ceremonies, a young girl behind me asked if I were going to sing the national anthem. Smiling, I nodded "yes," and she identified herself as Alyssa Smith, a relative of the man who had written it. Moments later, her father confirmed that Francis Scott Key was on one branch of her family tree. She was one of ten birthday children who threw out first pitches that evening, then a record number of participants for my season's pregame rituals. Sharing the opening ceremonies with one of Key's kin elevated my joy in singing "The Star-Spangled Banner" not only that evening, but throughout the season.

Even though the drama of fireworks had attracted a large local crowd to the Saturday-night game, the loudest cheering came from red-clad fans in three sections. They were supporting the visiting Carolina Mudcats, an affiliate of the Cincinnati Reds. Initially, it seemed odd that so many fans would follow a Double A team from North Carolina more than 600 miles to see a game on the muggy Gulf Coast. Yet the trek that this troupe had made was much shorter, merely having come across the state line from Florida. The following year the Mudcats would relocate to Pensacola, less than an hour's drive away. Despite the Pensacola fans' vocal presence, the Bay Bears blanked the Mudcats 8-0, thanks to the stellar pitching of Patrick Corbin and a grand slam by Paul Goldschmidt.

Sunday Baseball: Game 27 in Mississippi

Yes, it was a Sunday afternoon in Jackson, Mississippi, the city of my birth and my childhood and the city where my father had been pastor of one of the state's largest Baptist churches during those years. It was—and still is—a city with such a pious culture that churches and sports leagues and teams often mutually support each other. On this Sunday afternoon, the Mississippi Braves recognized several church and synagogue groups in attendance for the Braves game against the Suns. The Braves also reinforced church participation by announcing that, throughout the season, fans would be given discounted admission to a Monday game if they brought a church bulletin from the previous day.

That promotion recalled a similar bulletin policy established by the church softball league in Jackson. When I had lived there decades ago, attendance at Sunday services was a requirement for players' participation in church-league games. While it seemed that my church's team was always coming in second or third place, I wondered whether or not our rival team brought in ringers to play, offering them qualifying bulletins in exchange for potential home runs. Then the league also had a rule against Sunday-afternoon softball practices in order to "keep the Sabbath holy," as one of the Ten Commandments enjoins. Obviously, with Sunday ballgame restrictions no longer effective, choirs and Sunday-school groups endorsed the Sunday-afternoon Braves game as a special outing.

By contrast, the Chick-fil-A concession at the ballpark ironically remained closed on Sunday as an expression of corporate policy. Ever since the food chain's founder and CEO, Truett Cathy, had opened his first restaurant around 1950, Chick-fil-A's custom had been to respect Sunday as a day for spiritual practice. Adhering to this procedure of remaining closed on Sundays, the company also believed that it could express support for its employees by making sure they would have a day to spend in worship, family activities, or personal renewal exercises.

For the Braves game shortly after noon, there was no first pitch; no child selected from the stands to yell, "Play ball!"; no Little League team to caddie the home team's starting lineup onto the field. Instead, on this Sunday afternoon students from the secular Japanese Supplemental School in Mississippi sang "Amazing Grace," even retaining its original phrase: "...that saved a wretch like me." Their rendition contrasted with the popular bowdlerized version in several current church hymnals that preserves some self-esteem by reducing the sting of personal identification as "a wretch," referring instead to "sinners like me." The children and a few adult sponsors sang the first verse in English and repeated it in Japanese. Protestantism still suffuses Mississippi life.

Intentionally I had scheduled the Braves for a Sunday game, not for the purpose of examining how the relationship between baseball and religion in the city might have changed since my childhood years. More personally, since my nonagenarian mother lived in an assisted-living home twenty miles from the ballpark, I had targeted one of the few afternoon Braves games to make it possible for her to attend the game if her health had permitted. Although she did not feel well enough to join us for the game, Bonnie and I later enjoyed eating dinner with her, and following the game we were able to share our travel stories with her throughout the evening.

Before the game, I had mentioned to Braves assistant general manager Sean Guillotte that, this season, the home team had a 16-10 record when I had sung. Immediately he responded, "We'll have to hire you to sing for us the rest of the season." The Braves were 15-21 at that point, although they had shut out the Jacksonville Suns the previous night. Without knowing about my record for home-team success, Braves manager Rocket Wheeler introduced himself while I lounged by the dugout before the game. After I sang, he handed me a ball and said, "Thanks. Good job." That's the first ball that I was given on the trip. His evaluation was elaborated and elongated minutes later by a man wearing an Ole Miss baseball cap who drawled, "You sang it the way it's s'posed ta be sung."

In the second inning, the Braves strung together two singles and a walk, followed by a routine double-play scoring grounder—second to short to first. With a runner then on third, pitcher Brett Oberholtzer singled to drive in a second run. Anything but routine, his hit was the first by a pitcher that I had seen all season. Then, tossing seven strong innings, Oberholtzer and two relievers made the runs hold up before adding another for a 3-0 win.

During the middle innings of the game, I wandered out to a spot overlooking the Suns' bullpen where relief pitcher Jhan Marinez lay on his back lounging in the warm sun. One of his fellow relievers, Dan Jennings, noticed me also taking photographs of the young members of the grounds crew who were playing soccer beyond the centerfield fence. Dan called up to me, "Aren't you the guy who sang the national anthem? Weren't you at our place a couple of weeks ago?" Yes. I had sung in Jacksonville for the Suns three weeks earlier on another Sunday, Easter.

In our developing conversation, he asked where I was a professor, and learning of my affiliation with Whittier College, he offered, "That's where I wanted to attend more than anywhere else." At first I thought he was pulling my leg, but then he started recounting bits about his visit to campus: "Purple and gold. Aren't those the college's colors? And isn't it the place that has the rock that students paint?" Yes, again.

During his sophomore year in high school, Dan had toured several California colleges, thinking that he would pursue a baccalaureate degree rather than sign to play professionally. Although Whittier's team was out of town on the day that he had visited campus, he had left Coach Rizzo, one of my former students, a video of his pitching and a copy of his résumé. While he recalled positive impressions about the campus and the baseball program, what had most appealed to Dan about Whittier was its academic program, especially the faculty masters' program that expanded students' scholarly and cultural opportunities. I enjoyed sharing with him how Bonnie and I had served in that capacity and had hosted former Negro League stars to share their experiences—as well as, on a different occasion, former MLB commissioner Bowie Kuhn.

Dan also inquired about the book that I was writing about the national anthem for the national pastime. In part, his interest was piqued by difficulties his father—also a professor—had encountered in securing a publisher a few years earlier. At some length we talked about Whittier and my course on sports and religion, which he said he would have taken. When he expressed interest in my book, I tossed him one of the promotional, baseball-style cards for my book *Rounding the Bases*. Winds swirled, helicoptering the card back up to me on several occasions before it dropped to him beyond and below the bullpen wall.

Finally, we talked about the route and ballparks scheduled for the remainder of my tour and whether I would shine on the Suns again. When I described making the trip in Arbie with my wife, he responded, "That sounds like a dream come true."

"It is," I smiled.

Fathers and Sons: Game 28 in Memphis

For the first time in more than twenty-five games, I had to pay for parking near the ballpark in Memphis, where private lots and parking garages surround the stadium. In similar instances at inner city ballparks, like the one in Bradenton, Florida, I had persuaded the restricted lot attendant to let me park among the staff and players' spaces. While I had hoped for similar good fortune in Memphis, I couldn't find the entry to the small lot of controlled parking for team personnel. So Bonnie and I pulled Toad into a garage adjacent to Rendezvous, the Memphis barbecue restaurant that had been highly recommended to us. It was alive with excitement, and we could savor the ribs and pork from the aromas alone. But alas, it was Monday—a day when the place was closed to the public but open for a private party. It was tantalizing to smell the aromas of the hot barbecue wafting to the street though we could not relish its taste.

The Redbirds ballpark was the most urban of any stadium that I had seen, its left-field corner adjoined by an abandoned building whose facing wall had been decorated with a bright, five-story mural. The ballpark's entry was also one of the most engaging. The main gates were enhanced by a diptych sculpture whose hinge was an open space of sixty feet and six inches between the pieces: A pitcher and catcher, with backstop covered by a baseball-cap canopy, drew fans in from the street to the team store and ballpark offices.

As usual, the participants in pregame ceremonies were instructed to gather at an appointed spot—often the fan-assistance booth—before being escorted to the field. When I arrived at the designated place, I met Richard Farrell, who was carrying an antique glove and a paperback book about a ballplayer. Richard was scheduled to throw out the first pitch for Greek Night at the ballpark. One of the Memphis players—first-baseman Nick Stavinoha, of Greek descent—later received the loudest ovation each time he stepped into the batter's box.

Although Richard was not of Greek heritage, his wife was. While I wondered if his acceptance and integration into the Greek community resembled the transitions of Ian Miller portrayed in *My Big Fat Greek Wedding,* Richard and I talked baseball more than local Greek culture. I learned that a choir from the Annunciation Greek Orthodox Church, which had sponsored the Memphis Greek Festival a week earlier, was scheduled to sing the national anthem—the one for Greece. Whew! I was still on tap to sing

"The Star-Spangled Banner." By game time, however, the church choir had decided not to perform for the baseball crowd.

Richard's old glove and book about the ballplayer played significant roles in his enthusiasm. The glove had belonged to his father Doc Farrell, the second-baseman for the 1932 Yankees, who beat the Cubs in the World Series that fall. Stubby and flattened by age or weight from stuff piled on top of it in an attic, the old mitt required the use of two hands for grabbing and securing ground balls. It's doubtful whether an announcer would have used a verb like "snagged" to describe a diving catch of a line drive since the web of the glove was shallow and barely flexible. Even so, the glove epitomized the paternal bond celebrated in Donald Hall's panegyric to baseball and its familial bonding: *Fathers Playing Catch with Sons.*

The book that Richard carried was a biography written about his father, who was unusual because, during his career, Doc had been a teammate with more than twenty Hall of Fame players—headlined, of course, by Babe Ruth and Lou Gehrig. Doc had gotten his nickname because in the off-season he had practiced dentistry. Inordinately proud of his father, Richard was sharing the moment with his own son Matthew, a baseball player for Christian Brothers High School in Memphis. In a sense, they also reversed the mentoring role honored by Hall's book title since Matt was tutoring his father about how to hold and release the ball. As Richard took the mound to toss out the first pitch a short time later, he held high the glove, a trophy from and about his father.

His huge smile was almost as wide as the pitch he threw to the plate. His control contrasted sharply with that of the Fresno Grizzlies starter, Doug Mathis, who held the Redbirds hitless through his six innings. Finally getting hits off relievers in the eighth, Memphis scored four times in the frame, piecing together three singles, a walk, and a two-run, game-tying double by Stavinoha. Opah! Greek Night scored! And so did the Redbirds, who almost two hours later tallied the winning run in the fourteenth.

Traveling to the Travelers: Game 29 in Arkansas

Since the route from Memphis to Little Rock presented one of our shortest day's drives—just 150 miles—we were able to berth Arbie at a soothing site inside the flood wall and overlooking the Arkansas River. Unlike most of rivers that we had crossed earlier in the day, starting with the record-setting stages of the Mississippi and continuing over and past other swollen channels, the Arkansas River was not flooding.

Seeing the Clinton Presidential Library on the opposite bank of the river, we seized the opportunity to spend the afternoon interacting with the exhibits there. Inspired by the stories about Clinton's empathy for the poor and dispossessed, his advocacy for civil rights legislation and practice, and his success in economic development that produced budgetary surpluses during his terms in office, I was primed to sing the anthem for the Arkansas Travelers game against the Springfield Cardinals.

At various times in the team's history, the Travelers had barely survived in the area. Several decades earlier when the team had been in danger of folding, fans and local investors had purchased shares in the team to preserve its identity with Little Rock. And some years later when the team's former ballpark of almost seventy-five years had deteriorated, Warren Stephens, a Little Rock financier, donated eleven acres of riverfront property in North Little Rock for the site of a new ballpark, which was completed in time for the season opener in 2007. The ballpark was named in honor of the co-founding brothers of Stephens, Inc., an independent financial service that employed Hall of Fame catcher Bill Dickey and his brother Skeeter, also a major league player. Before starring for the Yankees, Bill had played the 1925 season for the Travelers, and following their baseball careers both Dickeys had worked for Stephens.

At the entry to the Dickey-Stephens Park, I had Bonnie take a photo of me with the plaque paying tribute to Bill Dickey. I have a fond place in my heart for him, not merely because he had played with Ruth and Gehrig but because he had interacted with me personally, if only briefly and in writing. In 1964 or 1965, a classified ad in *The Sporting News* had offered a mimeographed list of home addresses of current and former major league players for a few dollars plus postage. I could hardly lick stamps fast enough to place my order.

After receiving and reviewing the pages of data, I decided to develop my autograph collection, then consisting of several contemporary Yankees players, by writing to the Hall of Famers whose names appeared on the list. With slow typing skills, I pecked out brief letters to each, requesting that they sign the blank side of an enclosed index card and that they identify a career highlight on the opposite, blue-lined side. Bill Dickey was among about twenty Hall of Famers who responded, not only signing the index card and citing his career with the Yankees as the highlight, but also enclosing an autographed postcard of his Hall of Fame plaque.

Building on my childhood appreciation for Yogi Berra, Dickey's gracious gesture generated my fondness for Yankees catchers; and I have followed them closely ever since: Elston Howard, Thurman Munson, Rick Cerrone, Jorge Posada. Now spending the summer watching minor league games, I began to track the progress of a possible successor, the Yankees' top prospect at the time, Jesus Montero. (Failing to serve as the savior of the Yankees' catching tradition, Jesus was traded to Seattle the following season.) Although Little Rock was far from the Yankees' affiliates, I did note a distinct catching practice derived from Posada. Arkansas catcher Orlando Mercado duplicated Posada's practice of painting his fingernails white to improve the pitcher's perception of his signals for a pitch.

Even though Dickey-Phillips was among the newest professional ballparks, it was also the site of one of the most tragic events in baseball history—an extremely rare, on-field death by a player or coach. In the inaugural season of the ballpark, new hitting coach Mike Coolbaugh of the visiting Tulsa Drillers had stood in the coach's box along the first baseline in the ninth inning. Coolbaugh, who had played in the major leagues for forty-four games with the Brewers and Cardinals during the previous five years, had joined the Drillers as their hitting coach three weeks earlier. With Tulsa behind by four runs, Coolbaugh focused his attention on the Drillers baserunner who had started the inning with a single. Then Tino Sanchez, the back-up switch-hitting catcher for the Travelers, lined a shot that felled Coolbaugh, who died moments later despite CPR efforts. As I walked near the first base dugout while waiting for the pregame ceremonies to begin, I thought compassionately of Coolbaugh and prayed for his family, the Tulsa and Arkansas players, and the Travelers staff members who had been on duty that night.

In contrast to the mournful thoughts of Coolbaugh that the field evoked, I deeply enjoyed seeing children at the ballpark. With particular delight, I watched the players on the Mudcats, a local youth team that participated in the pregame ceremonies, tussle while trying to catch souvenir balls tossed to them by one of the Travelers; and later it was quite fun to see them get such a charge out of securing the signature of Shelly, the Travelers oil-company-sponsored mascot.

A pleasant tone for the evening was also set by live, pregame organ music, one of only two keyboard instruments that I heard in the ballparks on my tour. Young Trey Trimble sat at the organ console on the concourse behind home plate. Having learned of the Travelers organist position through an ad for the job, Trey auditioned well, got hired, and now played exuberantly from a list of titles that he had drawn up to set the mood for the games.

Yet the cheerful children and joyful music could not produce a hometown victory on this night. After the Travelers scored three in the first, they yielded six two-out runs in the second inning to the Cardinals, who held on to beat Arkansas 9-7 in a twenty-nine-hit slugfest. The highlight of the game for me was seeing the raw skills—quickly being refined—of Mike Trout. He ran like a gazelle on the bases and to the outfield alleys. He threw taut ropes from the warning track to cutoff men. And the ball leapt off his bat in ways unlike any other player on the field. For the record, he chased down two long drives in the gap, he stole a base, and he slammed a double and three singles.

And the Award Goes to...: Game 30 in Tulsa

If I were giving out the ESPY Awards for sports performances, I would surely designate one to go to the Tulsa Drillers for several reasons. For one thing, they displayed a living ESPY every night during their games, their manager Cecil Espy. For another, for the only time on tour the anthem introduction not only included information about me, the tour, and the book project; it also mentioned that I was accompanied by my wife Bonnie. Indeed, she deserved mention since she attended more than sixty-five of my games in as many cities. That number probably sets a minor league record for spousal attendance at different ballparks in a single season. When David Lamb (*A Stolen Season*), Ernest Green (*The Diamonds of Dixie*), and Cass Sapir (who tried to see games in all 189 professional ballparks) made their season-long tours through minor league cities and ballparks, they did so alone. While at least two couples whom I met during the summer were attempting to tally all professional ballparks over several years, I still would bet that Bonnie set the single-season record for wives. At the very least she should win an award for joining me on this jaunt, especially since she regularly sat through games out of love—not for the game, but for me.

The Drillers also should win ESPYs for a few other reasons, highlighted by the distinction of featuring the wildest promotion of the summer, wilder even than Whiplash, the Cowboy Monkey whose routine was well practiced. On this "Country Night" in Tulsa that was sponsored by two radio stations that encouraged Drillers staffers to dress in country "get-up," a between-innings competition featured an armadillo race. Three fans wearing thick gloves tried to cajole the critters to run the width of an Oklahoma roadway to win the race.

Having seen so much armadillo roadkill on and beside southern thoroughfares and byways, I laughed when the P.A. announcer indicated that the critter that could navigate the width of an Oklahoma highway would surely be a winner of this armadillo version of "Survivor." Two of the ugly creatures were named Speedy and ArmaDriller. When one of the armadillos started to veer and reverse course, a Drillers staffer corralled it with a fishing net. I had hoped to see them try to rope it with little lassos!

A few other fan activities also distinguished the Drillers entertainment. To increase the opportunities for children to participate in the pregame activities, the Drillers also created a "high-five corridor" through which the starting players ran, slapping hands with the kids, on their way to their field positions. On this night a Little League team of Braves enjoyed a low-fiving routine. About a half-hour later, one of the little Braves caught a pop foul in his glove and this time got high-fives from exuberant teammates who shared in his success.

During the seventh-inning stretch, all of the fans sang long and loud for two traditional songs in the region. Following the most accelerated rendition of "Take Me Out to the Ballgame" that I have ever heard, fans fervently joined in singing "Oklahoma."

Before the game while I had waited behind home plate, Drillers assistant manager of promotions Justin Gorski and I had talked about the enthusiasm that had been generated by the open auditions that the team had held months earlier for anthem performers. During the previous year, the first for the Drillers musical tryouts, more than 130 individuals and groups showed up, taking all day to compete for the dozen weekend dates available. This year, the team had limited tryouts to the first 100 performers. Even so, individuals had started lining up in the parking lot at 6 A.M., three hours before intoning the first phrases for the competition. On weeknights, the Drillers usually played a recording of the anthem. I was fortunate that Mike Tarranto, the Director of Promotions, had been willing to book me for a Thursday-night game and that Justin had made the effort to write the kind, inclusive introduction that also included Bonnie's role.

The only downer for the Drillers was that Salvador Perez, the catcher for the visiting Naturals from Northwest Arkansas, drilled a two-run homer while Tulsa was held to three harmless hits—sort of like the aimless armadillos—in their loss, 2-0.

Unnatural: A Missed Opportunity in Northwest Arkansas

Sooner or later, it was bound to happen. The only surprise was when and how the convergence occurred to cancel my singing at a game.

Eight months before the minor league season began, I re-contacted teams that had approved my online audition, and I suggested specific dates for me to sing the anthem. Amazingly, most accepted my proposed schedule. The Northwest Arkansas Naturals in Springdale, Arkansas, were among the teams that confirmed a date; and so my routing through Arkansas and eastern Oklahoma got set. Throughout the winter and spring I followed up with e-mails, seeking to re-confirm the date and to secure game-day instructions. Repeated follow-up e-mails to the Naturals scheduler proved futile, ignored like a pop foul over the press box. Certainly frustrating, that communication gap had also occurred with a few other teams. While I still anticipated singing for Arkansas on the evening after performing in Tulsa, I was naturally apprehensive about the team's unnatural unresponsiveness.

After the game in Little Rock, we had found an RV site in Springdale, Arkansas, where we could set up camp. Its relative proximity to Tulsa allowed us to drive Toad to Oklahoma for the Drillers game, followed by spending a night in a hotel and anticipating an easy return to Springdale the next morning in time for the evening's game at Arvest Ballpark.

Friday at dawn on my anticipated date with the Naturals, I sent yet another e-mail to the team's general manager, whom I had initially contacted during the previous summer, and I indicated that I had not received game-day instructions from the staffer whom I identified. I expressed concern about whether there were complications since I noted that the staffer's name no longer appeared on the team's office contact list. Still no reply.

Shortly before noon, I called another staffer whose title seemed similar to that of the absent scheduling staffer. Somewhat flustered, she informed me that the original scheduler no longer worked for the Naturals and that, as the new scheduler, she had been both unaware of the previous commitment and my project until her receipt of my e-mail that had been forwarded to her an hour earlier. In the meantime, she had gone to the AnthemTour.com website and checked out the legitimacy of my project and the restrictions of my schedule.

While she let me know that a group of 400 schoolchildren would be attending the game and their choir performing the anthem that evening, she graciously offered to let me sing "Take Me Out to the Ballgame" during the seventh-inning stretch. But since my project focused on the anthem itself and not merely singing at different stadiums, I declined her invitation. So Bonnie and I decided to remain in the security of the Tulsa hotel one more night while tornadic storms were predicted for the entire region. And that night, for the first time all season, my "scheduled" game got cancelled because of rain. No one sang.

Following our unexpected extra night in Tulsa, Bonnie and I returned to Springdale, detached Arbie from his electrical buoy in the RV park, and reconnected Toad before wending our way through the Ozarks and toward our next ballgames in central Kentucky.

During the routing phase of the tour, I had anticipated that Arbie would need recovery and rest at three intervals for possible tune-ups and repairs. Already, the unforeseen problem with the generator in Texas and Louisiana had been dealt with effectively without requiring delay in our travel. Even so, my wariness that road weariness might begin to weigh down on aging Arbie, now in his upper teen years, meant that I had set aside a few fallow days for the RV in West Kentucky. I had projected that he might need an oil change and tune-up after a month and four thousand miles on the road. So Bonnie and I had made arrangements to stay with friends in central Kentucky while leaving Arbie in a repair shop in Paducah and taking Toad to the games in Lexington, Bowling Green, Louisville, and Nashville before returning to Paducah to retrieve the RV.

To our surprise, Arbie hummed his way through Missouri and showed no signs of discomfort before his fluids got transfused in Paducah the following day. Although he seemed road ready, we decided to park him in a cousin's driveway while we made our way in Toad on toward Lexington, where we looked forward to visits with several clusters of friends who would join us for games in the Bluegrass.

A Legendary Evening: Game 31 in Lexington

The ballgame in Lexington proved legendary in multiple ways. It took place in the heart of the Bluegrass State, with which I have identified so closely for so long. Georgetown College, my undergraduate alma mater, lies only a tape-measure blast away from Lexington. A little farther to the east sits Mt. Sterling, where for three years during my college days I served as the music and youth minister for the First Baptist Church. Equidistant to the south of Lexington is Berea, the arts-and-crafts capital of Kentucky. There Bonnie and I had enjoyed the best parts of our honeymoon at the Boone Tavern Inn, which is serviced by Berea College students. Since then we have returned to Berea every few years, making sure that we get a chance to sample the spoonbread in the inn's dining room while we drool over the fine wood and fiber crafts that make Berea so special. And for more than a decade, Kent Gilbert, one of my former students, had served as pastor of the Union Church there. Not surprisingly, in central Kentucky clumps of friends from these various communities converged at the ballpark in Lexington.

The evening there took on additional mythic dimensions because of the severe weather that had attacked the region for the previous couple of days. Thankfully, while thunderstorms and downpours continued to strafe nearby communities throughout the game, the field itself was spared the worst, experiencing only a light two-inning shower that did not interrupt play.

When I entered the ballpark, I passed Maris: Yes, that was her divine name, calling to mind one of my childhood favorites and the home-run record holder of pre-steroid days. This Lexington Maris, however, was a young Legends fan who was distraught about the ineffectiveness of her ballpoint pen to imprint her name on the communal autograph ball adjacent to the parking-lot entry. I stopped and handed her a Sharpie. In her best five-and-a-half year-old penmanship, she then proudly printed her name, added a smiley-faced baseball, and said, "Now it'll stay there!" Like her namesake's accomplishment with sixty-one homers in '61.

At various ballparks I had seen banners or advertisements on foul poles, like the tributes to NASA Shuttles at Brevard County or the Carus dental ad in Round Rock that added the image of a vertical toothbrush as the screen in fair territory. The Legends ballpark added a twist to foul-pole displays. Hanging on the screens in fair territory were ads for Chick-fil-A: "EAT MOR FOWL." So if a ball hit the "fowl foul pole"—doubling or squaring its foul sound—would it still be fair?

Shortly before game time, friends from my undergraduate days arrived, followed soon thereafter by friends from Mt. Sterling. Ken Rich had been my roommate during our freshman year in college, and he and his wife Cheryl now lived in Williamstown, about an hour's drive north of Lexington. Weeks after we had graduated, I had enjoyed singing in their wedding, and in years since we had reconnoitered as often as either of us traveled toward the other.

From Mt. Sterling, Dorothy Sutton and her adult children Anna Ray Martin and R.T. Sutton, along with his son Robbie, found me sitting at a bistro table near the home-plate gate. Anna Ray had been one of the lively students in the church's high-school group that I had directed, and R.T. had been a kindergartner when I had persuaded Dorothy to help chaperone a week long youth trip to the church's retreat and conference center in North Carolina. I have always felt indebted to her for having assumed that leadership role, and we have kept in touch via Christmas cards and letters in the years since then. Still, I hadn't seen R.T. or Anna Ray in almost four decades. And yet we share good, strong memories of those formative years, now rekindled by my singing for a Legends game.

As I took my place to face the crowd and sing, I saw a smiling and waving family in the box seats twelve rows directly in front of me. There stood Laura Senkyr and two of her children, Connie and Tom Orme. During my years at Mt. Sterling, Laura had served as the church secretary, and Connie and Tom had sung in the youth choir and had participated in church activities, including the youth trip to North Carolina that Dorothy Sutton had helped to supervise. Like the Suttons, I hadn't seen the Ormes in years, and the deep delight in reconnecting with them intensified the already enjoyable gathering for the ballgame.

Adding to the entourage of old Kentucky friends who joined Bonnie and me for the game was my former stellar student Kent Gilbert, pastor of the Union Church in Berea. When I had posted my ballpark itinerary weeks before the season began, Kent had marked the Lexington date on his calendar, and in his typical, entrepreneurial way he had managed to synchronize multiple opportunities. Earlier in the spring, he had attended a fundraising event for a school in Lexington, and at its auction he had bid on a VIP suite for a Legends game. Making sure that he placed the winning bid, he then negotiated the night for my singing. In that way he also prevented the possibility of a conflict with a church meeting by putting the game on the church's calendar and hosting a dozen of its members for a church social.

With so many friends from so many nearby cities converging for the game, the Lexington evening took on a legendary character. Feeling buoyed by their presence, I sang the anthem with more enthusiasm and confidence than usual. And when I left the field and handed the microphone to Stephanie Fish, the Legends staff member in charge of anthem coordination, I asked her if there had been any distinct anthem performances this year. Quickly and briefly, she replied, "Yours."

The game itself featured an early-inning outburst by Lexington, only to see Rome's Braves knot the game 7-7 in the seventh. Even so, Lexington reignited its offense and tallied three in the eighth while their second-baseman Delino DeShields, Jr.—himself a baseball legacy of sorts since his father had been a major league all-star—completed a legendarily frustrating game on the base paths. After walking in the second, he was thrown out at third by the Braves left fielder as he tried to advance on a single. In the sixth he struck out into a double play when the Rome catcher nailed his teammate at second. And after singling to fuel the rally in the eighth, he strayed a bit too far down the line and got picked off third by the Braves catcher, curtailing the Legends rally.

Although there were no monstrous home runs, no record strikeouts, and no triple plays, the game and evening, enjoyed with so many friends from diverse communities, got classified in my mind as legendary.

All Automotive: Game 32 in Bowling Green

Cars seem to be the red blood cells of Bowling Green, which lies a warning track south of the Bluegrass region in Kentucky. The Corvette factory in the city provides thousands of jobs for its residents, and the 'Vette museum attracts tens of thousands of tourists each year. In addition, the Bowling Green Hot Rods play in the Midwest League and attract unusually large crowds for Lo-A level teams. On this Friday night, almost 4,500 fans showed up at the ballpark for the game between the Hot Rods and the Lansing Lugnuts, a contest of mascots that could put the evening in overdrive!

Prior to the game I encountered a number of ballpark firsts for the summer: a promotional giveaway night, an announced legal disclaimer, a ceremonial cleaning of home plate, a musical and visual patriotic display preceding the anthem, and an emphasis on going green—how "punny" in Bowling Green!

Before the gates opened, a hundred or more fans lined up to be among the first 1,000 entrants to receive a tee-shirt with the Hot Rods logo on the front and the names of the four sponsors on the back. While ballparks routinely schedule souvenir promotions throughout the season, this giveaway game was the first to coincide with my singing. When folks began to file into the stadium, announcements on the P.A. system began, as usual, with a welcome to the ballpark. For the first time, however, I also heard a disclaimer about liability. While other ballparks had regularly warned fans with announcements and signs about the danger of balls and bats flying into the stands and possibly causing injury, the opening series of announcements at Bowling Green included a statement that fans assumed the risk of injury from events "incidental to baseball."

After completing my facial and vocal exercises, I still had some congestion minutes before the anthem. Hoping to clear my throat, I unscrewed the cap on my water bottle as I walked past the home-team dugout. As I did so, I squeezed the thin plastic and spewed water, narrowly missing myself and Hot Rods hitting coach Manny Castillo. "Nervous?" he inquired. "No," I smiled. "This is Game 32 this season."

The pregame ceremonies featured choreography, but not of young ballplayers running onto the field with the starting lineup for the Hot Rods. Instead, a troupe of twenty-five girls from Dynamic Dance performed a routine that was followed by recognition of Special Olympians in Warren County. The final step in readying the field for play was a ceremonial cleaning of home plate with a large toothbrush sponsored by a local dental office, followed by eight participants tossing out first pitches. After these live activities, a short video tribute to the Armed Forces included images of American flags waving and Air Force jets soaring, accompanied by a recording of Ray Charles singing, "America, America, God shed his grace on thee, and crown thy good with brotherhood from sea to shining sea." How could I follow his impressive rendition? Now I *did* get nervous! Since I knew the recording of "America" was in a different key than the one that I use for the anthem, I paused longer than usual to get my pitch of C-sharp and to establish the key of F-sharp by humming the descending chord. All went well.

As I walked past the dugout, Coach Castillo said, "Good job," and manager Brady Williams and pitcher Chris Rearick gestured approval. Minutes later in the stands, a Korean War vet sought me out and said, "Thank you. I can tell you love to sing it." Indeed I do.

Continuing to share games with friends throughout Kentucky, I was joined for this one by Eric Bain-Selbo, his wife, and her mother. Eric is author of *Game Day and God*, a stimulating analysis of the religious significance of SEC football, and he and I had participated on several panels on sports and religion at academic conferences in previous years. Throughout the game, we talked about our baseball experiences and about the connections between sports and religion, specifically analyzing how the national anthem functions as a consecrating ritual for civil religion.

While we pursued such heady conversation, we also enjoyed the game. The Hot Rods narrowly escaped with a 5-4 win, in part because of a baserunning blunder by the Lugnuts in the sixth inning. Representing the potential tying run, K.C. Hobson got picked off third base for the third out on a throw by catcher Lucas Bailey. You might say "the wheels came off" the

Lugnuts' rally. Although I hadn't seen a runner picked off third in my first thirty games, I saw that put out for the second night in a row.

Going Home Again: Game 33 in Louisville

Arriving in Louisville was like returning home. Bonnie and I had met, courted, and married in Louisville while I was pursuing a seminary degree and she was beginning her teaching career. Our first apartment had been near Cherokee Park, a lushly wooded haven that was leveled by one of the tornados that roared through the Ohio River Valley in early April 1974. Days before our first anniversary, we had seen one of the whirlwinds approaching our duplex, sought refuge in the basement, and narrowly escaped its wrath as it veered away from us less than a hundred yards away. Despite the terror associated with that destructive event, Louisville holds romance for us. So it was especially gratifying that one of Bonnie's bridesmaids, Trudi Fastenow Bellou, and her husband Glenn joined us for an afternoon of retracing old paths and watching the evening game.

In the years since Bonnie and I had moved from Louisville, baseball had returned to the city and had garnered quite a few accolades. In 1982 the new Louisville team set a minor league attendance record, and the following year it bested that mark, becoming the first minor league team to exceed one million fans in attendance, even outdrawing three major league teams that season: Cleveland, Minnesota, and Seattle.

During our residency there, the old Louisville Colonels had departed and left the city without professional baseball for more than a decade. Finally, a franchise returned, a new stadium was built, and enthusiasm resumed. Three times during the last dozen years, the Louisville Bats ballpark has received awards for being the best playing surface in the minor leagues, and it often appears on national lists of the top ten ballparks to visit. I understand why. The facility is beautifully situated near the riverfront, and its architecture presents an enclosed entry that provides an energizing transition from the urban neighborhood. It also features several interactive sculptures and memorials that heighten its appeal.

The ballpark also distinguishes itself with the most unusual vendor whom I encountered during the season. Several other ballparks had hawkers who bellowed distinctly or sang their pitch playfully. Others had peanut sellers who tossed nut-bags with more accuracy than many minor league pitchers. But none had a cookie saleswoman like Louisville's. With native grace and ease, she carried her store in a basket balanced on her head. To make her display even more magnificent, she wore a smile that wider than home plate.

The Bats also surpassed most other stadiums and staff in the amenities provided to anthem performers. To prepare for and await the pregame ceremonies, staff members escorted me to the family waiting room near the team locker rooms. There, for only the second time on the tour, I was offered a secluded space where I could discreetly warm up. Finding overstuffed chairs and a comfy sofa in the room, I was able to relax and focus in a way that made me feel like the anthem really mattered as part of the game preparation and production.

In part because my participation was on Memorial Day weekend, I encountered my tour's largest, sold-out crowd by far: 11,641. The fans had come to see the Bats (especially starting pitcher Edinson Volquez, who was on rehab assignment from the Cincinnati Reds), the Yankees AAA farm team from Scranton/Wilkes-Barre (which featured Yankees prospect Jesus Montero, as well as several players who had been with New York during postseason play the year before), and BirdZerk (the most entertaining baseball act since the San Diego Chicken).

An independent, touring comic persona making a special scheduled appearance at the game, BirdZerk performed several entertaining routines—some featuring baseball players and actions—that reminded me of the classic antics of Max Patkin, the "Clown Prince of Baseball" who enjoyed a cameo appearance in *Bull Durham*. Before the bottom of the second inning, one of BirdZerk's wild skits highlighted Yankees infielder Kevin Russo, who seemed to hesitate before joining the energetic BirdZerk dancing around the left side of the diamond. The routine required that Russo drop his glove near the bag so that he could mimic BirdZerk's dance moves. Stealthily, BirdZerk then angled toward the bag, picked up Russo's glove, and teased him with it; then, holding it aloft, he stole the grounds crew's cart and took off toward the left-field corner. As Russo watched the cart turn along the warning track, he saw BirdZerk heave the glove so far over the fence that it went out of the ballpark. The crowd roared. Russo acted dumbfounded and horrified, then called for a new glove to be brought from the dugout. To make the act look unrehearsed, the equipment manager brought out two gloves, allowing Russo to select one to replace the glove confiscated and discarded by BirdZerk.

After the third inning another BirdZerk routine apparently involved the first-base umpire, who had actually gone into the Yankees dugout to allow BirdZerk's sidekick, dressed as an umpire, to take the ump's place along the first-baseline. This time, it seemed as though BirdZerk charmed the ump into a coordinated dance that ended with them twirling, legs interlocked, followed by the ump doing a flip and BirdZerk going berserk, lifting the ump and toting him into the dugout. From there the actual umpire, a few inches taller, emerged and resumed his duties of calling outs and fouls at first.

BirdZerk's tomfoolery also included two other acts that featured his sidekick. Together, they donned the single costume of DogZerk and danced to the song "Who Let the Dogs Out?" And an inning later BirdZerk duetted with a new persona, BabyZerk, presenting a well-choreographed comic routine that ended with BabyZerk mooning the crowd.

Shortly after I walked out to the home plate area, the Bats P.A. announcer introduced me as being from Whittier. In response, a fan in the front row behind the backstop looked puzzled as I walked past and inquired, "California?" Yes. "What brings you this far away?" We chatted about the anthem, baseball, and southern California. Matt McColgan, the fan, had grown up in La Canada, less than an hour's drive from Whittier, and he had played ball at UCSB with Chris Valaika, the Bats second-baseman who had been a third-round draft pick in 2006. Now living in the Tampa area, Matt had flown to Louisville for a long Memorial Day weekend and a reunion with his former teammate.

Following the anthem, several other fans and officials expressed appreciation in various ways. One woman was effusive: "Thank you for the anthem! You did a beautiful job. It was awesome." And Tom Slye, a Vietnam War veteran, excitedly inquired about my availability to join a barbershop group with him. Although his invitation was flattering, for sure, it would have required a wicked commute; so I declined. And for the first time, off-duty police officers working the game stopped me, thankfully not to cite me, but to express their satisfaction with my rendition and project. "We love baseball and, luckily, get to work all the games," Sergeant Paul Neal related. "We appreciate your efforts in singing the national anthem for the national pastime. Baseball deserves the effort." He had played college ball and his partner, Sergeant Brian Stanfield, had played in high school. Of the hundreds of anthem renditions that they had heard over the years, they expressed particular appreciation for the clarity and pace of my version.

The game matched the level of excitement provided by the large crowd. After the Yankees scored in the first following a leadoff triple, the Bats used walks to claim the lead, which held up until the eighth when Ramiro Pena hit a no-doubter homer to right for the Yankees. His shot was matched in the bottom half of the inning by Daniel Dorn, who hit a towering, two-run shot just over the reach of the center fielder. And in the ninth, the Yankees tightened the score with a homer by Justin Maxwell before loading the bases with one out. With the tying run on third, the batter hit a shot up the middle. Diving to his left, shortstop Kristopher Negron snared the short hop and, while prone, flipped the ball backhanded to Valaika, nipping the runner as Valaika pirouetted and made a strong relay to first to complete the double play and end the game with a flourish.

Perhaps Thomas Wolfe did not know baseball when he opined, "You can't go home again." Because baseball at home completes a circle. Baseball returns the runner to home. And on this fabulous evening, baseball had occasioned our return to Louisville, a place that I can genuinely call home even though I lived there only three years and now no relatives reside there. It was in Louisville that I had met and married Bonnie. It was in Louisville that I began to sing seriously, turning avocational practices into vocational possibilities. And it was in Louisville that I started to study the concept of civil religion, whose doxology is "The Star-Spangled Banner."

Bonnie, baseball, and my singing the national anthem converged in Louisville, transporting me again to a place of contentment and security called home.

4.

Record Heat

A Sound(s) Experience: Game 34 in Nashville

An odd sound persisted throughout the Sounds game in Nashville's Greer Stadium. I had expected to hear the crack of bats impacting pitches, the grunts of umpires calling strikes, or simply the ballpark P.A. system offering country music standards. Who would have thought that a cacophony of cicadas would prevail over such ordinary ballpark sounds? Returning in their thirteen-year cycle, the beetle-like, clear-winged insects chirped and cackled throughout the game.

Perhaps the Sounds and Oklahoma City RedHawks thought that the bugs might not be attracted to bright colors, thereby prompting both teams to wear red jerseys for the game. With both teams also donning blue caps, their similar appearance made it difficult to discern who was playing first base and who was base-running at the bag. Surprisingly, the pitchers made no errant pick-off throws during the game.

On this Sunday afternoon, in the shade the temperature crested in the upper nineties. The only problem was that there wasn't much shade. Bonnie and I traded our sun-drenched box seats for ones in the back row where the canopy provided cover. But I failed to follow the major league pattern in making trades, however, by not insisting that a bottle of water replace the proverbial "player to be named later" in order to complete the deal. Within a few innings my cousins Kent and Julie Price, who had driven from West Kentucky to see the game with their school-age children Joseph and Jenna, relinquished their blistering seats in the second row behind the dugout in order to join us in the upper reaches' shade. But there the cicadas whirled and hovered, flitted and lit.

To cool off, Joseph and Jenna chose ice cream treats, taking advantage of the ballpark's pitch that on Sundays all sundaes and other ice cream concessions were offered at reduced prices. Ice cream treats were also featured in one of the between-inning promotions that was intended to increase crowd noise. Inciting the fans to intensify their cheering, staffers tossed ice cream sandwiches to those yelling loudest. Yet one tosser chose to reward texting fans rather than screaming ones, aiming ice cream bars at two somewhat isolated young women who were silently working on their cell phones when the ice cream treats bounced off their shoulders and legs.

Not only was it "sundae Sunday" in Nashville, it was also autograph day. Before the game and under the blaring sun, nine Sounds players sat in chairs in front of their dugout, allowing children and fervent fans to file down their row seeking signatures. While they stood in line, Ozzie, the Sounds playful and graceful mascot, sidled over and addressed me by name. "How's the trip going so far, Joe?" Hmmm. The costume could hardly hide voice identification. Behind the feline mask of Ozzie was Buddy Yelton, the Sounds staff member with whom I had corresponded about my anthem project and performance. Before he began his daily mascot routines, we chatted about minor league ballparks, mascots, and anthem performances. At other ballparks the mascots had often slapped hands with me, hugged me, or even teased me as part of their routines. Ozzie was the first whose voice I heard, and it sounded familiar.

Built in 1978, Greer Stadium was one of the oldest ballparks in Triple-A. Distinguished by its original scoreboard in the shape of a guitar, it did not feature a videoboard or high-tech ads. Although the stadium was older than most that I had seen, I had expected that some of Music City's renowned recording studios would have installed a state-of-the art sound system to promote its artists and their releases. To my surprise, the sound system suffered a startling delay that caught me off guard when I started to sing.

As I mused about the irony that the scoreboard visually highlights Nashville's music culture while the audio system ignores it, I struggled to get several wads of sun-softened chewing gum off my shoes. Seeing my frustration with sticky soles, a fan in front of me bemoaned the condition of the stadium, not its cleanliness but its age. He expressed dismay about the defeat of an initiative that would have funded the construction of a new ballpark near the riverfront. He yearned for a new facility like that in rival Louisville where a riverfront ballpark had exceeded its projected impact on the area's economic redevelopment.

Still, there were charming aspects of Greer Stadium. Typically, older ballparks celebrated their historic feats or recognized former players and owners associated with the facility. In the old St. Louis ballpark, for instance, an oddly colored seat in the upper deck marked the spot where the longest home run had landed. In many older ballparks bronze plaques pay tribute to former players, team and league officials, and civic leaders instrumental in saving the team for the city or building the ballpark. In Nashville, there's a single such memorial posted in the grandstands—but not to Don Mattingly, who had played there when the Sounds had been a Yankees farm team; nor even to Herschel Greer, the Nashville financier who had spearheaded efforts to retain professional baseball in the city and for whom the stadium itself was posthumously named in 1978. Instead, the sole tribute is to a vendor, David Cheatham, a beloved beer salesman who had enjoyed and entertained the crowd for more than thirty years. Following his retirement to Florida some time before his death, David had returned each season to rekindle his friendship with the fans and hawk brew for the Nashville team.

It's also possible to increase the appreciation for older ballparks during friendly or family conversations. There's nothing like the experience of sharing memories of star-players' performances or weird plays: "One time when I was sitting about right here," a father might say to his son or daughter while gesturing toward the scoreboard, "I saw Prince Fielder clobber a homer so high and hard that it just missed hitting the last fret on that guitar!" Old ballparks are not inherently unlikable; they just need to be prized, as in Daytona and Savannah where wooden stands attract fans and overhead fans stir breezes above them.

Although there was the displeasing delay that I experienced in the Sounds' sound system, the anthem was well-received by ushers and fans, especially by Mary Catherine Dean. Expressing appreciation as I climbed the stairs toward my seat, she introduced herself as affiliated with Abingdon Press, whose offices are in Nashville. She was, in fact, the editor-in-chief of the publishing house that had issued the theological introduction and handbooks that I had authored and edited with Don Musser.

As my tour had begun to take shape a few months earlier, I had invited the Abingdon editorial staff to join me for the Sounds game. Remembering that my appearance would be on Memorial Day weekend, Mary Catherine had called the team, described my project, and learned that my singing would be on Sunday. I was flattered that she and her daughter Patsy, who had played basketball at St. Mary's College in Indiana, had made such an effort to attend. And I was delighted to spend an inning talking with her about Nashville, publishing ventures, and baseball—even if she was wearing a Red Sox tee-shirt.

While the near-record heat consistently tried to sap our enthusiasm and the cicadas occasionally tried to kamikaze themselves toward our heads and shoulders, the Nashville ballpark experience was sound. Enjoying the chance to sing the anthem in Music City and to spend the afternoon with family and friends, I was amused by the red jerseys mistakenly worn by both teams and by a first-inning, base-running blunder. With a runner on second and two outs, Sounds outfielder Erick Altamonte, who was on a rehab assignment from the Brewers, launched a drive to left. Thinking it was a home run, he went into his base-circling trot, only to be tagged out at second on a relay throw from the deep outfield corner. Sounds manager Don Money couldn't cash in on his argument with the umpire, who had ruled that the ball had struck the top of the wall before bouncing back into play. Even so, the Sounds hummed their way past the RedHawks by the score of 4-2.

In General: Game 35 in Jackson, Tennessee

While the sculpture at the entry to Pringles Park in Jackson, Tennessee, generally stood ready to welcome the crowd to every game, it provided a most appropriate greeting for fans coming to the Memorial Day contest between the Jackson Generals and the Montgomery Biscuits. Reminiscent of the iconic statue of the raising of the flag at Iwo Jima, the bronze piece portrays two children holding an American flag and expressing success in having ascended a mountaintop. Funded by an Armored Brigade Association, the untitled piece is dedicated to "The Children of Tennessee's Fallen Warriors."

The name of the Jackson team also fit the holiday. In recent seasons, the team had been known as the West Tennessee Jaxx; but during the previous off-season, the organization had changed its name to that of an early team in the area: the Generals. In keeping with the new name, the staff wore camouflage jerseys with the team's name emblazoned across the front, and the mascot became known as "Sarge."

Although the team's moniker and mascot demonstrated a deep appreciation for the military, the holiday to honor service men and women went otherwise uncelebrated. There was no pregame moment of silence to commemorate the sacrifice of soldiers. No special presentation of colors or celebration of the flag to accompany the anthem. No recognition of veterans in the community or the "Fallen Warriors" to whom the ballpark's entry sculpture was dedicated. Even a simple statement acknowledging the patriotic character of my project was missing in action.

Yet as usual at Pringles Park, the anthem singer was given some special treatment—a ride in a new, red F-150 from the entry gate, down the hill outside the ballpark, through the left-field access gates, around the warning track, and to the backstop behind home plate. The $40,000 pickup truck was provided by a local Ford dealer as a promotional feature. As we drove around the outfield wall, I teased the Generals staffer, asking if his perk for chauffeuring singers all summer would be to get the keys to the pickup at the end of the season. He laughed, but didn't consider suggesting the possibility to the dealer. Even so, when I got out of the truck, there was no introduction of the singer, no celebration of the anthem itself: only the identification and expression of appreciation for the sponsor. And there was still almost a half-hour wait until the pregame ceremonies would begin, during which time a couple of the staffers played catch and keep-away with the first ball tosser.

While the record-setting heat wave in the upper South slowed the scoreboard lights, which showed the names of the home team from the previous day's NCAA playoff game, it also stifled the crowd, which was surprisingly sparse for the holiday evening. There were so few fans that a solitary, cheering voice could be heard throughout the stands during the game. In the fourth inning following a walk and a first-pitch ball to the next batter, the pitching coach went to the mound to talk to the Jackson pitcher, Erasmo Ramirez. One fan yelled loudly and clearly at the pitching coach, "Don't go out there and talk to him! He's doing fine." The penetrating voice evoked a chuckle from fans and a cadre of scouts who had been aiming their radar guns repeatedly at Ramirez.

After a rough first inning in which he gave up four runs on three hits, a walk, a hit batter, and a stolen base, Ramirez settled down, yielding only a single during the next six frames and retiring the last thirteen Biscuit batters in row. Thanks to the Generals' seventh-inning, six-run surge that was capped off by a grand-slam home run by first-baseman Rich Poythress, the Generals prevailed 7-4.

A Baronial Game, If Not Classic: Game 36 in Birmingham

Shortly before the turn of the millennium, the first Rickwood Classic had been held in Birmingham to feature America's oldest professional ballpark, built in 1910. Annually now, the Friends of Rickwood sponsor the game between the hosting Birmingham Barons and a visiting team as the only scheduled game in the ballpark during the Southern League's season.

Knowing the historic significance of Rickwood, I had appealed to the Birmingham Barons, and then to the Friends of Rickwood, to allow me to sing for the contest. With the possibility that I might work things out with the organizing Friends to perform in Rickwood, the Barons graciously scheduled me for their home game the day before the 2011 Rickwood Classic, thereby putting me in the vicinity on the date for the Classic.

Alas, after several e-mail exchanges with the president of the Friends of Rickwood, I learned that the tradition for that game was to have a brass band play the anthem. That's certainly historically appropriate on two counts: The first ballpark amplification system in the major leagues was not installed until almost two decades after the construction of Rickwood; and at ballparks in the early 1900s, brass bands often played popular, patriotic medleys like "Columbia, Gem of the Ocean," "Yankee Doodle Dandy," and "The Star-Spangled Banner."

While I had been unable to schedule singing for the Classic, I also almost missed singing for the Barons because of travel delays. The drive from Jackson, Tennessee, to Birmingham was on the hottest day of the year in Alabama, and the route had taken us to Huntsville, where we had left Arbie on the farm of Dr. Don Ross, the brother-in-law of my good friend and frequent theological collaborator Don Musser. The day's drives to Birmingham in Arbie and Toad was the longest for any day on which I was scheduled to sing—almost 400 miles. The hours and hours of driving meant that we descended into Birmingham on I-65 at the height of commuter traffic and less than an hour before the pregame ceremonies would begin. Encountering grid-lock on the freeway south of the city's center, I feared that we would not make it to the ballpark in time for the pregame ceremonies.

But Bonnie came to the rescue. Using her iPad, she accessed a Birmingham traffic map that confirmed the traffic standstill for several miles until the interchange with I-459, our anticipated route to the community of Hoover and the Barons ballpark. She quickly searched for alternate directions and discovered a winding path along Shades Crest Road that was accessible from the next freeway exit. To our great relief, it provided spectacular views of the valleys and mountains southwest of Birmingham, and it guided us to the ballpark—with only a few minutes to spare.

At the ballpark: yes. Ready: no. I still wore the comfortable clothes for driving, not the fresh AnthemTour shirt and clean pants for performing. Since Toad was too small and cramped for me to change clothes on its back seat, I opened both driver's-side doors to the car to create a baffle with the side of the adjacent car. Then, easily stripping in the makeshift closet in the middle of the parking lot, I slipped on the khaki slacks of my customary anthem uniform.

While many minor league parks featured sculptures at their main gates, the Barons stadium presented a live exhibit to welcome fans to this game. Displaying animals from the Birmingham zoo, caretakers handled a large boa constrictor and a few other critters. I wondered if the large snake, wrapped around the waist and shoulder of its keeper, portended the execution of a squeeze play by the home team. Not fond of snakes, I was happy to pass the boa and check in with the Barons staff. For the second time—and on consecutive nights, at that!—I was given a ride onto the field in a new vehicle, this time in a Nissan sedan that was again provided by a local dealer as a promotional venture. Rather than waiting near the dugouts after the ride, as I had done on the previous night in Jackson, I was escorted up the tunnel to the family waiting room where I could warm up.

In the meantime, the keys to the Nissan got misplaced as game time approached, while the car remained parked between the batter's box and the backstop. Although the keys were located a couple of minutes before I sang, I had mused about what special ground rules might apply if the car were still sitting there during the game. Would a wild pitch going through the open driver's window allow an extra base for the runner, like an errant throw going into the dugout? Would a ball still be considered in play if it rolled under the car? What would the ruling be if a wild pitch caromed off the windshield? Would it be like one bouncing off the screen behind home or like one deflecting into the dugout? Or given that the opponent's name was the Chattanooga Lookouts, would there be a penalty for shouting, "Look out!" if the car should shift into gear and roll toward home? Ah, the possibilities!

I should have guessed that the glitches with the delivery of the anthem singer augured difficulties with the anthem presentation. Perfunctorily, the anthem was introduced with the simple statement: "Tonight's Coca-Cola national anthem performance presented by Joe Price." I might as well have been an employee at the soft drink magnate, the anthem's underwriter, not someone seeking to celebrate and study patriotism for an entire season. As I began to sing, the sound delay was so severe that I thought the microphone was dead—until I got to the second word on the third note and heard the first! Even so, the anthem went so well that Sean Pharos, the scheduling coordinator, became the first ballpark staff member to invite me back to sing again.

Usually, the concession stands at ballparks featured fried foods—always French fries, frequently fried chicken tenders, and occasionally distinct items like fried pickles. While Birmingham offered its share of fried entrées and sides, it also suggested a "Healthy Hits" menu of healthier food, a "Heart-Aware" selection of calorie-conscious options promoted by Baptist Health Systems. Yet I smirked when I saw that the list on the menu board of Baptist Health heretically included draft beer.

Although the Barons ballpark in 2011 couldn't claim historic appearances of Babe Ruth and Ty Cobb, as Birmingham's Rickwood Park could promote, it did enjoy the distinction of having been the place where two superstars in other sports got their professional starts in baseball. Bo Jackson, the running back for Auburn who won the Heisman Trophy in 1985, starred for the Barons in 1991 as he resumed playing baseball. Jackson became the first athlete to be named to all-star teams in two professional sports, having been chosen as a running back in the NFL while playing for the Oakland Raiders and later selected as an outfielder for the Chicago White Sox. And Michael Jordan, during his hiatus from basketball, tried his skills at baseball, initially for Birmingham before briefly appearing for the Chicago White Sox and then giving up the sport.

While I deeply admired both iconic players, my appreciation for former Birmingham players extended to a little-known player for the Negro League's Black Barons in the early 1950s. Joe Scott, a former Black Baron and roommate of Willie Mays, was one of the gracious guests at Whittier College during Black History Month in the mid-1990s when he had joined with four other former Negro League players to share their oral histories about life in segregated baseball of the mid-twentieth century.

On the field the Barons could have used a healthier offense. They played more like serfs than barons or lords, losing in undistinguished fashion to the Lookouts by the score of 6-2.

An Interlude

When we had parked Arbie adjacent to the barn on the farm of Don and Myrna Ross near Huntsville, shortly after noon and before driving in Toad to Birmingham for its evening game, I had still held unfounded hope that I would be able to attend the following day's Rickwood Classic and at least sing the anthem from my seat while it was being played by a brass quartet. But the record-setting heat wave had prompted the Rosses to invite us into their home rather than simply boon-dock by their barn; and our acceptance of their hospitality meant that we had to return Toad 128 miles back to their farm near Huntsville after the game.

Exhausted after fighting traffic in Birmingham, singing at the game, and driving Arbie and Toad a combined total of 483 miles that day, we were overwhelmed that the Rosses had waited up for us at midnight and greeted us with refreshments. Although we had never met them before midday, they opened their home and hearts to us. Myrna was the sister of my good friend and colleague Don Musser, who had hosted me during the first leg of the tour in Florida. For years, my friend Don had talked with Myrna and her husband Don about our collaborations and about my singing the national anthem. The Rosses' beautiful home, overlooking a bend in the Flint River in one direction and a Monet-worthy field of haystacks in another, provided a welcome interlude from the rhythms of driving and singing.

The unexpected day off from baseball the following day afforded me the opportunity to take Bonnie on a date focusing on some of *her* preferred activities—getting a haircut and manicure, eating a gourmet lunch, going shopping for clothes and accessories, and visiting and viewing exhibits at the Huntsville Museum of Art.

Luckily for me, the featured exhibit in the museum displayed a series of photographs taken by Edward Weston, one of the most innovative and influential photographic artists of the twentieth century. The show included photographs that Weston had taken during a cross-country expedition for shooting landscapes, landmarks, urban enterprises, and people in preparation for the publication of an illustrated version of Walt Whitman's *Leaves of Grass*. Issued in 1941, the book contained forty-nine photographs from more than 700 possible negatives that he had considered for inclusion. Remarkably, Weston avoided trying to take illustrative shots that might visually attempt to duplicate Whitman's verbal images. Instead, he focused on shooting scenes and people whose presence seemed to be inspired by Whitman's passages.

As I walked through the rooms of black-and-white photographs, I was rendered so speechless that I couldn't write more than a few words in my notes. I was consumed by the magnitude and precision of Weston's work, not only because of the grandeur of his subject, like Whitman's—the American self—but also because my own efforts to photograph my anthem quest paled in the light of his incredible images. I was humbled and inspired by the distillation of his months-long, 20,000-mile journey through half of the nation's states.

The day off also afforded me the chance to spend the evening reflecting on the expanse of my own journey, now one-third complete. When I had begun to conceive the project, I hadn't imagined how much the daily tasks would challenge me. In short, I had learned how hard it was to shift gears, often quickly, between so many different kinds of work associated with the anthem project—how difficult it was daily to travel, sing, write, and publish the blog. On a typical day, I would:

> rise at 6 or 6:30 A.M. and write for an hour before Bonnie would wake for breakfast;
> disconnect Arbie's electrical and plumbing systems, then clean and store the sewage line;
> drive Arbie about 200 miles;
> park and hook up the RV;
> unhitch Toad and drive it to the ballpark;
> do vocal exercises;
> deal immediately (and hopefully inconspicuously) with idiosyncratic sound systems;
> stay focused on the words, pitch, and phrases of the anthem;
> take photographs of fans, ballparks, and players;
> talk with staff, players, and fans;
> transcribe my notes and begin to elaborate them into a blog draft;
> sort through pictures;
> revise and revise the blog draft;
> upload and format pictures;
> re-contact teams about upcoming games and arrival instructions; and
> find food and sleep.

And on a couple of days each week I had to:

> deal with delays from late-afternoon traffic and road repairs;
> speak coherently with the press;
> write thank-you notes to the team staffers who had scheduled and hosted my ballpark visits;
> pay bills; and
> do laundry.

I also realized that maintenance issues for Arbie and Toad needed to be addressed (like getting oil changes and new tires), and that some afternoons should be spent sightseeing or visiting museums with Bonnie.

These challenges and tasks taught me to appreciate the skills of RV drivers, especially those who tow cars and those who troubleshoot and repair the mechanical systems in their vehicles.

I developed empathy for baseball scouts who undergo demanding travel and work routines and who sit through so many innings, make detailed notes on so many players, file crucial reports, and avoid eating ballpark food at dinner-time day after day.

I increased my admiration for sportswriters and other journalists who regularly write columns and meet deadlines.

I marveled at the artistry of photographers like Weston, whose imaginative eyes disclose new visions of their subjects, and for graphic designers who crop and position pictures in publications.

I became even more thankful for Bonnie's presence and patience. She made long journeys joyful, reading books to me, finding fun places to eat, talking to me about possibilities for exploration, and driving Arbie and Toad at times to give me time to write or recuperate. She eased my anxieties about travel delays by figuring out alternate routes when traffic snarled. And she tolerated so well my odd rhythms of eating and sleeping: when I regularly disrupted normal dinner times by singing at 7 P.M., when I delayed bedtime by staying up late to write, and when I disturbed her sleep by rising early to work.

A Starry Night: Game 37 in Huntsville

I love the wordplay that the multiple meanings of some teams' names connote. The Huntsville Stars were such a team since their current roster included players named to the Southern League's all-star team, and since one of their former players, Jose Canseco, had achieved Southern League MVP honors in 1985 before bashing his way to major league star status a few years later. Still, the Stars' name referred to more than baseball players' excellent skills and performances; it also reflected the primary industry in Huntsville by recognizing NASA, the starry-eyed space agency whose headquarters were nearby.

The Huntsville team also treated me like a star. General manager Buck Rogers, with whom I had originally corresponded about my anthem project during the previous summer, took Whittier College's press release about the endeavor and forwarded its information and the date of my Huntsville appearance to the Stars' listserv subscribers. During the game, several fans initiated conversations with me based on their familiarity with the profile that

Buck had provided. In addition, Stars director of media relations Jill Cacic set up a live pregame interview with sportscaster Ronnie Duncan on WAAY, the ABC television affiliate in Huntsville. The conversation was so lively that Ronnie returned for a taping of my anthem rendition, which was later featured on the station's evening sports report. Also picking up on the project, FOX-TV sent a videographer to the game and featured my rendition and tour in its newscast.

Jill indicated that the two television stations often worked closely with the team, with Duncan frequently doing the five-o'clock sports report live from the ballpark when the Stars were in town. Both WAAY (channel 31) and FOX-54 had also collaborated with the Stars on promotional nights that featured general admission tickets for 31 or 54 cents, respectively. The box office probably handled more pennies on those nights than during the rest of the season combined.

For my third game in a row, the anthem performance at a ballpark had a corporate sponsor. This time, it was the Musicology School in Huntsville. Having heard my introduction as a professor, several fans and Stars hitting coach John Curtis assumed that I was on the music faculty at the sponsoring school. Recalling the recordings of the anthem played in Yankee Stadium, Curtis likened my rendition to that of Robert Merrill, whom he considered the classic performer. I assured him that, although I am certainly not in Merrill's Met league, I modeled my rendition after his resonant, traditional, and up-tempo performance.

When Curtis learned that my field is religious studies, he posed several leading questions about possible connections between religion and sport. "How are you going to integrate your anthem tour into your teaching?" No one—no journalist, no professor, no friend, no Whittier alumnus—had asked me such a question in the first two months. Leave it to a coach!

Responding enthusiastically to his query, I suggested that the anthem functions as a consecrating hymn in the rituals of civil religion:

> Wherever "The Star-Spangled Banner" is played or sung, protocol requires solemn gestures of devotion. At ballparks, fans rise, remove their caps (often placing their hands over their hearts), and face the flag. The ritual posture and gesture resemble the acts and orientation associated with the consecration of the host in Christian celebrations of the Eucharist or that of the opening of the ark and the removal of the Torah in Jewish services. At the ballpark, the anthem ceremony frequently and immediately precedes the announcement, "Play ball!" and the lead-off hitter stepping into the batter's box. The anthem and the announce-

ment signify a kind of transition in time from the ordinary time of day to the special time of games that is measured in innings, not hours.

"It will be easy to incorporate examples and impressions from my tour into my teaching," I concluded. "Each year, I offer a course on 'Sport and Ritual' that includes several sessions that draw upon my book *From Season to Season: Sports as American Religion.*" He seemed genuinely fascinated by the ideas and the course; and although I would have loved to talk further with him about baseball and religion, the pitcher completed his warm-up tosses and the Smokies leadoff hitter stepped into the batter's box.

As I moved into the stands, a few fans who had received "the e-mail from Buck," as they put it, or who had seen the clip on the five-o'clock news also pursued conversations related to the project, its relation to religious studies, and their own experiences attending baseball games in Huntington and other cities.

"Good job with the anthem and good luck on your quest," a fan said as I walked off the field. Brian Allen caught my attention not only with his comment, but because his preschool daughter Katie Beth was so charming. Wearing a Brewers cheerleading dress that her godparents had brought her from their visit to the ballpark in Milwaukee, Katie Beth joyfully attended several of the Stars games each year with her mother and father. Brian indicated that he had learned of my project on the newscast a couple of hours earlier.

And thanks to Buck's e-mail, Steve Foley sought me out to talk about our mutual passion for baseball and ballparks. He and his daughter Ciera frequently attended the Stars games as well as those in major league cities during their annual summer travels. With a good bit of excitement, he shared their recent experiences of having been in Yankee Stadium on the night when Alex Rodriguez had hit his 600th home run. While Steve didn't expect most of the Stars games to be so memorable, he did express the ongoing, simple delight that an evening at the ballpark usually gave them a chance "to chill" together after a long day at work or school.

At the end of a blistering day of heat, Bonnie and I also enjoyed chilling at the game with our new friend and Huntsville host, Don Ross. After the home team had taken an early lead in the game, the Tennessee Smokies came back and held on for a 3-2 win. Although Huntsville's Stars were eclipsed by the Smokies, the clear sky in the cooling evening sparkled with stars; and our reception by Buck and Jill and the Rosses made Bonnie and me feel like stars.

At the Home of the Braves: Game 38 in Gwinnett

Re-boarding Arbie after a restful day with the Rosses, we left Huntsville and poked back up into Tennessee, skirting Chattanooga before descending into Georgia. As we approached the Atlanta area shortly after noon, we tried to circumvent its anticipated Friday-afternoon artery clogs by exiting I-75 and taking State Route 20 through Canton and toward Lake Lanier, where we had expected to hook up Arbie for the night. Then, that location would have allowed us to commute easily in Toad to Lawrenceville where the Gwinnett Braves make their home.

All went smoothly until mid-afternoon on a stretch of the two-lane road between the communities of Lathemtown and Free Home. There, an accident involving an eighteen-wheeler completely stopped traffic for thirty-five minutes on the broiling, sun-drenched pavement. The temperature on Arbie's exterior thermometer rose to 117 degrees. Some cars ahead of us turned back toward Canton. Others tried a possible cutoff, but soon returned to the line they had left, now further behind than the positions they had previously held. Given our size and position at the mid-point of our supposed time-saving route, we had little choice but to persevere on the route that we had selected.

Since Arbie's air conditioner had a twenty-degree differential, meaning that it could cool the outside air by that amount, we began to swelter as the interior temperature rose to the mid-90s. Figuring that we would start running short of time before the game and probably find it difficult to cool off Arbie's quarters before bedtime, we decided to book a room in the Lawrenceville Hampton Inn rather than in the RV park that we had targeted. Good idea. We checked into the hotel, changed clothes quickly, and made it to the Coolray ballpark eight minutes late—an incredible achievement!—thanks to Bonnie navigating me on back roads around the glut of traffic on Buford Highway that threatened to prevent our timely arrival. Moments after I reported to Maggie Neil, the Braves staffer who coordinated anthem performances, Bonnie and I were greeted by good friend Jon McRae and his wife Karen, who joined us for the game and hosted us for a marvelous dinner later that evening.

To begin the pregame ceremonies, one of the ministers of the 12Stone Church in Lawrenceville threw out the first pitch as a demonstration of outreach to the people in Gwinnett. While church groups had participated in the pregame festivities at other ballparks, I had encountered none that matched 12Stone's extensive promotional presence throughout the game.

For starters, the minister who delivered the first pitch was a statuesque woman bedecked in a gilded lamé blouse. A mega-church aligned with the Willow Creek Church, 12Stone provided information about its mission and ministries at a greeting table near the main gate, and it sponsored several giveaways between innings—the Best-Seat-in-the-House selection, the tee-shirt toss, and a Home Depot gift card for a lucky seat-holder.

Despite the difficulties of the hot afternoon, the dense traffic, and the slightly late arrival at the ballpark, I felt good while waiting to begin, in part because of the relaxed and convivial conversation with Maggie immediately before singing. She inquired about the progress of the trip as well as several of the ballparks with which she was most familiar—the stadia of her hometown Erie SeaWolves and the Myrtle Beach Pelicans, where she had worked the previous year.

My performance must have gone well since several fans passed along complimentary comments. One was most fun: "You shore do have a voice!" a man said as he approached. "I try to sing, but nothing like that. Wow. Good job." And during the game, Zach Weber from the Braves media relations office conducted an extensive interview for Gwinnett's website.

Perhaps because the ballpark was part of a green initiative, or perhaps because it was in such a burgeoning area of the region that it was subject to strict civic codes about adequate health warnings, it posted notices to distinguish "reclaimed" water from potable water. Whatever the cause for the notification, I was not tempted to drink the water in the urinals in the men's restroom even without the posted warning.

For the Braves there were few highlights until the ninth inning, even though they had executed one unusual defensive play: With a runner on second, Buffalo Bisons outfielder Lucas Duda singled sharply to right, and the runner held at third until Duda rounded the bag too widely. The Braves first baseman cut the ball off and started to run toward Duda, who headed for second. In the classic pickle play, the first-baseman threw to second, at which point the runner from third broke for home. The second-baseman whirled with the ball and threw to the catcher, who tagged the Bison trying to score while Duda took second.

In the ninth, however, Bisons pitcher D.J. Carrasco was working on a shutout and recorded the first two outs fairly easily on a pop fly and liner to centerfield. Then, yielding a sharp single to Braves shortstop Brandon Hicks, Carrasco was replaced on the mound. Braves third-baseman Shawn Bowman immediately lofted a homer to left, tightening the score 3-2 and bringing the potential tying run to the plate. But the Braves next batter lined out softly to end the game, allowing the Bisons to escape with a win at the home of the Braves.

For my first-grade class photo, I proudly wore the baseball uniform that my mother had sewn months earlier for my birthday.

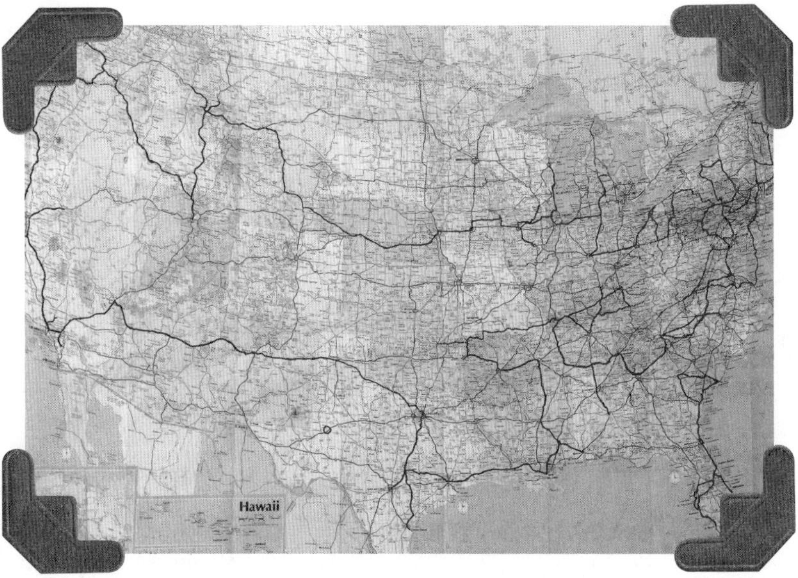

After plotting the cities of participating teams, I devised this screwball route to maximize games while minimizing mileage in the RV.

Mounting the Anthem Tour signage on Arbie,
I prepared for our "shakeout" trip in the RV.

Don Musser and I displayed two of the trophy bass we caught the morning before the first game in Brevard County.

Opening night in Brevard County—the wind whipped my tie while challenging the pitch of my anthem rendition.

Suffering the blistering sun in their section of box seats behind home plate, scouts recorded the speed and location of pitches.

Two visiting Lexington Legends ordered chicken and waffles—an award winning concession—in Savannah.

As a cart creates a wake in the "pond" behind home plate, head groundskeeper Mike Williams considers the challenge for getting the game started in Charleston.

Three members of the RiverDogs grounds crew fill buckets and cans with water before transporting and dumping beyond the ballpark.

It seemed unthinkable that the ballpark in Branchville, South Carolina, would be chain-locked to prevent kids' play during baseball season.

Following a home run by a Midland RockHounds player, passionate (and experienced) fans held up dollars bills to provide a bonus to the player.

The VIP suite in Adelanto where the High Desert Mavericks make their home was itself bittersweet with simplicity.

Among the sculptures in the Albuquerque ballpark, a series of players "in action" by Bill Arms enlivened fans' experience, particularly his "Batter II."

With typical Texas bravado, the VIP suites in Frisco, Texas, were not simply sky boxes; they were two story mansions with balconies.

One of the most spectacular centerfield views was of the Harbor Bridge that appeared like a tiara above the hillock in Corpus Christi.

The Texas heat on the asphalt or the horses' fondness for ice cream probably prompted riders to dismount instead of ordering a double-dip cone from the "ride-through" window in Amarillo.

The between-innings armadillo race in Tulsa presented the challenge of getting one of the critters to navigate the distance of the width of an Oklahoma highway.

Richard Farrell (above) displays the glove that his father, Doc Farrell, used when playing for the 1932 World Champion Yankees. From a book about his father, Richard shared a picture showing Doc wearing the glove.

As a religious studies professor, I naturally wanted to be embraced by a Cardinal, even if this one was only the Memphis mascot.

From left to right, Cheryl and Ken Rich (my first college roommate) joined Kent Gilbert (my former student) and Bonnie in the Lexington skybox where he hosted an outing for his church members.

Brushing home plate was a distinct pregame ritual in Bowling Green. Sponsored by a local dental clinic, it provided another opportunity for children to participate in the ceremonies.

Featured entertainer BirdZerk enticed Yankees third-baseman Kevin Russo to dance moments before stealing his glove and throwing it to the fans.

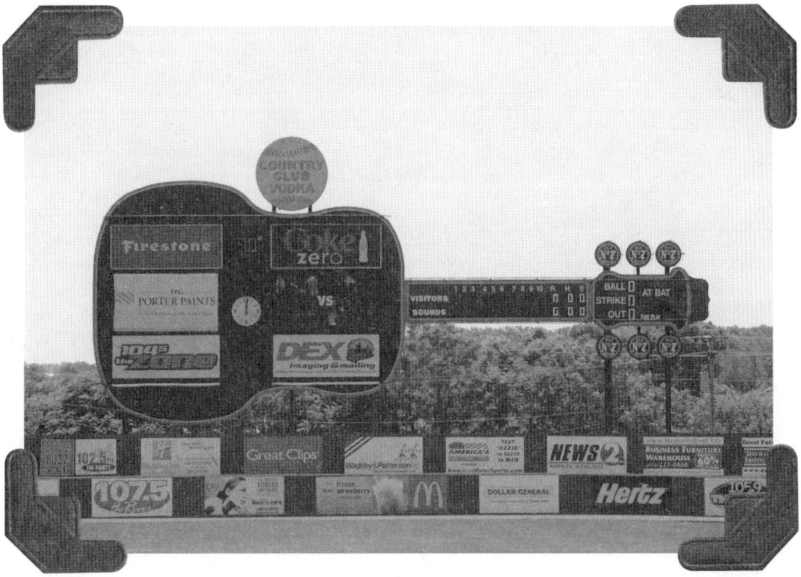

Nashville's scoreboard reflected the team's moniker
and the city's music culture.

Frequently, Bonnie displayed her patience and devotion by sitting alone
in the grandstands after we would arrive early for a game.

Members of Richmond's grounds crew wet the infield dirt while the rest ironically stood poised, ready to spread the tarp over the diamond in anticipation of the approaching storm.

Sculpted with old baseball gloves, "Horsehide" in Rochester was my favorite work of art in ballparks.

To a certain extent the Skyliner rollercoaster adjacent to the ballpark mimicked the historic Altoona Curve.

With Altoona at bat in the bottom of the first, the game suffered a "spray delay" when the sprinkler system malfunctioned.

Having encouraged Bonnie to undertake the anthem tour, her group of friends in Washington, D.C., welcomed us to the capital.

The ethereal lights at Scranton/Wilkes-Barre's ballpark lent it a sacred aura, confirming Ray Kinsella's belief that "a ballpark at night is more like a church than a church."

5.

The Reign of Rain

Intimate Baseball: Game 39 in Asheville

Some ballparks spread in open spaces where their foul lines point toward distant horizons. Some ballparks perch on river banks like wily kids poised above a swirling swimming hole. And some ballparks seem to huddle among urban buildings as though the stadium functions as a dugout for the field of surrounding high-rises.

Asheville's McCormick Field was different. It was nestled gently into a thickly forested hillside where great old oaks and majestic hickories seemed to dwarf and hide the light stanchions, and branches of the tallest trees bent over the twenty-five-foot-high walls and into the field of play.

While minor league ballparks are known for their intimacy, the Asheville Tourists ballpark pressed intimacy into the realm of a Buick's back seat at a drive-in theater. Left-handed hitters salivated when looking out to right: 297' down the line, and 320' to the power alley. And "dead centerfield" earned its nickname because, at 370', it often proved fatal to pitchers.

Not only did Asheville's ballpark enjoy distinct dimensions in its hillside position, it also sported the most aptly named souvenir shop: The Tourist Trap. Its playful spirit extended along the concession concourse where an Asheville-model Louisville Slugger towered opposite a food stand named "Crash's Kitchen." The name, of course, referred to Crash Davis, the veteran catcher in *Bull Durham* who taught flame-thrower Nuke LaLoosh and caught seductive Annie Savoy. It was while Crash ended the season with Asheville that, according to statistically and historically minded Annie, he set the career home-run record for the minor leagues.

The concessions were equally inventive. Among entrées, the Super Tostada could be anointed with any one—or more—of twenty different hot sauces, and there was the not-quite-so-tempting side order of a fried pickle basket. And for dessert, there was nothing like The Sweet Spot's fried moon pies, whose picture on the menu made it look more like a hamburger than a marshmallow-cookie sandwich.

On the field for the pregame ceremonies, I noticed the logo of Baseball Chapel on the shirt of Brent Besosa and asked, "What was your text this morning?"

"A couple of passages in The Book of Acts," he replied. "Luke's accounts of Paul's conversion stories."

Formally approved by Major League Baseball in the 1970s, Baseball Chapel is a Christian ministry that soon expanded into the minor leagues. Its mission is to inspire and nurture spiritual development of players and team personnel throughout professional baseball by sponsoring Sunday-morning Bible studies and worship services.

Brent had begun to serve the Tourists as chaplain several years earlier because he was already familiar with using sports to introduce his understanding of biblical faith. He had helped to set up www.4Outdoorsmen.net, an online ministry oriented to hunters. Not only had Brent led the Bible study for a group of Asheville players around noontime, he also immediately preceded me in the pregame rituals by offering a brief invocation for the crowd, the only ballpark prayer that I heard broadcast all summer.

Yes, it was Sunday afternoon in the South. And in Asheville the religious depth of the culture was displayed in the sponsorship of the bullpen by the First Baptist Church. Yet I never could figure out what the relationship might be between a tithe to the church and a reliever's ERA or WHIP.

More noteworthy than the ballpark's design or its pregame rituals was McCormick Field's history in regard to Jackie Robinson's exhibition game there in 1948. The anticipated appearance of Robinson for a single game prompted local officials to expect more than 2,000 fans beyond the ballpark's capacity. After rain had fallen for several days and saturated the field, officials feared the cancellation of the game, which could not be rescheduled. The Asheville groundskeepers came up with the idea of drying the field by torching it. But how could the sodden turf catch on fire to evaporate the moisture? By pouring gasoline on the grass, lighting it, and then making sure it would burn by accelerating the flames with helicopter fanning. Incredibly, the ploy worked.

Even though my anthem rendition was not quite that hot, it was among the very best during my first forty games. I felt in good spirits and good voice. The acoustics were fine and the crowd embracing. One of the umpires standing at home plate during the anthem turned at its conclusion, made eye contact, and slightly pumped his fist. I took that to mean "good job," not "you're out!" As I left the field, Tourists assistant general manager

Chris Smith, with whom I had worked to schedule my appearance, enthusiastically remarked, "You can come back and sing for us any time."

Having heard my introduction as a professor at Whittier College, a smiling man approached me as I walked past the box seats. "I'm an alumnus, class of '64," he said. "It's not often that I run into someone from Whittier in these parts. I'm Dean Kahl." A professor of chemistry and environmental studies at nearby Warren Wilson College, he attended several Tourists games each year, often, like that afternoon, with his daughter and grandchildren. As had been her practice for almost forty years, she had brought her old glove to the game, ready to slip it onto her hand to field a pop foul into the stands.

Dean and I talked about our baseball passions, our professorial experiences, and our connections to Whittier College. Like so many of Whittier's students throughout the years, Dean had been the first person in his family to attend college. When his chemistry professor, Roy Newsome (who later became president of the college), had suggested that he pursue graduate studies, Dean had wondered, "What's graduate school?" With Newsome's encouragement, he found out, completed his Ph.D., and followed Newsome's career path, becoming a professor at a liberal arts college.

As we discussed our respective joys in teaching, Dean expressed great appreciation for Whittier's continuing commitment to serve first-generation college students, indicated in part by its official designation as a Hispanic-Serving Institution. He had been a student when Martin Ortiz had initiated advocacy and support services for Latino/a students. Within a few years, Ortiz had created Whittier's Center for Mexican-American Affairs and then directed it for decades. Now expanded and renamed in his honor, the Ortiz Programs provide academic, financial, and career guidance to Latino/a students at Whittier.

While we mused about the campus and friends at Whittier in the sixties, I mentioned several of my recently retired faculty colleagues who, following their own graduate studies, had returned to their alma mater. He smiled with recognition as I went over the roster: Bill Geiger in English, Phil O'Brien in the library, and Les Howard in sociology. One of the enriching characteristics of liberal arts colleges is their cultivation of a sense of community that persists beyond the location of the campus or the time of one's studies.

Providing counterpoint to our conversation about the friendliness of Whittier, we also talked about the community of Minor League Baseball—

the Asheville ballpark and its various major league affiliations over the years; the stars whom he had seen play, including former Tourists and now Hall of Famers Eddie Murray and Willie Stargell, both power hitters who, he had said while pointing beyond right field, had "hit home runs into the trees"; and the Tourists' pitchers, who season after season ranked at the bottom of the league in team ERA, in large part a consequence of the field's short fences.

That profile of Asheville's pitching came to life as Dean and I watched Savannah's Sand Gnats score seven earned runs en route to an 8-5 victory over the Tourists.

A Knightly Event: Game 40 in Charlotte

To get to the Charlotte Knights ballpark in Fort Hill, I had to cross the border between North and South—Carolina, that is. The name of the team presented a quandary: It was named for a city in a different state than its ballpark's home. Even so, I counted the game in Fort Hill among the weeklong sequence of games I had scheduled for North Carolina teams, and I expected it to be a rather routine nightly game. It proved anything but ordinary. It was, in multiple ways, a knightly event.

The unusual character of the evening started with my customary reporting to staff members at the fan-assistance booth. There, Patty Hunter greeted me. As we exchanged pleasantries, she indicated that one of her best friends had attended Whittier.

"Who?" I simply asked.

"Alexandra Shelton," she said.

"Ah, Alex!" I blurted with delight. "She was in my course on 'Arabs and Muslims,' and she did quite a good job."

"No way!" Patty exclaimed. "I remember her talking about that course."

The conversation about the course was memorable to Patty, since Alex was then serving in the Peace Corps in regions of Africa where Islam exerts significant influence in ways that distinguish the practice of Islam from typical profiles of the faith as an Arab religion. There was little doubt in my mind that Alex would be making use of cultural, religious, and geographical information and insights that she had mastered in her studies.

The evening in Charlotte also featured a couple of other oblique connections with my California home and anthem project. Shortly before the gates opened, dozens of photographers, reporters, and television camera operators clotted the area around the batting cage. They were focused on Carolina Panthers lineman Geoff Schwartz (listed at 6' 3" and 331 lbs.) and several of his teammates. Taking hefty swings, Schwartz, a native of Los Angeles, hit several ground balls and then a routine fly to right. Although he made contact with most of the pitches, he didn't smash them like he did when blocking opponent linemen. Having displayed his modest hitting skills during batting practice, Schwartz then showed his ability to throw a strike in the pregame ceremonies as he tossed out the first pitch.

Shortly after I had completed my vocal exercises, I started up the stairwell from the field level when a person asked, "Are you singing the anthem tonight?" I nodded. "This will be my sixth time to see you," he said. Michael Juhl, a scout for the St. Louis Cardinals, smiled as he added, "I've seen you more often than some of the players I'm tracking! Let's see, Ft. Myers, Montgomery, Gwinnett a couple of nights ago, and a couple of other places, too."

Between innings, I sought him out, and we shared stories. A former professional player whose baseball career essentially paid for his education, Juhl had moved to the Charlotte area when he had begun his Ph.D. studies in sociology. For several years, then, he taught sociology courses in community colleges before returning to baseball as a Cardinals scout.

He understood the demands and opportunities afforded by my academic career, and increasingly I gained appreciation for challenges that scouts face. Although they are often envied by fans since they get to see so many games from such good seats behind home plate, scouts must catalogue the speed and placement of every pitch, record each hitter's eye for the strike zone and his ability to hit certain pitches, and chart the best defensive alignments given hitters' tendencies on certain kinds of pitches. They must keep detailed records of these multiple aspects of performances, often recording the data in adverse conditions with scorching sun, falling rain, or deafening noise from ballpark speakers.

While Juhl and I measured our workloads, compared our fatigue from frequent travel, and commiserated about the need to avoid a steady diet of ballpark food, we realized that we both used days off trying to catch up writing reports about baseball. I tried to write accounts of games and post them to my blog while he wrote profiles and analyses of players. His particular assignment in the coming weeks was to complete about 600 player reports, each of which would take at least fifteen minutes to compile and compose. The reports were due well before the major league trading deadline at the end of July so that the Cardinals could evaluate possible player transactions.

While my view of players was certainly nowhere near Juhl's discerning eye for their skills, I did appreciate their grace, power, speed, and heady play. And I also liked to report on noteworthy plays and accomplishments. On this night, the scouts' notes probably featured the strong arms of the Knights pitchers, who recorded thirteen strikeouts, and the uneven night at the plate by IronPigs first baseman Tagg Bozied. In the fifth inning, Tagg tagged a homer to tie the game, but in his other three plate appearances he struck out, while his team went on to defeat the Knights 4-2.

Two other bits related to the game—both involving fans—merit comment. One was a knightly oriented competition that took place in foul territory between innings. While a few other ballparks had featured inflated bouts between sumo-suited contestants, or balloon-ball rolls to knock over a bowling pin, or bloated water-balloon tosses, Charlotte highlighted its knightly fixation by having two fans joust with soft battering weapons. Clad in oversized inflated costumes with superimposed "heads," each contestant vied to knock the Velcro-attached head off his or her opponent.

The other observation involved fan behavior and an unseen player. Seated in the row immediately behind the Knights dugout were three boys—two young teens and a preschooler—and their father. After the first inning or so, one of the teenagers caught a ball tossed into the stands by an infielder who was returning to the dugout. For a couple of innings, the teen tumbled it gently in his hands, rubbing the horsehide and fingering its raised red seams. Eventually, he handed the ball to his younger brother who, moments later, rolled the ball slowly across the top of the dugout toward the field. As it disappeared into the unseen cavern of players, the father caught a glimpse of the youngster's actions. Rather than scold him severely, he calmly—but sternly—let the young boy know why the ball was special and how he should care for it. The teen, meanwhile, seemed unfazed: easy come, easy go. Within minutes, however, an unidentifiable hand appeared over the lip of the dugout and flipped the ball back to the boys.

Knightly courtesy characterized the night.

Sharing Anthem Singing: Game 41 in Hickory

Several weeks before the tour began, I received a message from the Hickory Crawdads requesting that, if possible, I shift the confirmed date for my appearance there. I checked with the other teams in North Carolina where I had scheduled performances during that week and learned that it would not be possible to change any of their dates to accommodate the Crawdads' request.

The Crawdads' problem—and now mine—was this: The Monday morning game in Hickory would be the team's school-day promotion during the final week of the school year before the students' summer vacation. The team expected about twenty elementary and middle schools to send busloads of students to the late-morning game.

While the Crawdads indicated that they would like to honor their commitment to me, they also wanted to feature a local school group performing the anthem. From nearby Newton in Catawba County, the Balls Creek Elementary School chorus stood ready to sing. The students at Balls Creek had a strong tradition of community involvement and social responsibility. In the previous decade, they had raised over $100,000 for the American Heart Association in their annual Jump Rope for Heart event.

Not wanting to break the hearts of these fourth-, fifth-, and sixth-graders, I suggested to the Crawdads that the choir join me in singing the anthem. The school's music director, Jennifer McNeely, expressed delight for the opportunity to accompany me. For the first and only time on my tour, I was able to count on support from good singers who knew the words.

Before the game, Conrad, the Crawdads mascot, also enjoyed interacting with members of the choir, giving them high-five hand slaps after he had teased the school librarian while she was taking their picture. Thankfully, he didn't try to harmonize with them using his crustacean voice.

The Balls Creek schoolmates created quite an enthusiastic climate for us. They cheered and clapped when the choir was introduced, and although the microphones had trouble picking up the students' joyful voices, it was apparent that they were excellent musicians. And most of the students standing in the bleachers joined with us in singing our allegiance.

Although baseball has historically been quite popular in North Carolina, Hickory's fielding of a professional team represented a relatively recent development. Prior to 1993, the team had played in Gastonia and had been affiliated with the Texas Rangers. In that year a group of citizens in Hickory succeeded in relocating and renaming the team, in part by constructing the L.P. Franz Stadium, which is named for two of the civic leaders and baseball lovers. The community's enthusiastic support of the team was evident in the ballpark, not merely by the presence of the fans but also by the number of local advertisements on the outfield wall. The right-field fence alone displayed more than thirty billboard ads.

Two pregame ceremonies were also distinct at Hickory. Unlike most ballparks, there were no first pitches. Instead of making a toss toward home plate, a child was offered the chance to crush the first hit by smacking a ball off a tee near the Crawdads dugout. And another child was given the chance to paint home plate white. Under the supervision of the groundskeeper, the official painter for the day could complete the final physical act of field preparation.

When Hickory's lead-off hitter stepped into the batter's box, the children began the rhythmic chanting and clapping of a pep rally: "Let's go, Crawdads!" Clap, clap, clap, clap. "Let's go, Crawdads!" Clap, clap, clap, clap. Amplified by the tiered formation of the seats and the hard surfaces of the stands, the enthusiastic noise encouraged the Crawdads, who scored early and often off the BlueClaws starter. To the delight of the young fans, Hickory built a ten-run lead over Lakewood and the Craws crushed the Claws 10-3.

Friendly Folks and Beasts: Game 42 in Greensboro

Anticipating a cluster of games in central North Carolina, Bonnie and I heeded the call of the wild and aimed Arbie toward the Zooland RV Park southwest of Asheboro. Located in a rural area at the edge of the Uwharrarie National Forest, Zooland was so named not because of rowdy activities possibly pursued by campers, but because the North Carolina Zoological Park was located about a lion's roar away. Despite its cagy name, Bonnie had selected the RV park because it provided Wi-Fi (which occasionally worked), cable TV (with a few basic channels), shaded sites (at least for a couple of early-morning hours), and especially its proximity to the historic Pisgah Covered Bridge, where we picnicked at lunch one day before heading out for an evening game an hour's drive away.

As we departed for the game in Greensboro, we turned away from Covered Bridge Road and toward the zoo before shooting straight north up Interstates 73 and 74. While I watched the highway signs as we approached the city and several interstate intersections, I kept wondering how an East-West, even-numbered interstate highway would overlap a North-South, odd-numbered freeway for more than twenty miles, especially since the numbers seemed to be in flux and the highway under reconstruction. Could we travel in multiple directions at once? Even so, the brief trip from Arbie to the ballpark proved easy, perhaps presaging our friendly encounters in Greensboro.

Arriving at the ballpark, we should have suspected that parking near Friendly Avenue would signal a good omen for our experience. While we walked along the sidewalk toward the front gate to Newbridge Bank Ballpark to pick up our tickets, a young woman standing on the concourse called out, "Are you Joe? Welcome."

As the anthem coordinator for the Greensboro Grasshoppers, Laura Damico had been reading our blogs earlier in the day and had recognized us from the pictures in our postings. Perhaps it also helped that Bonnie and I were wearing our AnthemTour logo polo shirts. Nonetheless, Laura's enthusiastic greeting set a gracious tone for the evening.

The general friendliness in Greensboro, evidenced in part by street names and ballpark hospitality, should not be surprising since the majority of British settlers in the area in the mid-eighteenth century were members of the Society of Friends—or Quakers, as they are more popularly known. In light of their employment of plain speech and their avoidance of using titles, it is somewhat ironic that they named the county "Guilford" after a titular Lord, the first Earl of Guilford, Francis North. In 1754 the Quaker immigrants established the New Garden Friends Meeting (their plain-speech designation for a congregation or "church"), and it continues to convene in Greensboro, along with several other meetings of the Society of Friends. In addition, Greensboro provides the home of Guilford College, which, like Whittier, was founded by the Quakers. While the name "Guilford" is historically significant for Greensboro, the name is also playfully important for its fans: It's the name of the Grasshoppers green mascot.

The ballpark, too, is impressive and inviting. Built to Double-A standards, the six-year-old facility featured several fan comforts: adequate seating for 7,500, wide concourses, picnic areas, kids' play spaces and facilities, and scores of concession stands. Certainly, it was the most elegant ballpark that I had seen for a Single-A team, especially in contrast to other, much more modest and relatively new stadia where I had been in Hickory and would find a few days later in Kannapolis.

Outside the ballpark, interactive sculptures invited kids—and grown-ups, too—to sit beside the likenesses of team mascot Guilford, an obese, fluffy caricature of a grasshopper; and Babe Ruff, the black Labrador retriever who served the team as bat-dog. Guilford and Babe vividly set a celebrative tone. Between the bench and the ballpark fence stood a bronze memorial to Sandra Bradshaw, a Greensboro resident and flight attendant aboard United's fateful flight 93 on September 11. The tribute expressed the city's pride and baseball's ties to patriotism. Nearby, kid-tall baseballs encouraged young fans to climb atop for photo opportunities while adjacent ball-shaped fountains burbled fresh hope for the hometown Hoppers. Even the security gates at the main entry featured the image of a baseball cap in their wrought-iron design.

While the ballpark's aesthetic features created a stimulating environment, the fans' excitement soared for the Grasshoppers' first game of their home-stand. Having won two out of three games on their short road trip to the home of the first-place Hagerstown Suns, the team had returned only a half-game out of the league lead. The fans' enthusiasm had been stirred not merely by the Hoppers' success, but also by an incident involving their starting pitcher, Zach Neal, a scene captured on video that had gone viral on YouTube the previous day. In the fourth inning of the middle game of the series against the Suns, Neal had yielded a home run to top minor league prospect Bryce Harper, who then blew a kiss to Neal as he rounded third and headed home. In response to the reprimands for Harper's unsportsmanlike gesture, the parent Washington Nationals management tried to protect their teenage "phenom" by calling Harper's flurry a "teachable moment."

In the first inning of this game against the Kannapolis Intimidators, Greensboro's starting pitcher again took center stage. After allowing two ground-ball singles, Jake Rogers induced a force play that left runners on first and third with two outs. Then he tried a standard, situational pickoff move that repeatedly fails: Rogers faked a pickoff throw to third, whirled, and threw to first. The feint-to-third and swirl-to-first is a pickoff play that never works even though it's taught to Little Leaguers, practiced by high-school teams, and tried again and again and again by every professional team: Fake a throw to third; pivot and peg to first. Runners are never deceived, and fans are rarely confused. Yet incredibly, this time the play worked. Dan Black, the baserunner, couldn't get back to the bag, took off for second, and slid into the tag by the shortstop who had taken the throw from the first-baseman. When I relayed this story to baseball-loving friends that I had witnessed this play's success, they groaned. Because the play had now worked, they reasoned, it would be likely that Rogers would continue to utilize it, although probably never again deceiving another first-base runner but always slowing down the game.

When the Grasshoppers came to bat in the bottom half of the inning, fireworks exploded—literally. One of the features of the ballpark was shooting off fireworks when a Hopper hit a home run. With one out and a runner on first, Christian Yelich launched a towering drive over the left-field fence, and the spray of sparks erupted to the delight of the Hoppers and their fans.

While the explosion of fireworks provided a contrast to the ballpark's non-violent, Quakerly atmosphere, other in-game entertainment manifested Greensboro's friendly character. As one of the promotions or distractions provided by the home team, Babe Ruff, a trained Labrador retriever and a representative of "man's best friend," was directed to the home-plate area in the bottom half of the third inning to fetch the bats dropped by the Grasshoppers' hitters. By that time, however, the Grasshoppers starting pitcher was probably already in his manager's doghouse since he had yielded four runs on nine hits and a wild pitch en route to taking the loss in an 8-3 decision to the Intimidators.

Compounding this friendly dog theme, one of the concession stands was named "The Dog Pound" since it offered classic "dogs" from major league ballparks: Dodger Dogs, Milwaukee Brats, Cincinnati Chili Cheese Coneys, and Chicago Dogs. Yet somehow, there seemed to be a disconnect: There was no distinct dog representing Greensboro's parent team in Miami. Then again, what kind of dog might adequately embody the relationship between grasshoppers and marlins? However friendly it might be, it would surely be a feature at the ballpark and at Zooland!

A "Dashing" Experience: Game 43 in Winston-Salem

Since I love team names that simultaneously feature grammatical elements and baseball plays, what could be better than a name that puns the punctuation mark within a city's name with the fleet-footed run from the batter's box to first base? The Dash. From Winston-Salem. Not that the team wanted to flee the city or its smoky heritage; there was yet another nominal twist: the team's name is a collective singular noun, a feature that underscores the group unity of teamwork. With the multiple meanings associated with the team's moniker, it's easy to see why I was so taken with Winston-Salem's dashing name.

While I found delight in wordplay about the Dash, what made the Winston-Salem game most enjoyable was that two former colleagues from Whittier, Laura Ammon and Randy Reed, drove down from their home in the mountains to join Bonnie and me for the game and dinner later in the evening. A specialist in the history of Christianity, Laura began her association with Whittier when she was appointed to replace me during a previous sabbatical leave. For several years thereafter, she continued to teach courses in religious studies while completing her Ph.D. at Claremont Graduate University. Her husband Randy, whose expertise lies in the studies of methods and theories related to religious studies, also began to teach for us while he completed his dissertation at my alma mater, the University of Chicago Divinity School. Incredibly, both now enjoyed tenure-track appointments in the same department at Appalachian State University.

Two hours before the scheduled start of the game, violent thunderstorms jolted the area and lightning struck in the parking lot about a shortstop's throw away from us. As the rain slackened, I still needed to complete a sound check on the field, and although the torrid portion of the storm had passed, I wondered whether the battery-powered microphone might attract residual lightning that still appeared in the distance.

As skies cleared and fans began to pour into the ballpark, they were greeted by members of the Knights of Columbus who passed out small flags in honor of upcoming Flag Day. What a great photo opportunity—a patriotic celebration by a religious group! I reached into my computer bag for my camera and realized that it was still on the dinette table in Arbie, which was caged at the Zooland RV Park fifty miles away.

Although it was a Friday night, the crowd appeared to be an ecumenical gathering for a North Carolina Christian conference. Not only were the Knights of Columbus from the Holy Family Catholic Church greeting fans; according to the welcome board, there were also groups attending from five Baptist churches, two Episcopalian churches, an independent religious community, a Catholic church, and a Moravian congregation. The series of groups could almost be sung to the tune of "The Twelve Days of Christmas"—a unifying celebration for which, like this baseball game, all of the diverse religious groups might gather together.

Given the throng of church folk in the audience, it was ironic—by omission—that the description of my affiliation and project didn't refer to the fact that I'm a professor of religious studies. Yet a more explicit irony was specified in my introduction. My identification was prefaced with the sponsoring phrase: "Performing tonight's anthem is *Winston-Salem Journal* National Anthem finalist and Whittier College professor Joe Price." What an irony! Several days earlier I had sent the *Journal*'s sports department a news release about me singing the anthem for the Dash's game and, as usual, my e-mail had been ignored, not even provoking a form reply. Yet now, getting ready to sing the anthem, I was claimed to be a sponsored finalist for a publication that had refused to recognize the anthem project that I had undertaken! Then following my rendition, I was also surprised by one woman's comment, especially in North Carolina: "Thank you for not singing it country."

The Dash's mascot, Bolt, was among the most energetic and inventive on-field entertainers encountered in the entire season. In one of his routines, he pretended to pilfer balls from the umpire's bag and then to pull out size 60 or larger briefs. The crowd roared. The underwear was so large that a later promotion could have featured a yoked race with two children using the leg holes of the underwear as waistbands, while competing against another pair of runners similarly tied together. Bolt also surprised me during one of the mid-inning toss-aways. While I was talking to Randy and Laura and oblivious to his antics, he threw a soft souvenir ball toward me. Bonnie said, "Look!" I turned and, with instinctive reactions uncommon for me, caught the spongy, small ball—a first for the season!

For the most part, the most dashing event during the game occurred when the grounds crew raced onto the field to cover the mound and home plate during a half-hour rain delay. Otherwise, play proceeded apace. Each team collected six hits while making a single error. The difference was that five of Wilmington's hits went for extra bases, including two round-trippers, leading to the Blue Rocks' 4-1 win over the Dash.

Almost Shut Out: Game 44 in Durham

By twenty-four hours, I missed seeing Dirk Hayhurst hurl a shutout for the Durham Bulls at home on Tobacco Road. Normally, Hayhurst wouldn't seem to warrant baseball's special notice since he was not a highly-rated minor league prospect, even though twice he had brewed a pot of coffee in "the Show." In twenty-five appearances for San Diego and Toronto in 2008 and 2009, he had struck out twenty-seven batters in forty innings, failing to win either of his two decisions.

But Hayhurst was noteworthy as an author—not of pitching gems but of books. Beginning in 2007, Hayhurst became a diarist for *Baseball America*'s website, honing his writing skills as he reflected on the routines and challenges of a minor leaguer. His 2010 book, *Bullpen Gospels: Major League Dreams of a Minor League Veteran*, achieved the all-star status that he had dreamed about attaining as a player when the book became a *New York Times* bestseller.

In *Bullpen Gospels,* Hayhurst avoided the polar temptations to expose teammates in clubhouse shenanigans or to sentimentalize his seasons in the sun. Instead, he explored the enduring lure of baseball while revealing his struggles with daily necessities and routines, all the while celebrating his good outings and acknowledging his failures. Shortly before I started the anthem tour, a friend had given me the book, which I inhaled. It's lively, entertaining, and poignant. Having the chance to see Hayhurst in action in the minors would have been more than a major highlight.

Like the Lehigh Valley IronPigs who had scratched out a single hit in their scoreless effort against Hayhurst the night before, I, too, was threatened to be shut out in Durham—not by a pitcher, but initially by parking challenges, then the box office, and finally torrential rain.

When Bonnie and I arrived at the ballpark almost two hours before game time, we were surprised by the density of the crowd and the impossibility of parking, even in little Toad. Although I had been warned that I would need to find parking on my own, I circled through the nearby streets, found no spaces, and finally drove toward the attendant at the entry to the small team lot. Rolling down my window, I inquired rather innocently, "I'm the anthem singer tonight. Where should I park?" Looking befuddled for a second or two, he waved me past his checkpoint and into the reserved spaces. With that good luck, I anticipated an auspicious evening.

The weather was warm and the crowd jazzed about evening promotions featuring former Durham Negro League players as well as two dozen Boy Scout troops. Walking toward the main gate, Bonnie and I paused to read names and tributes in the memorial bricks adjoining the ballpark. Several stood out, especially "Roger Craig: His dream started when he was a batboy for the Durham Bulls."

Among the markers identifying the affiliations of Durham's minor league players and teams over the years, one engraved tribute recognized the various professional Negro teams that had called Durham home during four decades—the Rams, Black Sox, Eagles, and Colts. Representatives from these teams would be honored during the evening: Roy Alston, Levy Barbee, Pernell Canady, Thomas Clark, Wesley Lee, Robert Pennington, Artis Plummer, Sterling Upchurch, Walter Wilson, and James Womble. Adding to the focus on historic Negro Leaguers, current players for Durham and Norfolk wore throwback uniforms, with the Norfolk players donning jerseys from various well-known teams like the Birmingham Black Barons and the Kansas City Monarchs, and the Bulls players sporting jerseys from Durham's several teams.

But the high spirits of the evening started to dampen when I arrived at the Will Call window to pick up the tickets. There the agent said that the game was sold out and that the only tickets available were for lawn seating beyond centerfield.

"Nuh uh," Bonnie protested. "He's the anthem singer and we need real seats."

A couple of minutes later, the ticket agent produced two separate reserved seat tickets, saying that they were all that could be secured. I was flabbergasted that at least two tickets had not been set aside for the anthem performer.

As I headed to the field for the pregame ceremonies, several of the Negro Leaguers were escorted to the home-plate area to await their introduction while the Boy Scouts paraded along the track in foul territory, starting from the right-field corner—thus reversing a player's normal route, rounding home and heading toward the third-base dugout. Meanwhile, the grounds crew started to cover the pitcher's mound and batter's boxes with rain tarps.

And when the last scout shuffled and scuffed his way through the grandstand gate beyond the dugout at 6:53 P.M.—minutes before the scheduled time for the anthem—the grounds crew unrolled the infield tarp, anchoring its edges with a tractor mower and whatever other heavy equipment could be found to weigh it down. While the crew spread the tarp over the infield, the pregame video featured Susan Sarandon in her seductive role as Annie Savoy in *Bull Durham*: Instead of reading the poetry of Whitman with Nuke or extolling the virtues of baseball with Crash, Sarandon's sultry voice simply urged the fans, "Now sit back and enjoy the best summer entertainment in the Triangle area—Durham Bulls baseball."

Even though I had witnessed deluges in Charleston, Lexington, and Winston-Salem, where I had seen tarps extend over the fields, I had not seen a grounds crew implement strategies to keep the cover from flapping in the wind and, depending on the vigor of gusts, perhaps blowing foul. I figured that a driving storm was imminent, and I dreaded the possibility of my first game rainout. After overhearing the grounds-crew chief tell the on-field announcer that the storm was expected to arrive at 7:10 P.M., I phoned Bonnie and suggested that she move to a covered area. Then I retreated to the shielded ramp behind the first-base dugout, hoping that the delay would be minimal, that a thunderhead would move through the area with greater speed than Lou Brock or Rickey Henderson.

In the ramp, I was joined by the director and accompanist for the Wake Baptist Grove Church choir from Garner, North Carolina. His distinct challenge was to shield his keyboard and amplifier equipment from the ensuing downpour. Since I had been expecting to sing the anthem alone, I was puzzled about his keyboard. Asking what his choir would perform, I learned that their participation was part of the celebration of the Negro Leaguers: They would sing the Negro national anthem, "Lift Every Voice and Sing," written and composed by James Weldon Johnson and J. Rosamond Johnson. Its first two stanzas call for all to celebrate hope based on the lessons that history has taught us.

> Till earth and heaven ring,
> Ring with the harmonies of liberty
> Let our rejoicing rise
> High as the listening skies,
> Let it resound loud as the rolling sea.
>
> Sing a song, full of the faith that the dark past has taught us,
> Sing a song, full of the hope that the present has brought us;
> Facing the rising sun of our new day begun,
> Let us march on till victory is won.

Yet on this night in Durham, like the previous year when this church choir had been disappointed by rain, the fans would not hear any of the Negro anthem's stanzas. After an hour or so standing in the ramp and shielding the amplifier, the discouraged choir director lifted his keyboard and left.

But because this evening was my only chance to sing for the Bulls, I remained hopeful and started to make my way through the crowd.

While the places of refuge in ramps, concourses, and concession areas were jammed tightly with fans seeking shelter, the Negro Leaguers set up a table to autograph their pictures and to tell their stories to interested fans. Although this night had expected to focus on these Negro League alumni, there were other tributes to Durham's African-American players displayed throughout the ballpark. In the entry, a memorial brick was inscribed to Durham's Negro League teams, and in the men's restroom, a poster of Nathaniel "Bubba" Morton was prominently displayed. Morton had been the first African-American player signed by the Detroit Tigers, and he was one of the first African Americans to play for the Durham Bulls, in fact, leading them to their first championship.

Interrupting my conversation with the Negro League veterans about their experiences and whether "The Star-Spangled Banner" or the Negro national anthem had been played or sung before their games, my cell phone rang. Bonnie was calling to let me know where she had huddled behind a pretzel stand. Weaving my way through the crowd's crush, I found her frustrated and amazed that I had been enjoying stimulating conversations. She was aghast that I wanted to wait for the possibility to sing. Normally, she entertained herself during my pregame preparations and later forays through the stands by playing games on her iPad and iPhone, or by doing Sudoku puzzles. But her iPad had been left in Arbie and the Sudoku book in the car. And after playing games for an hour on her iPhone, it was now out of juice.

Meanwhile, the rain poured, the wind whipped, and the crowd shrunk significantly. Bonnie and I moved from the concourse area back to the covered grandstands, now sparsely populated. Boy Scouts in uniform continued to dart in and out of the falling rain, splashing through puddles and playing tag while the baseball game remained remote. Down deep, I hoped that the Bulls would be highly motivated to get the game played, because hundreds of scouts anxiously anticipated camping out on the outfield grass following the game, and thousands of fans had already paid for admission, purchased concessions and souvenirs, and left.

As nine o'clock approached, I let Bonnie know that I would be willing to leave after 9:30 if, by then, there were no promise of the start of the game. But at 9:21 the grounds crew began to move the heavy equipment from the tarp's exposed edges, and I kindled whatever modicum of hope might remain. Sure enough, an announcement was soon made that the first pitch was anticipated shortly before 10 o'clock.

Before Durham, ballpark crowds always swelled after the performance of the national anthem. But this night, the announced attendance of 9,944 had almost evaporated by the time I resumed my place in the front row of the box seats, ready to move to the soggy sod behind home plate.

At 10:16 I finally started the star-spangled phrases. As I left the field, Frank Felicelli, the usher in the area behind home plate with whom I had talked at great length during the initial delay, gave me a grade of "A." Quite good, I thought, since he, a high-school social studies teacher, was a rigorous grader, having recently completed evaluating more than 500 essays for advanced-placement exams in U.S. history.

Although I appreciated Frank's endorsement of my rendition, I left the field and the game in some distress. I had imposed on Bonnie by persisting through the three-hour delay while she had nothing to do in the rain: her friends were elsewhere, her iPad asleep in Arbie, her Sudoku book marooned in the car, and her iPhone sapped of strength. As the Norfolk Tides came to bat, we left the ballpark; and the ninety-minute return drive to Asheboro, where Arbie was docked, was long, long, long in silence, much longer than the span of miles.

The following morning before I left alone for the afternoon game in Kannapolis, I checked the score of the previous night's game: the Tides had splashed their way to a 5-4 win.

Who's Intimidated?: Game 45 in Kannapolis

There was no way that I could cajole Bonnie to join me for the Sunday drive to Kannapolis for the late-afternoon Intimidators game, not after the fiasco of the rain delay the previous night in Durham. I was lucky she hadn't demanded that I drop her off at the airport in either Raleigh or Charlotte to abort her participation in the tour.

After starting a North Carolina week in the Smoky Mountains and then spending several days along the stretch of I-40 from Durham to Winston-Salem, I turned back toward the Charlotte area where Kannapolis provided my final stop in the state. During my Tar Heel tour, I had sung for teams in the Carolina League, the International League, the Eastern League, and the South Atlantic or Sally League (as it had been popularly known some years ago). And if the Appalachian League had begun its short-season schedule by this time, I would have added another team or two. Burlington had approved for me to sing; but, alas, they wouldn't begin their short season until two weeks after I had left the area.

Simply and thoroughly, I resonate with the Tar Heel region, not merely because of its baseball skeleton. While I love the landscape—the comforting haze snuggling down among the Blue Ridge Mountains and the hardwood forests hugging the rolling hills—I get inspired by the state's traditions of folk art, its celebration of multiple musical styles, and its passion for sports. In fact, I could easily have been a North Carolina native. My oldest sister was born in this state while my father had been on the faculty at Meredith College in Raleigh. But before I was born, he left the professorate to assume a pastorate in Mississippi.

Across the region's varied terrain, a sporting spirit characterizes the Tar Heel State, especially during spring and summer. The spring's sports-obsession begins with ACC basketball and March Madness, which almost always features Duke or North Carolina in the Final Four, not to mention that North Caroline State, Wake Forest, and Davidson also excel in round-ball. And NASCAR's circuit, which revs up with the Daytona 500 shortly before the NCAA basketball playoffs, traces its roots and rapid growth to the mountain regions of North Carolina, for which the stock-car fascination provides its pulse.

As much as racetracks at Daytona, Darlington, and Bristol draw NASCAR fans to desirable destinations, Kannapolis in North Carolina is probably the true mecca for the most fervent stock-car devotees. After all, it was in this historic mill town dominated by the textile industry that Dale Earnhardt was born, and throughout surrounding Cabarrus County dozens of NASCAR teams have their headquarters. It should not be too surprising, then, that the Kannapolis baseball team adopted Earnhardt's moniker by taking the name of the "Intimidators."

It is also fitting that one of the Intimidator's racecars—a "#3" black Chevy donated by the Earnhardt Foundation—paced most fans from the parking lot to the front gate at the Fieldcrest Cannon ballpark, so named to recognize the historic significance of the textile magnate of the area's economy.

While NASCAR certainly dominates the region, North Carolina still enjoys a summer love affair with baseball. The state was the home of Enos "Country" Slaughter and Catfish Hunter, Hall of Famers among the hundreds of Tar Heel players who became major league all-stars, and it routinely boasts the most varied slate of minor league teams of any state. If you count Charlotte's Knights among the North Carolina teams, the state then featured nine affiliated minor league franchises, fielding teams in all five levels of minor league play.

During childhood, I enjoyed learning about geographic regions by locating clusters of teams in aptly named leagues, like the New York-Penn League or the Texas League or the South Atlantic League. But since Kannapolis was set to play the Delmarva Shorebirds, whose home was in Salisbury, Maryland, I cringed at the geographic conflict between the team's location and the league's historic identity. Even so, the acceptance of a team from Maryland's eastern shore in the so-called South Atlantic League is less egregious than the league's inclusion of the Lakewood BlueClaws, whose northerly home in New Jersey at least peers toward the Atlantic, while the league's landlocked Lexington Legends home ballpark is a two-hour flight from the nearest Atlantic shore.

The discomfort of my final Carolina afternoon was not caused simply by the Sally League's geographic insensitivity. Kannapolis tried to intimidate the Shorebirds with such hot and humid conditions that even Earnhardt's number "3" sweated profusely—or so it appeared, since its black skin glistened like a middle-reliever facing a clean-up hitter with the bases loaded and none out. Other than the gleaming black shell of Earnhardt's Chevy, the most impressive aspect of the ballpark happened to be the size of the men's restroom, which seemed large enough to accommodate an entire team between innings. I counted nineteen urinals and twelve toilet stalls. And despite the name of the ballpark, there were no Fieldcrest or Cannon hand-towels adjacent to the dozen basins.

The miserable conditions of the afternoon were further intensified by the bleating sun that blistered all but two rows of seats directly in front of the press box. So I sought pregame refuge in the air-conditioned gift shop, where I resisted feeling intimidated by the barrage of team souvenir possibilities.

Leaving the comfort of the air-conditioned space, I made my way to the field, where I needed to tiptoe past the dugout littered with tobacco wads. Although Minor League Baseball forbids the use of tobacco products on the field, the dugout lip was stained with tobacco spit. (Still, this was North Carolina, home of Tobacco Road and a non-baseball kind of Lucky Strike.) Awaiting the start of pregame ceremonies, some of the Intimidators played hacky-sack with baseballs, with the added challenge of keeping the pristine balls out of the chaw debris.

Nearing the halfway point of the anthem tour, I was surprised by two previously unheard comments about my project and performance from Intimidators personnel, while I was also reassured by a fan offering the most common response about my style. I had grown somewhat accustomed to—but still frustrated by—my frequent minimal introductions, like this one, as "Joe Price." Perhaps the crowd thought that I must be the "Joe" whose bar and grill nearby via I-85 was advertised prominently on one of the left-field billboards. Without the simple recognition of my affiliation with Whittier College or a brief description of the anthem tour, I often had found that ballpark staff members were unaware of the anthem tour and their team's participation in my season-long efforts.

At Kannapolis, a staff intern's ignorance about my project was most glaring. She was astonished to learn about my progress in singing the anthem at more than 100 minor league ballparks. "All this season?" she queried. "Have you got the dates set? Or do you show up in town and drive to the ballpark and ask to sing?"

I was dumbfounded. How could she possibly understand the privilege of singing the anthem or the magnitude of my project, since it had taken hundreds of hours to contact teams, secure approval from senior staff members, develop feasible routes, propose fitting dates, and confirm acceptance—all before singing the first anthem in Florida or driving the first mile in Arbie?

The other comment was more affirming: As I walked past the Intimidators dugout after singing, manager Julio Vinas called out, "Good job again!" Three days earlier he had heard me sing the anthem when the Intimidators had visited Greensboro, where they had stomped the Grasshoppers 8-3. Today's outcome proved even more decisive. Perhaps Julio would like for me to intimidate their opponents more often!

Then, making my way up the aisle behind the dugout, I was stopped by "Red," a season ticket holder whose head of hair was fierier than the afternoon sun. He grabbed my arm to make sure I heard: "Thank you, Joe. Nothing funny, the way it's s'posed to be."

And that's the way Kannapolis played baseball that afternoon: nothing funny, the way it's supposed to be. In the bottom of the first inning, the Intimidators certainly sought to exemplify their name. Already leading 2-0 thanks to back-to-back doubles with two outs, Kannapolis placed runners on the corners. While Delmarva's pitcher Timothy Berry was coming to his set position in the stretch, Juan Silverio broke from third and slid across home plate before Berry could make a play. But because Rafael Vera, the Kannapolis runner on first, tried a delayed steal of second during Silvio's surprising dash, Berry whirled and threw to the shortstop, who nailed Vera before he reached the bag. Although Silverio scored before Vera had been tagged out, Silverio was not credited with the rare steal of home, which he had seemingly accomplished without a play at the plate.

Like Silverio, Intimidators starting pitcher Matthew Heidenreich did not get full credit for his season-best performance. By the top of the fifth inning, the Intimidators had built a 9-0 lead on their way to a lopsided shutout, 12-0. But an out later, they were threatened—not by the flock of Shorebirds from Delmarva, but by rain. Yet another torrential Tar Heel thunderstorm swept through the area, halting play for almost an hour. During the downpour on the field, Heidenreich headed to the showers in the clubhouse, thus losing his chance for a win in what would have been his five minutes and two outs later. In more than four strong innings, he had given up a harmless single and a lone walk. But because the deluge developed before the end of the opponent's fifth, he went unrewarded with "no decision."

While the grounds crew scurried to cover the field, I retreated past Earnhardt's memorial and headed northeast to Arbie near Asheboro, driving Toad through intermittent pounding rain that slowed traffic on I-85 to the pace of a caution lap on a NASCAR track.

Friendly Fans at Falwell Field: Game 46 in Lynchburg

While Wrigley Field might be known as the "Friendly Confines," I dare say it would be harder to find a friendlier ballpark than the one in Lynchburg, Virginia, where the Hillcats (Class-A affiliate of the Atlanta Braves) made their home.

In Lynchburg, assistant general manager Ronnie Roberts greeted me and introduced me to his boss, general manager Paul Sunwall. Both inquired about the progress of the tour and the reception that I had received at the ballparks. I indicated that, because I sing the anthem without embellishments and at a crisp tempo, the most frequent comment is, "That's the way it's supposed to be." Paul said that was exactly what he likes to hear. Ronnie added that, regularly, some singers audition in a traditional way, but when given the microphone at game time, they try to put their own spin on it. "They don't get invited back," Paul added.

Turning our conversation to baseball, Paul asked if I knew the story about Lynchburg's manager Luis Salazar. In spring training a few months earlier, Salazar had been hit in the face with a line drive that had caused him to lose an eye. By opening day, he was back in the dugout and, during the team introductions that day, he had individually greeted players on both teams with fist bumps. Although he had not yet resumed his typical on-field position in the third-base coach's box, he expected to do so during the second half of the season. Before then, he was scheduled to have advanced surgery to attach his prosthetic eye to the muscles and nerves in his eye socket, thereby enabling it to move in tandem with his "good eye." The friendly character of the ballpark extended to the dugout, where Salazar inquired about my next few games: Richmond, Potomac, Frederick. He grinned and added, "You know what it's like to be a bus leaguer."

Following the anthem, several fans expressed their gratitude for including Lynchburg on my itinerary. Also pleased with my rendition, Ronnie introduced me to Douglas Thom, a former professional light-opera performer. "I heard you at the game in Little Rock a month ago when I was visiting my folks," Douglas said. "You sounded great there and here again." What fun! Four years earlier he had sung the anthem on the final day of Lynchburg's season, and since then, he had become a regular performer for the Hillcats.

While I was talking with Douglas, Paul introduced me to Terry Falwell, son of Calvin Falwell, after whom the ballpark was named because of his instrumental role in bringing the Hillcats to the city. Terry also happened to be the cousin of the late Jerry Falwell, televangelist and founder of Liberty University, where Terry worked in community relations. Terry, in turn, seemed to know all of the regulars in the ballpark, and while talking with Bonnie and me about our grand adventure, he escorted us through the concourses and skyboxes, speaking to most folks by name and introducing them to us.

One was Gene Gallagher, one of the Hillcats' owners. Now a passionate Hillcats fan, Gene had not grown up loving baseball. In fact, he had not followed baseball until his children enjoyed attending their first Lynchburg game some years ago. After having a pleasant experience on the school-night promotion in their initial visit to the ballpark, his children requested the chance to return the following evening. They did, and Gene became a devoted Hillcats fan because of the wholesome, family entertainment provided by the minor league atmosphere.

In that first season of his children's fondness for the game and the Lynchburg team, which was then affiliated with the Mets, Gene and his family attended most of the home games and made several road trips with the team. His eight-year-old daughter Brittany fell in love with Paco Perez, one of the Hillcats players. Following the final game of the year, Brittany had teared up and said, "Now I won't be able to see Paco anymore." Seeing her cry and hearing her remark, Paco had put his arm around her and said, pointing to his heart and head, "But you'll always be here with me."

That tender moment of a minor leaguer's interaction with his daughter sold Gene on becoming more involved with the team. Now, decades later, he watched the game between Lynchburg and the Wilmington Blue Rocks with the keen eye of a businessman while cheering for the home team. The game itself was filled with unusual plays and blown calls. In the first inning, with runners on the corners and one out, a sharp grounder was hit to the first-baseman, who made a strong throw to shortstop Andrelton Simmons, who then leaped over the sliding runner and made a strong, accurate return throw to the first-base bag. But no one covered first, the ball sailed into foul territory, and the Blue Rocks runner from third scored. A group of six women behind me groaned in unison and loudly offered coaching advice to both the pitcher and the first-baseman: "Come on, guys! Cover the bag."

Cheering encouragement to Hillcats hitters, gently heckling the opponent in traditional ways, and criticizing close calls by the umpires, they provided great entertainment during the game. Lifelong residents of Lynchburg who regularly sat in the back row of the family section, these six women had been effusive in their expressions of appreciation of my anthem rendition. They initially endeared themselves to Bonnie when they pleasantly remarked to each other after the applause following my performance: "He's traveled all the way 'cross the United States to sing for us."

Immediately, Bonnie turned and interjected, "Me, too." And the friendly conversations with them began.

Inning after inning, they cheered and cheered so good-naturedly that we hated for the game to end so soon.

Responding to the Hillcats pitcher tossing over to first several times to keep the runner close, one who had leather lungs called out: "Come on! Let's get him at the plate."

But to the Blue Rocks' pitcher in a similar situation an inning later, she yelled: "Forget him! Pitch the ball."

Encouraging a Hillcats batter: "Good eye, Joey. Come on, Joey."

Or: "Base hit, Adam. Hit a homer."

Or advising a Hillcats runner on a tag play at home: "Slide. Slide. Slide."

Or badgering the ump on a blown call: "Blue, you're full of it tonight."

Their heckling of the home-plate umpire was not as biting as Terry's assessment, quoting his father: "He may have been cut out to be an ump, but somebody sewed him up wrong."

One thing's for sure, however. There was nothing wrong with a night at Falwell Field in Lynchburg. Despite the Hillcats losing to the Blue Rocks 4-3, the fans and ballpark were simply endearing. I credit the vocal gaggle of women with reenergizing Bonnie for the tour following the divisive experience in Durham a few nights earlier. Simply, it took a superb evening at a friendly ballpark to restore her enthusiasm for the summer's venture.

A Baseball Prism: Game 47 in Richmond

The site of Richmond's Diamond, the current name of its minor league ballpark, is a prism for many of my baseball experiences. It figured prominently in my acceptance of my family's relocation from our Mississippi home during my high-school years. It has material significance since it is the first ballpark where I caught a foul ball, now on display among several others in a wing of my study. It holds special memories since my sons and I went to games there during visits to their grandmother's house, it was the first minor league ballpark in which I sang twenty years ago, and now it could play a role in the anthem tour.

When my father had first suggested the possibility that our family might move to Richmond from the Mississippi home that I had known throughout my preteen years, he was surprised by my delight. "Why would you like Richmond?" he asked as he drove me to a doctor's appointment in Jackson. "It's where the Yankees farm team is," I replied.

Once we had moved, it didn't take many days for us to attend our first game featuring the Richmond Virginians and future Yankees second baseman Horace Clarke. Later that season at Parker Field, as the old ballpark on the same site was known, I caught a pop foul off the bat of Norm Sherry, a catcher for the Syracuse Chiefs. In addition to the charm of baseball, I also found a different kind of romance at the ballpark throughout my high-school years, taking special dates there to see the future—and sometimes former—Yankees.

Although I was disappointed when Richmond shifted its affiliation from the Yankees to the Braves, I still attended their games on return visits to my mother's home during my collegiate and graduate studies. And several years later when my sons were school age, my aunt and uncle treated our family to box seats. At the game that night, one of the promotions was a trivia contest, which my older son Jared, then age eight, entered with my assistance. The question: "What American League pitcher held the record for career strikeouts by left-handers?" We worked through several options and finally settled on Mickey Lolich. Jared printed the name with his best handwriting and handed his answer sheet to an usher.

An inning or so later, the P.A. announcer reported that there had been four correct submissions and that a winner's name had been drawn from them: Jared Price! He was thrilled to hear his name called aloud over the P.A. system. A picture of him smiling moments after the announcement hangs prominently among my cherished mementos in the baseball gallery in my office. When he went to retrieve his prize of a large pizza, several fans and staff members congratulated him on "knowing baseball." As much delight as he derived from winning the contest, he found at least equal pleasure in having earned supper for our family!

If these experiences years apart were not enough to carve a permanent place into the joy-box of my memories, a few years later I shared another delightful experience there. After I had sung the anthem for the Dodgers and Angels, I contacted the Richmond Braves and was approved to sing for them during another family trip to visit my mother. That afternoon, we were joined by Bill Kruschwitz, a friend from college and seminary years. More than three years later, I received a brief letter and Xeroxed page from Bill's former roommate Jack Birdwhistell, also a friend during seminary days. Having been told by Bill about my anthem performance the year before, Jack was surprised as he read David Lamb's *A Stolen Season*. From that book, he had copied page 183 and highlighted three sentences from Lamb's account of having seen a game at The Diamond: "A visiting college professor from California sang 'The Star-Spangled Banner' and someone from Napa Auto Parts threw out the first pitch. The Braves won in the eleventh inning. Dave Justice went 0 for 5." In the margin Jack had scrawled, "This must have been you." It was.

Lamb's somewhat anonymous account of my singing there almost two decades ago still makes me smile, especially since his mention was one of only three or four references that he made to anthem performances and receptions throughout his summer-long journey to minor league games.

After Richmond lost the Triple-A Braves to Gwinnett in 2008, The Diamond lay dormant for a year before the Eastern League relocated the Giants Double-A franchise from Connecticut. A fan contest was held to name the team, and more than 6,000 local entries were submitted before a national surge added another 9,000 suggestions. For proposing the winning entry—"the Flying Squirrels"—the fan received lifetime season tickets. In preparation for the shift, a number of renovations were made in the ballpark, primarily to improve seating comfort, upgrade luxury boxes, and redesign the restaurant and souvenir shop. The concourses now also provide a gallery for children's artistic renderings of Nutzy, the Flying Squirrels mascot.

Even so, the sound system was still as poor as it was when Lamb had heard me sing two decades earlier. The sound delay, one of the worst that I encountered, was described by some of Richmond's staffers as being a couple of seconds. While singing with earplugs packed as tightly as possible into my ears, I heard both "then and now" simultaneously, almost like listening to a simulcast on TV and radio with both sound systems on, but with one delayed. The experience was disjointed, to say the least, as I tried to block the continuous echo. In part, the audio difficulties were masked by fireworks that were shot off from beyond the centerfield fence when I reached the phrases about "rockets' red glare" and "bombs bursting in air." Despite the audio difficulties and visual distractions, the anthem went well.

After hearing pathetic introductions at so many ballparks in the first weeks of the tour, I had begun to request that I be introduced at least by mentioning my affiliation with Whittier College, whose sabbatical support made it possible for me to undertake the journey. Yet my request had gone unheeded, even after pointing out my history in Richmond. The evening's truncated introduction—"Tonight's national anthem presented by Joe Price"—was quicker than an Aroldis Chapman fastball. Perhaps the P.A. announcer cut the planned introduction because of the length of other pregame events—a rain delay, a parade of Little League players, and eleven first pitches.

In the Richmond dugout during pregame warm-ups, I had hoped to connect with Tom Vessella, who had pitched for the Poets while he had attended Whittier. Although Vessella had begun the season with an impressive win for the Flying Squirrels in his first start in Double-A, he had been sent back to the Class-A San Jose Giants by the time that I got to Virginia.

Though my pregame experience was not as gratifying as I had hoped, I was glad that the game was able to be played after a downpour drenched the area less than an hour before its scheduled start. The preparation for the oncoming rain provided one of my favorite images from the tour. While members of the grounds crew unrolled the tarp and stood ready to cover the infield, the core of the crew hosed down the infield dirt in customary preparation for the game.

Gradually, the capacity crowd filled the ballpark and cheered enthusiastically as Richmond took an early and commanding lead. In the first inning, Richmond scored a run in a way that I had never seen in person. Leadoff hitter Justin Christian hit a ball to the shortstop, who muffed it, allowing him to reach first safely. Another grounder to short advanced the fleet-footed Christian to second on a fielder's choice. With one out, Roger Kieschnick hit a towering drive to centerfield. Anticipating that it might be caught against the wall, Christian returned to second, tagged immediately as the catch was made, never hesitated as he rounded third, and slid across home as the relay came in chest high. The catcher didn't bother to sweep a tag.

If he hadn't convinced me with his first-inning feat, Christian made a believer out of me the next inning when he crushed a home run with two on and two out, and two innings later when he singled in the middle of another Flying Squirrels rally. Led by Christian and Kieschnick, who also hit a three-run homer, Richmond scored eleven runs on only nine hits while Binghamton tallied seventeen hits but only nine runs, four of which they got in the ninth.

The Deluge: A Rainout in Potomac

Sooner or later rain was bound to drown one of my games. Narrowly, I had escaped cancellation in several cities during previous weeks. A torrential storm in Charleston had swamped the field in April and threatened cancellation of the game. A steady, soft rain during a couple of innings in Lexington weeks before hadn't interrupted play, while days earlier thunderstorms in Winston-Salem and Durham had delayed the start of their games. And the night before Potomac's deluge, rain had complicated matters in Richmond. Yet each of those games had proceeded.

The game in Woodbridge, Virginia, would have pitted the two last-place teams in the Carolina League. Potomac sat at the bottom of the Northern Division with a 28-39 record, and Salem had slumped to the bottom of the Southern Division with thirty wins and thirty-seven losses. The good news about the evening was that neither team would sink farther—that is, unless they sloshed through the flood in the field or splashed through the puddles in the undercroft of the grandstand.

As recently as mid-afternoon in northern Virginia, no rainstorms had appeared on radar, but at 6:03 an intense isolated storm erupted. Lightning cracked and thunder rolled. A torrential cell had developed southwest of the ballpark around 5 o'clock and seemed to have targeted the municipal recreational ballpark in Woodbridge for its fury. Because the field didn't drain well, a short shower could cause significant problems, and a downpour often prompted the postponement of a game. Steady rains sometimes left the field in such an unplayable condition that Potomac had to play its home games in Frederick, not only a rival team's ballpark but a location in an adjoining state.

While both teams forewent batting practice, the field remained covered in hopes of the storm being merely a passing shower, but a deluge ensued for forty-five minutes. An odd thing: At 6:30, I learned of the postponement of the game and phoned Bonnie, who was driving to the ballpark with one of her friends. Although they were only four miles away, they were shocked since it wasn't raining on their car. So, too, was Ann Lindner, a friend from Chicago. For months, she had planned to synchronize her visit with family in the Washington area with the time that Bonnie and I would be there. Having paid the parking fee minutes before receiving my phone call, she and her entourage of cousins and nephews could hardly believe that the game had been cancelled since the skies had begun to clear and the parking lot had begun to drain and dry.

Despite Potomac's losing record, the list of its recent alumni was impressive, featuring former National League MVP first-basemen Albert Pujols of St. Louis and Joey Votto of Cincinnati. I had wanted to see who would now be playing first for the team—perhaps the National League MVP for 2020!

6.

A Different Curve

Stars for the Suns: Game 48 in Hagerstown

It's not often that a Class-A team has drawing power because of a renowned player on its roster. Players with high promise and profiles usually progress quickly to more advanced leagues. But the Hagerstown Suns had been fortunate in their affiliation with the Washington Nationals who, because of their ineptitude on the field for several years, had enjoyed premier selections in MLB's drafts.

For the first few months of the season, the Suns had basked in the starlight of Bryce Harper, the number-one draft pick the previous year. At the unusually early age of seventeen, Harper became eligible for the draft because he had completed his GED and had enrolled in the College of Southern Nevada in order to play at the collegiate level. There he had competed in a wood-bats league, where he was named the Player of the Year while setting school offensive records by hitting above .400 and averaging a home run every other game. Following his incredible performance at the community college, he had signed with the Nationals. Although he had started the 2011 season slowly with the Suns, he caught fire after getting contact lenses. By the time that I sang for Hagerstown in mid-June, he was already headed to the South Atlantic League's all-star game as one of its leaders in batting average and home runs.

Because the weekend game between the hosting Suns and the visiting Delmarva Shorebirds supported breast cancer awareness and research, players wore pink jerseys, each of which would then be offered in a blind auction to raise money for breast cancer research. Harper's jersey, of course, promised to create frenzied activity and a whopping winning bid. Harper also wore pink shoes, the only player to be so creative. Prior to the game, which he sat out because of a slightly injured wrist, I teased him playfully about the shoes, pointing to them, nodding my head while smirking and raising an eyebrow, and then gesturing "thumbs up." He grinned in return.

Following my anthem rendition, Harper walked to the opposite end of the dugout to shake my hand. I felt like an all-star, even if in a league very different from his. It also gave me a moment to share a bit of fun. Before the game, fans had petitioned him for autographs, calling out time and again, "Bryce. Hey, Bryce!" Each time, I instinctively turned, thinking they were calling out, "Price. Hey, Price!" and wondering who would be calling me at Hagerstown! He laughed about my presumptive mis-hearing.

The Suns' introduction of my anthem performance mentioned simply my name, which was a bit of a disappointment to several of Bonnie's friends who had driven up from the Washington area to see the game and hear me sing. Since her friends were not attentive baseball fans, they weren't aware that they were missing seeing Harper play, especially because Kevin Keyes, his replacement in right field that night, hit two home runs and a double, propelling the Suns to a 7-3 win over the Shorebirds.

Seated near us in the grandstands was a retired couple who groaned each time Keyes launched a shot. Paul Lasky and his wife Janet had come to the game from their home in Montgomery County, Maryland, to socialize with their nephew, Delmarva's play-by-play announcer Bret Lasky.

A few days earlier, Janet had retired after teaching for more than thirty years, and she celebrated her new freedom with another hug of congratulations from Suns mascot Woolie. When the Laskys learned that I would be singing the following week at Frederick, Paul indicated that he would come to that game, too, which he did. Paul also graciously set up the possibility of my meeting with Bret when I was scheduled to sing for Delmarva's day game in late June. Regrettably, that was one of the two performances I had to cancel when Arbie blew his alternator near Farmville, Virginia.

Surprisingly, the concessions at Hagerstown offered the most extensive array of foods and concoctions out of all of the first fifty ballparks of my season. One stand proved particularly alluring. It featured buffalo burgers, country-ham sandwiches, and an inventive sandwich called a Roller Burger. Richard Hollsinger, a sixth-generation butcher and chef, had created a rolled "hamburger" made of ground chuck, grated cheddar cheese, salt, and pepper—a mixture that he then stuffed into a sausage case and smoked. Shortly before serving it, he grilled the Roller Burger. Even though I had tried to minimize my consumption of ballpark foods, particularly ordinary ones, I couldn't resist trying the Roller Burger, which was quite good: lean and somewhat smoky, with a pleasantly chewy texture like kielbasa. The Hollsingers also routinely catered the meals for the Suns players, who, Richard said, favored the lasagna, pork tenderloin, and green beans.

"Green beans?" I intoned as a question. "What's your secret? Why do they like them so much?"

"Must be the country ham that we add to them," Richard replied.

That was it: green beans, Southern-style.

Capitalizing on Hagerstown's affiliation with the Nationals, another of the food kiosks featured "The All-Angus Stephen StrasBurger," named in honor of the fast-balling "phenom" who had set a record for initial contracts when he had signed with Washington for $15.5 million. In his inaugural season with the Nationals, Strasburg suffered a career-threatening elbow injury that required Tommy John surgery and a year's physical therapy. Six weeks after my appearance for the Suns, he was scheduled to make his first rehab start in Hagerstown.

A third distinct concession menu could be found at Hartle's Fry Tent, which offered everything fried except its wings and sodas. Hagerstown was the second ballpark where I had found fried Oreos available, and the first to offer fried Twinkies and candy bars. About the only missing possibility was fried frog legs, which could double the fun or fear of frying by calling a single serving "A Fried Fry." And if its sale could be restricted to Fridays, it could be marketed as a triple fry—a Friday Fried Fry. My mind was almost fried as I imagined these possibilities.

For more than thirty years, the Hagerstown minor league teams had been known as the Suns, even while their affiliation had shifted from one major league team to another and while their league and minor league level changed from Carolina to Eastern to South Atlantic. Earlier teams in the twentieth century had been known as the Hubs, the Owls, the Braves, and the Packers, while the quality of teams improved from Class-D in the Blue Ridge League before the Great Depression to Class-B for the Interstate and Piedmont Leagues in the early 1950s.

Although the earliest Hagerstown team had begun its play in another ballpark, it inaugurated Municipal Stadium in 1930 after the ballpark had been completed in six weeks, and all subsequent Hagerstown teams had called this stadium their home. Before the end of World War II, the ballpark hosted several games for Negro League teams, including the Indianapolis Clowns, the Pittsburgh Crawfords, and the Homestead Grays. While some improvements had been made to the facility over the years, the ballpark retained its intimate and vintage character.

The historic significance of the ballpark was noted with posters of bygone teams and prominent players on walls near the concession stands. The team also posted retired numbers above the bullpen bench, including #24 for Willie Mays. Although Mays never played for Hagerstown, he played his first integrated, regular season game there on June 24, 1950, for the Trenton Giants, who took the field against Hagerstown's Class-B Braves, then in the Interstate League.

Joining the ballpark's recognition of star players and historic accomplishments was an inconspicuous memorial tribute in the grandstands along the first-baseline. There, a sign in front of Section C indicated that, in honor of longtime season ticket holder and devout Suns fan Fred Ziegler, that section would be known as Section Z. This simple recognition of an individual's devotion to the team exemplified the ballpark's personable style, which was displayed in multiple areas: Near the front gates, a white board with hand-lettered greetings welcomed specific community groups to the game, and the hand-operated scoreboard in left field featured numbers that were hand-hung inning by inning, then removed to accentuate the final score: Visitors 3, Hagerstown 7.

Tossed a Fatherly Curve: Game 49 in Altoona

My favorite team names are ones that connote multiple meanings, especially when the name reflects both a distinct character of its community and an element of baseball. When the name also happens to be a collective singular noun, I find that it somehow exemplifies the essence of teamwork that bonds individuals into a unit. (I do experience difficulty, of course, in knowing what kinds of agreement need to be made with the collective singular noun, such as whether to use a singular or plural pronoun. Should I refer to the Curve as "they"—usage that would correspond to a reference to a plural name, such as "the Nationals"; or should I specify the Curve as "it"—thereby spinning the emphasis to the collective entity?)

While fans might associate the Curve's name with baseball's breaking pitch, the Altoona Curve's name derives from the famous horseshoe railroad curve that rises through the mountains of central Pennsylvania a few miles west of the city. Now designated as a national historic landmark, "Horseshoe Curve" opened in 1854. An engineering feat that conforms to the contour of the mountains without the aid of a trestle, the tracks rise more than 100 feet over a distance of less than half a mile, a slope that is more than two and a half times greater than the average grade that trains usually negotiate. That slope is further complicated by the severity of the tracks' half-circle, whose degree of curvature is nine degrees, twenty-five minutes.

In the mid-nineteenth century, Horseshoe Curve enabled rail traffic to move uninterrupted through the region, making the nearby Allegheny Portage Railway obsolete. Prior to the completion of the curve, the portage system had combined canal barges and rail lines with ten incline engine stations, using counterbalances to lift and lower cargo and passengers, for a thirty-six-mile stretch across the mountain ridge. When completed in 1834, the Portage Railway had also featured the first rail tunnel in the United States, and its combined barge and railroad system had accelerated the exploration and commercial development of territory west of the Alleghenies.

But back to baseball and Altoona: Until the late 1990s, history threw a curve to Altoona's turn for professional baseball. For less than two months in the inaugural season of the Union Association in the late 1800s, Altoona had served as the home of a team in the new league that challenged the professional dominance of the National League and the American Association. Within weeks, however, Altoona's team flailed and failed, drawing poorly and losing frequently. After compiling a record of 6-19, the team was basically railroaded out of town, going far to Kansas City.

In several years before the depths of the Great Depression, Altoona fielded minor league teams, twice watching them depart for other cities before the end of their first season. When the Altoona Engineers left for Beaver Falls in 1931, more than six decades would expire before professional baseball would return to the mountain town in the mid-1990s with the establishment of the Rail Kings in the independent North Atlantic League. While that team enjoyed relative success and enthusiastic support from the community, the league itself folded, forcing the team to join the equally independent and hapless Heartland League the following year.

Then came Major League Baseball's expansion in the late 1990s. Accompanying the development of two new major league teams—the Arizona Diamondbacks and the Tampa Bay Devil Rays (as the team was initially known)—affiliated minor league franchises were also awarded to prospective cities, with Altoona winning out over Springfield, Massachusetts, for one of the new Double-A teams. So was conceived and born the Altoona Curve.

My predisposition to like the Curve because of the playful complexity of its name was heightened by the hospitality that I received in the mountain community and the special features aligned with the game on the date of my singing. It was Father's Day. I had anticipated missing my family since Bonnie had remained in Washington to spend several days with friends, and my sons, both of whom phoned me before evening, were a continent away in California. I also had left Arbie in D.C., having set aside several days for him to rest and get maintenance work done.

What I had not expected on Father's Day was that I could share the afternoon with the father of a friend and colleague, Art Remillard. Baseball brought the three of us together. A professor of American religious history at Saint Francis University, Art had presented papers on religion and sport at various conferences that I had attended, and he had reviewed some of my books. When he learned of my project, he invited me to stay in his home for the nights when I would sing for Altoona and State College, an hour's drive away. The odd thing: Art and his family would be out of town for two months surrounding my time in the area. Art said that I could get access to his house from his father Vincent, an ardent Curves fan who lived close by and who planned to attend my games in Altoona and at State College.

Although the age difference that I had with Vincent was hardly sufficient to allow for him to be like my father, we began our relationship on the basis of my friendship with his son and our mutual love of baseball. To a very real extent, Vincent and I experienced Father's Day with vicarious delight, recognizing that, while each of us missed being with our own sons that day, we could relate as father and son. The following day we continued to enjoy each other's similar company while Vince showed me great sites in the region—the Horseshoe Curve, the Franciscan Monastery in Loretto, and the nearby Saint Francis University campus—before we headed down the mountain to State College for its evening game.

In Altoona, the ballpark is one of the most imaginative in all of baseball. A couple of years after the Blair County Ballpark had opened in 1999, *USA Today* played with its description of the facility: "A minor league ballpark is one thing. An amusement park is another. But tucked in the Allegheny Mountains is a place where there's really no difference." That description is apt. In large part, the ballpark's entertaining ambiance was set by Lakemont Park's Skyliner roller coaster, whose high tracks abutted the right-field fence. While the amusement park dates from the late nineteenth century, the fifty-year-old Skyliner was purchased from another amusement park and installed at its present site more than a decade before the baseball team was formed and the adjoining ballpark conceived. The high wooden scaffolding and sweeping curves of the Skyliner's structure not only add a playful backdrop to the ballpark; they also mimic Horseshoe Curve, from which the team derives its name.

At Altoona's ballpark on Father's Day afternoon, a sense of poetry also prevailed as a pregame promotion allowed parents to play catch with their children in the outfield. Generations of families participated in the activity, while many of the pairs of tossers and catchers again called to mind *Fathers Playing Catch with Sons,* poet Donald Hall's celebration of the transmission of baseball passion from parent to child.

The game also proved distinct in several other ways. Squeals of delight Dopplered into the stands from the roller-coaster riders swooping along the Skyliner's dips and turns. Sprinklers spattered the infield during the bottom of the first inning, causing a brief spray delay. For the first time on the tour, I was interviewed as part of the pregame entertainment by local ESPN radio host Josh Ellis. And in his Double-A debut, Curve Phil Irwin hurled six impressive innings, showing good control after hitting the first batter that he faced, yielding two harmless singles (one on a hanging curve), and holding the Harrisburg Senators scoreless during his team's win, 4-1.

Spiked Interest: Game 50 at State College

During summer 2011, Central Pennsylvania continued to be affectionately known as "JoePa" country several months before the dismissal of Joe Paterno as head football coach at Penn State University, a termination that was quickly followed by his diagnosis, demise, and death from lung cancer. The winningest coach in major college football history, Paterno had spent almost a half-century leading the Nittany Lions to five undefeated seasons, numerous bowl game victories, and two national titles. Because he had become the icon of the region, it's not too surprising that the State College Spikes played in football's shadow, both figuratively and literally.

The university's football stadium looms above Lubrano Park, which is a facility shared between the Spikes and the Penn State baseball team. By contrast, the football stadium dwarfs the baseball park by expanse and capacity. Although the State College team is known as the Spikes, both Coach Paterno and the Nittany name frame the baseball field: Beyond the outfield fences, undeveloped Mount Nittany stands tall like Randy Johnson towering atop the mound, and opposite the preferred parking area for the ballpark, a dynamic statue of Paterno then defined the entry to the stadium.

There is a sense in which the name of the Spikes reflects the intellectual climate of the city and the literary bent of Paterno, who had earned his master's degree in English literature. Their name generates a double entendre related both to the State College vicinity and to baseball, for "spikes" is the name of the pair of undivided antlers on young deer that are so prevalent throughout the region and that provide the logo for the team. Metaphorically, the hopeful players on the short-season Class-A team were young baseball spikes. And "spikes," of course, designates the pair of cleats that baseball players wear. I love the use of such a homonym, especially when variant meanings of "spikes" equally apply to the team.

After spending the morning with Vincent Remillard exploring mountain scenery and sites near Ebensburg and Loretta, he and I descended by Horseshoe Curve in Altoona and on to State College, where we parked at the home of Louise and Bob Griffin, one of Vincent's colleagues whom I had met at the game in Altoona. While the Griffins chauffeured the Remillards and me to the game, showers threatened the evening and eventually delayed the game for almost an hour. During the rain delay, which had become a fairly common experience for me during the previous month, Spikes mascots Ike and Nookie entertained the crowd even more than the wind gusts that wrestled the tarp that covered the diamond.

At the State College ballpark, I encountered several distinctions, in addition to ducking a wicked foul line drive that sliced past my head. There I saw the professional debut of a "bonus baby," I experienced my first "Bark in the Park" night (and I wondered if dog owners were given free admission if their dogs were named "Spike"), and I shunned the thousands of calories in the most distinct hamburger of the summer: "The Endless Love Burger." It was a standard bacon cheeseburger, but with a unique twist: It was served on a glazed-donut bun! I'm certain that the special burger expanded some heart throbs, but I imagine they were ones associated with cardiac arrest, not eternal passion.

While the spirit of "JoePa" certainly hovered over the area, it was the initial appearance of Stetson Allie that dominated attention this night. Drafted out of high school in the second round by the Pirates in 2010, Allie had delayed inking his contract until the deadline, finally settling on a signing bonus exceeding two million dollars. His first professional assignment was to State College, the Pirates affiliate in the short-season New York-Penn League. Allie's first professional pitch followed my singing the national anthem to open the Spikes' second home game of the season.

With his fast ball routinely registering in the mid-nineties and occasionally clocking in triple digits during high school, Allie commanded center stage. He blazed his first pitch past the Auburn Doubledays leadoff hitter en route to striking him out. But the next batter singled and, following another strikeout and a stolen base, a two-out double brought home Auburn's first run. Although Allie recorded a third strikeout in the second inning, he lost command in the third, walking three batters and allowing two more stolen bases. He was charged with three earned runs in less than three full innings of work, and his first professional decision was a loss: an inauspicious beginning, and typical of his season totals, which eventually showed no wins, two losses, twenty-six innings pitched, twenty-eight strikeouts, but twenty-nine walks.

If the debut of Stetson Allie weren't enough to draw the large crowd, the promotion known as "Bark in the Park" added to the attractions for the evening. It was my first encounter with such a canine celebration. Encouraging fans to bring dogs on leashes to the ballpark, it came at an opportune time on my trip. Halfway through the tour, I keenly missed my two dogs: Winston, a lovable black-and-white Havanese that often walked to campus to share my office hours with me; and Tucker, a playful white cockapoo puppy that we had rescued six months before beginning the tour. While I didn't find look-alikes of Winston or Tucker, I did get to enjoy meeting another of my favorite breeds—a handsome Bernese mountain dog named Toby—and his owner Bella.

Because quite a few teams had introduced me with the simple phrase, "Please rise for the national anthem, performed tonight by Joe Price," I had begun to e-mail team personnel requesting that the P.A. announcer identify me as "Whittier College professor Joe Price." And I suggested that, if a supplemental sentence could be added to stimulate conversation with fans, I would appreciate the announcer adding, "During the 2011 baseball season, Professor Price is singing 'The Star-Spangled Banner' at more than 100 minor league ballparks in forty states as he examines how the national anthem and baseball combine to shape the national pastime." As I had hoped, following the Spikes full introduction, several fans approached me during the game. A graduate student at Penn State inquired about the tour, especially my field of expertise. Both he and a fellow grad student had bet that I was in sociology (like themselves), music, or anthropology. When I confessed that I am a theologian, he looked as stunned as Tony Kubek after the bad hop grounder deflected off his Adam's apple in the eighth inning of Game 7 in 1960.

Undeterred, the student began to talk about his love of baseball and the sociological observations that he often enjoyed at the ballpark. As our conversation developed, he inquired about my work relating baseball to religious studies, and I summarized two chapters in my book *Rounding the Bases: Baseball and Religion in America* that utilize sociological and anthropological methods of analysis. In one, I explore the possibility of interpreting baseball in continuity with the ancient Greek *omphalos* myth, and in the central chapter, I apply sociological methods to examine how baseball functions as a denomination in American civil religion.

At the ballpark, we engaged in serious scholarship! I loved it, and so did he. When I stepped toward the concession stand to get a look at the Endless Love Burger, I playfully chided him: "Don't bet against religious studies, which can make sense of baseball *and* the ritual significance of the national anthem."

Following the game, which Auburn won 7-6, I accepted the Griffins' gracious offer to sleep in their guest room rather than return to the Remillards' house in Ebensburg, since it would reduce my drive the next day by more than an hour. It was a delight to extend the evening with Bob, an aficionado of Minor League Baseball. He knew the strengths and weaknesses of players throughout the Pirates farm system, and he reported on records and distinctions of teams and ballparks across the region. When I put my luggage in the guest room, I immediately understood more: Artfully framed on the far wall were ticket stubs from the ten minor league ballparks in Pennsylvania. The caption read: "Best Road Trip Ever," a ball-planned vacation Bob had taken with Louise some years earlier. Yet as heartwarming as this display of mementos was, adjacent to them hung photos of Forbes Field and the end of the 1960 World Series.

Since I had become a devout fan of the Yankees during childhood, I recall having shed tears when I heard Ralph Terry hang a curve ball to Bill Mazeroski in the bottom of the ninth in the seventh game of that series. Now, in the Griffins' guest room above the bed hung photographs of Mazeroski rounding third on his Series walk-off homer and of the ecstatic celebration of the Pirates. I wasn't sure that I would be able to fall asleep beneath this bleak reliquary. Finally, as sleep began to seep past my sorrowful memories, I hoped that I wouldn't have nightmares about Yogi Berra turning to watch Maz's blast clearing the left-field wall at Forbes Field.

Like a Church: Game 51 in Scranton/Wilkes-Barre

It was perhaps fitting and certainly restorative that the night after I had spent in purgatory beneath the Pirates altar, I could return to the chapel of "the True Church," as I affectionately and playfully call the Yankees. Scranton/Wilkes-Barre basically serves as the chapel to the cathedral, Yankee Stadium, since the major league Yankees virtually run a shuttle from the Bronx to the eastern Pennsylvania city, where they often ship players for rehab with their Triple-A affiliate.

The evening experience at the Scranton/Wilkes-Barre ballpark reminded me of a wistful scene in W.P. Kinsella's magical novel *Shoeless Joe*, a bit omitted from the story's film adaption into *Field of Dreams*. After leaving Chisholm, Minnesota, and picking up the hitch-hiking kid Archie Graham, Ray Kinsella asks him and J.D. Salinger (who is transformed in the movie into computer programmer Terrence Mann) if they have ever been to a ballpark at night. "There's something both eerie and holy about it," he says. Excited by this simple tease, they leave their hotel room to explore nearby Metropolitan Stadium in the dark. Continuing to muse about the mysterious atmosphere of such an experience, Ray adds, "A ballpark at night is more like a church than a church."

The ecclesial metaphor applied particularly well to old PNC Field in Lackawanna County, Pennsylvania, home of the Triple-A Yankees, even though the ballpark there was neither vacant nor dark like the one at Bloomington that had captivated Kinsella and his companions. Built in 1989, the Lackawanna ballpark resembled a smaller version of the cookie-cutter, multi-use stadiums that had become popular in major cities during the 1970s. Like them, it had declined in appeal, so much so that it would be razed, reconfigured, and restructured following the end of the 2011 season. Despite the stale character of the Lackawanna edifice, the field exuded an ethereal aura. A halo seemed to sanctify both the diamond and the night itself, and the spotlighted field beckoned the faithful to leave the darkness to bask in the light and the sacrament of the game.

In several additional respects, the ballpark near Scranton resembled a church. Like cathedrals that embody tradition by honoring saints with relics, the ballpark's undercroft was lined with portraits and tributes to bygone Yankee luminaries—DiMaggio and Dickey, Mantle and Mattingly—as well as other fan favorites, such as Catfish Hunter and Goose Gossage, Wade Boggs and Roy White.

Several impressions of this gallery of saints leapt to the forefront of my mind. For one, I didn't find beatific tapestries featuring Ruth and Gehrig, or Whitey Ford and Yogi Berra; but their banners might have been hanging in the upper-deck corridor, which was closed for the evening service like the balcony of a Baptist church for week-night prayers. In any case, I wondered why the pantheon more prominently featured some shorter-term Yankee stars like Hunter (who enjoyed his best years in Oakland) and Boggs (who spent more than twice as much time in Boston, where he won five batting titles, than he did in the Bronx, where he won none), while White was a lifelong Yankee whose fifteen-year major league career might have garnered little notice had he not been playing for New York. During a decade of down years for the Yankees, he had been a solid but not great player. Did he ever lead the league in any category? Yes, but... He was a two-time all-star who did lead the league twice in sacrifice flies, once in walks, and once in plate appearances, seemingly insufficient accomplishments to warrant beatification.

Finally, since the Yankees had begun their relationship with Scranton/Wilkes-Barre barely a decade earlier, I was surprised that none of the tapestries in the shrine featured former players for SWB. Unlike several other communities that celebrated the record-setting success of their former players who might not have starred in the majors, Scranton/Wilkes-Barre recognized the heroes of the Mother Church in the Bronx. Even the composite banner of pancake portraits focused on New York since it included players like Jason Giambi and Roger Clemens, who had minimally appeared in SWB while on rehab assignments.

Like many urban church sanctuaries that were built to accommodate huge congregations in previous generations, Scranton's cavernous size far exceeded its current seating demand: Simply, like the waning attendance at many traditional church services, the ballpark crowd tonight would hardly have filled a single section in the lower deck. With a seating capacity of more than 10,000, the team announced game attendance as 2,876. Although I would wager that fewer than a thousand fans saw any inning of the game, that generous count of the crowd, which included all tickets sold, also corresponds to a tent-revival report of number of attendees.

Still, there were apparent differences between the perspectives of Scranton fans and those of worshippers in a sanctuary. For one, unlike the pattern of seating in most churches where the back rows and balcony seats usually fill first, the SWB fans preferred to sit between first and third. And unlike the prominent appearance of the altar or pulpit from a front-pew view in a sanctuary, home plate could not be seen by a fan seated in the front-row seat adjacent to the far end of the visitors dugout.

Despite the small crowd, I was enthusiastically received like a Sunday-morning guest soloist. As I moved to different sections throughout the game, two school-age boys in box seats behind home plate asked for my autograph on their scorebooks. When I also signed AnthemTour postcards for them, you would have thought that I had just given them a foul ball.

Moments later, Ellen Watkins, a season ticket holder, stopped by my seat to introduce herself. "Thanks for a beautiful anthem," she said. "It was the best all season. The tempo was right, and you didn't do anything weird." Another fan nearby commented on my clear articulation and asked if I were British. That's always a surprise to me since I routinely hear echoes of my Southern drawl despite having moved from my native Mississippi more than forty years ago.

For the most part, the game itself offered few opportunities for the home-team fans to cheer. Tides designated hitter Rhyne Hughes outslugged and outscored the Yankees, going four for four with two home runs. After SWB bunched a walk and two singles into a run in the first inning, the Yankees managed only a feeble bingle the rest of the game, finally losing 8-1.

But an unusual set of plays at first base made the game memorable. In the top of the second inning, Norfolk scored four runs while no batter made an out, grounded into a force play, or hit into a fielder's choice. In that inning, every Tides batter got a base hit, with the team going seven for seven. After two inning-opening singles and Hughes's first home run, Brenden Harris's base hit was followed by Tyler Henson's line drive to right field, where Jordan Parraz threw toward third. But the second-baseman cut the ball off and whirled to relay the throw to first to nail Henson, who had rounded the base too far. One out, runner on third. Kyle Hudson restarted the Tides rally by singling Harris home, but Yankees starter David Phelps quickly picked Hudson off first. Two out, none on. Matt Angle then singled for the Tides for the seventh consecutive hit. But before the next batter could complete his plate appearance, Phelps picked Angle off first for the third out. Inning totals: four runs on seven hits and three put-outs by Brandon Laird at first, each by a tag of a runner trying to get back to the bag.

Perhaps the weird sequence of these put-outs also aligned the ballgame with an ecclesiastical service by lending a sense of otherness to an encounter, by providing a manifestation of the unexpected.

On a Wing and a Prayer: Game 52 in Rochester

The worn metaphor of coming in on "a wing and prayer" has come to identify the frailty of hopes and faith for one's deliverance from trying times, not simply to implore a safe landing after a harrowing flight. During my drive to Rochester, that stale figure of speech—differently applied—

characterized my goal and my spirit, probably because of the Rochester team's name, "the Red Wings," and because I thought that prayer might be the only way to get the pelting rain to subside and permit the game to proceed.

While Arbie rested back in Falls Church, Virginia, and while Bonnie used Toad to hop around the D.C. area, I drove a rental car for a week through portions of Pennsylvania and New York. After singing in Scranton/Wilkes-Barre, I headed north in steady rain the following morning. Tracing I-81 through Binghamton, I briefly bemoaned the fact that I hadn't been able to schedule their mini-Mets among the teams on my tour. On toward Syracuse I pressed through increasingly driving rain, praying that my destination two hours west in Rochester might not be caught in the same storm system, or that it would have cleared the area. As hackneyed as the metaphor might be about coming in on "a wing and prayer," it certainly seemed applicable to my destination and attitude.

Shortly after my arrival at Rochester's ballpark in late afternoon, the skies above downtown Rochester began to clear, and I was welcomed into the administrative office's reception area where I sat and worked on transcribing notes about recent ballgames. There I saw a gesture that typified the graciousness of the Red Wings staff. One of the senior administrators brought the receptionist a baseball bouquet.

Matching the elegance and spirit of the flower arrangement, the Rochester ballpark graciously and artistically ushers fans into the game. Outside the main entry to Frontier Field is a statue of Morrie Silver, and inside the left-field gate is a tribute to Joe Altobelli. Silver is credited with having saved professional baseball for Rochester in 1957 when he spearheaded a drive to get more than eight thousand local investors to purchase the team and the ballpark from the St. Louis Cardinals, who had owned both. In recognition of his effort, the old ballpark, where the Red Wings played until their move to Frontier Field in 1997, had been named "Silver Stadium" in 1968. Now his congenial likeness, positioned next to a child wearing a baseball uniform and representing future Red Wings fans, welcomes attendees to Frontier Field.

Inside the left-field gate, another statue salutes Rochester devotees in the ballpark. There a sculpture of Joe Altobelli stands as a reminder of the many ways to affiliate with and support the team. After playing for the Red Wings in the mid-1960s, he became the team's manager in 1971, guiding Rochester to more than 500 wins (the most by any Red Wings manager in history) en route to multiple championship seasons. Following his successful leadership on the field, Altobelli assumed the position of general manager before shifting his voice to the broadcast booth, where he achieved an enduring level of popularity.

In addition to these graceful bronze figures, other artistic sculptures are exhibited along the concourse. Inside the main gate two images of red-winged raptors oversee fans' arrival, and an impressionistic, textural sculpture of a horse, whose medium is old baseball gloves, stands proudly at the heart of the entry. Given my fondness for names that convey multiple, appropriate meanings, it's not surprising that "Horsehide," positioned at the ballpark entry, remains one of my two favorite sculptures of the tour. While I was unable to find the name of the artist, the plaque bearing the sculpture's name credited several season ticket holders for their contributions to acquire and display the piece.

In keeping with the elegant bronze statues and sculptures that greet fans as they enter the ballpark, and reflecting the personal style of the Morrie Silver statue at the main gates, the Red Wings general manager personally welcomed fans to the game during pregame ceremonies by taking the microphone behind home plate, alerting the crowd to upcoming events, and informing everyone about in-game attractions and concession specials like the "Wednesday Wings Night Special" and the Josh Whetzel Pretzel. Named after the Red Wings chief broadcaster, the salty snack was an oversized treat intended to serve a family of four.

Among all of the ballparks that I encountered on the tour, the staff at Rochester was the most traditional and professional in appearance and demeanor. Male staffers wore starched, long-sleeve shirts with button-down collars, even in the hot, humid weather. They looked crisp as they complemented their shirts with color-coordinated ties, frequently sporting artistic designs of the Jerry Garcia label. Yet they often relaxed the formality of their appearance a bit by rolling their shirt sleeves to the elbow.

Among other announcements, the general manager anticipated the appearance and participation of Davey Johnson, who was scheduled to interact and sign autographs on the following Sunday. However, two days after my singing in Rochester, Johnson had to cancel his appearance because he assumed the reins of the Washington Nationals after the sudden resignation of their manager Jim Riggelman. Rochester's personal touch extended also to in-game entertainment, which was provided by live organ music, one of only two ballparks all season to include such a feature.

At various ballparks, I inquired about distinct anthem performances that the staff coordinator recalled during the season. Since I deliver an operatic rendition, I like to think that I surprise staff, players, and fans with my own performance by exceeding most that they hear during the season. I was delighted to learn from the Rochester staff that the team annually enjoyed performances by Greg Kunde, a local "product" who had gained acclaim internationally as an operatic performer. Knowing of his appearances and inspired by the staff's demeanor and support, I enthusiastically delivered one of my better renditions. A distinct addition to this anthem performance was that two interpreters—one flanking me along the first-baseline and the other standing in a mirrored position toward third—signed the anthem for hearing-impaired fans in the audience, the only time during the season that I was so accompanied. Although I had not known this was one of Rochester's cultural distinctions, the city enjoyed recognition for its sensitivity to and accommodations for persons with hearing disabilities.

When I entered the stands after singing, a fan in the front row hailed me in a way that I had not heard in other ballparks: "Are you really from Whittier, California?" Kathleen Joyce Melrose asked. "I grew up there and went to Cal Hi."

"That is the high school where my two sons attended," I replied.

For a couple of innings then, I sat with Kathleen and her husband to talk about Whittier, baseball, and the national anthem. Kathleen said that when she finally writes her memoir, she'll feature baseball, using the title *Life of a Season Ticket Holder*. Among other reflections in it, she'll propose several rule revisions to speed up games. For one, if a batter hits four foul balls, he'll be out. And since nine lives are enough for a cat's longevity, she reasoned, so, too, nine innings should be enough for baseball: no extra innings.

Enjoying Kathleen's proposed rule revisions, I trusted her recommendation for which concession to select—Rochester leads Triple-A ballparks in its array of desirable and healthy foods—and I headed for the Red Osier stand, where Dom the sandwich-maker treated me to a prime roast beef sandwich on a special kimmelweck roll, a Kaiser-style bun with caraway seeds. While I salivated and waited for the beef to be dipped, Tom Hober, a local high-school coach, thanked me for the anthem's clarity and brilliant tone.

In addition to ranking first in the smorgasbord category, Rochester was also the first ballpark where I encountered a "nut-free zone" in the grandstands as well as an "allergen-free" concession stand offering a range of "free" items: peanut free, gluten free, dairy free, tree-nut free. Yet since I am allergic to sucrose, I chuckled to myself that the menu did not identify any "sugar-free" products.

While I was photographing artworks near the main entry and the displays about the inductees in the Rochester Hall of Fame, Blaze Dinardo, the Red Wings' chief of security, asked me if I were a professional photographer. I was flattered. When I told him about my project, he seemed fascinated and directed me behind the third-base foul line to the stone tribute to Cal Ripken, Jr., a piece that simply featured his name and number. Later, he introduced me to one of the Red Wings board members, Priscilla Astifan, a local baseball historian who had researched and written about nineteenth-century baseball in Rochester.

An authority on the subject of Rochester's early embrace of baseball, she had published several short books about the early days of the sport in the city: the first organized game in the city between two collegiate teams in 1858, the first professional game in 1877, and the initial competition in the International League in 1885. In keeping with the public ownership of the team initiated by Morrie Silver several decades earlier, the board now was comprised primarily of lawyers and business executives, as well as herself and the bishops of the Catholic and Episcopalian diocese.

When Priscilla learned that I am a theologian, she identified several parallels between baseball and religion, starting with the similarity between the umpire and God. But adding a new twist to the metaphor, she reversed the basis for their comparison from "the umpire is God-like" to "God is like the umpire." "You have to be pleased," she suggested, "when 'The Great Umpire' calls you safe at home."

She followed up this playful trope by sending me a copy of a "prayerful toast" wherein she had encountered this inverted comparison. Offered at a baseball banquet in Rochester in 1858, the toast had initially appeared in a Buffalo newspaper before a portion was reprinted in the *Rochester Democrat and American* shortly thereafter:

> This game of ball is but a miniature of the rivalry of life. In both, may you and all of us play our parts manfully. May the blows you deal send the *balls* of truth down the *right field* and always *within the bounds*, may your *foul balls* never be caught by your opponents; may you make every *base* in the round of duty upon which manhood has set its impress; may your *innings* at the fire side hearth be the best of all, and when the *short*

> *stop* is put by the Great Umpire to your *runs*, may you find our *Home Base* where celestial music is struck by angel hands on golden lyres.

These pious musings about the value of baseball to a spiritual practice are among the first recorded reflections on connections between baseball and faith in American journalism.

Although lacking the reverential references that permeate the nineteenth-century toast, the fans at Frontier Field enthusiastically expressed their support for the Red Wings and their love for the game. While individual fans at many ballparks had loudly challenged ball and strike calls by the home-plate umpire, a few had chattered throughout the game like bench jockeys. In that spirit, Red Wings fans repeatedly harassed the visiting players with ongoing jeers: "Pitcher's got a rubber arm!" "Swing, batter!" "New ball!" "You're out!"

Their expressiveness also extended to their cheering for other fans. When a kid got his glove on a foul ball, only to watch it glance away to a man who picked it up, the crowd booed until the man offered the ball to the kid. But the kid, knowing that he had missed his real chance to catch a game ball, refused the offer, showing the highest of baseball integrity: It's not the ball itself that matters; it's the act of catching it or making the play. Minutes later when another kid caught a foul ball on a rebound off the façade, fans applauded more loudly than at any point in the evening, even more than when Joe Nathan, the former all-star closer for the Twins, pitched an inning on his rehab assignment, or when the Red Wings scored runs in their 8-7 loss to the Charlotte Knights.

Beyond Little League: Game 53 in Williamsport

During the last two weeks of August each year, the eyes of the baseball world turn toward Williamsport, Pennsylvania, for the summer's second World Series—this one for kids. Unlike the season's first World Series held in Omaha to crown the NCAA champion, or the professional one pitting the pennant winners from the American and National Leagues, the Little League World Series is truly for the World Championship. It features representative teams from Europe, Asia, Africa, and Latin America, as well as regional winners from the U.S. In fact, Little League claims to be the world's largest youth sports organization.

Among the impacts that the Little League World Series has on the Susquehanna Valley, hotel rooms rent for premium rates during the period of the playoffs. While blocks of rooms are guaranteed for competing teams and their entourage, media personnel and baseball pilgrims of all ages book space years in advance. Although I would have enjoyed trying to double-dip while in the area—singing for one of the LLWS games *and* for the Williamsport Crosscutters, who play in the short-season New York-Pennsylvania League—I chose the better bet for room and rates by scheduling my visit to Williamsport several weeks before the region's saturation with Little League fans.

Even so, my lodging possibilities were challenged by the recent discovery of an enormous natural gas reservoir underlying most of the region. Halliburton, among other exploratory enterprises, had sent so many crews to the area that hotels had filled for miles around in late June. I felt lucky to secure one of the last two rooms in the city at the historic Genetti Hotel. For the second time on the tour, fuel exploration and extrapolation created explosive hotel rates: the first in Midland, Texas, now in Williamsport.

According to the waitress at breakfast the following morning, Williamsport is a town crowded with banks, bars, churches, and Little League baseball. During the eleven months when the LLWS is not in play, the Little League Museum and its new complex of fields, located in a pastoral stretch of South Williamsport above the Susquehanna River, attract thousands of fans of all ages. The centerpiece of the complex is Lamade Stadium, whose grandstands seat more fans than many minor league ballparks. While most of the interactive exhibits at the museum are designed to appeal to preadolescents, significant numbers of adults make their way through its turnstile. They embrace the idea of Little League—a project by adults, an activity for kids.

To players and their parents from generations past, Little League signifies much more than childhood socialization through sport. It represents a person's early and innocent hopes, dreams that extend beyond the fading horizon of maturity, desires keenly felt that have gone unfulfilled, possibilities unpursued that still mold memories of what once shaped promise. It's not uncommon for men to recall their batting averages from their best year of play in Little League, or the strikeout pitch that froze the big kid with the winning runs on base, or the name of the outfielder who made a stumbling catch to save the game. A single significant win or game-turning play in Little League is often remembered as one of the formative events in childhood, if not of life itself.

As prominent as Little League is for Williamsport, it was an even older baseball tradition that drew me to the city. The Crosscutters of the New

York-Pennsylvania League call the city home, as did their predecessor the Williamsport Grays, a minor league team that had played there in the 1920s. After competing against the team from Bucknell University, the Grays had inaugurated professional play in Bowman Field against the Harrisburg Colored Giants in 1926, more than a decade before Little League founder Carl Stotz organized three teams to compete on an adjacent playground.

Bowman Field, where the Crosscutters play, is historic, claiming to be the second-oldest minor league ballpark in regular use. When it was constructed, the ballpark expanded over acres of outfield, with distances from home plate extending 367 feet down the line to right, 400 to left, and 450 to center. Because only ten home runs were hit in the first seven years of the ballpark's use—including one in the first professional game by Harrisburg's future Cooperstown enshrinee Oscar Charleston, and others by barnstorming major-leaguers—an inner fence was "temporarily" added. It stood for almost thirty years. Although still spacious, the outfield now conforms to typical dimensions at other ballparks.

While the outfield fences no longer stand in their original position, several of Bowman's architectural features survive undisturbed. Behind the third-base grandstands, the ballpark's wooden outer wall requires buttressing to remain erect, and the small dugouts, which retain their original, open position farther down the baselines than usual, can't accommodate a full roster of players. During the 1950s, the ballpark had slipped into such disrepair that the Little League World Series refused an offer to assume its supervision. When the city took over its operation as a last resort, several improvements began to be made, notably the installation of lights that came from the Polo Grounds in the 1960s after the Mets moved into Shea Stadium. Yet Bowman's deterioration continued for another decade, prompting professional baseball to desert Williamsport until the mid-1980s.

Now renovated, Bowman Park still exudes its early aura, which made my unamplified performance there seem fitting for its history. As I stepped to my position behind home plate, the microphone went dead. Not hearing any sound delay after the first few notes, I realized that the amplification system was not projecting my voice, and I simply ratcheted up my volume, intensified my resonance, and kept going unperturbed. My voice carried throughout the ballpark so well that I could hear natural echoes tossed back to me from the wooden wall in centerfield toward which I was facing.

When I came off the field, Crosscutters Vice President and Game-Day Operations Manager Gabe Sinicropi apologized and said that he could hear me from the far end of the distant dugout. Fans also uniformly expressed their appreciation with loud applause and frequent comments of "good job." And a couple of days later, I learned from Jack and Louise Thomas, shirttail relatives of Ruth Musser and musicians who had attended the game, that my a cappella performance without amplification had been splendid and appeared planned.

In contrast to the sound system failure during the pregame ceremony, amplified recordings generated entertaining highlights throughout the game. When a downpour interrupted the otherwise sunny early evening in the bottom of the third inning, the guys on the grounds crew enjoyed hearing their own "walk-on" music. While they sloshed through the puddles to extend a half-tarp over the left side of the diamond and then pulled a second one into place on the right side, they heard the familiar refrains of Creedence Clearwater Revival blaring over the loudspeakers: "Have you ever seen the rain coming down…?" After the passing shower delayed the game for almost an hour, an incredible sunset smothered the sky before the seventh-inning stretch on summer's second-longest day.

Another brief soundtrack had been routinely played at a number of other ballparks. When a foul ball would disappear over the grandstand, the crash of breaking glass often crackled over the loudspeakers. Yet at Williamsport, the timing for that sound effect was different: When a foul ball soared out of the ballpark and into the parking lot, there was a slight delay, allowing time for the ball to fall and for the crowd to settle. Then, suddenly, the clash of glass shattering jarred the fans, and the playful soundtrack became a prompt for an ad for a local insurance agent whose featured line was: "If that was your car, you'd be covered by the agent."

Things getting fouled up seemed to be a recurrent theme for the evening. When another foul ball rolled into the bullpen, a Batavia reliever picked it up and tossed it toward a fan, but it hit the wall. He retrieved it and tossed again, this time with the fan dropping it. Finally, he picked it up and handed it to the fan before returning to his seat in the middle of bullpen bench.

Meanwhile, in the grandstands one of the vendors hawked peanuts by threatening to throw them to the fans. One joked with him, "If you hit me, I'll sue." "Won't matter," the young man replied, keeping up his banter while also offering two-for-one sodas. "When you bought a ticket, you signed a waiver," he grinned.

Before the rain had erupted, Williamsport had scored a run on a couple of doubles in the second inning. But in the third, an error led to the first run for Batavia and extended the inning for the Muckdogs to score again. Minutes later, the offensive productivity of both teams drowned, and Batavia held on to win 2-1.

Bowie Louie: Game 54 in Bowie

Mascots at minor league ballparks appeal particularly to young fans, who frequently hug the silly creatures or slap high-fives with them while posing for photographs taken by their moms and dads. Occasionally, the gargantuan critters appear as though the team's icon has ingested bowls full of steroids instead of acorns, like Nutzy of the Richmond Flying Squirrels. Yet frequently, the playful beasts bear no relation to the team's name or an identifiable breed, like the one for Montgomery's Biscuits. There the mascot wasn't the Pillsbury Doughboy—an unexplored marketing alignment—but the mutt of multiple stuffed animals.

Throughout games, mascots entertained fans, dancing atop the dugout, bazooka-ing tee-shirts toward the upper grandstands, racing children around the bases between innings, and tossing buckets of confetti on box-seat fans. Several ballparks featured an autograph inning when the mascot, always beating with the heart of a clown, sat at a table in a designated area. So it shouldn't be surprising that one of the game promotions for the Bowie Baysox featured the birthday bash for their mascot Bowie Louie. Like most mascots, the name of Bowie's creature, "Louie," related neither to the identity of the team nor the character of the region. In this case, Louie's handle revealed his comic spirit by playing with the title of the rock hit "Louie, Louie," which had become a musical home run in the 1960s after the Kingsmen recorded the Richard Berry tune. Hence, his anthem could be "Bowie Louie."

Like the twist of using the song's title to name the Baysox mascot, the shape, color, and size of Bowie Louie also appeared to be a mongrel of various kid-fascinating creatures: the fuzziness of Cookie Monster, the color of Oscar the Grouch, the two dorky eyes of Snuffleupagus, and the feet with sneakers too large for Shaq—all with an added pink cranial tuft that must have come from DNA shared with My Pretty Pony.

Whatever the name, appearance, and character of Bowie Louie might have been, I was fortunate to sing on the night of his birthday party, which meant that several mascots from nearby teams, universities, and corporations attended his party: Sherman the Shorebird from the Baysox Eastern League rival in Delmarva; the iconic and ironic buffoons from Bowie State (the

Bulldog) and Towson State (the Tiger) universities; and among several corporate mascots, "Peeps," the chick from the maker of the namesake marshmallow candy, and "Wally Goose," from Wawa stores, a convenience store featuring several fresh foods.

Clowns in gowns were also invited to the park that night to lead the singing of "Happy Birthday" following the third inning, as were several different live animals, including an impressive iguana, whose exhibition required clearance by the county's animal control officers. Yet the animal agents weren't the least bit concerned about the unusual breed of Louie, nor the animal versions of the clowns.

When I inquired about Louie's birth certificate and its accuracy (we were, of course, within a home run's call from the White House, where birth certification was still a topic for some who continued to challenge Obama's presidential eligibility at the time), I was assured that June 24 might as well be his birthday as any.

As congenial a mascot as Louie was, and as festive as the evening became with other mascots, clowns, and animals providing entertainment, I most appreciated the pleasant ambiance at Prince George County Stadium, where parking was free for all. At the entrance to the ballpark, families of fans are welcomed by the sculpture of a baseball player and a young girl. Together, they model the transfer of baseball love and lore from parent and player to child, an inter-gender, inter-generational image. Sporting his uniform, stepping with cleats, and squeezing a ball for a split-fingered pitch, the father in the artistic piece leads the young girl by her throwing hand. Twisting her head slightly toward her father, the girl wears a smile almost bigger than the glove on her left hand, tilted expectantly. Standing tall, they peer together toward possibilities of baseball. They move together, together through baseball.

While the entry to Bowie's ballpark was distinct, its pregame activities and ceremonies corresponded to those at many other ballparks. Music blasted over the sound system during the teams' warm-ups and the fans' arrival, and children thronged to the field to perform particular exercises. This evening, a group of Tae Kwan Do junior Olympian contestants practiced their martial arts behind home plate, and they were followed by dozens of Boy Scout troops who paraded through the outfield. Amid such noisy clamor, I found it challenging to maintain focus for the start of the anthem.

Another common challenge that I encountered during the start of the anthem was a delay, often significant, in the rebound of sound from ballpark speakers in multiple directions. Few of the teams—in fact, only five all season—required or allowed rehearsal of the anthem on their audio system. As common as the problems with the sound system were, I never grew comfortable with the delay. In Bowie, as sometimes happened, my descending triad at the start of "The Star-Spangled Banner" was muddled by the ongoing echo. Nonetheless, I adjusted quickly to the instant replay and finished strong at the minor league ballpark nearest Baltimore's Fort McHenry, whose defense had inspired Francis Scott Key to pen the four stanzas of his poem almost two centuries earlier.

Tonight proved no different regarding commotions and distractions, but it did provide a new accent in another respect. While my name or image typically might appear on the scoreboard during my introduction, here—for the first time—the game program included my name as the national anthem performer.

Even as the ad-enriched scorecard presented this simple highlight, the game itself featured a once-in-a-career feat for Binghamton Mets third baseman Josh Satin: He hit for the cycle. With two outs as he batted in the first inning, Satin fouled off several two-strike pitches before connecting with a curve ball for his ninth home run of the season. Two innings later when he came to the plate with a runner on first, he hit a one-hop shot wide of third. Although the shortstop was able to make a diving stop of the ball deep in the hole, his throw to second was too late; and Satin was credited with an infield single. In Satin's next plate appearance in the fifth, he doubled to centerfield. Not known for his speed, Satin was often teased by teammates about shrinking triples into doubles.

In the seventh inning, as he stepped into the batter's box, he stood a triple shy of the cycle, an unlikely achievement since he was not fleet-footed and since the triple is the rarest kind of base hit. Of Satin's thirty extra base hits in this season before this at-bat, only one had been a three-bagger. Although on several occasions in previous seasons he had encountered a similar situation of needing only a triple to complete a cycle, he had not been in this position in a ballpark where the ball often caroms off the outfield fence at an oblique angle. He lined a ball to the left-field corner and, as the ball hit the wall, it ricocheted oddly past the Baysox fielder. Immediately, Satin shifted into overdrive and legged the hit into a triple. His cycle was complete, but not his night: In the ninth, Satin added to his perfect effort by coaxing a walk. Altogether, his historic performance propelled Binghamton to a 5-3 win.

7.

The Original Key

Searching for a Key: Game 55 in Frederick

While conceiving and setting up the tour, I became aware of the gravesite memorial to Francis Scott Key across the street from the Frederick Keys ballpark, and I made sure that my travel schedule would permit me to spend some time there. Early on the date of my scheduled singing for the Keys, I drove Toad to Frederick to ensure ample time to explore tributes to Key, one of the city's native sons.

A statue of Key perches above the entry to Mount Olivet Cemetery, and behind the figure is a small stone chapel erected in 1911 and named in his honor. Inscribed on the bronze plaques around the base of the statue are the four stanzas of his poem, as well as a bronze relief of the first bars of the chorus in its most popular key of B-flat. To make sure that all entrants into the cemetery know whom the statue represents, his name is sculpted in the hedge at its base.

Although the cemetery prominently memorializes Key, I had hoped to find his historic home or a local museum with exhibits and artifacts related to his life and work. While a few of those pieces of material history are on display at the Smithsonian, there is relatively little in Frederick that celebrates Key. The city's welcome center provides minimal information about him in a small exhibit that also features two other notable Frederick residents during the nineteenth century: Elizabeth Ann Seton, the first American-born Christian to be canonized by the Roman Catholic Church; and Barbara Fritchie, immortalized in a poem by John Greenleaf Whittier about her flying of an American flag during the Confederate occupation of the city. Even though the community memorialized the houses associated with both of these women, I could not find a historic marker for Key other than the memorial in the cemetery.

While the flag above Fort McHenry had inspired Key to write his poem, I was surprised that the cemetery's tribute to him did not fly a replica of the Stars and Stripes that had survived the British barrage, especially since other historic flags flew prominently throughout the cemetery. Among them were an American flag adjacent to Fritchie's tomb and the flag of Maryland beside the gravesite of the first governor of the state. At the very least it seemed incongruous that the only flag that I could see immediately beyond Key's memorial was the one of the Confederate States of America. In addition to individual tributes to Key and Fritchie, the cemetery in Frederick also commemorates the collective service of Confederate and Union soldiers, especially those who died in the nearby battles of Antietam and Monocacy.

Although the Stars and Stripes had occasioned the composition of the two poems—"The Defence of Ft. McHenry" and "Barbara Frietchie's Defiance"—the flag of another aspiring nation flew more conspicuously than the American flag by Fritchie's memorial. And while the flag of the Confederacy at best represents the period of history during which the Southern soldiers had served and died, the flag at Fritchie's tomb was the current version with fifty stars, not a replica of the flag that could have flown in front of her house during the 1860s.

Enriched and perplexed by the history commemorated in the cemetery, I turned along Mount Olivet's outer drive and found baseball insignia on two tombstones facing the ballpark across the street. In an odd way these two grave markers seemed to provide an effective transition for me from considering the moral and political significance of Key, Fritchie, and the war dead, to appreciating the playful spirit by which two baseball fans wanted to be remembered.

When I first had contacted the Keys, I had not realized that their name refers to the author of the stanzas of "The Star-Spangled Banner." In his response to my query, Keys general manager Dave Ziedelis had let me know that Francis Scott Key's burial place was across the street from the ballpark. Then I understood multiple meanings of "Keys," a plural noun used to identify the team of Frederick players with the poet. The name enjoys a musical ring since it often matters in which key the anthem is sung, so that its wide range can be scaled. And the puns extend to art in the ballpark. Greeting fans inside the main gate was an oversized model of the key to the city or, perhaps, baseball's key to the fan's heart.

At the Will Call window where I picked up my tickets, Cheryl McClain was delighted to learn about my singing the anthem. She related that in the 1980s, she had sung the anthem for the Keys when they had played at the old ballpark. A special memory of that occasion was that her grandfather, "a war veteran and an avid baseball fan," she said, had been there to celebrate the occasion with her. He had introduced her to baseball, which she had enjoyed ever since. Now working for the Keys, she was pleased that her daughter Melissa was scheduled to sing the anthem for the Keys later in the season, as she had done last year, as well as having sung for the Delmarva Shorebirds, the team nearest Melissa's home. When I asked Cheryl if she had been more nervous when she had sung or when her daughter had performed, she replied quickly, "That's easy. Hers!"

Joining Bonnie and me at the ballpark were Alan and Sandy Yamamoto, friends from Alexandria, Virginia, who had been hosting Bonnie during the week while I had traveled across Pennsylvania and into New York to sing in several ballparks. Bonnie and Alan had known each other since her high-school years in Watsonville, California, and through the years our friendship has spanned the continent. In recent decades during our biennial visits to Washington, D.C., we have frequently stayed with Alan and Sandy and their lovable black Labs.

On one of our trips to the area a dozen years ago, the four of us celebrated one of Bonnie's numerous teaching awards (this one as a Milken Educator) with an extravagant culinary event—having dinner at the Inn at Little Washington, then rated as the favorite restaurant in the nation by award-winning chefs. And when I first had sung for the Orioles in Camden Yards several years earlier, Alan and Sandy had driven to Baltimore to link up with us for the game. It was a delight to share another evening of baseball with them. Among the varied topics of our conversation throughout the game, Alan and I dissected the placement and possible effectiveness of the eighty billboard ads—often triple-decked—on the outfield fences.

Also finding us at the ballpark was Paul Lasky, who had sat in the row below Bonnie and me a week earlier in Hagerstown. He had come to the Frederick game to enjoy another night of Minor League Baseball. For several innings we shared stories about baseball players and broadcast personalities since his nephew provided radio play-by-play for the Delmarva Shorebirds. Before the evening was over, Paul set up an interview for me with his nephew during our scheduled visit to the Shorebirds ballpark several days later.

At Frederick, like my game the night before in Bowie, troops of Boy Scouts paraded behind the diamond before the game and anticipated spending the night camping out on the outfield grass. One result of the promotion at Frederick was that the team enjoyed its largest crowd in four years with more than 9,000 attending the game. The density of the crowd was so great that the lines at the concession stands seemed to stretch farther than those for airport security at O'Hare. They were so long and slow that we actually missed almost three innings of play while waiting to buy a crab pretzel. "Is it standard pretzel dough twisted into the shape of a crab claw, or is it somehow filled with crab meat?" I wondered aloud to Alan. Alas, it was simply a long stick pretzel with a reasonably good crab dip. But it certainly wouldn't rival any of the hors d'oeuvres that we had sampled years earlier at the Inn at Little Washington.

One effect of the long lines was that they apparently voided the ten-second rule for contaminating dropped food, at least for one parent. When Alan and I saw a child drop a hot dog near the condiment counter, we sympathized with his plight of losing dinner. He tapped his mother on her hip and pointed disappointedly to his spill. We were dumbfounded by what we saw next. The mother finished putting ketchup and relish on a couple of hot dogs, then bent down to retrieve the fallen wiener, wipe it off, and tuck it back into the bun—an act of ballpark hunger desperation and line-wait exasperation.

While Alan and I waited for service and food, Frederick catcher Adam Donachie homered for a second time in the game even though before this game he had not hit a round-tripper. His five RBIs led the Keys to a dashing 6-2 win over Winston-Salem, while highly touted prospect Manny Machado, who had been promoted to the Keys three days earlier, had an unremarkable game, hitting two ground-ball outs, walking twice, and muffing a grounder that was generously ruled a hit.

Facets of an Appalachian Gem: Game 56 in Pulaski

Friendliness seems to be endemic to Southwestern Virginia. In the small mountain town of Pulaski, Mariners staff and fans were as welcoming as a dugout of teammates to a slugger following a grand-slam home run. Of course, folks there might have been prompted to be so cordial to me because they had read Dan Casey's Sunday column in the *Roanoke Times* that had featured my anthem adventure.

While several of the specific greetings that were extended to me were probably stimulated by the newspaper article, I'm fairly certain that the fans' affability was a reflection of the community's spirit. They intensely love their community, which had been severely damaged by one of the tornados that had ripped through the region several weeks before, and they genuinely expressed appreciation for me having come to Pulaski, where the Appalachian League's Mariners had opened their rookie-level season several days earlier.

With scaffolding still erect in one section of the grandstands and foliage still in pots awaiting transplanting into the ballpark landscape, an expectant attitude seemed to emanate from the field as well.

Because the Appalachian League plays a short-season schedule, my travel route overlapped the Mariners' late-June start by only one game. So I was especially appreciative that Pulaski allowed me to sing during their first home-stand, giving me my lone opportunity to sing for a team in that league. The 2011 season marked the 100th anniversary of the founding of the original Appalachian League, which has been reconstituted on two occasions, most recently fifty years ago.

When I picked up my ticket, Wayne Carpenter, one of the owners of the Pulaski team, greeted me and offered me something to drink and eat, one of a handful of such hospitable ballpark receptions. And Abby Lyman, the assistant general manager with whom I had corresponded during the scheduling phase of the tour, gave me a copy of the souvenir program, also a rare gift on the tour. An hour or so later when I stood ready to sing the anthem, my introduction was most thorough, focusing on the objectives of the tour, promoting the anthem itself, and detailing the expanse of my travel.

Following my rendition, Dave Hart, the director of ballpark operations, mentioned that, after having read in my blog about the dead microphone at Williamsport, he had made sure to put a fresh battery in the one at Pulaski. His enthusiasm for historic ballparks was unmistakable. He asked about my perceptions of and reactions to the older facilities in Daytona, Savannah, and Williamsport, and he expressed personal appreciation for Rickwood Field in Birmingham. Several years earlier when he had attended a regional conference of civic parks and recreation directors in Alabama, the group had organized a softball game that was played on the diamond at Rickwood. As he told me the story, he glowed like a rookie standing on base after his first hit.

Historic Calfree Park, the home of the Mariners, is one of the oldest ballparks in the minor leagues. Built in 1935 as a WPA project, the ballpark had been refurbished in 1999 when stands along the first base line were renovated, new locker rooms constructed, and the concessions area expanded. The grandstands along the third base line, however, were left intact and merely repaired. One of the charming features of that original section is that its wide rows do not have separate seats or even benches. With expansive space, fans could sit on the widely tiered platforms or bring their own folding chairs—as many did—to place comfortably under the canopy of the grandstand.

As a Rookie League affiliate, Pulaski annually features a roster filled with quite young prospects, some drafted as recently as a few weeks before the season opener, and others having played professionally for a single year. The highest draftee on the Mariners was a tenth-rounder, while the visiting Princeton Rays featured Tampa's first-round pick of the 2011 draft, eighteen-year-old infielder Jake Hager from Las Vegas, and its first-round pick from the previous year, catcher Justin O'Conner.

Half of the players on Pulaski's team had signed as free agents, most of whom seemed to be nineteen-year-olds from Venezuela and the Dominican Republic. Another international Mariner was an eighteen-year-old pitcher who hailed from South Africa. Whether drafted as a prospect or signed as a free agent, each of the players appeared thrilled to be pursuing the dream of playing in the major leagues.

As delighted as the players were about getting paid to play baseball, the Pulaski fans reciprocated with an enthusiastic embrace of the team. The community's exuberant acceptance of the minor leaguers and their lifestyles more closely resembled the snapshot of minor league life in *Bull Durham* than any that I had seen. Each year, fifteen or twenty community members adopted players to provide them with family-style connections and support. But nowhere did I encounter anyone like Millie, the cinematic daughter of the Durham Bulls owner, or Annie Savoy, the sultry seductress of Nuke and Crash.

One of the local Pulaski adopters sought me out as I walked through the reserved seats. Mont Quisenberry, the retired choral director at Pulaski High School and the music director at nearby Memorial Baptist Church, extended his hand as he complimented my rendition. "Thanks for singing it as the national anthem," he said, "and not as a voice exercise. Since it has a difficult range, you don't need to add thirty extra notes to try to show off your voice."

With courtesies exchanged, we talked at length about the national anthem, baseball (especially the Pulaski fans' support of the team while his adopted player came to bat), and our musical training. He had honed his vocal skills and choral directing at Berea College, "a little Kentucky school that you probably wouldn't know," he added. When I chimed in that my former student Kent Gilbert was pastor of the Berea Union Church, he was surprised. And he was more amazed that Bonnie and I had been on the college campus and that we had dined at the Boone's Tavern Inn when I had sung for Lexington a month earlier.

For a number of the Rookie League players, the challenge of professional play is compounded by the need to make adjustments in their first move away from home and in relocating to a distant community. A mountain town in Appalachia proved to be quite distant in miles and culture from a Midwestern city, suburban Los Angeles, or especially, Merida Menda, Venezuela, the home of one of the young Mariners.

In previous years sponsoring families had provided housing for players, often feeding them and driving them to the grocery store or Walmart for routine shopping. During the previous year, Meredith McGrady, the coordinator for player sponsorship, had put 10,000 miles on her Explorer transporting players on errands and trips. For the 2011 season a new process of sponsorship was being introduced: The players were living together in a motel, and the ball club's owners had purchased three vans for the coaches and staff to use to drive the players on errands and to the ballpark. Still, the sponsors would offer ongoing support by providing family interactions with the teenage athletes.

One of the attractions that draws fans to adopt a player is the chance to extend personal hospitality and to strengthen the community's cohesiveness and reputation. Another is the possibility that the adopted player might become a major league star. Within the past few decades, a roster of major-leaguers who had played for Pulaski included 2011 starting pitchers Aaron Harang (Cincinnati) and Colby Lewis (Texas), as well as former Atlanta Braves all-stars Dave Justice and Javy Lopez, and Hall of Fame slugger Mike Schmidt.

The close relationship between players and fans was displayed before the game when players stopped to talk at length to children, often giving them batting tips, as did Daniel Paolini, the highest draft pick on the Mariners team. And there was a familiarity that youngsters also enjoyed with players. When one of the little "dream-team" players who participated in pregame ceremonies approached Reynaldo Sabala, a Venezuelan-born pitcher, the kid proudly exclaimed, "I get to go on the field with you!"

Looking a bit baffled, as though the catcher had called for a pitch out with no runners on base, Sabala smiled broadly and said simply, "Don't understand you." Indeed the challenges of adjusting to life in the Appalachian League often extend far beyond those of geographic relocation. They frequently involve unfamiliar language and cultural immersion in the life of a small mountain town.

Although the Mariners had won their first five games during the season, they were plagued by sloppy fielding, making six errors that led to eight unearned runs in their 14-2 loss to Princeton. Even so, the evening was a gem that revealed the camaraderie that could grow between players and their adopting community. And the joyful expressions on the faces of both players and fans showed that baseball helps to bridge racial distinctions, ethnic differences, and linguistic barriers.

Tributes in Salem: Game 57 in Salem

When I entered Salem's ballpark and saw the Red Sox warming up for their home game against the Myrtle Beach Pelicans, I took one look at their uniforms and wondered what was going on. Since popular *Roanoke Times* columnist Dan Casey had written a feature story about my project for the Sunday edition of the regional paper, I briefly wondered if there were a connection between it and the players' garb. There wasn't. They wore mock-tux uniforms for another reason.

In an attempt to break the June-long hex that had sunk the team into last place, they had resorted to wearing tuxedo-style jerseys. The Sox' last victory at home had been almost a month earlier on Memorial Day; then they had won on a walk-off grand-slam home run. For the entire month of June they had been winless in their own ballpark, going 0 and 6 and compounding their misery on the road with a 6 and 12 mark. With such an abysmal record, they reversed from first (having blasted off to a 17-5 record in April) to last in the semblance of biblical judgment.

On the night of my singing they had hoped that, by "dressing to impress," they could break their streak. Impress whom? The gods of the gopher ball or the demons of the diamond? Whatever their motive and target, the ploy didn't work. They lost to the Myrtle Beach Pelicans 10-8, even though they had taken a lead into the late innings. As only a losing streak can seem to generate, the poor June luck of the Red Sox continued when their promising relief pitcher Mitch Herold suffered an arm injury that forced his exit with none on and two outs in the eighth inning. Alas, before the inning was over, his replacement had yielded four hits, hit a batter, balked, walked a batter, and allowed a stolen base, all of which produced four runs and effectively sank Salem, allowing the Pelicans to fly away with the win.

Although I couldn't claim partial credit for ending their streak the following night when they shut out Myrtle Beach, I thoroughly enjoyed my one evening in Salem, spending it with old and new friends. Carter Turner, a professor at nearby Radford University, and I had worked together on conference panels and projects dealing with sports and religion, and he had pitched the story of the anthem tour to Dan Casey, the Roanoke journalist who was also able to join us for the game.

While the story by Casey had not affected the Red Sox, it certainly had influenced interactions with fans and awareness of other media about the anthem tour. Mid-afternoon I had received a call from Elizabeth Harrington, a reporter for WDBJ-TV, requesting an interview that we filmed before the game in the ballpark. Her short feature ran on the evening news and the morning show the following day. As stimulating and enjoyable as the interview was, it was even more engaging to be approached by fans throughout the game who had seen Casey's story the previous day and who had heard my introduction before singing.

When I had entered the ballpark, Dave Spangler greeted me at the gate, congratulating me on the project and indicating that he had read about it in Casey's column, which was accompanied by a picture of me in my customary performance attire of an anthem-tour polo shirt. Another fan passing by said, "Mr. Price. We're glad you came to Salem. Keep up the good work around the country." Later while I was standing in one of the concession lines, Bruce Briggs approached and asked me to sign the back of his ticket. I know that the autograph will never amount to much worth, but his request reflects the kind of hope that many minor league fans have about one of their players making it big in the big leagues. A few do—and their early autographs rise from sentimental significance to monetary value.

At most minor league parks where I had sung, hanging banners or expandable wall boards identified recent team alumni who had made it to The Show. A few ballparks—like the ones in Asheville or Scranton/Wilkes-Barre—also displayed colorful portraits or bronze plaques of former players who starred in the major leagues and became enshrined in the Hall of Fame in Cooperstown. At Salem, a different level of respect is accorded to the team's former heroes. Rather than using a concourse wall to display the roster of successful bygone players, the team devoted a separate facility in the ballpark complex to serve as Salem's Hall of Fame. It commemorates the pacesetters among the team's former stars as well as local baseball personalities who contributed to the community in significant ways.

The building is located beyond the children's play space, a Wiffle-ball diamond with a miniature replica of Fenway's Green Monster looming over left field. This free field encouraged kids to throng to the site to play their own game within earshot of the Salem-Myrtle Beach game a few hundred feet away. They appeared to be more excited by their competition in this baseball set than the bouncy-room attractions that typified most of the play spaces at other minor league parks.

Salem's Hall of Fame intrigued me for personal reasons. I wanted to see if a shirttail friend—a recurring acquaintance through our mutual good friend Don Musser—was honored there. Having been told by an usher that the facility was open, I was disappointed to find its doors locked. Undeterred, I sought one of the senior staff members to get access. Sure enough, a stadium security officer unlocked the doors, turned on the lights, and allowed me to survey the walls until I found the tribute to Art Howe, whose plaque he removed from the wall so that I could photograph it more easily.

Forty years earlier, Art had been a semi-pro player in Pittsburgh and a member of the church where Don Musser had served as pastor. Signed to a contract with the Pirates after showing his skills at a tryout camp, Art soon led the league in hitting in the year that he played for Salem. Thereafter, he progressed through the minors and finally was promoted to the Pirates as a reserve infielder in the mid-1970s, a year or so before Don and I met during graduate school in Chicago.

When Pittsburgh came to the Windy City to play the Cubs during summer our second year of studies, Don phoned Art and secured complimentary box-seat tickets at Wrigley Field for a record-setting game. That afternoon, Pirates second-baseman Rennie Stennett became the first player to get seven hits in a nine-inning game, and John Candelaria pitched Pittsburgh to a sunny shellacking of Chicago—22-0, the largest margin of victory in a shutout in major league history. After the game, Art persuaded Stennett to autograph a ball (his sixth hit), date it, and mark its significance before handing it to Don. And when the Pirates enjoyed a rare day off in Chicago the following spring, Art came down to the Midway at the university to watch the divinity school's intramural softball team, on which both Don and I played, and to cheer for us as we beat the business school that afternoon. The "biz school" players were flummoxed that a major-leaguer was rooting in person for the "feebs"—the "impotent holy guys," as they had pegged us.

After finishing his playing career in Houston about a decade later, Art shifted his role to that of coaching, progressing to become the manager of the Astros, then the A's, and finally the Mets. Our paths crossed again in the early 1990s when I had sung the anthem in Atlanta. Conveniently, Don and his wife Ruth were in the city while Don was doing academic research at

Emory University; and the three of us attended the game and talked with Art during batting practice. Adjacent to the Astros' dugout, I was able to take a posed picture of Don, Ruth, and Art, later getting the photograph enlarged and signed by Art during one of the Astros' visits to Los Angeles. The poster-size photograph now hangs in Don's study.

My last encounter with Art solidified my respect for his friendship with Don. After Art became the manager of the A's, I was able to sing the anthem on several occasions in Oakland. Prior to one of the pregame ceremonies there, I informed him that Don, who had conquered lymphoma while serving as his pastor, had contracted a new case of the cancer now thirty years later. A few weeks later while Don was completing rounds of chemotherapy and awaiting an autologous stem-cell transplant, Art phoned him to check on him, reversing the pastoral role that had bonded them together years earlier. My deep friendship with Don motivated me to search out the tribute to Art in Salem's Hall of Fame exhibit.

It's not surprising that I fell in love with the people, the setting, and the tributes at Salem's ballpark. Yet while romance at a ballpark is a common desire and experience of baseball fans, marriage proposals offered there are less frequent. Following the fifth inning of the Red Sox game, Mike and Melanie were "invited" to participate in a trivia contest and dance atop the third-base dugout. Unbeknownst to Melanie, Mike had connived their selection to participate. On cue then, Mike knelt and proposed to her, and she accepted.

Love at the ballpark and love of the ballpark: Baseball in Salem stimulated both.

Arbie's Distress: Not Quite Games 58 and 59

Ten days after Bonnie and I had left Southwestern Virginia for my swing through Northern Virginia, Maryland, Pennsylvania, and even New York, we returned to the Blue Ridge region for two more games, each exceedingly important in its own way. The game at Pulaski provided my only experience in the Appalachian (Short Season A) League, and Salem offered the opportunity to explore the recognition of former major league player and manager Art Howe, whom I had met on multiple occasions.

During our earlier stay near Lynchburg at the Thousand Trails RV Park, we had docked Arbie in the most idyllic RV site that we had found. Nestled between trees and overlooking a lake, Arbie had relaxed for an infrequent day when I neither was scheduled for a performance nor needed to drive for several hours to a new city. So we took advantage of the chance to explore nearby Appomattox Courthouse where we toured the National Historical Park, the site of Robert E. Lee's surrender to U.S. Grant. The theme of the exhibits and presentations is neither the conquest by the Union forces nor the defeat of the Confederate army, but the reunion of the nation.

For our return to Southwestern Virginia, Bonnie secured an unbeatable rate at the boutique Craddock Terry Hotel rather than trying to recapture the serenity of our earlier experience in the RV park a few miles farther south. Located within an outfielder's throw of the James River, the hotel was an artsy conversion of a former shoe factory. Our room retained distinct features of the architectural integrity of the building while enjoying stylish upgrades and furnishings: the ceiling seemed as tall as a pop fly, the drapes rivaled the size of some infield tarps, and a walk-in shower seemed to stretch the length of a home-team dugout. Decorated with art and artifacts relating to its stylish history, the hotel delivered continental breakfast to our room in pristine, shoeshine boxes.

After two restful nights in the hotel and two most peaceful, unoccupied nights for Arbie parked at the curb, we re-boarded the RV and headed east along Highway 460 through Appomattox. Then reversing the route of Lee's retreat, we aimed toward Petersburg with the afternoon's goal of reaching Norfolk. There, at five o'clock I was scheduled for a sound test since the Tides' audio system was known to suffer the worst delay in the league. To make sure that we could arrive in the Tidewater area around mid-afternoon, Arbie needed fuel. Recalling which of the service stations in Appomattox offered the lowest price, we stopped for gas, pumping fifty-nine gallons for $197.43. But shortly after pulling back onto the highway and nearing the little community of Evergreen, Arbie began to complain. The dashboard warning light flashed: SERVICE ENGINE SOON.

Okay, I thought. We should be able to get the Chevy 454 engine serviced in about twenty-four hours in Salisbury, Maryland, if not in Norfolk later that afternoon during my rehearsal at the ballpark. If all went well, we could get to the Tidewater area by two or three o'clock; and if no attention could be given to Arbie then, we could call ahead to Salisbury, where I would sing for the Delmarva Shorebirds before a late-morning start the following day. To make the schedule work, we had calculated that we could leave the Norfolk game after the fifth inning, drive across and through the Chesapeake Bay Bridge/Tunnel to the Delmarva Peninsula, and stop in Salisbury for the evening.

But the biggest problem with our tight plan was Arbie's distress, indicated by the persistent warning on the instrument panel even as we eased through the little community with the hopeful name of "Prospect." Watching the incessant omen refuse to fade, we pressed on toward Farmville and passed its exits. Then, belch, burp, spasm: Arbie clanked as though something had fallen off the front end near the engine, then trailed under the passenger's side. Immediately, I pulled over, got out, looked under the engine, and scanned our trail for metal debris. No damage was apparent, but Arbie heaved. It was 11:02. I was due in Norfolk, about 150 miles away, by 5 o'clock.

As a member of Good Sam RV Club and AAA, Bonnie phoned both assistance services, and found that Good Sam could offer little more than information that we could access via the iPad. By contrast, although the AAA dispatcher had trouble identifying our precise location, she was able to contact an approved automotive shop in Farmville, describe our plight, and learn that we could be serviced that afternoon. I remained hopeful, even when I learned that the tow would not arrive until 1 o'clock. Meanwhile, I set out warning flares and orange triangles, expressed appreciation to the state trooper who stopped to inquire about our situation, turned on the generator to run the coach's air conditioning, and telephoned the Tides about the vehicular difficulty while Bonnie retreated to the bed for a nap.

Minutes later, my phone buzzed with a call from Lisa Bryant, one of the television reporters for WBOC in Salisbury, Maryland. She wanted to set up an interview the following morning in conjunction with my singing for the Shorebirds. Regrettably, I let her know about Arbie's incapacity and the probability of my cancellation for singing at Delmarva's game.

Shortly after one o'clock, a heavy-duty tow truck crossed the overpass behind us on State Highway 696, turned down the entry ramp onto Highway 460, and pulled forward to our position a few feet beyond its merge. While we disconnected Toad and watched Arbie getting hitched to the truck, I really sensed that I would be unable to make it to the Norfolk game. Seeing Arbie's reversed position as the towed vehicle, I began to agonize about the uncertainties of repair and delay or, worse yet, of Arbie's possibly prolonged disablement. Already on the tour, I had experienced the cancellation of two games: one in Northwest Arkansas because of duplicate scheduling, and weeks later a rainout for the Potomac Nationals. Obviously, I knew that I couldn't bat 1.000 on the tour; still, I desperately wanted to capitalize on every singing opportunity to reach my goal of 100 ballpark performances, a target that permitted less than a ten-percent margin of error for travel woes, rain, and my health.

Initially, the truck towed Arbie away from Farmville for several miles before reaching a point where it could make a u-turn, safely swinging the twenty-nine-foot RV back toward the East End Motor Company in Farmville. When the tow-truck driver dropped Arbie in the lot, I went inside the shop to describe the problem, only to learn that the mechanics had left for lunch.

With little to do, I left my cell phone number with the office manager, Bonnie checked Yelp's reviews for nearby restaurants, and we hopped in Toad to hustle over for a late lunch at Charley's Waterfront Café in a restored industrial area along the Appomattox River.

I worried and wondered as we ordered. Before our sandwiches arrived, my phone buzzed with good news from East End: Arbie's diagnosis was a bad alternator, an easy repair that could be completed quickly once the right part could be located. Alas, at 4:30 the repair shop called back to report that none of the auto parts stores in Farmville had the correct alternator for Arbie's engine. The mechanic indicated that he had ordered one from a supply house in Richmond and that its delivery was anticipated at dawn the next day. If all went well in receiving the part and completing the replacement, he said that Arbie should be ready for the road by noon the following day.

Frustrated by the situation, I phoned the Tides, the Shorebirds, and WBOC-TV with the bad news about being stranded in Farmville. Separated from Arbie for the night, we checked into a Hampton Inn and rested easily in its comfort and security during violent evening thunderstorms.

Getting Back on Track: Game 58 in Wilmington

Although I had missed my scheduled anthem performances for the Norfolk Tides and the Delmarva Shorebirds because of Arbie's faulty alternator, we got back on track en route to Wilmington, Delaware. Having missed Norfolk meant that we no longer needed to head toward the Tidewater area. Instead, when we left Farmville we took an isosceles cutoff on State Highway 307 at Rice. Now a well-marked and truck-traveled route through high, rolling hills, it had been a little-known shortcut forty years earlier. Then spending the summer at my parents' home in Richmond, I had learned about that time-saving way when I had preached nearby at the small Baptist Church in Rice where my father had served as interim pastor.

Back aboard Arbie, Bonnie and I angled on up to and through the capital of the Confederacy; there we turned due north on the East Coast's aorta, I-95. Before reaching Fredericksburg, however, we veered acutely toward Bowling Green and its intersection with US 301, thereby hoping to circumvent Washington's glut of traffic. By taking this route toward Wilmington, we missed the anticipated adventure of crossing over and through the twenty-seven-mile Chesapeake Bay Bridge Tunnel from Norfolk to the tip of the Delmarva Peninsula; but we were able to cross two impressive bridges spanning the Potomac River and the Chesapeake Bay. From Dahlgren, Virginia, to Newberg, Maryland, we arched over the Potomac on the magnificent Harry W. Nice Memorial Bridge; and an hour or so later as we left Annapolis, we transcended the Chesapeake on the spectacular, curving, double-span, four-mile bridge on US 50. Safely on the eastern shore of Maryland, we made our way on toward Wilmington, where we rejoined I-95 and passed the Blue Rocks ballpark on our way to the Tohickon Family Campground in Quakertown, Pennsylvania, an hour's drive north of Philadelphia. By docking there, we figured that we could easily tether in Toad back to Wilmington the following day and on to Trenton the day after.

Making the final turn from the narrow rural roads toward the campground east of Quakertown, I knew that our travel woes must be over. Our luck was changing. The Sheard's Mill Covered Bridge over Tohickon Creek, through which we must pass, showed clearance of 12' 6"—not quite a foot above the full height of Arbie. Still, I eased through the portal, into the darkness of the tunnel and then the brilliance of sunlight at the other end.

Our luck also was changing in ways that I had not yet anticipated. While we had approached Philadelphia, Bonnie had called the Barnes Foundation to inquire about possibilities of securing tickets for the following morning to see the Barnes collection of French Impressionists and Post-Impressionists, especially portions of its huge collection of works by Renoir, Cézanne, Matisse, and Picasso. The educational institution—a concept intentionally designed as an alternative to a "museum"—had been founded by Albert C. Barnes, a pharmaceutical chemist in the early twentieth century who had begun to collect art after he had made a fortune developing an anti-gonorrheal drug. Although Bonnie learned that admission had been sold out months earlier because of the impending year-long closure required for the collection to be relocated from its current historic site, she left her number on the recording device, indicating that we would be glad to change last-minute plans if notified about ticket cancellation. Perhaps, I thought, some ticketholder's alternator might fail!

Whatever the cause, Bonnie's cell phone rang after breakfast the next morning with the Barnes representative offering early-afternoon tickets. Of course we claimed them. Undoubtedly, Bonnie's first love after her family is the group of French Impressionists. And over the decades of our marriage, I have been comforted by a replica of Renoir's portrait of a young girl with a watering can hanging in our bedroom at home, I have grown fond of paintings by Matisse and Monet, and I have increasingly resonated with works by Cézanne.

Shortly after Bonnie had conveyed her excitement about getting to see "the Barnes" (which held a place on her bucket list of art museums comparable to Yankee Stadium on my roster of ballparks), we dressed for the evening game in Wilmington and headed to suburban Philadelphia for the penultimate exhibition of works at the original foundation location.

If there is a visual counterpoint to the narrative form of hagiography, the display of works in the rooms at the Barnes institution certainly would fit. The audio tour directed viewers' attention to Barnes's perception of a work, its position in a room, and its relation to other pieces and artifacts nearby. The purpose of the exhibition seemed to align the viewer's perception with Barnes's distinct appreciation rather than allowing each piece to engage the viewer on its own terms. And faithful to the directives of Barnes's estate, the placement of the clusters of paintings and other artistic pieces would be duplicated at the new facility housing the collection.

The philosophical and educational design of these "wall ensembles" emphasized the structure, power, and drama created through color, form, and light. Rather than being able to focus on a single work or to see the world through the eye of a particular painter, the viewer was presented with pieces displaying the collector's ideas (and often his words) about "volumes of color." Memorable phrases from the audio about a room's cluster of works included: "spatial intervals felt as color relations," "color extends over contour" creating an "indissoluble entity," and "color gives substance."

While the dense displays throughout the building often seemed contrived, the works themselves exerted the power to evoke a depth of contentment, an expression of energy, and an invitation to contemplation. Even so, a couple of hours after leaving the exhibition at the Barnes, I was delighted to engage the simplicity of Wilmington's ballpark—its open spaces and its transparent celebrations of accomplishment.

Unlike the style of the Impressionist works at the Barnes, a realistic sculpture of Judy Johnson greets fans and graces the pedestrian spaces between the parking lot and the ballpark's main gate. A lifelong Delaware resident and the Negro Leagues' premier third-baseman, Johnson had batted over .400 in one season and had been enshrined in Cooperstown in 1975.

Banners identifying successful Blue Rocks players who had made it to The Show hung above the concession concourse. And numerical tributes to Wilmington stars added a personal character to the splay of ads on the outfield fence. Affixed to the light standard in right field, a baseball featuring Robin Roberts's jersey number (#36) represented the first number retired by the Blue Rocks. Inducted into the Hall of Fame in 1976, Roberts had won nine games for Wilmington in 1948, his only partial season with the team before being called up to the Phillies before mid-summer.

Above the left-field wall, two other numbers appeared, one retired, the other marking an accomplishment. A Sweeney jersey with "#33" honored former Blue Rocks first-baseman Mike Sweeney. A five-time major league all-star with a career batting average of .297, Sweeney was widely respected for his community service and his vibrant faith, exemplified by his serving as president of Catholic Athletes for Christ.

The other honorific number—871—appeared with a microphone and the name of John McAdams, the original P.A. announcer for the Blue Rocks who had died in 2005. The figure identifies the number of games that he had announced during his tenure with the team. Known for his smooth, booming voice, he had taken great pride in making sure that players' names were pronounced correctly.

His successor in the booth provided me with a precise introduction about the anthem tour that ended with the request, "Please welcome Joe Price, professor from Whittier College." And the fans did. They applauded *before* I sang—and afterward as well.

My warm reception in Wilmington had begun months earlier in pleasant correspondence with Blue Rocks general manager Chris Kemple to set up the date for my singing. Chris personalized the coordination of the scheduling process by letting me know that he had Southern California roots. He had grown up in Whittier, attended high school nearby in Hacienda Heights, and then graduated from San Diego State University. Recognized by *Baseball America* as Minor League Executive of the Year in 2004, Chris completed the gracious welcome in person by greeting me in the conference room where I was given a chance to warm up.

Several additional factors contributed to the delightful experience at the ballpark. For starters, the team name was intriguing: the Blue Rocks. I wondered whether that was the name of a species of shellfish native to the Chesapeake Bay, but I learned that the name instead refers to blue granite that is found nearby in outcroppings along the Brandywine River.

The mascot's name was similarly charming. With a moniker of "Rocky Bluewinkle," the mascot impersonated a blue moose whose name plays upon the popularity of the cartoon characters Rocky (a flying squirrel) and Bullwinkle (an anthropomorphic moose). Like most of the friendly mascots at ballparks, Rocky enchanted kids, joyfully posing with them for souvenir photographs.

And the food was unusually fresh and flavorful, with carved meets available at a make-your-own sandwich station. Even so, one young fan added to the flavor of his pizza after it tumbled from his plate beneath his seat. Undeterred by dirt on the concrete, the boy then downed most of the pepperoni, smearing cheese and sauce across his face while sharing his hatful of popcorn with his sister.

Adding to the elements of the ballpark's ambiance was the chance to see Wilmington's highly touted starting pitcher, Jake Odorizzi. A first-round draft selection out of high school by the Milwaukee Brewers three years earlier, Odorizzi had been the key acquisition by Kansas City in its trade of Cy Young Award winner Zack Greinke to the Brewers during the previous winter. On this night, however, Odorizzi gave up five runs in six innings, with Wilmington losing to Salem 5-3. Summoned to the manager's office after the game, Odorizzi was surprised by the manager's message—that, despite his lackluster performance that evening, he was being promoted to Kansas City's Double-A affiliate in Northwest Arkansas.

Still, the most significant factor in making the ballpark experience so enjoyable was that I could see several fans joining me in singing "The Star-Spangled Banner." Among them was Ron, a staff member assigned to monitor the VIP suites. He told me that, as a tenor, he had harmonized with my low-key rendition, and he was pleased to let me know that he regularly served as the relief performer for the Blue Rocks when scheduled singers failed to show up.

As I left the ballpark, Matt Robinson stopped to congratulate me. "Thanks. Good job," he said. "Thanks for singing it the way it's supposed to be." Before the game, he had learned of my project from one of the Blue Rocks interns who had been his student in sports management at the University of Delaware. After the disruptions in my schedule earlier in the week, it was certainly good to get back in the game with baseball and an appreciated performance of the national anthem in Wilmington.

Beating Derek Jeter: Game 59 in Trenton

By one game I beat Derek Jeter to Trenton, and missed seeing him on his rehab assignment for the next two days. As the Yankees Double-A affiliate in the Eastern League, the Trenton Thunder occasioned a frequent final stop for players recovering from injuries and preparing for return to New York's active roster.

Although I didn't get to sing for Jeter this time, I did get to meet and greet Thunder usher Mike Nolan who, after hearing my introduction and rendition, requested that I come to his section to talk for an inning or two. For four years, Mike had been pursuing a goal of seeing a game in every professional ballpark in the country. His tally had climbed to 166, and he expected to add to that number a few weeks later on a trip to Columbus and Indianapolis, where our schedules would converge.

Mike was curious about the multiple attractions and passions that lure fans to baseball games. He estimated that at minor league games about ten percent of the fans would be die-hard devotees to baseball. So he wondered what would prompt the majority of attendees to spend an evening at the ballpark. Its relatively low cost for entertainment? Its outdoor setting on a summer evening? Its playful dramas during mid-inning antics? Its featured guest performers like BirdZerk? Its frequent promotional giveaways of tee-shirts, caps, and bobble-heads? On and on he mused about the possibilities.

He classified his favorite ballparks according to level. In Triple-A he preferred Durham's bullish image and Memphis's urban landscape, with its wafting smells of barbecue from the Rendezvous Restaurant close by. In Double-A he liked Altoona, with its roller-coaster backdrop, and Jacksonville, where he had learned the ballpark's ins-and-outs from the head groundskeeper. And in Class-A—well, before we got around to discussing his selections for that level, we were interrupted by fans needing to be seated in his section.

While I was delighted to find new friends at the ballpark, I found much greater joy in sharing the experience with longtime friends Jerry Fiddler and Missy Alden. In August 1991 Bonnie and I had met Jerry and Missy during an educational technology tour that we had made to the Soviet Union, where each of us made presentations in a conference hosted by Soviet physicists. A unique event occurred during that trip: While we had entered the USSR, we returned from Russia. Although we didn't cause the Soviet coup and the dissolution of its union of socialist republics, we had arrived in Moscow at dawn, disembarking from the overnight train from St. Petersburg while tanks rolled into Red Square. Two days later we aborted our plans to spend another week touring the country, and we boarded a flight to Helsinki. Upon arrival there, I was so thrilled to enjoy the freedom of an American that I sang "The Star-Spangled Banner" for our group after we deplaned.

Jerry, Missy, Bonnie, and I had bonded during the two weeks that we had spent working with Russian scientists and educators, and in years since we had enriched our friendship in various educational and recreational activities. Annually we had convened at ed-tech meetings; and Jerry, who had studied music theory and composition before becoming a computer programmer and co-founder of Wind River Systems, had made two visionary presentations to my students and faculty colleagues about technologies' impacts on—and possibilities for—liberal education, organizational structures, and economic and environmental sustainability. More leisurely, during one August we had sailed together for several days in the San Juan Islands, and on multiple occasions we had attended baseball games in Oakland and Los Angeles.

When we arrived at the ballpark, Jerry accompanied me to the green room where I could warm up. And incredible though it now seems to me, I let him take photographs of me doing some of the odd facial exercises to loosen up before singing scales and a "vowels-only" run through the anthem. As zany as my exercises might seem, a weird thing also happened to Jerry before we left for the field. When Chad Heidel, my contact with the Thunder, came to get us, Jerry bumped the phone on the table, and it rang. No one was calling—but the jostle of the Nortel phone had caused it to ring. Jerry laughed: "I wrote the software for this phone." Then while he pressed other buttons and reset the receiver, he quipped that he must have left that bump sequence out of the program!

My anthem performance was among my best of the season, and I am sure that the luxury of sharing a few days with good friends put me in an upbeat state of mind. Natalie, one of the fans near our seats, observed, "I could see the joy of the anthem come through when you sang." She inquired about the tour, places where I had been, and destinations in the coming days. As I turned back to my seat, she calmly and compassionately said, "Grace in your journey." While many along the way had commented about the challenges of travel, she was the first to offer a blessing. Others also expressed appreciation for my enthusiasm, especially at the start of the patriotic holiday weekend.

Another fan introduced himself as Stephen and asked if I had sung the anthem in the key of G. "Close," I replied. "Although I sometimes sing it in that key, tonight I sang it in F-sharp." Since he taught orchestral strings, specializing in bass, he expressed particular appreciation for the lower register in the descending triads in the first few lines of the tune. He said that as a baritone he was delighted to hear the rendition in a lower key. At various times on the tour, I had been asked for my autograph. Stephen became the first person to ask me to be photographed with him and his fiancée.

To say that it was a wild night at Trenton's ballpark would be an understatement. The ballpark's tributes featured a wild disjunction of sorts—a memorial to a Red Sox all-star seemed to hover over the Yankees prospects. Featured on the face of the press box directly behind home plate was the retired "#5"—not for the parent Yankees DiMaggio but for the former Red Sox favorite Nomar Garciaparro, whose name also appeared there. Garciaparro, who had grown up and played Little League ball in Whittier, had played for the Trenton team when he had been rising through the minors.

A temporary wildness of sorts also characterized the evening. Dogs were everywhere. They had been admitted on leashes as a project to raise funds for a charity. For every dog that entered the park with its owner, a donation would be made. Seeing all of the friendly dogs (except for one yappy Chihuahua mix), I realized how homesick I was for my dogs Winston (a three-year-old Havanese) and Tucker (a year-old Cockapoo). So when I saw Lisa and her ten-month-old Havanese named Elvis, I went wild taking their photographs.

And the outcome of the game was also largely determined by wild Thunder—at least their pitchers' lack of control. Although the Curve hadn't won in the dozen days since I had sung for their home game in Altoona, they didn't act Thunder-struck this night, using six walks, three hit batters, and three wild pitches to supplement their hits en route to a 10-5 trumping of Trenton.

Northern Heights: Game 60 in Burlington, Vermont

The Vermont Lake Monsters make their home in Burlington, which was the northernmost point in the eastern portion of my tour. Whether it or Lowell, Massachusetts, was the ballpark city farthest from Whittier might be determined by how distance was determined—by air miles or by highway route. In either case, the Lake Monsters game on the Fourth of July weekend became a Northeastern peak of the anthem tour.

For this final game on their home-stand on the holiday weekend, the Lake Monsters' pregame festivities featured Vermont Governor Peter Shumlin. Waiting for the governor to arrive, Vermont's assistant general manager Joe Doud gave me a tour of the ballpark and expressed his delight in scheduling my anthem performance in conjunction with July 4 and the governor's appearance. Following his arrival and introduction to several civic leaders, the governor and I chatted briefly about pregame routines of throwing out the first pitch and singing the anthem. He had heard advice about aiming high for the target since he would be throwing downhill from the mound, and I had received instruction about the stadium's microphone idiosyncrasies.

Before taking the mound to throw out the first pitch, he spoke briefly about the significance of Independence Day, the importance of Vermont as the greatest state in the Union, and the prominence of the Lake Monsters as the best team in the league. Indeed, at the beginning of the game, Vermont had stood atop the league standings. In addition to the governor's participation, the first-pitch ceremony featured an innovative way to promote the service of a sponsor. Rather than the P.A. announcer simply saying that the ritual was sponsored by Brick Oven Pizza, the ball for the first pitch was delivered to the mound in a pizza box. I wondered when was the last time the governor had received personal delivery from a pizza guy.

Moments later, I was introduced as touring the country during the season to sing the anthem in as many minor league ballparks as possible, perhaps justifying to Vermont citizens why a Californian would be on the pregame program with Governor Shumlin. Following my rendition, the governor said, "You hit it out of the park. You're a better singer than I am a pitcher!" That was true. Standing in front of the rubber, he had thrown a fifty-five-foot slider. Actually, his pitch wasn't intended to be a breaking ball. It simply hit the dirt in front of the plate and slid past the catcher.

The ballpark in Burlington is one of the most historic in the nation. Of course, Rickwood Field in Birmingham is the oldest, but it schedules only a single game each year for the Birmingham Barons. Also built earlier than Burlington's ballpark is one in Pittsfield, Massachusetts, where the first collegiate game was played. Now restored, the one in Pittsfield has hosted various minor league franchises over the years. In 2011, it provided the home for the Pittsfield Colonials, an unaffiliated minor league team in the CANAM League. Still, Centennial Park in Burlington could claim to be the oldest ballpark that provides a home for an affiliated minor league team.

During its earliest years the ballpark had served as the home for the team at the University of Vermont, and in 1955 it hosted its first minor league games. The original wooden grandstands at Centennial had been erected in the early part of the twentieth century, and the aged character of the ballpark was apparent before reaching its grandstand with a steep pitch and narrow rows. As I entered the vomitory on my way to the field, I heeded the warning of low clearance and ducked to avoid hitting my forehead.

Like other municipal ballparks of the era whose area for general admission was open space, Centennial Park didn't have seats or benches in the area, merely wide risers. But unlike the custom at Pulaski's vintage ballpark, which shared a similar structure, none of the fans in Burlington brought folding chairs to prop up on the wide tiers. Instead, they simply sat on the cement and used cushions to soften their perches.

The playing field was also quirky in a couple of other ways, one affecting a possible home run, the other a fair ball. In dead centerfield the grounds crew's access gate was hung about six inches higher than the adjoining outfield wall. Consequently, the yellow home-run line atop the outfield fence jutted up a half-foot in that section. Somewhat similarly, the foul poles displayed banners for Fairpoint Communications, a regional telephone service. Grinning about their placement, I wondered if the Fairpoint signs really helped the umpires determine whether a long-lofted ball was fair.

The antics of the Lake Monsters mascots also added to the fun of the afternoon. A new mascot, Chippy the Chipmunk, was making his debut in 2011 to complement the actions of and attraction to Champ the Lake Monster, who had been a local celebrity for a number of years. Chippy's featured activity was leading kids on a run across the outfield before the bottom of the fourth. While the visiting Tri-City ValleyCats were making their between-inning warm-up throws, the children chased Chippy along the edge of the outfield grass from the third-baseline to first.

Champ's efforts were even more energetic than those of darting Chippy. When the Lake Monsters put runners on first and second, Champ climbed atop the ValleyCats dugout and began to lead a cheer for the home team as only a mute mascot could do. Using his clown-oversized shoes, he stomp-stomped the top of the dugout, followed by clap-clapping. Again. And again. The crowd quickly joined in and the noise became quite a distraction to the players in the dugout, especially with Champ's feet thudding above their heads. Although the ValleyCats in the dugout soon surrendered, tossing out paper cups rather than waving a white flag, their teammates on the field yielded a run but didn't relinquish the lead.

The Lake Monsters delayed their game-winning rally until the ninth inning. Entering the frame trailing 6-3, Vermont started to rebound on an unusual play. With one out, Jordan Tripp swung and missed a third strike, a wild pitch reminiscent of the governor's pregame toss. Escaping the catcher, the ball rolled toward the backstop and allowed Tripp to trip to first. Following a walk to the next batter, two teammates singled in runs to cut the deficit. Then with two runners on base, Jacob Tanis struck out before Diomedes Lopez tied the score with a line-drive single. Following a pitching change and yet another base-on-balls, Seth Jamieson fought off two two-strike pitches before delivering the game-winning single and sending the Lake Monsters crowd home celebrating the holiday-weekend victory.

Even having shared the opening ceremonies with the governor, the good times that Bonnie and I enjoyed in Vermont were more personal than political. They were rooted in good friendship. A couple of days before the Burlington game, Jerry Fiddler and Missy Alden had joined us in Trenton and had accompanied us in Arbie for a couple of days as we trekked north to enjoy Missy's family's retreat atop a mountain at Royalton before making our way on to Burlington with them.

8.

A Human Home Run

Shots Abounding and Resounding: Game 61 in Lowell

Perhaps Toad was homesick. Having spent most of his odometer's 75,000 miles in and around Whittier before our purchase of him and Arbie, he experienced intense distress during his dislocation to remote New England.

While corkscrewing up mountain roads in Vermont where Arbie could not venture, Toad had begun to fret about feeling feverish. In an effort to cool him down before leaving the mountaintop at Royalton, I had given him a dose of antifreeze after noticing that his fluid looked rusty. At that time I hoped that our excessive use of the air conditioner during weeks of record heat had really been the cause of his temporary high temperature.

Reconnecting with Arbie in Brattleboro where we had left him to avoid difficulties with Vermont's slaloming and sloping highways, we descended into Massachusetts, turning on the Mass Pike east to Palmer, exiting on US 20 toward Brimfield, before veering south on State Highway 19 to Wales. A month earlier a series of tornadoes, a freakish storm cluster in the Northeast, had swept through the region, leveling homes in Brimfield and cutting a half-mile-wide swath through the dense forests along the route to Wales. When we had Googled the RV park where we had set up reservations, the images still showed the hillsides draped with lush forests before the storm had scoured the landscape. Thankfully, the Oak Haven Campground in Wales had narrowly missed the destructive path of the whirlwinds, and we were able to nestle Arbie among several RVs in a shaded area.

Although Wales was more than an hour's drive from the nearest minor league ballpark, it was somewhat centrally located for games in Lowell, Pawtucket, Norwich, New Britain, and even New Hampshire. For several days then, we could remain anchored at the single site while bungee-ing back and forth in Toad to scheduled ballparks.

En route to the first game in the region, however, I began to suspect that Toad's circulatory problem was more critical than I had perceived on Vermont's mountain roads. And during the late-night, ninety-mile return to

Wales from Lowell, it was necessary to stop twice to give Toad a break and let his engine cool. Yet Toad's distress did not diminish the shot in the arm that I had experienced during the doubleheader for the Spinners in Lowell.

The association of shots with baseball usually means that a home run has rocketed over the fence. But in Lowell on the evening following July 4, the dramatic shots were not tape-measure home runs; instead, they were fired from muskets by fans dressed as Colonial soldiers from North Middlesex County. Often throughout the Lowell Spinners baseball season, these minutemen presented the colors at the beginning of games. But because their flagbearer had not arrived in time for this pregame ceremony, Courtney, a staff intern with the Spinners, volunteered to carry the flag. Her presence seemed incongruous even though she bore the colors. She was the lone woman among the minutemen who carried guns, while she carried the flag. The men wore costumes from the eighteenth century while she wore shorts and a Spinners staff tee-shirt from the twenty-first century. And following my singing of the anthem, they fired their muskets in salute while she winced at the explosion.

During the game they also fired their arms when a Spinner would cross home plate. Since the home team scored eleven times in the seven-inning first game of the twin bill, the minutemen were hardly able to reload their muskets fast enough to shoot repeatedly for each run.

Despite the frequency of their firing, the musketeers were not the main shooting attraction of the game. The Human Cannonball—David Smith, Sr., who held the world record for human projection from a cannon at more than 201 feet—became the first "Human Home Run." The attraction had been publicized in ads and blogs and media in days leading up to the event.

When I had first learned of the promotion, I had hoped to see a cannon placed in the batter's box and a stuntman then propelled over one of the outfield fences. Even at a cozy ballpark like the one in Asheville where the distance down the line was less than 300 feet, a human home run would have bettered the world record by almost fifty percent.

I was a little disappointed when I saw that Smith's cannon was rolled to an outfield position about halfway between second base and the right centerfield wall. When a kid in the grandstands watched the Spinners staffers place a tarp to protect the field while the cannon was being rolled out, I heard him muse, somewhat prophetically, "What's the worst thing that could happen? Damaging the field?"

No. We all knew that the worst thing might be that Smith could hit the outfield wall head-first, or that he might land in the trees, or that he might miss the acrobat's net beyond the outfield wall. Yet what appeared to be of most immediate concern to the Spinners was the condition of the outfield grass.

Because Smith's son, who had been scheduled to be the first Human Home Run, had withdrawn from the production a few days earlier, the senior Smith, age sixty-nine, had inserted himself into the event. He climbed into the barrel of the cannon and, after a launch-like countdown, he was shot over the fence.

The spectacle was incredible. The crowd oohed and aahed, cheered, and applauded.

After emerging through the outfield fence like an astronaut opening the hatch to his space capsule after an ocean splashdown, Smith waved to the fans and began a victory lap toward home. Stopping at first base, he was interviewed about his experience of flying over the fence.

Excerpts: "What does it feel like when you're up there?"

"It feels free."

"How did you get started as a human cannonball?"

"I was a schoolteacher," he said, "and that was too tough!"

Oh, too true!

While athletes often use interviews as a means to offer a brief testimony, Smith used a different vehicle to express his faith. In big bold letters he emblazoned the base of his powerful cannon with a single word: JESUS.

Indeed his feat of clearing the right-field wall—and the row of trees behind it—was spectacular. Even ESPN had taken notice. Thomas Neumann, one of its online editors, attended the game to document the event. Having arrived early enough to catch the first game of the doubleheader, unlike most of the fans, Thomas also caught my anthem rendition, interviewed me during the middle innings, and blogged his story on the ESPN website the following day.

Not only is Lowell known for its Colonial reenactments and its modern fascination with rocketry, it is also well-known for its inventive promotions. Over the years it has become legendary for its creative bobble-head giveaways, one of the most famous being the image of Jack Kerouac, a sample now archived in the Baseball Hall of Fame. And when Jonathan Papelbon, then the ace closer for the Red Sox, was recognized with his own likeness, fans had lined up for blocks before the front gates opened.

For the most part the Spinners had designed their bobble-headed features to promote fan devotion to the Red Sox, Lowell's parent club, or to notable Massachusetts persona. Unusual selections joining Kerouac included a piece representing Stephen King, who certainly claims at least princely stature in Red Sox Nation. His bobble-head likeness was distributed on a Friday the 13th, and its base listed the titles of his three favorite novels among those he has authored: *The Dark Tower*, *The Dead Zone*, and *The Green Mile*. Another baseball-fan favorite was the bobble-head of Massachusetts's native Emeril Lagasse that was given out on the day that Katrina struck New Orleans. (I wondered if his image came with a sound chip exclaiming, "Bam!")

In a way the Lowell ballpark seems to typify the democratic identification of a community with a team, not merely by the inclusion of Massachusetts notables in the series of souvenir figures but also by the design of the grandstands. There was little distinction in viewing angle or closeness to field between the box seats and general admission; and there were no elegantly appointed luxury boxes atop the stadium or at dugout level. Instead, the VIP suites were a couple of rooms adjacent to the press booth and accessible from the concourse level. The named one—a Yawkey suite, of course—had no fans in it during the first game of the evening, only a staff member retreating to text her friends.

After Smith, who was wearing Spinners jersey #37, had soared over the fence, the pitching coach for the Spinners, also wearing uniform #37, looked up at me in the right-field stands and said, "Are you the guy who sang the national anthem?"

I nodded yes.

"Aren't you from Whittier, California?"

Again, yes.

"Didn't you sing last year at Fullerton?"

Score my replies a triple! Pitching coach Paul Abbott of the Lowell Spinners had heard my introduction and made the association of my singing with the previous summer's rendition for the Orange County Flyers, an independent minor league team in the Gold Coast League. Having been in the ballpark in Fullerton that afternoon, he had heard the introduction of me as a professor at Whittier College. That bit of info had lodged in his mind like a ball stuck in the web of a glove.

Still, I wondered why Smith had worn the pitching coach's number as the uniform when he became the first Human Home Run: Shouldn't identification with the pitching coach suggest a strikeout possibility? Shouldn't Smith have preferred a powerful slugger's number? Wouldn't a home run embarrass a pitching coach?

In the doubleheader's first game, home-run power was provided by Seth Schwindenhammer, whose surname clobbered the season's competition for having the most letters. In the fourth inning, Seth blasted a grand-slam home run, prompting shots by the Middlesex militia and propelling the Spinners to an insurmountable lead against the Connecticut Tigers. Final scores: Spinners 11, Tigers 7. And Smith, Sr., 1; Smith, Jr., 0.

A Long Way from Home: Game 62 in New Hampshire

After overheating on the return from Lowell to Arbie in Wales, Toad rebuffed the chance to see Manchester, New Hampshire, by one measure our itinerary's farthest point from Southern California. So I dropped Toad off at the D&M Auto Repair at the eastern edge of Palmer several miles from Arbie's resting place. Because the mechanics couldn't complete a circulation diagnosis and radiator flush until the following morning, I faced a big problem: That very evening, my one game scheduled in New Hampshire was about 125 miles away. Understanding my predicament, the manager of the shop called a used-car rental operation on the other side of town.

About forty-five minutes later, the owner arrived with a wreck rental, which I was delighted to see even though it looked more decrepit than Toad and smelled like a high-school boys' bathroom—scuzzy and smoky. Yet I couldn't beat its rental rate—$38.52 for the day—and especially its availability. Despite its questionable aura, it easily ambled along the Mass Pike and the interstate highways around Worcester, northward through Nashua, and on to Manchester to get me to the game ahead of schedule. Later, of course, I was equally pleased that, battling inclement weather and running well past its normal curfew, the car behaved respectably during our safe return to Wales.

By renting the wreck, I defeated the automotive demons, but the weather wizards threatened to undo my singing in New Hampshire. When we arrived in Manchester, the darkening sky foreboded thunderstorms, and as the pregame ceremonies started, the thunderous rumble grew suddenly louder although there had been no apparent lightning zaps nearby. Surprisingly, the booms weren't the reverberations of thunderclaps but the deafening sounds of an approaching jet in a direct flyover. Although I had been accompanied by honor guards for the presentation of colors at several ballparks, I had not experienced the tribute of an Air Force squadron or Navy fighter timed to coincide with the final strains of the anthem. Alas, there was no transcendent military salute to the anthem that night. A UPS transport was altering its final approach into the Manchester-Boston Regional Airport in order to circumvent the threatening thunderheads.

Unlike the pregame preparations at all of the other ballparks on the tour, the New Hampshire Fisher Cats cordoned off an area for participants. Was the rope there to prevent us from straying onto the field? Or was its function to discourage players from hitting on the frilly-dressed intern who assumed a ceremonial role as the tooth fairy? Or was it intended to set prowling limits for fisher cats, a possibility that raised a more essential question: What is a fisher cat?

I had no clue. But a staff member at the information kiosk gave me a profile of the small mammal that grows to a little more than ten pounds. The odd thing about the critter is that it is so misnamed. It is neither a member of the feline family—it's akin to a weasel—nor does it fish. Incredibly, it is one of the few predators of porcupines. More striking than these specious characteristics of the fisher cat is its haunting cry.

Even more difficult to understand than the fisher cat's genus was the name of New Hampshire's opponent, the New Britain Rock Cats—which aren't really cats, but the name of a mascot concocted by one of the team's officials who had probably loved rock music and the moniker's pun with the "Rockettes" from Radio City Music Hall.

At a few ballparks where some fans had occasionally remained seated during the national anthem, I could often see others continuing to talk while I sang. But in Manchester, I enjoyed a radically different experience. Beyond the warning track and wall in left-centerfield, a Hilton Hotel rose higher than the grandstands behind home plate. In many respects, it resembled—at least in concept—the integration of the Renaissance Toronto Hotel into the design of the Blue Jays SkyDome, as that ballpark had been initially known. In Manchester, the terrace of the Hilton Garden Inn adjoined the fence, faced the ballpark, and provided patio umbrellas to shield guests from the shriek of the sun more than the splash of rain, all the while enabling patrons to enjoy bleacher views of the ballgame. As I began to sing "The Star-Spangled Banner," I noticed that the Hilton's guests stood at their tables and faced the flag briskly waving beneath the light standard in left field.

In the second inning, rain delayed the game for about an hour, during which I huddled on the first base concourse with Brian Moynahan, a blogger for the Bus Leagues Baseball site. For more than half an hour he interviewed me about the anthem tour.

When play resumed in the third inning, New Britain scored a run without a hit. Its second batter reached base on a fielding error—a sloppy throw by the third-baseman that allowed the hitter to reach first safely and advance to second. Moments later, the pitcher also lost his grip on the ball and threw a wild pitch, allowing the runner to advance to third and then score on a routine grounder. After the third out, the rain intensified and the grounds crew was summoned again to cover the field. Although I had already experienced rain delays on multiple occasions, and although I had suffered a soggy cancellation at Potomac (as I would again two nights later in New Britain), this game was the only one throughout the tour that got suspended: New Britain 1, New Hampshire 0, middle of the third inning. The next day while Bonnie and I were driving rejuvenated Toad to Hudson Valley, the game picked up where it had left off with New Hampshire trailing. Twice in the eighth and ninth innings, the Fisher Cats scored to tie before eventually losing to the Rock Cats in the twelfth.

Even though our ballpark experience had been cut short, I did notice a cream theme among its concessions and ads. Most striking was the forty-foot high image of a milk jug in foul territory beyond the left-field fence. While I had seen huge banners attached to outfield light stanchions and enormous billboards extend above scoreboards at other ballparks, I had not seen such a gigantic ad placed in foul territory, which was somewhat ironic since the Hood Dairy jug promoted its light-blocking plastic that would protect milk from turning foul. Still, if a long fly ball hit the big image of the jug, it would indeed be foul and would leave a sour taste in the batter's mouth.

Two of the concession stands also rose to the cream theme. One served Hoodwich ice-cream sandwiches, a bewitching treat created by New Hampshire's Hood Dairy that featured chocolate-chip cookie wafers. And nearby, as might be expected in New England, the alluring Chowdah House offered bowls of creamy clam chowder as well as lobster rolls.

Doubling Up: Game 63 in Hudson Valley

Near the Military Academy at West Point, the Hudson Valley Renegades count on the availability of the institution's staff members to work part-time during the short season of the New York-Penn League. While I was not sure if they might be considered renegade employees, I wondered when they might be considered AWOL from the academy.

Although none of the fans at the Hudson Valley ballparks wore military uniforms or sported Army tee-shirts in mid-July, it was apparent from their haircuts, demeanor (especially their crisp salute of the flag during the anthem), and conversation that many of them were affiliated with the academy. Rather than displaying military apparel, many fans had slipped on the Renegades jerseys given to the first 1,500 entering the turnstiles.

Since Bonnie and I had arrived at the Hudson Valley ballpark later than usual, all of the shirts had been snagged by fans who had stood in line waiting for the gates to open. Although we didn't get the promotional item, we were thrilled that we did receive the support of two Whittier friends who joined us for the game: Michelle Cervantes, one of my former students who worked in the United Nations, and Mike McBride, a close colleague in political science whose campus office is almost adjacent to mine.

Michelle's responsibilities at the U.N., I think, are reflected in her job title, whose length rivals the distance of our drive from Wales. Officially, she served as "the Senior Policy Coordination Assistant for the New York Office of the United Nations High Commissioner for Refugees." On occasions when she had returned to California to visit family, Michelle had attended Angels and Dodgers games when I had sung the anthem.

Mike, too, was a repeat attender at games for which I had sung, and several years ago he had persuaded a tour guide at old Busch Stadium in St. Louis to let me sing the anthem at home plate in the empty ballpark a week before the season opened. Amazingly, the cavernous edifice there resonated like a shower stall since its empty wooden seats, artificial surface, and concrete and steel structure reverberated my voice. Staff members emerged from offices to hear and see what was happening, and maintenance workers in the outfield stands paused during the anthem, applauding after I reached the final note. As much fun as singing in St. Louis had been, I don't count that ballpark among the twenty-one major league stadiums where I have sung for games.

Mike's love of baseball rivals my own. He regularly teaches a writing seminar on baseball history. For the course he usually takes students to see a Dodgers game, and for another assignment he has them play Town Ball, often inviting me to join in the fun. Mike's devotion to the game extends well beyond his familiarity with its history and literature. In the mid-1980s after the publication of the book about the original Rotisserie League, he organized a fantasy league for Whittier College faculty. For more than three decades, he has continued to compile and calculate the weekly statistics for the league. In a more significant respect, I owe my hobby of singing the anthem at ballparks to him because he was the one who won the bid in the fundraising auction for the lunch with Don Sutton, and he was the one who invited me and my two sons to join his entourage for the noon meal at which Sutton urged me to contact the Dodgers to sing for them.

In the ballpark at Hudson Valley, multiple surfaces were used to feature former greats of the game—none, however, dating back to its primeval Town Ball days. Ushering fans toward the entry gate, one wall displayed plaques honoring members of the Pro Baseball Scouts Hall of Fame, and inside the turnstiles a Wall of Recognition familiarized fans with two Hall of Famers from the nearby area. Eddie Collins, who had grown up in Millerton, is ranked among the best second-basemen of all time. During a quarter-century playing at the keystone for the Philadelphia Athletics and the Chicago White Sox, he excelled at bat and on the base paths. Seventeen times in his career, he stole home, and twice he stole six bases in a single game. He and Ty Cobb were the pair of preeminent base-stealers in their day, like Lou Brock and Rickey Henderson in the latter half of the twentieth century. Also celebrated with a plaque on the Hudson Valley wall was Dennis "Big Dan" Brouthers from Wappingers Falls. He had begun his nineteen-year big-league career in 1879 with the nearby Troy Trojans in the National League. During the dead-ball era, he was considered the greatest power hitter, slugging more than 100 home runs in his career while compiling a lifetime batting average of .342.

A different wall tribute of sorts displayed the retired numbers of two players: Discs with "#42" and "#45" peered like binocular lenses above the left-field fence. Of course, #42 had been unilaterally retired by Major League Baseball as a way of recognizing the contributions of Jackie Robinson. "But #45"? I wondered aloud to several uninformed staffers until one identified it as the number of Kevin Brown, the first Hudson Valley player to star in the major leagues. Not to be confused with all-star pitcher James Kevin Brown who won more than 200 games, mostly for the Rangers and Dodgers, Kevin Lee Brown had been a catcher for Hudson Valley in his first year of professional play. Appearing in most of the team's games that season, he compiled a non-descript record, averaging a strike out more than once a game and batting less than .250. His defensive skills, however, eventually advanced him to the major leagues where he served effectively as a back-up catcher for seven seasons.

The walls in a more private area of the ballpark also provided an opportunity for displaying baseball themes, not in tribute to bygone heroes but in a playful effort to appeal to the youngest possible fans. Because I often found that the quietest, most out-of-the-way space to warm up at ballparks was in the family restroom, I was able to see the multiple murals of animals playing baseball on the walls of that sequestered space at Hudson Valley. While other ballparks had provided diaper-changing tables in their facilities, none had been as clever and inviting as this one with murals of animals engaged in baseball and circus activities.

Beyond such wall decor, the ballpark at Hudson Valley also distinguished itself by offering several unique concessions. The healthy choices exceeded those at many other ballparks, adding gluten-free beer and a tastefully named sandwich, the Thai Cobb Veggie Burger. And the grill-to-order stand continued the playful approach to burger names, calling its monster sandwich the Eben Burger, in honor of the team's general manager Eben Yager. The Eben Burger, which was subject to continuous modification according to Eben's tastes, started with a half-pound hamburger stuffed with cheddar cheese and A-1 steak sauce, then grilled to order.

While I salivated for either of these burgers, I knew that I shouldn't eat one before singing the anthem. At 6:25 participants in the pregame ceremonies were called to the first base dugout, and I joined the throng. In contrast to the confined space on the previous night in New Hampshire, where theater chains had cordoned off the place for pregame participants to stand until time to fill their roles, the area in front of the Renegades dugout almost looked like a flash-mob scene. There, fifty-three young ballet dancers in pink and maroon costumes playfully "plíed" and pirouetted in preparation for their pregame routines. They were joined by a score of their parents wielding video cameras and cell phones, a dozen softball players awaiting introduction, and the usual cadre of Little Leaguers preparing to take the field with the starting lineup. It was almost as crowded on the field as in the grandstands.

Inspired by the ambiance of West Point and the presence of good friends, I sang about as well as possible; and my rendition was enthusiastically embraced by the crowd, which respected the anthem with impeccable protocol. I was surprised, however, by the response of one of the fans. While returning to my seat, one woman stopped me and said, "Thank you. You sang it better than the people who were born here." Then she continued, "You're a foreigner, aren't you? You sing with an accent."

"No ma'am," I replied. "I grew up in the South, but I try to sing crisply and articulate each word clearly."

A few days earlier at another ballpark, a person had asked if I were Scottish because of the roundness of my vowels in "the dawn's early light." I guess that my attempts to enunciate each word clearly disguise some of my Southern accent.

For the most part, the game itself was a rather ho-hum affair. Both teams scored a single run in the first few innings, and then matched records through regulation: one run on three singles and one error apiece. But there was a twist to the action in the sixth when Renegades pitcher Mickey Jannis, who had entered the game at the top of the inning, gave up a questionable single, a soft line drive that had glanced off his glove toward the second-baseman. An odd sequence then developed. Jannis approached the foul line where he was met by the trainer, manager, catcher, and umpire. It didn't look like he had hurt his arm or leg since he didn't try to twirl his arm, rub his leg, or flex his knee. Pausing at the first-baseline, he simply left the field and went into the dugout; yet the manager and umpire summoned no new reliever.

A few minutes later Jannis returned and started toward the mound but turned back, calling for the trainer to supply tissue for his nose, which he had hit with his glove when he had deflected the weak liner. After Jannis had stuffed tissue into his nostril, the home-plate umpire determined that the white protrusion from his nose might distract the hitter. Back to the dugout Jannis went. After a twelve-minute delay, he finally resumed pitching, missing the strike zone on his first two offerings before getting the batter to ground into an inning-ending double play.

Following the ValleyCats' futile turn at bat in the top of the seventh, I led off the traditional mid-inning stretch by singing "God Bless America." In anticipation, players emptied from the dugouts, lined up and toed the grass, and took off their caps and held them at their side or dropped them by their shoes. They placed their hands over their hearts as though they were pledging allegiance to the flag. Impressed by their reverential respect for the song by Irving Berlin that Kate Smith had popularized, and inspired by the presence of friends and the proximity to West Point, I doubled my singing pleasure that evening.

With the score knotted 1-1 in the bottom of the eighth, fans along the third-baseline tried to rally the Renegades by starting a wave. It didn't work—neither the rally nor the wave. But in the tenth inning, the Renegades scratched out a run on Chris Winder's single and stolen base, followed by his advance to third on a ground out. With two outs then, he scored the winning run on a wild pitch.

For the second time in a week, I watched the ValleyCats suffer a catastrophic final inning because of a battery muff—a dropped third strike in the ninth had led to their defeat in Vermont, and now the extra-inning wild pitch in Hudson Valley allowed the Renegades to double their score: Hudson Valley 2, Tri-Cities 1.

All in all, it was also a kind of Wrigley-esque evening of doubling my pleasure and doubling my fun by singing twice and sharing the game with a duo of Whittier friends.

Sunshine and Shadows: Game 64 in Pawtucket

Located in a vintage neighborhood with triple-decked dwellings and irregular, narrow streets, Pawtucket's McCoy Stadium is distinct in several ways. Erected shortly after World War II on the site of Hammond's Pond, the ballpark had suffered from tales of vehicles disappearing in the continuing muck. And because of the ballpark's swampy location, the team had often been derided as the BogSox. Following its most recent renovation on the eve of the twenty-first century, McCoy became one of the statelier minor league ballparks, featuring elevated concourses with multiple levels of seating above and below the access aisles. In keeping with ballparks of yesteryear, the stadium's name was not auctioned to the highest corporate sponsor. Instead, it befitted the community, bearing the name of the former Pawtucket mayor who had engineered its construction. And unlike the recent tendency to elevate luxury boxes to the "sky level," the prime seats in Pawtucket were located at ground level, beneath box seats, open to the field, and adjacent to the dugouts. Symbolically read, the luxury boxes provided support for ordinary fans rather than peering down on them from an elitist perch.

While I was courteously received by staff at most ballparks, few proved as hospitable and gracious as the welcome that I received from the Pawtucket Red Sox. Immediately after Bonnie and I entered the pass gate, Jeff Bradley invited us into a hosted buffet to enjoy barbecue, baked beans, potato salad, and cold drinks. Not only did the party tent offer these refreshments; it also provided late-afternoon shade from the brilliant sunshine that had bathed us hours earlier when we had picnicked nearby at Oakland Beach, where we had feasted on Iggy's clam bellies and chowder.

Jeff's gestures of appreciation quickly began to restore Bonnie's pleasure at ballparks, which had been dampened—both literally and figuratively—the previous night in New Britain, Connecticut, home of the Rock Cats. Since a steady rain had fallen throughout the afternoon in New Britain, I had phoned the ballpark before leaving Starbucks to make sure that the game was still being played. As we approached the stadium parking lot, a young, summer city worker had been arrogant and rude, even when I explained that I was the anthem singer and had never been to the ballpark before. When I asked his name, he refused to give it, only willing to share his supervisor's name, who, he said, was not on site. Reluctantly, I paid the six-dollar fee, drove to a spot near the ticket window, and shielded myself with an umbrella while I approached the Will Call window, only to learn that the game had just been rained out.

Within minutes, we returned to the attendant's station, finding him as aloof as an imaginary Rock Cat and as sensitive as the hot tin roof on which the Rock Cat might prance and prowl for unsuspecting prey like me. He refused to refund our fee, in effect charging us simply to drive up to the gate to learn that the game was cancelled. The real parking rate thus computed to forty-five dollars an hour, more expensive than the tolls on the New York Thruway or a parking garage in Manhattan. To say the least, our impressions of New Britain put a major crimp in our minor league string. That sour experience in New Britain was especially disappointing since Rock Cats staff members—particularly, Kim Pizighelli—had been most accommodating and encouraging in scheduling and anticipating my anthem performance there. After the rainout, she had offered me the chance to sing the following afternoon for the make-up game; but my scheduled opportunity to sing in Rhode Island hours later took precedence.

By stark contrast to the New Britain fiasco, the experience at Pawtucket was most pleasant. The hospitality tent also offered us a relatively quiet place to sit before the pregame ceremonies, which featured two different elements for me—my position on the field and my sequence in pregame routines. I stood between home plate and the pitcher's mound, and I sang the anthem before the umpires had taken the field.

Not only were we cordially greeted by PawSox staffers when we entered the stadium; we also were joined for the game by Charlie Burke, one of my recent students, and his mother. Following his graduation at the end of the spring semester with a double major in French and Religious Studies, Charlie had returned to the Boston area for the summer, and he had corresponded with me for several weeks to make sure that we could get together during my time in New England.

In his first year at Whittier, Charlie had been assigned to my advising group and writing seminar on "Humor and Faith in Southern Fiction," in which he excelled. Throughout his four years, he continued to improve his writing skills, consummating his religious studies with a remarkably sophisticated research paper for my course on "Latin-American Liberation Theologies" a few months before I began the anthem tour.

On the opening day of students' registration when he had been a freshman, Charlie had made one of the most compassionate gestures by a student that I had witnessed in more than three decades of teaching. Learning that one of his fellow classmates would need to commute seventy-five miles to classes and would need to consolidate her schedule, Charlie offered his own opportunity for advanced registration to her and he encouraged and persuaded the rest of his group to do the same. Of course, getting registered for courses in a desirable schedule is a cherished goal, especially for an untested, entering student. To forego the chance to get a head-start with registration at that anxious and vulnerable time was an amazing gift to Dana. With that genuine gesture of team spirit, Charlie became an all-star in my book even though he was a voting citizen in Red Sox Nation. Throughout the game, we enjoyed reminiscing about Whittier, discussing religious studies, and considering possibilities for his career moves.

Interspersed throughout our academic conversation, Charlie took time to provide player profiles of former BoSox now in Pawtucket's lineup, and I reflected on the longest baseball game in history. Baseball, of course, has been deemed a timeless game, not simply because its rules are rarely revised, or because its pace occasionally lags, but because it is possible for a game to go on forever—like the mythic 2,000-inning game between the Chicago Cubs and the local all-stars from Big Inning, Iowa, in W.P. Kinsella's magical novel *The Iowa Baseball Confederacy.*

A generation earlier at Pawtucket, myth had infused history and history had elevated to myth. On April 18, 1981, the Rochester Red Wings, whose lineup featured Cal Ripken, came to bat at the usual time for the start of an evening game on Holy Saturday. A detailed account of the game is provided by Dan Barrry in his riveting narrative, *Bottom of the 33rd.* By the time of the seventh-inning stretch, the PawSox trailed 1-0 but, in the bottom of the ninth, tallied a run to tie the score. And that's the way things stood for more than another nine innings of shutout ball. Finally, in the twenty-second inning the Red Wings scored the go-ahead run, only to be matched in the bottom half of the frame by the rallying PawSox. Again, another stretch of more than nine innings of shutout ball ensued until 4:09 the following morning when, after thirty-two innings, the score was still knotted while a few of the remaining nineteen fans in the stands nodded off.

At that point the president of the International League intervened, ruling that the game could be suspended until the dawn of a new day, much like the fictional, multi-day game in Kinsella's account. When Rochester next visited Pawtucket on June 23, play resumed, with Bobby Ojeda pitching for the PawSox, who set the Red Wings down in order. Taking the mound for Rochester in the bottom half of the inning was a pitcher who had not been on the roster when the game had begun weeks earlier. In the bottom of the thirty-third, the PawSox loaded the bases with none out and scored, winning the longest game in history 3-2. Other future Boston stars who played in the game were catcher Rich Gedman, infielder Marty Barrett, pitcher Bruce Hurst, and Hall of Famer Wade Boggs, who happened to go four for twelve. And getting two hits for Rochester in the game was future Orioles stalwart shortstop Cal Ripken, Jr. In all, the play of the game stretched more than eight hours and took more than two months to complete. Often identified by fans as "a foretaste of eternity," baseball in this game in 1981 came about as close as possible to fulfilling that description.

As historic as McCoy Stadium was, it also featured several popular attractions for fans, young and old. With the setting sun warming their backs and the rise of the hill shadowing left field, fans of all ages could picnic on the berm beyond the fence. For younger fans, inflated bouncy rooms offered the chance to jump to their hearts' delight, and even the mascot's autograph and photograph station at Paw's Pavilion invited childish interaction, enticing kids to climb and slide down the slope of the glove-shaped sculpture.

The ballpark also displayed an unintentional comic curve—at least to Yankee fans—with the placement of one of the outfield ads. Hovering above the PawSox bullpen was an advertisement for a prominent liquor store in Massachusetts, Yankee Spirits. How ironic it appeared that future Red Sox relievers should warm up beneath a promotion for Yankee Spirits! The ghost of Babe Ruth and the spirit of Bucky Dent probably chortle loudly at that juxtaposition.

McCoy's diamond was also oriented in an unusual way. Left field lay in the west, meaning that, at sunset, the glare came directly over its outfield wall. The blinding light caused two successive errors that I had never seen. On multiple occasions I had seen fly balls lost in the sun or in stadium lights at night, even a line drive misplayed from its blending into the white shirts of fans behind the batter, but never had I seen a first-baseman lose sight of the ball on a throw from a fellow infielder. Yet the first baseman lost a throw from an infielder releasing the ball into the trajectory of the sun's blaze—not once, but twice, in the same inning.

On consecutive plays in the Sox unlucky seventh inning, Buffalo Bisons batters hit routine ground balls to the middle infielders. The second-baseman gloved the first one and made an easy throw that first-baseman Lars Anderson lost in the sun, shielding his face with his forearm as he thought the ball was approaching. The hitter reached second on the fielding error, and—to my surprise—the official scorer awarded an assist to the second-baseman on his throw, even though an out was not recorded. The next batter hit a broken-bat hopper to the shortstop, who cleanly fielded it and made an accurate throw to first that Anderson again lost in the setting sun! And again, the official scorer awarded the shortstop an assist on the play, even though no out was recorded.

Then with runners on the corners and one out, the batter hit a grounder to the shortstop. He shuffled the ball to the second-baseman, who pivoted at the bag and rifled a throw to first for the inning-ending double play. The catch of the relay by Anderson this time evoked both derisive and delighted cheers from the home crowd.

With the sun sinking and the shadows spreading into the blanket of dusk, Pawtucket held on for a 2-0 win; and Bonnie and I left the ballpark refreshed by the hospitality of the PawSox, our contact with the ballpark's history, and our friendship with the Burkes.

Legacies in Norwich: Game 65 in Connecticut

What do you call the offshoots of stars? Perhaps "asteroids," if you're focusing on heavenly bodies, or "starlets," if you're thinking of Hollywood. But if you're talking about ballplayers, their names might include Colin, Bo, and Patrick, all of whom played for the Connecticut Tigers in 2011. As offspring of former major league stars, Colin Kaline and Patrick Leyland seemed to have been born with the gene of Tiger stripes. Colin's grandfather Al, of course, had been a perennial all-star for Detroit for more than two decades, and Patrick's dad had managed the Tigers to a divisional championship in the American League during the previous season. They were joined in their Tigers legacy by pitcher Nick Avila, the son of one of Detroit's vice presidents.

But what about Bo McClendon? Although he did not come naturally by his Tiger paws, his father Lloyd had played for the Pirates in the late 1990s before becoming their manager for five years at the beginning of the twenty-first century. Although Bo had been drafted by a different team than his father's, he had earlier followed in his father's footsteps as a university ballplayer, having starred, like his father, at Valparaiso University.

Unlike his Hall of Fame grandfather, Colin did not enjoy an outstanding start to his professional career. Even so, there seemed to be something prescient about Donald Hall's musing about baseball and Kaline in his lead essay in *Fathers Playing Catch with Sons*: "Baseball is a game of years and of decades. Al Kaline's children grew up....And Kaline kept on hitting line drives." Drafted and signed a month before my appearance in Norwich, the twenty-one-year-old Colin was assigned to the Tigers short-season affiliate to begin his two-year pro career. By contrast, Al had been one of a handful of players who skipped the minor leagues altogether and made his major league debut as an eighteen-year-old outfielder for Detroit in early summer 1953.

Yet on this afternoon, Colin starred. In the second inning his single advanced a teammate to second, positioning him to score the game's first run on a subsequent hit. And in the sixth inning Kaline singled again, enjoying one of his best offensive outputs of the summer. A second-baseman, Colin finished the season with a .222 batting average, striking out in one-fifth of his plate appearances while collecting only six RBIs with no home runs.

While Patrick Leyland, a catcher, sat on the bench throughout the game, he fared about the same as Kaline during the season, getting an equal number of hits in one more at-bat, but also tagging one home run while doubling Kaline's number of RBIs.

The influx of Tigers prospects was most welcome to the Connecticut team since the 2011 season represented only the second year of its affiliation with the Tigers and the ballpark's demotion to a Short Season A-level schedule. In previous years the Connecticut team had operated at the Double-A level in the Eastern League, first for the Yankees, who moved their franchise to Trenton, followed by the Giants, who then moved their team to

Richmond. The last Connecticut Giants team had included six players who had been on San Francisco's World Championship roster in 2010. After losing these and other highly touted Giants prospects, the fans were delighted to welcome the arrival of recognizable Tigers names in Dodd Memorial Stadium.

While the pride of the Detroit Tigers' progeny honed their skills on the field, the Connecticut Tigers mascot—C.T., the Tiger—flubbed a couple of his standard routines. Typically, a team's mascot tries to tease fans, often playfully embarrassing them. This afternoon, however, C.T. got his own tail twisted, twice to the point of blushing through his feline mask.

After the third inning, C.T. invited a young fan to race him from first to third, with a planned joke coming at the foul line when C.T. would shoot the winning kid with a water gun. But this time, eleven-year-old Alex Russo upstaged C.T., not merely winning the race, as would be expected, but foiling the water gun ambush by cartwheeling safely across the third-base bag and sprinting on into the stands behind the dugout. Dumbfounded, C.T. merely put his hands akimbo on his stripes and shrugged. A couple of innings later, the mascot muffed another effort. This time, C.T. was supposed to shoot a souvenir tee-shirt into the stands. But his slingshot aim went awry, and the shirt *thwanged* into the dugout, narrowly missing manager Andrew Graham.

Somewhat like C.T.'s wild pitch, I threw a pregame curve to Dave Schermerhorn, the team's director of community relations and promotions. Having alerted the parking-lot staff to reserve several spaces for Arbie, he was disappointed to see us arrive in Toad, whose maneuverability had prompted us to follow blue highways from Wales to Norwich, first wending our way through Stafford Springs and then Willimantic before tracing a scenic, low ridge above the Shetucket River.

Following the pregame ceremonies, an appreciative usher asked Bonnie and me if we wanted to move from our assigned, sun-bleached boxes to more comfortable seats. Without hesitating, Bonnie turned to follow him up the aisle and staircase to the air-conditioned suites and their concession lounge. Officially, the temperature at the time of the first pitch of the afternoon had been ninety degrees, a reading that must have been registered in the shade of trees beyond the parking lot. Elsewhere, the sun's direct rays raged.

As memorable as the skybox was because of its relief from the heat and glare, the space made a greater impression because most of the other patrons in the room paid more attention to the game on telecast—the U.S. women's soccer miracle against Brazil—than to Connecticut's contest on the field with Brooklyn. One who was more interested in baseball than the Women's World Cup was the brother of Eric Ammerer, the broadcaster for the Tigers. Confessing that he had been a philosophy major in college, he queried me for several innings with philosophical concerns about the nature of good and evil, the relation between justice and peace, and the prospects for universal salvation. While we puzzled through these issues and shared stories about our love of baseball, a foul ball crashed off the glass in front of my face. I didn't react quickly enough to duck or to throw my hands up. Talk about divine protection! It was clear that possible headers should have been restricted to the women's soccer game on TV!

By 3:30 the game was over. The Tigers had slipped past the Cyclones, 2-1, and Bonnie and I leapt into Toad and headed south, not north back to Arbie. In half an hour we wound our way toward the harbor at Mystic and parked at the Captain Daniel Packer Inne. Descending its narrow flight of stairs, we imagined that we might be moving down the steps like Ben Franklin or John Adams, either of whom might have visited the Inne when it had been new. An open table by the crackling fire in the stone fireplace beckoned to us. What a contrast to our high seats in an air-cooled skybox two hours earlier! Now sitting adjacent to the hearth in an eighteenth-century pub overlooking Mystic's harbor, we reveled in the romance of the lapping fire while we enjoyed the daily specials featuring shrimp and scallops.

After dinner, we strolled along historic streets lined with rock walls and sprays of blue and yellow flowers, and we sat on a bench by the harbor listening to weekend sailors tying up their skiffs as we inhaled the salty air. With dusk beginning to enwrap the evening, we headed back to Arbie, retracing our path along the state highways. Surprisingly, Toad drew attention from a Connecticut state trooper who kept pace with us for six or seven miles while we cruised leisurely a bit below the posted speed limit. Perhaps he was bemused by the California plates on a little sedan that hardly looked roadworthy for a cross-continental drive. Whatever the case, he followed us closely until he turned back at the state line while we continued on to Wales.

Nursery-Rhyming Ironbirds: Game 66 in Tri-City

At Tri-City in New York, the words and tune of a different song competed in my mind with the familiar strains of "The Star-Spangled Banner."

Lines from a nursery rhyme—"Four and twenty blackbirds baked in a pie"—kept humming through my mind because the ValleyCats' opponent that evening was the four and twenty Ironbirds from Aberdeen. Not that their roster was comprised of twenty-four players: their record stood at a dismal four wins and twenty losses.

Named "the Ironbirds" because of their affiliation with Baltimore and their ownership group headed by Cal Ripken, himself the Iron Oriole, the team from Maryland began the game watching the ball spray beside the plate like buckshot. The leadoff batter was hit by a pitch and scored on a wild pitch later in the inning. And that run would prove decisive for the tinfoil birds as they held on for a 7-6 victory over the ValleyCats who, despite a losing record of their own, had been favored to win as the NYP League's defending champion.

Before the game, I assured the ValleyCats manager that my anthem renditions did not produce bad luck for his team. When Tri-City had played at Burlington, Vermont, a week earlier, the team had lost the game when their opponent's rally was ignited in the bottom of the ninth when the ValleyCats catcher had dropped a third strike. Days later when I had seen them play in Wappingers Falls, New York, they had lost to their Hudson River rivals when, again in their opponent's final at-bat (this time in the tenth), the ValleyCats reliever unleashed a wild pitch that had brought the winning run home: a walk-off wild one.

"Really, I'm not a jinx," I bantered with Stubby Clapp, the ValleyCats manager. "You'll win tonight."

"What's your cell number?" he countered. "If we win, you're coming back."

So I quickly handed him my card.

It's no wonder that he was superstitiously searching for any answer to improve his team's performance. At that point in the season, the ValleyCats were four games under .500. Three of his starting players were hitting below .150, and one a paltry .040! Alas, not even the launch of distracting fireworks during the anthem's phrase about "the bombs bursting in air" could turn the fortunes of Tri-City. For the third time in less than a fortnight with me singing, the ValleyCats would lose by a single run.

Our interchange anticipated my interaction with the sports reporter for News 13, one of the TV channels in the Albany area that had sent a film crew to the game. While I had been singing the anthem and thinking about "A Song of Six-Pence," I had noticed that there were five TV cameras positioned on the media pad at the concourse level behind home plate. When I moved to my box seat during the early innings of the game, I asked the sports anchor why there was so much attention on the game between two losing teams. I wondered if a recent high draft choice had signed and were making his professional debut. Not the case. "Simple," the reporter said. "It's a slow Monday sports night."

Immediately, I handed him my anthem-tour business card, described my project, and suggested that he had a distinct story to tell, leading it off by playing a phrase or two of me singing. "Wow! I didn't run the tape then," he responded. "Tell me ahead next time."

Right! As though there might be a next time for me, a Californian in Troy, New York. Regrettably, during the pregame introductions, the ValleyCats had identified me merely by name, which meant that no one in the stands—including the reporters—knew about the anthem project or my journey until I approached them.

Nevertheless, overhearing my conversation with the reporter, usher Dan Carubia expressed enthusiasm for my patriotic mission. During the next few batters, he recounted stories about memorable anthem performances in Shea Stadium and Madison Square Garden, where he had also served as an usher for several years. His stories were inspiring, mostly about respectful and robust performances that he had heard. A few innings later, after entertaining the entire crowd by dancing atop the dugout, he made the evening for two young teens with general-admission tickets by escorting them to vacant seats behind the backstop.

Even as it was a slow sports night near the Berkshires to the east and the state capital a few miles to the southwest, so, too, the pace of the game was equally lethargic: there were five walks, four wild pitches, three errors, a hit batsman, a passed ball, and a balk. These plodding plays must have affected the P.A. announcer as well since he apparently sought to intersperse his game description with filler announcements, such as one about preventing the spread of a destructive tree beetle. He urged homeowners and campers to avoid burning firewood away from the premises where it had been cut.

While the home team's loss might have merited little news coverage in the region, and while the P.A. announcer's repartee might have strained for sporting relevance, the ballpark itself prominently paid tribute to baseball legends who had played in Troy. Positioned near the entry to the ballpark were plaques and portraits honoring Hall of Famers Johnny Evers (of "Tinker to Evers to Chance" fame), Buck Ewing (the first major-leaguer to hit ten home runs in a single season), and two nineteenth-century stars, Tim Keefe and Roger Conner.

More so than other ballparks in the Northeast, the outfield fences at Joseph Bruno Stadium featured an extensive range of commercials for local businesses, regional enterprises, and national products like JIF peanut butter, Sunkist citrus, and Dunkin' Donuts. Among the more than seventy displays double-decking the fence from foul pole to foul pole, several of the billboards were noteworthy because of their particular placement. Above and beyond the highest sign in the left-handed hitter's power alley was Cooley's lure to win a car by hitting a home run through a basketball-size hole. Nearby, the ad for a fence company seemed oddly placed because it was positioned *above and beyond* the outfield fence. And a right-field placard plugged the law office of Hank Bauer. Although the lawyer was unrelated to the former major league player by the same name, I wondered whether right field had been strategically chosen for the placement of his ad because of the familiar association of the name with right field, where Hank Bauer had starred for a decade with the Orioles and then the Yankees.

Following the seventh inning stretch, with the Ironbirds leading by five runs, I retired from the game as quietly as the ValleyCats batters had been prone to do. Back-to-back homers in the second inning had been the only solid contact that Tri-City's hitters had made, a bunt single in the fifth being their only other hit until the ninth. Although I then missed their rally, during which they scored four runs and advanced the tying tally to third with only one out, I faced almost a two-hour drive back toward Monterey, Massachusetts, in the heart of the Berkshires. Mid-afternoon I had parked Arbie at a friend's house there so that we could enjoy two days off in the beauty of their home, the serenity of the mountains, and the comfort of their companionship. And the return drive along the New York State Thruway beneath flooding moonlight provided a good beginning to a recess in my schedule.

A "Goulden" Recess between Games 66 and 67

After a week of tethering out in Toad from Wales to ballparks in Connecticut, Massachusetts, New Hampshire, New York, and Rhode Island, I looked forward to two unscheduled days that Bonnie and I could spend with her friends Pam and Bill Johnson in their home in the Berkshires. Months earlier when I had been developing possible itineraries and scheduling the anthem performances, I had bemoaned the fact that, during my stay in the area, I couldn't coordinate my schedule with home dates for the Portland Sea Dogs in Maine or the independent minor league team close by in Pittsfield, which recently had restored one of the oldest ballparks in the country. Yet at that time my colleague Charles Adams had cautioned me about compacting my schedule, suggesting that I'd benefit from a few days off now and then, here and there.

During my scheduling frenzy, I had scoffed at the idea of needing a break. Now, as I returned to the Johnson's home in Monterey following the evening game in Troy, New York, I reveled in the prospect of a respite from daily driving and interacting at ballparks. I lowered the windows in Toad and let the cool night air blow freshly across my forehead and through my mind, and I savored the picnic supper that Pam had packed for me a few hours earlier. Although I couldn't see the salad in the dark while I was driving, I enjoyed feeling the texture of the lettuce, cucumbers, carrots, and pepitas as I fingered bites to my mouth. I followed this first course with a marinated chicken breast, amazingly moist despite having been chilled for a few hours. And then there was fruit—sticky and delicious chunks of melons and berries. Only hours earlier had I met Pam and Bill, and I already thought of her as my newest friend, someone who sensed my needs and catered to my tastes.

When I entered the Johnsons' house shortly before midnight, Bonnie and Pam were catching up on their mutual interests in art and gardening and literature. Among her many talents, Pam is an accomplished fabric artist whose primary medium is quilting. The design of two of her pieces hanging in the house rivaled award-winning quilts on exhibit at the National Quilting Museum that Bonnie and I had toured weeks earlier during our stay in western Kentucky.

Meanwhile, Bill offered me a chance to be soothed and stimulated simultaneously by listening to one of Dvorak's symphonies on his theatrical sound system while we sipped a nightcap and shared perspectives about our professions, mine in academics and his in corporate leadership. Initially, he had served as an executive in the computing industry, and recently he had assumed the role of executive director of Gould Farm, a residential therapeutic community located in Monterey.

Tired though I was, I was enthralled by his characterization of the mission and therapy afforded by Gould Farm, which had been founded at the beginning of the twentieth century to provide a radical alternative to the treatment of persons suffering from mental instability and illness. Even more than my fascination with Bill's enthusiastic description of the program and several of its recent successes, I sensed a moral integrity in Gould Farm's distinct, restorative method, which offers guests (as its participants are called) an opportunity to pursue mental-health by engaging in meaningful agricultural teamwork, individual counseling, respectful relationships, and a healthy diet—all in the context of a supportive community that provides ongoing encouragement and progressive levels of independence.

Before we left their home two days later, Bonnie and I walked through a pasture on the 650 acres of Gould Farm, toured its dairy and cheese production facility, and saw and smelled its goats and chickens and cows. Daily the guests gain familiarity with dairy chores, and regularly they harvest sap and refine maple syrup, bake breads and pastries, and blend granola—all of which could be purchased by the public at the Farm's Roadside Store and Café along Route 23. On our return to the Johnsons' house we stopped by the Gould Farm store to replenish Arbie's cereal supplies with a bag of the granola, which didn't last long. Bonnie claimed that it was "that good."

During much of the two days that we spent with the Johnsons, I enjoyed the freedom to write in a refreshing retreat in Bill's study that overlooks a wooded hillside sloping down from their house to Stevens Lake. Not only was the Internet access uninterrupted; the setting was secluded, spectacular, inspirational.

Regrettably, my writing and walking through their lush gardens and surrounding woods were disrupted when Arbie begged for special attention. Because the Johnsons' driveway is so steep and twisted, Pam had arranged for us to park Arbie near a neighbor's house. But when we learned that workmen needed access past Arbie, I went to move it and discovered a red oil leak near the right front tire. Ugh! Dabbing my finger in the wet spill and fearing a transmission malfunction, I gingerly drove Arbie to a truck repair shop in Lee, where mechanics easily and efficiently replaced the cracked hydrolytic line controlling the right front automatic leveler. But they also diagnosed a bushing failure that we could address days later in Chicago.

Even the frustration of this vehicular problem could not dim the deep refreshment of our visit. The Johnsons engaged us with stimulating conversation, inspired us with their commitments to Gould Farm, and served incredible meals. Turning her artistic skills to the kitchen, Pam created amazing salads with fresh produce and cheeses from Gould Farm, and she baked a delectable fig torte garnished with fresh raspberries. I was convinced that she could compete with the Iron Chefs. Taking on the air of one of the show's judges, I imagined myself describing the presentation and taste of her creations: "The salads blended the artistries of Brahms and Baryshnikov," I would begin, "by permitting the béchamel sauce to lift and twist the harmonic flavors of the chilled shrimp, fresh greens, and blanched asparagus beyond two octaves." But unlike the food judges who sit conference-style at a table under floodlights, we enjoyed the ambiance of an elegant table set with colorful china and situated on the porch beneath towering trees.

To prepare for our final evening meal with the Johnsons, Pam took Bonnie to the fresh fish market in Stockbridge to pick up live lobsters, which sloshed in the bucket that Bonnie stabilized during their return drive. I do believe that my lobster must have weighed more than two pounds, and I savored the experience for the rest of the month.

After two days of nourishment and hospitality with Pam and Bill, Bonnie and I descended the mountain from Monterey in Toad, slowed to avoid a frequent speed trap in Tyringham, and made our way back to Lee where we picked up Arbie from his repair. Accessing the Mass Pike there, we joined the New York Thruway a half-hour later and aimed toward Allentown, Pennsylvania, for a doubleheader that night between the Syracuse Chiefs and the hosting Lehigh Valley IronPigs.

An Ironic and Elegant Sty: Game 67 in Lehigh Valley

I love teams and ballparks that display a sense of humor like the Lehigh Valley IronPigs who called Coca-Cola Park in Allentown, Pennsylvania, their home. When I had first seen the team's logo of a steely-faced boar, I had assumed that the name "IronPigs" suggested the character of the baseball team—that it plays with a kind of pig-headed determination. Yet the team's name really derives from the region's primary industry. Pig irons are smelted ingots produced in the process of refining steel, and the steelworkers in Eastern Pennsylvania who produce the bars of pig iron are themselves often called "iron pigs."

Ballpark references to the region's dominant industry also extended to the names of the team mascots, Ferrous and FeFe. Certainly the pair must have been male and female representatives of their fuzzy species, for "Ferrous" connotes a male creature with iron strength (even if *not* the man of steel himself, Superman), and "FeFe" playfully fuses the effete pet name Fifi with the chemical symbol for iron, Fe.

While "iron pigs" refers to a by-product of local industry, the team nonetheless puns its name with porcine images and labels throughout the ballpark. Posted at the entry are signs displaying ballpark rules and decorum—what's not permitted inside the stadium, like chairs and coolers, "outside" food and drinks, as well as pets, except for service dogs. Oddly, then, the final order to fans encouraged, perhaps, other behavior: "Go Hog Wild!"

As they entered the concourse, fans could pick up free copies of the program—"Pork Illustrated," whose lettering resembled the font and format of the banner of the iconic magazine *Sports Illustrated.* Not only did the "I" in "Illustrated" feature a swine's swirling tail, it also represented the iron ingots produced in steel refining.

Immediately past this trough filled with information for fans' consumption was an "IronPiggy Bank" emblazoned with the Coca-Cola logo. Painted annually from a winning design submitted by a child (in 2011, there had been more than 2,000 entries), the big piggy invited donations to raise awareness of IronPigs Charities presented by the Air Products Foundation. With a mission to provide educational and recreational opportunities for youth in the region, IronPigs Charities eventually collected and distributed a record total of more than $106,000 in 2011, despite the economic woes that affected the Lehigh Valley. Recipients of awards ranged from a local school system, regional Boys and Girls Clubs, nearby churches with sports teams and leagues, a community bicycling group, and the area's Special Olympics.

Most of the funds for IronPigs Charities had been raised from a golf tournament, a winter banquet with silent auctions and a bat raffle, and a mid-season luncheon with manager Ryne Sandberg and several players—a luncheon that, coincidentally, had taken place a few hours before my appearance for the anthem. Still, the IronPiggy Bank also proved to be effective in encouraging fan participation in the charitable efforts. On average, about ten dollars in loose change was slipped into IronPiggy's slot at each home game. And the ban on pets at the ballpark was lifted during summer on two evenings, when dogs were welcomed—on leashes—with the purchase of a one-dollar ticket whose proceeds then went to IronPigs Charities. During 2011, more than $700 was collected in this way for distribution to the Animal Food Bank and the Center for Animal Health and Welfare.

Part of the charm associated with IronPiggy was the playful tone of its solicitation: "that good fortune goes to ye who feed me change and then rub my nose." So if feeding the IronPiggy and rubbing its nose might bring good luck, then what greater benefit might come from kissing its snout, as one young boy did?

Certainly one might expect that the food stands would also play with the piggish theme. One of the permanent concessions was known as "Pig Out," and a temporary tent offered pulled pork. Although the Philadelphia Pretzel Factory didn't offer a bacon-infused treat, it did exhibit a playful spirit, naming its pretzel bits for one of the products associated with the steel industry. The box of bites was called "rivets."

A whimsical spirit characterized the young ballpark, and it was also distinguished by its architectural design, which provided superb sightlines throughout the stands and wide concourses. In 2008 *Baseball Digest* had recognized Coca-Cola Park as an ironic and elegant sty, naming it the new Ballpark of the Year. One of the artistic—and playful—facets in its design is the scoreboard, which features a gigantic Coca-Cola bottle "Roman candle" that fizzed with fireworks when an IronPig hit a home run.

Other sportive, artistic expressions could be found at the main gate, where the sidewalk welcomed fans to traverse a giant baseball with red-brick seams, and adjacent to the doors to the executive offices, an eight-foot IronPigs bat leaned into a corner beside the coin-operated newspaper stand shaped like a baseball.

As distinct as these features were at Lehigh Valley, the ballpark shared with most other minor league ballparks the intimate contact between its seats and the field, between the fans and the players. And like many other stadiums, Coca-Cola Park touted scores of advertisers on outfield fences. At few other ballparks that I visited, however, were there as many as the seventy-six billboards on the fences in Allentown.

It's not surprising that, during the 2011 season, attendance at attractive Coca-Cola Park topped all other minor league venues. Since the IronPigs were enjoying the best record in the International League, and since a doubleheader—the regularly scheduled game plus a make-up game caused by a rainout earlier in the season—was on tap for this evening, more than 10,000 fans flooded to the ballpark on this night, about ten percent more than the IronPigs average attendance during the year.

While the crowd was among the largest that I encountered during the summer, so, too, was the number of "first pitches" that were thrown: sixteen! I sometimes saw first innings with fewer pitches than the number of first pitches that were tossed in the pregame ceremonies. And despite the outstanding architectural features and the multiple forms of entertainment at the ballpark, the delay in the sound system was among the most challenging that I encountered. Even so, as I left the ballpark, a woman clasped my arm, looked me in the eyes, and echoed the fan in Daytona: "Thanks for not making it a funeral dirge like so many."

For sure, when there is a significant delay, the temptation is to slow down. But to minimize "overlap," my own response is to accelerate the tempo.

The seven-inning contest, the normal length of games in Triple-A doubleheaders, was distinct in a couple of ways. With Syracuse leading by two runs in the bottom of the fifth inning, Jeff Larish took a lead off second, rounded third on a single to left field, and collided with the catcher as he slid into home. Not only was he out at the plate, he also was out for the season, suffering a compound fracture of his right leg that required the application of an inflatable cast before he was carried off the field.

After Syracuse tallied another run in the top of the sixth, the IronPigs finally scored in their half of the inning when Brandon Moss hammered a two-run homer to right centerfield, prompting the Coke bottle atop the scoreboard to fizz its fireworks. Following Moss's blast, Josh Wilkie relieved the starting pitcher and smelted the rally, striking out three of the IronPigs to secure the victory for the visiting Chiefs, 3-2.

An Erie Birthday: Game 68 in Erie

In Amish country near Randolph, New York, I awoke on my birthday thinking about baseball and birthdays while anticipating a leisurely drive in Toad to Erie for the afternoon game between the SeaWolves and the Altoona Curve. When I was a child, two of my birthday celebrations had featured trips to St. Louis, where I saw Musial hit a home run, and Chicago, where Mantle and Maris homered in two games during their record-smashing summer of 1961. For another birthday amid the lean years of grad school, Bonnie had bought us box-seat tickets for a game again between the Yankees and White Sox. And, of course, throughout their childhood years my sons had found that mid-summer baseball gifts—caps and shirts and license-plate holders and autographed balls—would bring me certain delight.

In a distinct way my birthday had already proved pivotal for my anthem tour. A year earlier when I had sent out my requests to teams for preapproval to sing the anthem, I had included a link to a streaming video of me singing for a game between the Rockies and Reds in Cincinnati on my birthday several years earlier. Like that day in Southern Ohio, this sunny birthday in Erie was a scorcher, with the temperature in the shade—if any could be found—settling in the nineties, and the humidity level…well, next to the Great Lake, there needn't be an attempt to measure it.

In most of the grandstands and on the field, of course, the sun proved tenacious, blistering fans and fielders alike. Although I tried to be cool when I sang the anthem a cappella, intense heat vied against my performances. In recent weeks Bonnie and I had encountered record-high temperatures in Texas, Tennessee, and Alabama, and within subsequent days and weeks we would continue to swelter through another record-setting heat wave sweating its way slowly across the Midwest. Even so, Erie's singeing afternoon could not match the on-field temperature on my birthday in Southern Ohio some years earlier. Then, on the artificial turf at Riverfront Stadium, the game-time temperature had crested above 120 degrees—a few degrees cooler, believe it or not, than two days before when a thermometer on the field had registered more than 130! A vivid series of non-anthem images comes to mind when I recall that afternoon. After the fifth inning, the batboys took a liter of water to each of the umpires. Standing behind second base, one ump quickly guzzled a portion, then removed his cap and splashed some on the top of his head, and finally poured the last half of the bottle in a circle around his feet, letting the immediate evaporation cool his cramping legs.

In Cincinnati, I had been offered a chance to view the game from an air-conditioned suite where my college alumni group was holding a reception. Yet in Erie the only shade and breeze that we could find was in the row of seats in front of the open broadcasters' window, through which we could faintly feel the wafting of their words past our ears. So there we sat in semi-shade for several innings, enjoying the announcers' play-by-play descriptions and color commentary, and imagining how we might have differently filled the long pauses between their narration of action on the field.

Despite the scalding heat at birthday baseball games, my anthem performances on those days were well received. As in Cincinnati, the Erie team provided me with a video of my performance, the third ballpark on the tour to do so. In Frisco and Winston-Salem the new ballparks had benefitted from the chance to utilize their sophisticated recording systems. By contrast, Erie's Jerry Uht Park seemed to emit a demi-archaic aura. So I was surprised at the stellar quality of the video and sound systems, as well as the all-star caliber tech crew, at this seemingly unsophisticated urban ballpark—not simply because they recorded my performance but also because they personalized my introduction with comments about my making a national tour and celebrating a birthday.

Politely, the crowd preceded my rendition with applause and, following my straightforward performance, two fans approached me, one with the familiar expression of appreciation that I had sung it as written and another with terse praise: "You did a damn good job. That's a hard song to sing."

The sense of history that fans get at "the Uht," as the SeaWolves ballpark is familiarly known, derives in part from its memorials, its simplicity, and its neighborhood placement. Constructed in 1995 and renovated about a decade later, the ballpark honors civic leadership and baseball achievements rather than corporate sponsorship by its having been named for a longtime area resident. Jerry Uht had established an endowment with the Erie Community Foundation for the maintenance of the ballpark and support of its operations.

In addition to its recognition of Uht, the ballpark also celebrates Erie's baseball history by displaying bronze steles of former Pennsylvania Governor Robert Casey, who had been instrumental in securing funding for the ballpark's construction; Dick Agresti, who had been the founder of Erie's Boys Baseball, for which he built fields and organized volunteers to enrich the lives of the areas youth; and Mike Cannavino, who had been a mid-twentieth-century city council member responsible for saving the Erie Sailors, the SeaWolves' predecessor.

The other historic plaque honored Sam "the Jet" Jethroe, a notable major-leaguer who began to play baseball in Erie *following* his professional career. After achieving stardom in the Negro Leagues where he had won two batting titles, Jethroe became the first African American to play for a Boston team, breaking the color line in Beantown when he won the Rookie-of-the-Year award in 1950 for the Boston Braves. That year, he also led the National League in stolen bases, and for three years he roamed centerfield at Braves Field before the team departed for Milwaukee. For most of the rest of the decade, he played in the International League before retiring and settling in Erie. While employed in a factory in the city, he resumed playing baseball in the Glenwood League, Erie's prominent amateur league that operated as a wooden-bat league for most of a century.

Jethroe's jersey (#5) was also one of only two retired numbers displayed on the outfield wall. When I saw the baseball with his name and number, I asked a staffer who he was and why he was associated with Erie. She didn't know but suggested that the memorial was from "long ago." The other recognized number in left field was uniform, Jackie Robinson's #42—uniform both in the sense that it was the numeral on his jersey, and uniform in the sense that it is the single number mandatorily retired throughout the major and minor leagues. Oddly then, the only honored numbers at Erie were for former Negro League stars who became major league pioneers yet who never played for an Erie professional team.

Even though kids at a twenty-first-century ballpark might not seem to be drawn to history and its traditional practices, the children at Erie this afternoon enjoyed their time at "the Uht" in old-fashioned ways. Without the lure of techno-pitches and swings or the chance to careen off the walls of bouncy rooms, they anticipated foul balls with eyes glued toward home and gloves poised; and later they lined up for the simple run from the centerfield fence across the outfield to the first-baseline during a between-inning dash known as the "Kids' Stampede."

To a certain extent, the SeaWolves also enjoyed a stampede of singles in the fifth inning when six consecutive batters connected for base hits en route to their 9-3 victory over Altoona's Curve.

Featuring a Different Ball: Game 69 in Jamestown

Outside the front gates of seventy-year-old Diethrick Park in Jamestown, New York, a historic marker pays general tribute to baseball—its players and fans. Yet the community in this grape-growing region of the state more specifically and significantly celebrates its love for a different "Ball"—comedienne Lucille Ball, who hailed from the city. And if Lucy herself weren't one for the birds, the other famous former citizen of Jamestown is Roger Tory Peterson, the ornithologist who published the world's most popular guidebooks for birdwatchers.

Inside the ballpark one of the signs on the left-field wall publicized the anticipated, centennial celebration of Lucy's birth, an event that would attract to a single site a world-record number of Lucy impersonators aflame with red hair and red lipstick. I know that almost everyone loved Lucy, but a hundred impersonators at a single event might be too many for even rerun TV networks to enjoy.

However, the comic spirit might come naturally to the Jamestown Jammers and their fans. With a name that conjures up flavors of the fruity spread for toast, the team personifies its logo by placing a face on a cluster of grapes and calls its mascot "Bubba, the Grape Ape." That playful spirit prompts creative expressions by the fans, demonstrated by one small girl dressed in pink who, after hugging Big Bubba, turned to her mother and asked, "What color bananas does Bubba eat since he's purple?" I grinned at this budding Lucille Ball.

The young girl was ready to take the stage—not at a comedy club, but on the field with the other children participants in the pregame "Dream Team" that accompanied the Jammers to their respective starting positions. Obviously already dreaming of his professional possibilities, another small member of the Dream Team bent down to touch the rubber as he crossed the mound on his way to his second baseman position. Did he perform this ritual act routinely in his Little League games, or was his gesture the response to some dare from a brother or teammate? Or was his simple move a genuine expression of his love of the game?

While these images and actions caused me to smile, I did not otherwise enjoy my experience at Jamestown. When I had checked into the ballpark as the anthem singer, the staffer asked me what my name was, not for the purpose of verification but for the purpose of knowing whom to announce. Minutes later, the P.A. announcer identified me simply as "Joe Price." Miffed by the minimal, impersonal character of the introduction, I sensed that they might as well have mocked Ed McMahon on *The Tonight Show*: "Heeeeere's Joe!"

Although I was disappointed with the introduction at Jamestown, I realized that their inattentiveness wasn't a personal slight. The staffer who had met me upon arrival was consistently careless. She spent much of the pregame period complaining about kids who show up late and still ask to participate in one of the "in-game" entertainments. Even so, she hadn't selected someone to throw out the first pitch until three minutes before the ceremony, nor had she secured a player to sign the bat that would be given to the "fan of the game." And once he had agreed to sign, she turned to another player and asked, "What's his name?"

For the record, the game itself seemed unremarkable, other than eleven runs, twenty hits, and five errors. Jamestown played more like Roller Derby jammers than grape jellies, beating the Mahoning Valley Scrappers 6-5 by coming from behind with three runs in the seventh and, despite an error advancing a runner to third with two outs in the ninth, by holding off the visitors for the victory.

Although I was disappointed in the overall Jammers experience, I loved western New York. Earlier in the day Bonnie and I had explored the Amish country near the Village of Randolph, where we had anchored Arbie in the Pope Haven Campground for a couple of days coinciding with my singing in

Erie and Jamestown. During the morning we had meandered in Toad on backroads past family farms, many also selling different items such as lawn harnesses or buggy wheels, cedar chests or hickory rockers, birdhouses or wicker chairs, as well as women's handiworks in rugs and quilts and baskets and, of course, pastries, pies, and canned goods.

Lured by the simple sign "Hill Top Toy Shop," we had stopped at Dan Raber's workshop where he designed and supervised the construction of wooden toys. To our surprise, when we entered we could hear and see craftsmen working with power tools in an adjacent room. How could these Amish artisans use power saws without electricity? After generations of the Amish requiring that their craftwork be hand-tooled, this western New York community had begun to allow generators to power some tools used for making initial cuts, as long as the finishing touches could be completed by hand. While we looked over toys and other items on display, one of the customers rocked back and forth on a rope-hung horse-swing in the middle of the shop, and two friendly dogs nuzzled Bonnie and me, encouraging us to pet them. It was reassuring that good old dogs can bridge cultures and generations.

Shortly after leaving the toy shop, we pulled into a neighbor's place to see his ironwork before we headed to a younger Raber's shed to admire the simple designs, fine woods, tight joints, and lustrous finishes on his furniture. If only Arbie could have opened his storage bay wide enough to carry a chest, we would have bought and uploaded a bureau into one of his holds.

In our interactions with the Amish, two of their particular products intrigued me since they seemed incongruous with my understanding of an Amish lifestyle. At the toy shop we saw a bin full of clothespin-loaded, rubber-band guns selling for $2.50. Not only was I confounded by the fact that gun culture was being marketed to children by pacifists, I also wondered how many mothers, in response to their young sons' and daughters' fondling of the toy, had repeated Santa's line of maternal worry uttered to Richie in *A Christmas Story*: "Not a chance, kid. You'll shoot your eye out."

The other incongruous item we found in a leather shop, where belts could be punched and custom-cut to fit. The sale of belts seemed to mismatch Amish ways since Amish men wear only suspenders. Impressed by this irony and concerned that I needed to tighten my belt both physically and metaphorically, I bought two of the tooled black straps and wore one daily during the last six weeks of the trip.

Having paid for the belts with the remaining bills and coins in my pockets, we needed to find an ATM to replenish our cash. Looking at the map, Bonnie saw that the nearest town was Dayton, toward which she directed me along rural roads through fields and fields of flourishing, sun-drenched crops.

A half-hour later as hunger started to gnaw at us, we drove into the charming community—no traffic lights, no fast-food restaurants, no national hardware stores. What we found was diagonal, unmetered parking in front of the Jenny Lee Country Store and the County Bank of Cattaraugus. There, two tellers standing behind an open counter pleasantly greeted me. When I asked where I could access an ATM, they directed me to the only one in town, two blocks south, inside the South Dayton Super 303 grocery store. The bank itself had no teller machines; it relied on humans.

Feeling somewhat alien standing in front of the ATM machine a few minutes later, I inserted my card, punched in numbers, and got crisp twenty-dollar bills. Now reloaded with these yuppie food coupons, we returned to Jenny Lee for hot meatloaf sandwiches before resuming our wander through the countryside, where we discovered a world-class quilt shop run by Elizabeth Wengerd and assisted by six-year-old Amanda, one of her twenty-eight grandchildren. Although Amanda responded to our smiles and facial expressions, she did not understand our conversation since German is the language spoken in Amish homes. Elizabeth explained that Amish children begin to study English when they enter their schools, which continue through eighth grade. Typically then, the boys begin to apprentice within their extended family or community while the girls focus on improving their craft-working and homemaking skills. As we talked with Elizabeth and admired her handiwork, little Amanda joined her in turning back the stack of quilts.

On a wall-map of the world close by, pushpins located the hometowns of quilt purchasers, and Bonnie showed Amanda that we lived near the cluster of customers whose location was in Los Angeles. "California's far away," Elizabeth translated into German. So far, in fact, that she wondered how many days it had taken us to drive across country. She glanced toward Toad, which probably looked no more comfortable or efficient than the buggies in which she often rode.

Learning of our circuitous route, she then asked why we had come to the area. "To sing tonight in Jamestown," I replied.

"At the baseball game," Bonnie added. "He's singing the national anthem at ballparks throughout America."

Now I wondered how she might respond, especially since non-Amish families throughout the area often distinguished their identity by painting American flags on the roadside of their barns. But as we left, Elizabeth simply said, "Sing tonight for me."

And I did, still mystified by her polite expression of patriotism, the sight of Raber's power tools, and the snug fit of my new Amish-crafted belt against my waist.

A Quality Start Amid Base-Running Blunders: Game 70 in Niles, Ohio

In baseball terms, a quality start for a pitcher means that he completes at least six innings and gives up three runs or fewer, keeping his team in the game. Former Whittier colleague and perennial fantasy-league competitor Jon Moody dubbed my anthem progress a quality start since he attended performance number seventy with me for the Mahoning Valley Scrappers game against the State College Spikes. With seventy games completed and thirty-four still scheduled, the game in Niles, Ohio, marked the two-thirds point in my project—or, in baseball terms, the end of the sixth inning.

Call me an old warhorse or a performer from bygone years: I expected to go the distance. I didn't see a reliever in sight, and I certainly didn't have a closer waiting in the pen to come in to sing or play for the final inning—or dozen games.

If baseball metaphors apply to my anthem tour and performances, then my appearance in Mahoning Valley also was fueled by a rally of enthusiastic reception. Publicity about the anthem tour by Scrappers staff on the team's website prompted TV journalist Dan Martin to conduct pregame interviews with Bonnie and me for the evening news on WKNB. The Scrappers' respect for the project energized my anthem performance, as did the presence of Jon, his wife Jane, and their son Jonathan.

After I had sung, Scrappers manager Dave Wallace shook hands with me, and I wished him better luck than the night before when I had sung for their game in Jamestown, when they had lost to the Jammers 6-5. "If we lose," Wallace quipped, "I'll hold it against you."

On the outfield wall in Niles, two names and numbers appeared to be retired. As usual, one was Jackie Robinson's number, "42." The other Scrappers number was "13," which was identified with the name "Wolcott." Two things puzzled me about the sign: Wolcott's name did not appear on the roster of former Scrappers who had made it to the majors, and the number

"13," which I assumed to be retired, was being worn by starting catcher Alex Lavisky.

I wondered aloud to Jon about the conundrum and told him how, in Erie a couple of days earlier, I had seen two retired numbers on the outfield wall. There I had inquired of a couple of staff members about the identity of the companion number and name to that of Robinson: "Jethroe #5." None knew.

Immediately, Jon effused, "He was my favorite Braves player when I was growing up in Boston. I'm not sure why, and I didn't understand his significance until later—what he meant as the first African-American player for Boston and the Braves—but he was somehow my favorite." Sam "the Jet" Jethroe, had starred in the Negro Leagues before playing in the major leagues during the first wave of signings of black players.

In the year following Jackie Robinson's debut with the Dodgers, Jethroe also signed with the Brooklyn team and played two seasons for their Triple-A team in Montreal before being traded to the Boston Braves following the 1949 season. As the starting center fielder for the Braves in 1950, Jethroe had made an immediate impact, hitting a home run in his first game, leading the National League in stolen bases for the season, and being named the league's Rookie of the Year—the oldest player ever to be accorded that honor. Yes, there were plenty of baseball reasons why Jon might have identified Jethroe as his favorite Brave, even without recognizing Jethroe's significance in breaking Boston's baseball color barrier.

Although Jon and I enjoyed musing about the numerical memorial to Jethroe in Erie, we were mystified by the number "13" associated with Wolcott in Niles. The only Wolcott listed with a minor league record on Baseball-Reference.com is Bob Wolcott, a former pitcher whose minor league career never intersected with the Ohio team.

Throughout the game Jon and I caught up on each other's professional work. Meanwhile, it looked like the young players in the NYP League had trouble with a number of fundamental skills and baseball savvy. Their fielding was often erratic, especially when they failed to make intelligent decisions about where and how to throw to a base on a fielder's choice; and their base-running frequently produced blunders when they failed to take an extra base or foolishly ran into an out.

In the first inning the Scrappers leadoff hitter slapped a routine bounder toward the second-baseman. Taking a wicked hop, the ball hit Ashley Ponce in the face, felling him and forcing his removal from the game. Base-running blunders began on the next play when the batter hit a grounder to the replacement second-baseman. Running from first, Cody Elliott failed to stop in the base path in order to delay a tag or force a throw to second to get the lead runner. Instead, he ran directly into the tag that easily led to a double play.

The Scrappers continued their inept base-running a couple of innings later. With men on first and third with one out, Jake Lowery hit a deep drive to the right-centerfield alley. The runner on first advanced to second, where he paused to watch the flight of the ball while the runner on third retreated to the bag to tag in case the ball should be caught. It was. While Evan Frazer tagged and scored from third, Tony Walters, who had paused at second, simply proceeded toward third. The relay throw from the second-baseman to first was fumbled but retrieved easily to double-up Walters, who had never attempted retreat.

The mystifying misadventures of base-running were not restricted to the Scrappers and the Spikes. The umpires also joined in their confusion. In the top of the third inning with Walker Gurley on first, Justin Bensko hit a line drive to the third-baseman, who got his glove on the ball, juggling it up in the air a couple of times before watching it drop beyond the sweep of his bare hand. The base umpire ruled that the ball hadn't been caught, and the base-runner Gourley, already retreating toward first in anticipation of a catch, was caught off guard. The third-baseman tossed the ball to the second-baseman, who tagged the retreating runner; and his throw to first failed to beat Bensko, who, after crossing the bag, started back toward the dugout before being told by the first-base coach to return to the bag. The base umpire had called him safe. Befuddled by the whole sequence—as though this description might be any clearer—both runners stood on the first-base bag while the plate umpire convened near the mound with the base umpire to sort things out.

The result: A double play was ruled because the home-plate umpire had had a better view of the play by the third-baseman, who supposedly had snagged the line drive before fumbling the ball in the exchange between his glove and his hand. The umpires determined that the runner who had been on first had been doubled off by the tag that had been applied as he had retreated toward the bag.

While I had enjoyed a quality start to the tour, Scrappers starting pitcher Will Roberts didn't fare quite as well even though he didn't allow a run. Because he reached his pitch count after four innings, he left with a five-run lead. Not only did he fail to go six innings, he also didn't qualify for the win in Mahoning Valley's 6-1 victory.

Triple Jumping in Ohio: Game 71 in Lake County

To include as many Ohio teams in my itinerary as possible, I had to execute a triple jump through the state. In sequence I had agreed to a night game in Niles, where the Mahoning Valley Scrappers made their home, reserved the next evening for Dayton, and planned to hop back to Columbus for the following midday start. But when the Dayton Flyers, who hold the record for most continuous sellouts, stepped back from their initial willingness to work with me on scheduling and wanted me to participate in their on-field auditions in March, I skipped them and jumped instead at the chance to include the Lake County Captains in Eastlake, a suburb of Cleveland. This sequence also meant that I could mimic the childhood counting song from the 1950s "One Little, Two Little, Three Little Indians," since Mahoning Valley, Lake County, and Columbus are affiliates of the Cleveland Indians. However, the distance from Eastlake to Columbus posed a logistical problem: After singing for a night game for the Captains, how could I arrive in Columbus by late morning the following day in time for the noon game?

Throughout the first half of the tour, I had devised and completed a number of jagged routes to Oklahoma, through Alabama, and around Massachusetts. When I tried to figure out how we could minimize Arbie's expense, work with his pace, and get from the Cleveland area to Columbus well before noon, the solution seemed to be to split the distance.

Consequently, when we left Niles on the morning after the Scrappers game, we turned south toward Columbus rather than north toward Cleveland, drove three hours over the roughly plowed surfaces of Ohio freeways, and secured a room at a Hampton Inn—now quite familiar—in Mansfield, just seventy-five miles north of the Columbus ballpark. Then, leaving Arbie in the hotel parking lot and Bonnie in the comfort of the room, I boomeranged in Toad up to Eastlake for the early-evening game before swinging back to Mansfield a little before midnight.

At the entry to the Captains ballpark, I found evidence of a conundrum that had gotten resolved when Lake County shifted its alliance to the Midwest League in 2010. Until then, Lake County had fielded a team in the South Atlantic League. Only a few miles from Lake Erie, the ballpark in Eastlake is hardly in the South or near the Atlantic shoreline. Even so, like so many of the other facilities in the Sally League, the ballpark pays tribute to the league's former president John Henry Moss with a bronze plaque featuring a relief of his bust. During his fifty years of service in that capacity, Moss led the South Atlantic League and its predecessor, the Western Carolina League, to locate teams in more than forty cities in eight states. Even though the plaque does not specify Eastlake's former participation in and departure from the South Atlantic League, the Captains continue to honor Moss.

Before the game I roamed through the concourses taking pictures of Classic Park's distinct concessions, exhibits, and architectural elements. Two of the more interesting features were the nautical attire worn by the ushers and the lighthouse rising beyond the centerfield fence. (I wondered if it, like the Coke bottle scoreboard at Lehigh Valley, might serve as a silo to launch fireworks when a Scrapper hit a homer.) As playful as these elements were, the Captains' most innovative feature appeared at the bottom of the erasable, daily lineup board. Although the posting of the starting lineup was common at ballparks, the creative twist at Lake County was the addition of the QR Codes that could be read by smartphone apps.

Also meandering through the stands before the game was a fan snapping photos of the ballpark rather than the players. Armed with a lens as large as home plate, Ron Vetter seemed as fascinated by Classic Park's design as I was. Hailing from western New York, he enjoyed making excursions to ballparks in the region. As we shared stories about our baseball adventures, he inquired about my anthem project, and he recalled a few, distinct national anthem performances that he had heard. The best, he said, were by Charlie Pride, Mudcat Grant, Tony Tenille in Buffalo, and Josh Groban, whom he heard sing twice on a single day in different ballparks.

First he had seen Groban perform for an afternoon major league game in Pittsburgh before hearing his anthem reprise at a night game for the Washington (Pennsylvania) Wild Things in the independent Frontier League. Talk about your day-night doubleheaders: That's a feat that I couldn't manage to schedule on the tour, even with the night-to-noon sequence between Lake County and Columbus. Ron also brightened when he related that, although he hadn't heard John Elway sing the national anthem, he had seen him hit a triple while going two for five when Elway had been a Yankees baseball prospect playing for Oneonta.

Overhearing our conversation about anthems at ballparks, usher Bob Dew chimed in that Lake County's most distinct anthem performances had been on heritage nights, when ethnic groups—especially the Italian Americans—performed the national anthems of their heritage nations as well as "The Star-Spangled Banner."

Shortly after my interchange with Drew, Andrew Grover, the Captains staff member who assisted me with preparation for the anthem, learned of my tour and asked, "Do they put you up in a hotel?"

"I wish. Most teams provide free parking along with a couple of tickets to the game. Otherwise, teams provide few perks."

Astonished, he snorted, "You really must be a fan! Where are you going next?"

"To Columbus for a noon game tomorrow."

"How will you get there in time? Are you staying for our game?"

"As long as possible."

Within the past few days he had attended a ballpark staff conference that Columbus had hosted, and he raved about their stadium, calling it the Trump Tower of minor league facilities.

For my anthem performance at Eastlake, I took the field in an unfamiliar position—at the base of the pitcher's mound. Immediately after I voiced the "V" in "home of the brave," Lake County's starting pitcher Cole Cook, who had been standing at the rubber, tapped me on the shoulder, extended his hand, and introduced himself by saying, "My brother attended Whittier College!"

Regrettably, I couldn't delay his warmup tosses with questions, nor could I find him after his departure at the end of the fourth inning. But from Ben Hill, the blogger for the Minor League Baseball website who had followed my tour since its inception, I soon learned more about Cook from an interview that Ben had conducted with him a month earlier. Because Cook's father was a character actor in Hollywood, Cook had grown up around movie lots, even getting to play inside the brain set on *Herman's Head*, the FOX sitcom in which his father had filled the recurring role as Genius. With such routine stimulation, one could anticipate that Cook eventually would major in creative writing. I wondered if he would, like later biblical authors Luke or John, follow baseball's first gospel writer (Dirk Hayhurst, who had published *Bullpen Gospels* the previous year) and put his own spin on the truths about the minor leagues.

While I made my way to my seat where longtime friend Jon Moody waited to greet me for a second successive game, I got intercepted by two fans who commented, "Great job, not like some yahoos."

A former colleague at Whittier, Jon was an emeritus religious studies professor at nearby Hiram College. The previous night, Jon and I had struggled to sustain discussions over the blaring music broadcast on the ballpark P.A. system. By contrast, thankfully, Eastlake's ballpark proved friendly to ongoing conversation.

I always look forward to talking with Jon since he is so passionate and reflective about his favorite teams and about sports in general, not to mention our shared passions related to social justice. A lifelong Boston fan, Jon years ago had told me a personal story about the true measures of baseball joy. During childhood his father had given him a baseball that he and his playmates had played with day after day on makeshift diamonds, hitting it again and again across rough fields and into streets. With great delight they played until the scuffed seams gave way and the cover fell off. Even tattered as a ball, they continued to play with it until its tautly wrapped threads finally unraveled or disintegrated.

A few years later Jon's father told him that he had been given the ball by Babe Ruth. Telling me the whole story, Jon derived great joy from the fact that the ball had brought such deep delight to so many children for so many games and hours. Forget its possible value as a relic for auction on Ebay! What greater tribute and connection to the Bambino might there be, Jon concluded, than that the ball had provided such extensive and enduring baseball pleasure for kids?!

Watching a game with Jon is special, in large part because of the range of our conversation. While we developed a proposal for Jon to return to Whittier to teach a short-term course on comparative ethics, which he was able to offer the following year, we interspersed our ideas with observations and evaluations about the two levels of play that we had seen on consecutive nights. Although we couldn't determine whether the players at Eastlake were significantly more skilled than those at Niles, we did agree that the umpires seemed to be more secure and steady in the Midwest League than in the short-season NYP League.

For the record, the Quad Cities River Bandits didn't get docked by the Captains. Instead, the visitors pounded out seventeen hits en route to a 15-3 win over Lake County, which meant, regrettably, that Cole Cook didn't pass the test that night, giving up four home runs in as many innings.

Still, Jon and I were able to enjoy another night of baseball—watching the game, sharing stories, and completing a trade between our fantasy-league teams, a move that buttressed Jon's position in first place and allowed me to build for the following season.

9.

More Heat and Rain

Voyage to Columbus: Game 72 in Columbus

I'm not sure whether our old RV Arbie felt a kinship with La Niña, La Pinta, and La Santa Maria—the pioneering vessels of Columbus; but like them he did encounter a new horizon in a venture associated with Columbus. Of course, Arbie's relation to Columbus was hardly that of a seagoing captain, merely the capital of Ohio.

For the first time on the summer's venture, Arbie went to a ballpark simply because we were on such a tight schedule. Immediately after breakfast we had left Mansfield, about two hours north of Columbus, and we approached Huntington Park at the time of my scheduled arrival. In its urban setting, the ballpark enjoys more than 14,000 automobile parking spots within a ten-minute walk of an entrance. Yet Arbie was challenged to find an accessible lot with enough contiguous spaces where, with his twenty-nine-foot length, he could cool down with Toad in tow. Unfortunately, we did stall traffic for three or four minutes while a parking assistant walkie-talkied for directions to a large, open lot, whose entry required our backtracking a couple of blocks. So we paid for three spots—only the third time that we had had to pay for parking at any game—and pulled Arbie over the curb, onto the grass, across the dirt field, and to a spot in a partially shaded area adjacent to the lot's far fence.

From our approach along the street and sidewalk, Huntington Park—built in 2009—looked inviting by, in a sense, looking backward. At its main entry a bronze sculpture of Howard Cooper stands tall, seeming ready to make a pitch for Columbus baseball. The previous ballpark in Columbus had been named for Cooper, a former county commissioner, general manager of the Columbus team, and president of the International League, including the night (and days) of the thirty-three-inning game in Pawtucket in 1981. At the foot of Cooper's statue multiple steles trace the storied, local history of professional baseball, each with plaques providing blurbs about the teams in Columbus: the Senators (1900–1930), the Red Birds (1931–1954), the Jets (1955–1970), and the current Clippers (starting in 1977); its Negro

League teams in the early twentieth century (the Black Tourists, the Buckeyes, the Keystones, the Turfs, the Blue Birds, and the Elite Giants); and its late-nineteenth-century major league predecessors, the Buckeyes of the International Association and the Reds of the Western League (a team that eventually became the American League's Cleveland Indians).

Even more striking than Cooper's statue and its adjoining foyer of foliage is the ballpark's stunning design. Along the left-field line a picnic terrace as wide as an infield is framed by the promise of eventual shade from a few young trees. Close by, the sculpture of an oversized bat, ball, and glove entices young fans to get a feel for the game, and the installation of the victory bell, which had hung at the Clippers previous ballpark, reminds everyone of the home-team wins that its ring had signaled. Beyond left field a multipurpose, three-story pavilion rises above the bleachers. From the promenade adjacent to its first level, fans can enter the team store thematically named "Clippers Cargo." Hanging in the stairwell to the second-floor restaurant, color sketches of starting players from select Columbus teams enliven the walls. The gallery effectively demonstrates the roster of star players who had worn Columbus uniforms, including Don Mattingly and Deion Sanders.

So popular that it's always crowded, the air-conditioned restaurant upstairs provides refuge for hundreds from the blistering heat and blinding glare of midday sun. While one side of the restaurant opens onto decks overlooking the field, its opposite wall is decorated with photographs of bygone players, memorabilia from earlier teams, brass plaques identifying Columbus record-setters and their sensational seasons, and framed quips and quotes by baseball notables about the game itself. As my students might expect, one of my favorites was Herbert Hoover's epigram: "Next to religion, baseball has furnished a greater impact on American life than any other institution." And for its humor, I particularly enjoyed Lefty Gomez's wisecrack: "We lost thirteen straight one year. I decided, if we got rained out, we'd have a victory party." Jerseys from various teams over the years were also suspended from the exposed pipes in the ceiling. And on the open-air floor above the restaurant, a section of bleachers resembled the popular rooftop seats across the streets from Wrigley Field.

Different areas of the ballpark proved equally fascinating to younger fans. Behind the centerfield fence in a public area accessible from the sidewalk during games, a water fountain drew children to play in its spray, and a perch above the wall in right centerfield allowed kids a narrow view if they chose to mimic knothole viewers at ballparks long ago.

On the field players also found the layout stimulating—and challenging—with its asymmetrical outfield dimensions and quirky fence. Extending the power alley in right field, a long bay juts out from the fence line, and a green mini-monster looms above the short warning track along the line in right. Even the foul pole incorporates artistic curvature—not in a twist of the pole but by overlaying its fair screen with various crescents.

In addition to these distinctive design elements and ornaments, several other factors contributed to Huntington's appeal, especially its amenities and its creative array of advertisements, most of which featured historic or playful baseball themes.

Fan friendly throughout, the ballpark enjoys wide concourses and a large concession stand set in the round so that hungry and thirsty folks can approach from any angle while keeping an eye on the field rather than watching a TV screen to keep up with the action. With food in hand, then, fans can either return to their seats or to one of several open spaces: the sloped lawn where blankets can be spread for lounging; the bar and bistro-style seating in the balconies above the little green monster; or the spacious, covered picnic area deep down the right-field foul line.

Rarely has a ballpark offered so much. Because of its dynamic design, its artistic and historic features, its welcoming amenities, and its excellent sightlines of the field, Huntington Park was recognized by several publications as the best new ballpark in the country in 2009, trumping Yankee Stadium, which also opened that same season.

On the field before the game I chatted with Yankees third-baseman Kevin Russo about his experience cavorting with BirdZerk several weeks earlier in Louisville. When I let him know that his acting job had sold me on the stealth of his glove, he smiled and acknowledged that he had had fun dancing and faking surprise during the routine. Russo's teammate Austin Krum also expressed delight when he saw the familiar face of Mike Nolan, the "super-usher" from the Trenton Thunder where Krum had played earlier in the season. Weeks before when I had met Mike at Trenton's game, he had indicated that his annual journey to select minor league parks would coincide with my schedule in Columbus.

While they reconnected, I was joined near the dugout by Allen Hye, a friend from the Dayton area who had driven up for the game. Two decades ago, Allen and I had met when we participated on a baseball panel at a meeting of the Popular Culture Association. On several occasions in recent years, we had continued to collaborate on various projects. On one occasion he had invited me to lecture at Wright State University on baseball and religion, and a few years later he published *The Great God Baseball: Religion in Baseball Fiction* in the series that I edit for Mercer University Press. Allen also had attended the game in Cincinnati when I had sung for the Reds some years earlier.

A lagniappe joy that I experience when singing at ballparks derives from seeing the expressions of delight on the faces of friends when they accompany me to the field during the pregame ceremonies. For many, it is a unique experience, almost like a child being chosen to play a game—with permission—in a sacred place. Like others, Allen smiled while joining me behind home plate, and he added a different twist to my appearance by taking photographs from atypical angles.

Also unusual for my performance in Columbus was the fact that the staff assistant told me that the anthem should start *precisely* at 12:02 following my brief introduction. Because the game was being televised as the featured minor league game of the day, the timing needed to be exact. The staffer also reminded me that my rendition should last less than ninety seconds, which didn't mean that I would be on camera during that time. Instead, it ensured sufficient time for ads and a prompt beginning of the game's telecast.

Attendance for the final game between the Yankees' top farm team and the Triple-A National Champion Clippers exceeded 7,000. But during the anthem the grandstands looked empty because the official game-time temperature, which was probably recorded in some undisclosed spot adjacent to an open ice chest, registered in the low nineties. And in Ohio in July the discomfort level could be more effectively gauged by the fact that the bleaching sun and the adhesive humidity beat almost everyone into retreat, including Bonnie who, after three innings, returned to Arbie, cranked up the generator, and turned on the air conditioner.

Sharing our mutual passion for baseball, Allen and I spent the rest of the game exploring various parts of the park, examining the old photos and framed aphorisms in the restaurant, and evaluating the major league potential of players on the Yankees and Clippers. Russo already had appeared in more than two dozen games for the parent Yankees during the previous season, and his teammate Greg Golson, who started the game in centerfield, likewise had played for New York in several games. The Clippers starting lineup similarly included two players who had spent time with the Bronx Bombers: Shelley Duncan, who had clubbed seven homers for them in his initial appearance in the big leagues at season's end in 2007, and Nick Johnson, who had played extensively for multiple teams during nine seasons in the major leagues.

While we speculated about the performance of several players, I focused on Russo and Krum, wondering how pregame interactions with fans and friends might affect a player's performance. Does it matter if the fans merely exchange pleasantries with a player rather than ask him for his autograph? Does it help or hurt if fans provide encouragement rather than distracting banter? Does a player perform better when he has been smiling and laughing before a game?

Considering the micro-sample of the performance of Russo and Krum in a single game, the answer to the last question would certainly be "yes." Russo had three doubles in five at-bats, and Krum went three-for-three with a double. In short, Russo and Krum were responsible for all of Scranton/Wilkes-Barre's runs, knocking in three and scoring the other three in the Yankees 6-5 win.

When Indians Might Not Be Indians: Game 73 in Indianapolis

For three consecutive games in Ohio I had sung for minor league teams affiliated with the Cleveland Indians; but none were named "the Indians." In sequence, the teams were called the Scrappers, the Captains, and the Clippers. Yet when I arrived at Victory Field in Indianapolis, the string of the Indians non-Indian-named teams took on an ironic twist: the Indianapolis Indians hadn't been aligned with Cleveland for more than half a century. In fact, for only a five-year period since the team's founding in 1902 had the Indians been associated with the major league team in Cleveland.

This nominal duplication of a major league team by a minor league team affiliated with another organization is highly unusual. Most frequently, teams either adopt their parent club's name or they identify with a distinctive regional characteristic that expands merchandising prospects. But since 2005, the Indianapolis Indians had been the Triple-A affiliate of the Pittsburgh Pirates, a connection that later in the evening occasioned one of the more serendipitous and delightful encounters with fans during the season.

Like the weather the previous day in Columbus, temperatures soared to record levels in central Indiana. When we arrived at the ballpark a couple of hours before the game, we sought an air-conditioned space where we might retreat from the afternoon swelter until game time. Even the souvenir store didn't prove alluring, perhaps because it was named the "Hot Corner Gift

Shop." Told that we could not wait in the team offices, Bonnie and I walked across the street to the JW Marriott Hotel.

From our perch in the hotel overlooking the centerfield gates to the ballpark, we sipped iced coffees while we watched early fans line up to claim their Indians tee-shirts—the evening's promotional giveaway. Wondering how long it would take some of them to wither in the sun, we overheard a brief heat-exchange between two staffers leaving the hotel. Looking out onto the crowd waiting to enter the ballpark, one intoned with rising pitch in her voice, "There's a game tonight?" To which, the other replied, "It's too hot for baseball."

But not for me. Probably never.

Even as "there's no crying in baseball," there's no weather too hot for baseball.

The hottest game for which I ever sang was in Palm Springs, where the Angels California League team had operated until 1993. Following an afternoon brown-out caused by a transformer overload, the August temperature had soared to 119 even though, by game-time, the official temperature had cooled a bit—to 116. On the sunny field, however, a thermometer almost burst as it surged a dozen degrees higher. While the heat had been dry in Palm Springs, the humid broil in Indianapolis was comparably uncomfortable since the temperature at dusk in the city officially registered at ninety-five degrees.

Avoiding as much of the scorching heat as possible, we lounged as long as we could in the cool of the Marriott, where we discovered that a baseball meeting—the Jerry Malloy Negro Leagues Baseball Research Conference sponsored by the Negro Leagues Committee of the Society for American Baseball Research—was adjourning for the day. Several of its participants began to make their way past us, proceeding down the escalator, across the street, and through the turnstiles, since several of the former Negro League players would be participating in the pregame ceremonies.

Although I was unfamiliar with the local Negro League veterans who attended the conference and appeared during the pregame events, I recalled having met Andy Porter, a pitcher for the Indianapolis Clowns. Fifteen years earlier he had spoken at Whittier College for a Black History Month celebration. During their brief membership in the Negro American League, the Clowns had won the pennant in 1950, Porter's final year with the team, and they also had become the first professional men's team to hire a female player, second "baseperson" Toni Stone in 1953.

Accompanying the group of former Negro League players and conference participants to the game was Rebecca Alpert, a friend and author of *Out of Left Field: Jews and Black Baseball.* Although I was then unaware of her presence at the game, I learned of the coincidence of our gigs in Indianapolis when, months later, she introduced me as a panelist at a religious studies conference on sports and religion. The surprise of learning later that friends have been at games when I have sung is one of the great delights that I associate with my anthem performances. Days or even months after several of the major league games for which I've sung, I have occasionally found out that friends attended one of "my" games and shared in the fun of telling seatmates about their connections with the performer.

Nearing the time for my scheduled re-check-in with the Indians' in-game staff, I left Bonnie in the comfort of the hotel to await the arrival of my youngest sister Fan and her son Samuel, both of whom lived nearby. Before the game I also had arranged to meet Tom Akin, a friend of the organist and choirmaster at Tustin Presbyterian Church where I regularly sang. A retired timpanist for the Indianapolis Symphony, Tom had also served for years as a broadcaster for the Indians games. Familiar with the radio booth, its adjoining suites, and the ushers controlling access to the area, Tom later took me to an unoccupied ballpark penthouse where we could view the game in comfort for a few innings. A more avid and accomplished baseball-card collector by far than I, Tom shared his love and lore about the Indians history and the city's ballparks; and I was pleased when he complimented the pace and pitch of my performance.

Yet the life of a ballpark and the temper of its crowd cannot be fully enjoyed from the isolation of a luxury suite. So back to the grandstands and their open concourses we went.

From our seats behind home plate, we enjoyed more facets of a minor league night: the antics of the mascot, interactions with ushers and fans, the score-keeping of the scouts, and of course, plays of the game. Most obvious was Rowdie, the Indians mascot who played with fans throughout the game, personally interacting in ways that typify a minor league ballpark experience. After posing for photographs with one ardent fan, he demonstrated a particular nose for the action by chomping her head.

As usual, in rows directly behind the backstop a troupe of scouts sat making notes about players, especially two of the Pirates highly touted prospects, outfielder Andy Marte and third-baseman Pedro Alvarez. Although we had routinely seen and interacted with scouts at other ballparks, for the first time on the tour we saw one using a different method to keep score, this time in Japanese.

With the evening heat continuing to sear our senses, I retreated toward the concession stand to get an icy treat for Bonnie. En route, Matt Wolfert stopped me to express appreciation for my traditional and enthusiastic performance of the anthem. As our conversation expanded, our encounter became one of the most serendipitous and felicitous experiences of the summer.

An associate athletic director at Ball State University, Matt was intrigued by the scope of my project of singing the anthem at so many parks throughout the country. Gesturing to his brothers to join our conversation, he introduced me to Dan and Mike, both of whom also worked in sports management: Dan as the athletic director for Yorktown High School near Muncie, and Mike as a sports marketer for IMG College in North Carolina.

Curious about how I had set up the tour, where I'd been, and where I was headed, they focused on the Pirates affiliates that fed Indianapolis. In particular, they expressed interest in my experience in the Florida State League. When I described my process of making initial queries to general managers a year earlier, Dan revealed that he had held that position at Bradenton at that time.

"Did I respond?" he quizzed. "What did I say?"

"Yes, I remember your e-mail address and reply," which I later confirmed with my e-mail records. "You indicated that it'd work out."

"I knew that I'd be gone and I'd let others make it happen," Dan grinned again.

On my way back to give Bonnie the frozen lemonade dessert, usher Joe Zaharako expressed appreciation for my unembellished anthem rendition. As we talked about my tour and our mutual love of baseball, he shared with me his copy of the program from the day's Negro League conference presentations and invited me to join him the following morning for the final sessions. Alas, I couldn't. Bonnie and I needed to be on our way to Fort Wayne for the night game there between the Tin Caps and the Quad Cities River Bandits.

While our eyes and ears often turned and tuned to these genial encounters and subtle observations, the game itself repeatedly reclaimed our attention because of so many "team" efforts, a contrast to the spectacular, individual achievements that often thrill the fans. One of the plays was one that I had never seen. In the Indians' second turn at bat, Marte stepped into the batter's box with runners on first and second. When he scalded a ground ball past the pitcher, Rochester's center fielder Brandon Roberts rushed toward the diamond, scooped the ball cleanly, and threw a bullet to the shortstop covering second base to get a force out on the runner sliding into the bag. What normally would have been a single to centerfield, loading the bases, ended up being a force play at second.

Less unusual was a pick-off move by Indianapolis pitcher Garrett Olson, although it did catch the runner so far off first base that he fled for second, where he was tagged out by the shortstop on a quick relay from the first-baseman. Another dramatic defensive play demonstrating close teamwork occurred at the plate when Rochester's third-baseman stabbed at a wicked hopper and threw home to nail the Indians runner, who slid into the sweeping tag by the catcher. Adding to these collaborative efforts were five double plays: three routinely turned on ground balls, another initiated on a liner caught by the pitcher, and a final one featuring a soft infield fly on a hit-and-run play. Sacrificial teamwork also typified the offensive efforts for both teams, who successfully laid down three sacrifice bunts and lofted a sacrifice fly.

After Rochester tied the score in the seventh inning, the game went into extra innings. With two outs in the bottom of the tenth, Indians centerfielder Gorkys Hernandez slapped his third hit of the night to right and collected his fourth RBI of the game when Pedro Alvarez slid past the tag of Rochester's catcher with the winning run on the game's final play: Indianapolis 5, Rochester 4.

Replacing Hubcaps with TinCaps: Game 74 in Fort Wayne

The morning after the game in Indianapolis we left the RV park near Greenfield, and Arbie was happy for a change in traffic patterns. For hundreds of miles since leaving New York, he had been restricted to interstate highways, mostly in Ohio. Now heading north, we followed county roads and state highways for an hour or more through flat fields and fields of blistered corn and soy. The rural route provided much needed refreshment from the thick truck traffic and furrowed surfaces of interstate highways 71 and 70 across Ohio and Indiana. Two days earlier in his trek along those freeways, Arbie had lost three of his four hubcaps, each of which had been bolted on. The cracks and holes in the highways that opened almost to Hell had won the wheel-cover battle. By contrast, we now made our way along a smoother, more remote route through Eden—really, that was the small town's name—

on our way to Anderson, where we merged onto I-69 North to Fort Wayne, home of the TinCaps and our destination for the day.

Although the territory in northeastern Indiana was new and refreshing to Arbie, Bonnie and I had traveled this way before. In summer 1974 when we had moved out of our first apartment in Louisville, we headed north for a summer job in Bluffton, Indiana, which lies halfway between Ossian and Petroleum south of Fort Wayne. There Bonnie and I sweated through July and August in an attic apartment provided by the church where I served as the summer assistant pastor. The apartment was so inadequately wired that it required a gas refrigerator because the simultaneous use of an electric skillet and a fan blew the entire circuit. To escape the sultry and claustrophobic condition of our rooms after dinner, we regularly drove to the local, air-conditioned grocery store to wander its aisles and to window shop the icy treats in its open-chest freezers.

Arbie must have intuited our dismal history in the region since he didn't blink while we peered straight ahead when we passed the Markle exit, the nearest freeway access to Bluffton. We cruised on through and beyond Fort Wayne, continuing north for about twenty miles to Auburn where we docked Arbie at an open RV site in the Fireside Campground within earshot of the interstate. By driving a few extra miles that day, we reduced our travel time the following day since I was scheduled to sing in Lansing for a late-afternoon Lugnuts game.

Although Bonnie had thought that she would take a night off from the TinCaps game after the extra-inning affair in Indianapolis the night before, roiling dark clouds rolled across the fields toward us and prompted her to reconsider plans. Accessing a weather website to track the density and direction of the approaching storm, the park's manager pointed out that Fort Wayne was beneath the path of the isolated thunderheads, and he showed us the shelter where we might find safety if, in the meantime, we needed to retreat from Arbie. Looking at the thunderheads and hearing the gusts whir past Arbie, Bonnie decided to join me as I left for the TinCaps game.

What a spectacular and surprising evening it turned out to be! The ballpark was as open and aesthetically stimulating as any that we had seen. The fans—especially young Asa Eames—were as charming and cordial as any. The in-game entertainment was absolutely delightful, particularly the dancing spoofs of the grounds crew and the comic routines of BirdZerk and his sidekicks. The game itself featured the play of Cory Spangenberg, the tenth overall selection in the baseball draft held a month earlier. And the threatening weather dissolved into an expansive sunset that lingered through the seventh-inning stretch.

The impressive home of the TinCaps is Parkview Field, a dually appropriate name since its naming rights had been purchased by Parkview Health System prior to the ballpark's opening in 2009, and since its architectural design—especially its integration of various performance and leisure spaces—creates such a park-like ambiance.

Beyond deep centerfield and its picnic patio, the stadium expanse includes an amphitheater whose angle of vision overlooks centerfield and home plate so far away that even Mark McGwire couldn't launch one of his steroid homers to the front row of the outdoor theater's tiers. Emphasizing the significance of this section of the ballpark's grounds, a bronze plaque recognizes the area as the Robert E. Meyers Park and acknowledges how the facility advances the city's "parks and recreation" mission: "to enhance the quality of life in Fort Wayne by providing positive opportunities for leisure time, and by being stewards of our parkland facilities, public trees, and other resources placed in our care."

Additional attractive areas of the ballpark resembled other new and theme-oriented stadia. Most notable was the elevated section above the right-field concourse and picnic concessions. But unlike the third-floor bleachers above the restaurant at Huntington Park in Columbus, the rooftop section at Parkview was reserved for large groups, and its seats appeared like those at a bistro bar rather than backless bleachers.

The TinCaps derived their name from the tin-pan hat that Johnny Appleseed reputedly wore backwards as he crossed the upper Midwest planting apple trees in the early nineteenth century. During his crisscrossing of Ohio, Indiana, and Illinois, he frequently stopped in Fort Wayne, eventually settling and dying there. Until its move to the new ballpark in 2009, Fort Wayne's team had been known as the Wizards. But in conjunction with the completion of the new stadium, the team adopted the TinCaps signature, an identity deeply rooted in the region.

Throughout the ballpark the apple theme also came into play. A large mural of the team's apple-face logo branded the wall behind the right-field rooftop grandstand named "The Treetops." In the opposite corner of the ballpark, a rock-climbing structure in the kids' play area featured the image of an apple tree on one face that was fed by a waterfall painted on the other side. Fans could pluck sweet souvenirs from the shelves in the team store called "The Orchard," and the suite level of exclusive seating was known as "J. Chapman," the legal name of Johnny Appleseed.

Apple names also applied to the team's entertainers and food selections. TinCaps mascot Johnny roamed through the stands personifying the team's namesake—and the grounds crew, known as "the Bad Apples," also regularly high-stepped into the playful act. Pausing amid their mid-innings raking of the infield dirt, the group of guys mocked Rockettes routines.

Since their infield manicure and dance took place between innings, many fans missed their missteps while getting snacks, several of which were apple-related. At multiple concession stands, TinCaps punch and salads could be purchased, and the Apple Cart situated on the concourse near the main entry offered a range of apple-only treats: turnovers and pies, dumplings and wontons, sauce and cider, and of course, caramel- and candy-coated fruit.

I guess that I must have seemed rotten, breaking this apple momentum since I didn't take photos or record the anthem with my Apple iPhone.

During the prolonged pre-anthem ceremonies that included sixteen first pitches, I chatted with Dominic Latkovski, the entertainer who dons the BirdZerk costume and portrays that playful character. Having been amused by his shenanigans in Louisville—particularly his dancing antics with the first-base umpire impersonator and his stolen-glove frolic with the visiting team's third-baseman—I told him that his skits were the most entertaining baseball routines since Max Patkin's gags as the Clown Prince of Baseball. Like Patkin's parody of players and umpires, BirdZerk's stunts engage players on the field while lampooning their work. As we talked about the ball-glove sketch, Latkovski let me know that Quad Cities first-baseman Jonathan Rodriguez would be his prank partner a few innings later.

While I enjoy the playfulness associated with ballpark names, exhibits, and entertainments like those in Fort Wayne, I am much more of a traditionalist when it comes to performances of the national anthem. I prefer that "The Star-Spangled Banner" be sung at a crisp tempo and without embellishment so that all might embrace it as *our* nation's song, not as an individual's improvisation. Simply, I consider the anthem to be somewhat sacred, a hymn of our civil religion. Even the dramatic accompaniment of the anthem with fireworks, which the TinCaps provided during the phrases about "rockets' red glare" and "bombs bursting in air," seems to make the anthem more of an entertainment than a patriotic canticle by detracting from the historic significance of the words and by distracting the audience's orientation toward the flag. A few innings after I had sung, a woman approached me at the concession stand and said, simply, "Thanks for not doing something crazy." I wondered whether she had regarded the fireworks as crazy or coordinated.

More accustomed to the harmonization between the fireworks with the lyrics, usher Sam Stokes also expressed appreciation for my straightforward rendition. As an elementary-school music teacher, he indicated that he wished that fans would routinely join in singing the anthem. If they had simple choral lessons in grade school, he mused, they would more easily overcome their hesitation about singing "The Star-Spangled Banner," which he regarded as a "sing-able tune, even with its wide range." The anthem, he concluded, "brings together the joys of patriotism and singing."

A particular source of joy for me throughout the tour was observing preschoolers during games. Occasionally, they would pay close attention to action on the field, watching pitchers wind up and batters swing while they waited expectantly for a foul ball to ricochet their way, as did the little girl in Fort Myers. More often, they invented their own games, like the enchanting child in Jackson, Tennessee, who climbed over, under, and through the handrails as though they were a jungle gym. And a few, like Samantha in Augusta, drew pictures in a sketchbook or colored portions of a scorecard. But no child captivated my attention more than three-year-old Asa Eames in Fort Wayne. His brother Eli—older by four years or so—had been one of the first pitchers preceding the anthem. That meant that, as pregame participants, his family's seats and ours were in adjacent rows.

When Asa's father Billy showed him the program blurb about BirdZerk, Asa enthusiastically shared the information with his brother. Then he turned excitedly to me and, pointing to BirdZerk's picture, told me that we would see him soon.

Asa and I struck up a conversation about everything—his piece of chicken, his brother's name, his trip to the game, and so on. I was further charmed when he set his soda cup in the holder in front of my seat, making it easier for him to turn and sip through the straw without losing his balance by leaning forward. Of course, it also made it much easier for him to talk with me. He was happy, uninhibited, and well-mannered, except for not having asked permission to use my cup holder. Even that I found charming.

When BirdZerk started to dance with his partner impersonating the first-base umpire, Asa smiled and talked on and on, describing in some detail BirdZerk's gymnastic display with "the ump." A short time later Asa gurgled with laughter when BirdZerk pulled the stolen-glove trick with the River Bandits first baseman.

My delight in chatting with Asa and his family extended beyond our mutual enjoyment of BirdZerk's entertainment. On the occasions when I left my seat to buy an apple snack or simply walk the stands to interact with fans, Asa would turn to Bonnie and inquire, "Where did your guy go?"

Asa won our hearts throughout the TinCaps surprising win, especially given their pitching woes and fielding miscues. While hometown fans groaned during the TinCaps inept defensive play—which included seven walks, one balk, one hit batter, three wild pitches, two passed balls, and four errors—they applauded the play of Cory Spangenburg and Wes Covington. A hot prospect and recent addition to the TinCaps roster, Spangenburg collected three hits, equaling the total of his output in his first ten games, and Covington knocked in six runs, setting a career high. With two outs in the bottom of the ninth, they combined to produce the walk-off run for the TinCaps 8-7 win.

Old(s) and New: Game 75 in Lansing

Leaving the RV park in Auburn just north of Fort Wayne early Sunday morning, we headed three hours north to Lansing, Michigan, old home of the Oldsmobile factory (until 2004) and still home of the Lansing Lugnuts. Initially named "Oldsmobile Park" for the oldest brand of American automobiles, Lansing's relatively new ballpark, built in 1996, oddly stands as a kind of relic to the automotive industry since it witnessed the demise of the trademark car's manufacture within less than a decade following its construction. Now the ballpark is legally known as the Cooley Law School Stadium—a paradox of sorts since Cooley Law School, which purchased the naming rights, doesn't field any athletic team. Even so, the ballpark's old "Olds" name is a cherished one, and one emblazoned in my memory.

For the decade preceding its death, Olds had promoted a television ad campaign that featured a slogan designed to appeal to a new generation of prospective Olds owners: "This is not your father's Oldsmobile." But for me, that is exactly what the car had been. My father's Olds 88, a cherished gift in 1963 from the church that he had pastored for almost twenty years, was the car in which I had learned to drive.

Although I had never been to Lansing, the name of its ballpark evoked the deep sense of satisfaction that the 88 had prompted decades earlier. Completed in anticipation of the inaugural season for the Lugnuts,

Oldsmobile Ballpark hosted its very first game between Big Ten, in-state rivals Michigan and Michigan State, with the Wolverines winning an extra-inning decision by a single run over the Spartans. About the time that the nearby factory towed the last Olds off the production line, renovations to the adolescent Oldsmobile ballpark were completed, and various fan pit stops in the ballpark assumed names aligned with the automotive industry and its products. The picnic porch was designated as Gasoline Alley, and the souvenir store was tagged as Nuts and Bolts, while the hot dog and burger stand—the Chrome Plated Grille—crouched under the hood of the grandstand.

Even though the concession stands adopted automotive names, they didn't thematize their super-size snacks with names like a "trunk full of fries" or a "tank of tea." Yet they did toss a change-up toward the downhome favorite of a fried bologna sandwich, which they distinguished by serving the seared and warped deli slice on a toasted waffle bun. Still, it's too bad that they didn't label that snack as a "tire-tread delight."

As usual, I arrived at the ballpark well before game time, indicating to the parking-lot attendant that I was the anthem singer and asking where I should park. "Not here unless you have a printed pass," he offered. "But you can park in that space while you go to the office to check on the availability of a pass." I did. And there I learned that all of the lot's spaces were designated for the day. "So where should I park?" I asked Nick Grueser, the assistant general manager who was working at the ticket window. "In a metered space on the street," he replied, "since parking is free on Sundays." Then shoving a five-dollar bill into my hand, he added, "If you can't find a spot close by, this should cover the charge of one of the lots across the street."

Welcomed by Nick's gesture, I smiled at the attendant as I exited the small reserved lot, turning right toward the state capitol hovering at the end of Main Street less than a mile away. Toad hopped into the first open spot about a block away, prompting the return of the five-spot to Nick a few minutes later.

The walk back to the ballpark was surprisingly stimulating. Several sidewalk sculptures and brilliant banners, which had been installed as part of Lansing's street exhibition, remained on display. Nearest the ballpark's entry was an intriguing and interactive installation, "C'ood: a democracy experiment," by Margaret Parker. Airy, the colorful sculpture invited fans and even passersby to detour through its space to see the Lansing world and sky through its steel-laced portals.

Also welcoming fans to the ballpark were memorial and tribute bricks interspersed throughout the walkway leading to the main entrance. Curious about who might be honored with sentiments, I found a grandchild's tribute to "Clare Warner—1880–1953/Grandpa Loved Baseball," and the simple affirmation "Friends of Joe," offered by "Le Legion du Lugnuts."

Before Lansing, Sunday-afternoon games had produced several unpredictable spiritual expressions. At my first Sunday-afternoon game in Fort Myers three months earlier, I had witnessed a genuine act of grace when a six-year-old girl had dashed for a foul ball bouncing through the box seats, retrieving it gleefully and then giving it to a disappointed preschool-aged boy whom she had beaten to the prize. Weeks later at a Sunday game in Mississippi, muted recognition of the Christian Sabbath was ironically displayed: while the P.A. announcer acknowledged several church groups attending the game, the primary evidence of its being Sunday was the closure of the Chick-Fil-A concession, a corporate policy to permit employees to join their families for worship, and the pregame singing of "Amazing Grace" by a choir from a secular school. And prior to the Sunday game in Asheville, I had heard—for the only time all summer—a public invocation delivered from behind home plate before my singing of the national anthem.

Yet in Lansing, Sunday manners and patterns appeared more typical, even if more secluded than in the other ballparks. In the undercroft where I was taken to warm up or wait for the pregame ceremonies, a sign on the door to the Lugnuts' locker room invoked silence and respect: "Chapel in progress." Minutes earlier, Baseball Chapel had concluded its home-game Sunday Bible study and meditation under the leadership of two chaplains, both members of Lansing's South Church.

Rolando Quiroga had led the Spanish-language Bible lesson, focusing on the challenges of sexual temptation and biblical teachings about resisting temptation. Although members of the visiting team often participated in the Sunday services, none from Beloit had joined the four Lugnuts and ballpark staff members who had attended this morning. During the Bible studies for Spanish speakers, seminary student Jeremy Focu had led an English-language devotional. In his first year serving as a leader for Baseball Chapel services, Jeremy was in the process of assuming the mantle of his father-in-law, who had served as Lansing's chaplain since the team had been founded. Like Rolando, Jeremy focused his morning message on the epistle to Titus, emphasizing the need to exercise control over temptations.

By the time that I entered the locker room, the evangelistic service had ended and the space had resumed its function as a dressing room. While I began my facial exercises, the staffer assigned to play the role of Big Lug—the team mascot—entered and looked at me strangely. Moments later as he donned the costume and mask with large nuts depicting open nostrils, I returned the quizzical look.

Often at Class-A ballparks, interns who escorted me to field had little interest in the anthem or my tour. That was certainly not the case in Lansing, where staffer Gabe Esquivel inquired about my singing of the anthem game after game, each with different settings, procedures, and acoustics. She acknowledged that earlier in the season she had performed the anthem at a Lugnuts game as a last-minute replacement. Hours before a performer had been scheduled to appear, she had received a call to pinch sing. The most memorable part of her experience, she recalled, was that she had rehearsed her rendition in the car while driving to the ballpark.

At Lansing, my rendition a short time later continued a week's run of stellar performances. My evaluation was confirmed by a vacationing Methodist minister who remarked on my performance as "crisp and undecorated," as she put it, "making it possible for all to join in, like a congregational hymn." That's success—because it's *our* national anthem, not *my* theme song, however much I might be associated with it.

During the fourth inning a carefree kid abandoned his ball and glove, shoving them under the bench a row or so behind his grandfather Leonard Burns, who angled back toward the boy's stuff while I focused my camera on the innocent equipment. Assuring him that I was simply photographing the deserted gear, I enjoyed another serendipitous encounter, learning that he had been on Whittier's campus decades earlier. When he had served as the superintendent of Bellflower schools near Los Angeles, Dr. Burns had attended the inauguration of Eugene Mills as president of Whittier College a few years before I joined its faculty.

At most minor league ballparks, a roster of players who have made it to The Show is prominently displayed, and often banners or posters throughout the concourse celebrate current major league stars who had played for the home team. At several of the ballparks, there were team "halls of fame"—bronze plaques or photographic exhibits that identified the most outstanding players of bygone years. At Salem, Virginia, an elaborate building dedicated to their recognition stood adjacent to the children's Wiffle-ball diamond.

At Lansing there was a different pitch for its few Hall of Fame inductees, who included accomplished major-leaguers Carlos Beltran and Carlos Zambrano. Also celebrated by Lansing with Hall of Fame honors was Brian Dopirak, a former Lugnut inducted in 2010 after toiling in the minors for almost a decade. The impressive thing about his inclusion is that, after eight years playing primarily for small-town teams, he had not sipped a cup of coffee in the big leagues. Still, he was honored because in 2004 he had set Lansing records for home runs and RBIs in a season—thirty-nine and 120, respectively—also socking thirty-eight doubles while batting .307. Now he had risen for a full season to Triple-A; and I had seen him in a single plate appearance for the Oklahoma City RedHawks when they had lost to the Nashville Sounds, also on a Sunday. Then he had carried a .259 average into the game and walked as a pinch hitter in the sixth inning.

In this game between the Lugnuts and Snappers, no plays or players stood out other than the Lugnuts starting pitcher, Marcus Walden, who departed with a nail-biting win after five strong innings of one-hit ball before the Snappers chomped the lead to a single run before the home team held on for a 6-4 victory.

A Loony Christmas Tune: Game 76 in Midland

Months before I had hummed the starting pitch for my first rendition on the anthem tour, I had mapped out desirable routes for connecting sites to minimize mileage and maximize landscape beauty and other passing attractions. While trying to figure out how I could pass through areas of the country that I had not previously seen, I had wanted to align consecutive games in Midland, Michigan, where the Great Lakes Loons make their home, with other teams in the Midwest League. And because I had never been to Michigan's Upper Peninsula, I had hoped that it would be possible to aim Arbie north from Midland, crossing the bridge at Mackinaw City, looping through the U.P., and then descending through Wisconsin to Appleton for a Timber Rattlers appearance. Although that route would have exceeded my daily mileage limit, I figured an extra night between games would be worth the northern exposure. And if the trek north could not have been successfully projected, then taking Arbie and Toad on a ferry ride across Lake Michigan from Ludington to Manitowoc, just an hour's drive from Appleton, might have been equally adventurous.

Alas, neither schedule could be worked out. Meanwhile, Midland didn't seem to lie along a route to anywhere, much less midway to somewhere. Even so, I set up a date with the Loons following a game in Lansing and two days before one for the Kane County Cougars in suburban Chicago.

While Bonnie and I headed north in Toad from the comforts of the Cottonwood RV Park in Lansing, I wondered if Midland would be worth our jaunty spur since neither the Mackinaw route nor the Lake Michigan crossing had become feasible. Added to my concerns was the fact that the Midland team enjoyed the support of Dow Chemical, whose home office and primary plant are in Midland. As an ardent supporter of ecological initiatives, I could hardy fathom appreciating the alignment of the Loons with Dow. Yet few teams, ballparks, and cities proved as receptive, supportive, innovative, and community-oriented as Midland. And it also enjoyed an affiliation with one of my hometown teams, the Dodgers, as their Lo-A affiliate.

Often, staff members who escorted me during the pregame ceremonies were unaware of my anthem project, and some had to request my name, which occasionally had been omitted from the day's flowchart of pregame activities. More than two dozen times, I had been introduced simply by name while first pitchers and dream-team players frequently received more extensive introductions. On a number of other occasions, staff had greeted me appreciatively and graciously—and Midland led the leagues in this category. The credit for such incredible hospitality goes to Linda Lones, the game-day staff member who coordinated my visit.

During the staff meeting before the gates opened to fans, Linda informed ushers and game-day entertainers about my tour while emphasizing the evening's theme of "Christmas in July." The meeting ended with a cheer, and the staff, appearing jubilant like carolers, dispersed to their respective duties, many stopping to welcome me and thank me for including Midland on the tour.

Familiar with positive experiences that I had written about in my blog, especially the fun at Altoona where she had worked the previous year, Linda indicated that she wanted to do something special to distinguish my visit to Midland. She proposed that I throw out the first pitch, an opportunity that I had not been offered. Moments before the anthem, then, I joined Santa on the mound and threw a pitch over the heart of the plate—but on a single bounce!

Thankfully, my delivery of the anthem went without a hitch or hop. Then, for only the second time all tour, the home-team manager—John Shoemaker—approvingly stopped me and handed me an autographed ball.

Fans also expressed their appreciation in more typical comments: "Thank you for your project." "What you're doing is good." "Thanks for coming to Midland."

After I joined Bonnie in the stands, Linda appeared with Santa sacks filled with Loons loot: tee-shirts and blankets, trinkets and candies, and two bobble-head dolls, both from earlier promotions—one of Michigander Kirk Gibson and the other of former Loon and then-Dodgers pitcher Hong-Chi Kuo. When we returned to Arbie later that evening, we mounted the mini-Kuo on the shelf above the door to the RV, letting him function for safe-keeping like old St. Christopher statuettes mounted on dashboards of sturdy station wagons.

Modeling yuletide joy, staff members wore Christmas ties and tucked Santa hats into their belts. Their merriment extended to the introductions of the Loons, whose representations on the scoreboard featured the winter holiday theme by using a candy-cane font to identify uniform numbers. When right fielder Nick Akins came to bat, he was depicted as St. Nick with a white beard and Santa's cap. At the plate, Akins experienced a game like Christmas, getting on base in all five plate appearances, slapping two singles and working three walks.

And other Loons joined him in the Christmas hit parade: doubling was "Cold" David Iden, who was represented in ice attire; and singling were John Garcia, portrayed in an elf costume, and lumbering first-baseman Chris Jacobs, depicted as "the Grinch who stole Christmas," even though he had not stolen a base all season.

Despite the scoreboard's festive presentation of the Loons, the game itself featured umpires almost as much as players. In the top of the sixth inning after a close play at the plate, the home-plate ump, Dane Ratajski, tossed the Loons catcher Michael Pericht who argued the call. And in the next inning Ratajski ejected designated hitter Bobby Coyle after striking out. While it's not uncommon for a player to argue a called third strike, or even a checked swing, it's unusual to see a player tossed after swinging and missing strike three.

Not to be out-argued by Ratajski, base umpire Mario Seneca blew two calls, prompting protests before reversing his rulings. With runners on first and second and none out, Iden hit a soft liner to the edge of the infield grass in front of the shortstop. Too low for the infield fly rule to be called, the Wisconsin infielder snared the ball on a short hop while the runners, thinking it would be caught on the fly, returned to their bases. The shortstop tossed the ball to the third-baseman, who tagged the base, forcing the runner who had retreated to second. Then he threw the ball to the second-baseman, who tagged second—and the base-runner, standing on the bag, just to make sure. Finally, he threw the ball to first, where the runner had crossed the base and stood with his teammate who had retreated.

In the confusion of runners and throws, Seneca called a triple play, and the Rattlers left the field. Iden, meanwhile, was instructed by his first-base coach to stay on first—alone.

Shoemaker argued mildly, asking Seneca to consult with Ratajski, the home-plate ump. He did. After they sorted through the sequence of tosses and tags, Iden was ruled safe and the Timber Rattlers returned to the field to record a different final out of the inning.

I never did see a triple play.

In the next inning Seneca blew another call, another based on familiarity with the rules rather than simply a judgment decision, like calling a strike, a balk, or an out on a bang-bang play. This situation was different. With a runner on first and none out, Wisconsin's batter bunted down the first-baseline, and it was fielded by the first-baseman who made a sweeping tag attempt on the hitter. Seneca called him safe. Again Shoemaker argued and asked for him to confer with Ratajski, who ruled correctly that the batter had been out for swerving out of the baserunner's lane. The score: Shoemaker 2, Seneca 0.

As magnetic as were the plays and calls in the game and as gracious as was the reception of my appearance by staff and fans, the experience in Midland was made even more engaging by the character of the Loons organization and the architecture of the ballpark. While some minor league teams like the Arkansas Travelers are community-owned, the Great Lakes Loons are unique in their ownership by a non-profit public charity, the Michigan Baseball Foundation. At the end of each baseball season, the foundation awards its year-end balance to various Midland and mid-Michigan charities. And the previous year's donations had exceeded $100,000.

The salutary mission of the organization was also reflected in the ballpark's design and facilities. Built on the site of the original headquarters for the Dow Chemical Company, the stadium had been completed in 2007 in time for the Loons' inaugural game after the purchase of the Southwest Michigan team and its move from Battle Creek. In that initial year, the Dow Diamond won *Baseball Digest*'s award for the Best New Ballpark.

The organization and the ballpark are the only ones that I encountered with a thorough commitment to sustainability, evinced by their pledge to cut their water, waste, and energy use by half in the next decade. For starters, the huge videoboard was powered by more than 150 solar panels installed adjacent to the park's right-field gate. Although there was no direct connection between the panels and the scoreboard, the energy annually generated by the solar system essentially equaled that required for the videoboard's operation.

Manifesting its ecological initiative in a different way, the ballpark's construction crew crushed and repurposed the red brick salvaged from the original Dow complex for use as cinders in the warning track.

A distinct ballpark design element also enhanced the Christmas in July promotion. A grand fireplace dominated the intersection of the main entry and the concourse, allowing stockings to be hung by the chimney with care. Adding warming possibilities to the ballpark in another way, two fire pits on the terraces beyond left field were set to lure "Loony" fans on cold, early-season evenings—hardly the situation on the ninety-plus degree day when we were there.

All said, you gotta love the Loons, even though they got struck 6-3 by the Wisconsin Timber Rattlers.

Chicago Promotions: Game 77 in Kane County

Once Bonnie had decided to join me in the cross-country journey in Arbie, I wanted to make sure that we could be in the Chicago area at the end of July for her birthday. She loves to visit friends in the city where we had spent almost a decade during my graduate studies. And since art, not baseball, is one of her passions, Chicago also inspires her with the Art Institute, especially its collection of works by French Impressionists and its proximity to Millennium Park.

When we arrived in suburban Chicago three days before her birthday, we anticipated enjoying tourist sites during our free time before and after my appearance with the Kane County Cougars, the only minor league team within earshot of a Harry Caray home-run call at Wrigley Field. Usually when we had returned to Chicago, we typically had stayed with friends on the South Side or at one of the hotels on the Miracle Mile near the river. But with Arbie to care for, we selected an RV park in north suburban Volo, a location near one of the commuter rail lines to the Loop and within a few miles of a truck repair shop where we had scheduled a mechanic to replace the bushings on our bouncing beast.

To this point on our trip—to our great surprise—we had found that few of the RV parks where we stayed were peopled with RVers on the move. Most were locations where permanent RV residents lived, as in Springdale, Arkansas, which had a single space unoccupied by "long termies"; or the RV parks served primarily as vacation locations, like the one in Wales, Massachusetts, where most of the sites were set up as second summer homes. Sometimes the sites were simply destinations for multi-day stays, such as the Zooland Park in Asheboro near the North Carolina Zoological Park and the Potter's Museum in Seagrove. Yet few parks had been like the ones near Memphis, Richmond, and Fort Wayne, ones that we had expected to find more frequently: easily accessible from a freeway and with plenty of pull-through sites and clean facilities. Our place at the Fish Lake Beach RV Park in Volo fit the vacation-home category: Of the 550 sites there, ninety percent seemed to be permanently docked motor and mobile homes for weekend and summer escapes for folks in the Chicago vicinity.

Throughout the week before our arrival there, record-breaking heat had blanketed the upper Midwest, making afternoon and early-evening games miserable. The Chicago area greeted us with a different weather threat. During our first night there, thunderstorms raged and the downpour continued past the second pot of morning coffee. Finally as the storm started to break, our site resembled the shallows of Fish Lake itself. Puddles had swelled into ponds.

Concerned that my Kane County appearance might be rained out, I began to wonder whether Ann Lindner, one of our Chicago friends who planned to join us for the game that evening, might be a thunderstorm jinx. A month earlier she had coordinated her family's vacation to Washington, D.C., to coincide with my schedule for singing for the Potomac Nationals. But that game had been rained out by a microburst that had deluged the municipal ballpark but not the shopping mall a few miles away.

During the day several calls to the Cougars front office assured me that the evening game would proceed as scheduled. Even so, I hoped that there would be at least one shift from the standard guidelines that the Cougars anthem coordinator had sent to me several weeks earlier. They included the recommendation that I should purchase my tickets early. Hmm. Purchase tickets? For several ballparks along the way I had been warned that I would need to pay for parking—a fee that was waived by appreciative lot attendants on all but two occasions—but no team had suggested that I would need to pay for entry to the game for which I would sing.

When we neared Elfstrom Park in Geneva thirty-five miles south of Arbie's flooded site, I took the late-afternoon sunshine as a brilliant omen. Walking toward the ticket office I spotted the spotless pants of a Cougars player hanging from a branch in the tree near the exit from the home-team clubhouse. While the sunshine might have been a good omen, I didn't know how to interpret the half-scarecrow of trousers: Had #45 been found guilty in the Cougars kangaroo court? Or did the dangling pants portend me getting "pantsed" during my tickets request? Warily, I approached the Will Call window and identified myself as the anthem singer, indicating that assistant general manager Jeff Ney had set things up as part of my national tour. Twisting her mouth to the right side and raising her eyebrows, the Cougars staffer then shrugged a little and handed me three tickets, probably in Ney's own box since they were in the first row behind the backstop.

To a certain extent Minor League Baseball attracts fans in relation to the promotions that are offered. Each Wednesday at Kane County, attendees received a "Winning Wednesdays" scratcher, which might hide a discount coupon for a featured concession, tickets to a subsequent game, or the chance to throw out a first pitch.

During the game, an upcoming celebration of promotions was also advertised. The extravaganza would feature 100 different promotions offered throughout the game, and it would spotlight Nancy Faust (the Chicago-sports organist extraordinaire who had accompanied me at old Comiskey Park in 1977 when I first had sung the national anthem for a major league game) and Mike Veeck (son of the promotional innovator Bill Veeck, part-owner of five minor league teams, and the person who had set up my initial singing for the White Sox). Mike himself also proved to be an inventive promoter, once having arranged for a pig to deliver baseballs to the home-plate umpire and on another occasion having offered fans a chance to receive a therapeutic massage from a Roman Catholic nun. I only wished that I could have stayed in Kane County long enough to attend the Cougars promotional festival and witness the shenanigans that promised to be in store.

In a different way I also experienced a promotion at the ballpark. On the announcement board along the concourse behind home plate, the Cougars had posted an article from the *Kane County Chronicle* about my appearance at Elfstrom Stadium. Standing a few feet away while I read and photographed the piece was its author, Kevin Druley, who had talked with me several days earlier following a feature that had run on the University of Chicago's website.

The university's story had also prompted Manya Brachear, a feature writer for the *Chicago Tribune*, to send one of the newspaper's staff photographers to shoot my performance so that a picture could accompany her story the following day. After Jeff Ney saw the *Tribune*'s photographer videoing my performance, he seemed stunned that the *Trib* was finally noticing the suburban Cougars. "I've tried over and over to get them just to print our scores," he bemoaned, "and they always ignore us. How did you get them to come out here?"

While the publicity about my appearance at Kane County was unusual, there were customary displays and experiences at Elfstrom. Like several other minor league ballparks, current major leaguers and former team stars were recognized with banners and images. On the awnings above the entry to Elfstrom, action images of Cougar alumni Josh Beckett, Joe Blanton, Ryan Dempster, and Adrian Gonzalez greeted fans. And inside the ballpark former Cougar catcher Charles Johnson was recognized by his retired number—"35"—the only one so honored by the team. Twice a first-round draft pick (initially by the Montreal Expos after graduating from high school and then by the Florida Marlins in 1992 when he was finishing his collegiate career at the University of Miami), Johnson had slugged nineteen home runs and collected ninety-four RBIs for Kane County in 1993, his first season as a pro. Within two years, he was playing regularly for the Marlins, and during his twelve-year major league career, he won five Gold Glove awards and twice was named to the all-star team. Since both Josh Beckett and Adrian Gonzalez had worn number "19," I would expect that number to be the next one retired by the Cougars.

Like clusters of fans at a number of other parks, a quartet of regulars—Sue, Dan, Pam, and Judy—sat in a shady set of seats behind the backstop and congratulated me, commenting specifically on my tone, pace, and articulation, as well as the fact that I appeared to enjoy singing the anthem.

Over the years Dan had attended games in about 100 ballparks, and Judy enjoyed watching her grandson play for the Cougars. They let me know that they regularly grade anthem performances; and so I asked about my score: a 93, a low "A," a grade that fit with the Low-A level of the Midwest League. Curious about how my rendition might rank with others that they had heard, I inquired about distinct anthem performances that they recalled. While they assured me that they would remember mine favorably because of my tour, they recounted face-puckering ones with sour pitch that they routinely had heard season after season.

The game itself also caused the hometown fans to cringe during a seventh-inning disaster. After starting pitcher Yordano Ventura and reliever Antonio Cruz had shut Cedar Rapids down following a first-inning run, the Cougars seventh-inning pitchers created distress rather than relief, allowing three singles, issuing three walks, adding a wild pitch, and permitting the Kernels to score four times, enough to assure the visitors' victory, 6-3.

A Second July Birthday Celebration

Rarely did Bonnie and I remain in an RV site or a city for a day following my scheduled game, much less for two days. Routinely we felt the need to press on to the next location and enjoy the freedom of resting or refreshing in the next ballpark's town, thus reducing anxiety about travel complications that might arise during a final approach.

But Bonnie's birthday called for a different tactic, a break from baseball, my meager gift to her.

On the morning after the Cougars loss in Kane County, we boarded the commuter train in Grayslake and headed to downtown Chicago for a day of dining, viewing art, enjoying friends, and meandering along the Magnificent Mile. There we strolled through Millennium Park, walked along Michigan Avenue, and savored lunch at the Capital Grille before spending a couple of hours with two of my mentors.

Martin Marty and his wife Harriett hosted us for wine and cheese in their spectacular home on the eighty-fifth floor of the Hancock Tower overlooking Lake Michigan. The view extended beyond the University of Chicago (our mutual academic home) ten miles to the south. When I had reached a critical juncture in my graduate studies, Marty had invited Bonnie and me to his home to talk with him about my academic pursuits and our family life. His counsel that evening was cogent and compassionate, as it had been on several previous occasions. Incredibly, his graciousness—as always—matched his scholarly excellence (an amazing tribute given his productivity of more than fifty books authored and edited). And Harriet, a professional music instructor and advocate, engaged our venture with great enthusiasm. Enlivened by our afternoon with the Martys, Bonnie and I walked the Chicago streets near the Water Tower before ducking into the Museum of Contemporary Art for an hour or so.

Weeks before the anthem tour began, my initial graduate-school advisor Tony Yu, who also served on my dissertation committee member, invited Bonnie and me to celebrate her birthday with a Chinese dinner of Peking duck prepared by one of Chicago's premier chefs. Tony, who had made one of the signal contributions to world literature in the last generation by translating the Chinese epic *The Monkey*, had long been more than an academic guide and scholarly model for me. An accomplished pianist, Tony accompanied me when I would sing operatic arias at luncheons at the university.

After Bonnie and I had left the exhibits at the Museum of Contemporary Art, we walked through the Near North area of Chicago and arrived at the elegant home of Tony and Priscilla Yu. He greeted us with fabulous champagne, handed me a copy of Manya Brachear's story from the *Chicago Tribune*, and invited me to sing the anthem with his accompaniment. How could I resist? The course work that I had completed with Tony about the spiritual significance of secular literature had provided the conceptual foundation for me to begin to think about how sports might function as a civil religion. We sang, we sipped, we laughed, and we reminisced. Then he drove us to the Phoenix Restaurant in Chinatown where he had preordered the celebratory Peking duck.

I cannot adequately describe the honor that I felt in the Yus' embrace of a special day for Bonnie. The dinner was spectacular, the conversation unlike anything that can be explained other than to say that it was stimulating, thoroughly University of Chicago, and personally affirming. That energy was one of the wonderful gifts that Tony and Priscilla directed to his students. And following the meal that included an array of customized entrees that Tony entreated the chef to prepare, they drove us to Union Station where we boarded the train back to Grayslake and then, eventually, Arbie.

While I found a mechanic to replace Arbie's bushings on the following day, Bonnie's actual birthday, she returned to the Loop to view the exhibits at the Art Institute with her friend Ann, followed by lunch in Terzo Piano, its elegant restaurant, and their departure for a weekend women's retreat.

Rattled by Routes and Rain: Game 78 in Wisconsin

Routing headaches and traffic miseries rarely had worried me on our way to ballparks, partly because of Toad's maneuverability, partly because of Bonnie's access to Web reports about alternate routes, and partly because I insisted on having an arrival cushion that often deposited us at ballparks well before my scheduled pregame meeting with staff.

In San Antonio, road construction in the heart of the city had prompted us to Google a different approach to the Missions ballpark, only to find that we had been directed to an authentic San Antonio mission on the opposite side of the city. Even so, we made it to the baseball park a half-hour before the game's start, exactly at the time I was scheduled to meet the game-day staff. Approaching New Orleans, we had learned that the causeway over Lake Pontchartrain was clogged or closed, prompting us to take a more circuitous route that still gave us plenty of time to get to the Zephyrs ballpark. And the miracle of iPad access allowed us to circumvent clogs in Birmingham and Gwinnett. Yet in Massachusetts, while Arbie still had Toad tethered, we found no escape from the freeway repair that kept us inching along for more than an hour, a pace so slow and with an unknown cause and unforeseen end that we worried about reaching Lowell in time for the Spinners doubleheader.

Not since that Northeast construction delay had I fretted about getting to a game on time. Even having budgeted extra hours for driving from the northern Chicago area to Appleton, Wisconsin, on a Saturday, I started to get anxious about my arrival because of a sequence of unusual obstacles and hazards as I departed. This time, since Bonnie had taken a weekend leave from ballgames to join a women's *non*-baseball retreat at her friend's home on the Rock River, I could not rely on her troubleshooting and rerouting.

The road woes unfolded in this way: From the RV park in north suburban Chicago to Appleton, the most direct route coursed like a crooked river over county roads, which, on a weekend, I feared might be slowed by tractors and farmers and in-laws reluctantly heading to remote reunions. Instead of starting on these backroads, I turned east, not north, heading toward Lake Michigan and the I-94 corridor between Chicago and Milwaukee. I hoped to capitalize on its regular freeway flow on a seemingly innocuous Saturday in July.

To get to the interstate, however, I had to drive through several villages and towns crouching toward Lake Michigan. Near Grayslake around noon, traffic backed up on the single lane of Route 120, causing Toad and me to wait through three changes of the traffic signal before I could move through the intersection at Milwaukee Road. I probably should have perceived the difficulties as an omen from the travel deities and immediately turned north. Yet I persisted in my direction toward Lake Michigan.

Rather than being relieved when I reached the interstate, I thought that I had returned to the L.A. freeways. Seeing that its traffic was at a standstill and not wanting to chance that the clog might be only temporary, I continued on 120 to US 41 North, not far beyond the freeway. There I found an easy flow toward the Wisconsin border a dozen miles away. But a few minutes later, an orange sign alerted me to construction and delays on 41 North as it merged with I-94. While a smaller sign marked an alternate 94 route to the right, I naïvely persisted in my move toward the freeway ramp until the traffic stopped. Luckily, a gravel lane crossing over the grassy median provided a means to escape, and I u-turned toward Illinois 173, which was identified as the alternate 94 route.

Alas, traffic stalled right away on 173 because a one-lane bridge restricted movement, which also was controlled by another traffic signal. Delayed by an inning's worth of red lights in that construction zone, I was relieved to resume normal speed momentarily for about a mile before having to stop in the line waiting for a freight train to clear the road's crossing. Once it had passed and the arms blocking the tracks had lifted, traffic accelerated to the posted limit.

What else might impede my progress, or lack thereof, I wondered, since I had come less than twenty miles in the first hour of an anticipated three-hour drive? I didn't have to think long. Ahead, police action—merely a traffic citation being issued to a motorist—constricted traffic to a single lane before I could turn north on Illinois 131, approaching the Wisconsin state line. Still, another delay ensued. Some event was being held at the stadium near the crossroads, and traffic clotted yet again when turning vehicles slowed to pay for parking while pedestrians—some daring and darting, others ambling unconcerned—crossed my traffic lane.

Four miles later, I finally felt deliverance as I entered Wisconsin, finding its highways wide, clear, and without potholes. I didn't even mind that there were partial barriers on I-94 as I approached Milwaukee and made my way through downtown since traffic there slowed only moderately. Beyond the city, skies cleared until I reached the Oshkosh area, where I could see dense storm clouds to the northwest. I hoped that I would be spared another rainout since there was a chance that the ballpark might lie south of the storm line that was visibly moving toward the northeast.

At a few minutes after 4 o'clock, I finally reached the Appleton exit for the Timber Rattlers ballpark and noticed flags briskly slapping toward the east. I looked heavenward, to no avail—other than noting the imminence of the approaching storm. Yes, at 4:20 the downpour—that's putting it mildly—began while I sat in Starbucks, sipping coffee, writing about the day's delays and frustrations, and worrying anew about whether I would get to sing that evening. Mid-deluge, my hope started to slip like the person sloshing and sliding through the parking lot, finally spilling his coffee, not into a puddle but into his SUV.

For almost two hours the skies emptied time and again with arpeggio flourishes. But after 6 o'clock, the thunderheads started to break as I splashed in Toad toward the Timber Rattlers ballpark a mile or so away. What an incredible surprise! Despite the intensity and duration of the thunderstorm, hundreds of fans had already convened for parties in the parking lot, setting up tailgate barbecues.

Perhaps they knew that the Timber Rattlers promotion for that night was an umbrella giveaway to the first thousand fans entering the ballpark! Although Charleston and Durham had deeper outfield ponds and more splash pools behind home plate that required drainage before their games, I hadn't seen players assist the grounds crew in sweeping water away until T.J. Mittelstaedt, the Rattlers starting left fielder, picked up a broom and began to sweep the dugout's swamp into the trap.

During the game I also saw an unusual pitcher's move. In the second inning, Wisconsin pitcher Matthew Miller, perhaps rattled by Burlington runner Yordy Cabrera's break from first, dropped to the ground to avoid the catcher's throw to second, which never happened on Cabrera's uncontested steal.

Other "firsts" also distinguished my experience at Appleton's ballpark, whose concessions featured several unique snacks and drinks. I guess that I shouldn't be surprised Wisconsin was the only place where cheese curds were available. Another unusual offering from the grill was "Fang's Venom Burger," dressed with hot spices, peppers, salsa, and cheese—although it was made with beef rather than rattlesnake. And two of the microbrews adopted complementary serpentine names: Snake Tail Ale and Rattler Brau Scottish Ale. Similarly, the team store picked up on the herpetological motif, identifying itself as the "Snake Pit." One can only imagine its merchandizing possibilities, especially novelties associated with the team mascot Fang. In most cases, a team's mascot looked lovable, huggable. But Fang provided a stark contrast, even with his baseball cap impishly reversed.

Fox Cities Stadium also featured fan interactivity via smart phones. By accessing an in-game website, fans could order concessions to be delivered directly to their seats, and they could play various Rattlers games, post ballpark pictures, provide Twitter feeds, and link Facebook posts. Socializing more immediately were groups in the picnic pavilion. While various wedding celebrations occasionally had been held at other minor league ballparks, the picnic area at the Rattlers ballpark simultaneously hosted three distinct wedding groups on this last Saturday in July: Bridget's bachelorette party, the Geiser and Knier wedding party, and Dave Selan's bachelor party. One can only hope that specially ordered cakes were appropriately delivered to each group.

Other gathering spots in the ballpark included the berm along the right-field line and the sandbox beyond the centerfield fence. With so many activities supplementing the game, it's no wonder that, despite the rain, the ballpark sold out for the evening.

After finishing the final notes of the anthem, I detoured past puddles in front of the Rattlers bench, and their third-base coach applauded my rendition, calling out, "Good job!" Since he had heard me sing when the Timber Rattlers had struck the Loons in Midland at the beginning of the week, he added, "Are you following us?" Then Wisconsin had won handily, 6-3. But this night the venom of the Rattlers couldn't match the sting of the Bees from Burlington, who prevailed 8-2, thanks in large part to a bases-loaded double and a two-run homer by A.J. Kirby-Jones.

An Iowa Anthem Caucus: Game 79 in Clinton

In Clinton, Iowa, for only the second time on the tour, Arbie accompanied us to a game. Like his first ballpark visit in Columbus, Arbie's appearance was necessitated by the timing of the midday game in a ballpark between overnights in different cities. This time, his mooring at dawn had been near Chicago and the evening's destination and next day's game were in Davenport, Iowa. But unlike Arbie's earlier urban-lot parking in Columbus where he had waited while I sang for the Clippers, he was able to get street parking adjacent to the ballpark in Clinton. Having arrived early, we rolled out the awning, turned on the generator and the air conditioner, and read and wrote for two hours before Alliant Energy Field opened.

Sandwiched between two transport corridors, Clinton's Riverview Stadium—its original name—had been constructed as a WPA project in 1937 and renovated sixty years later. The left-field wall adjoins the road atop the levee holding back the mighty Mississippi River, and the parking lot adjacent to the first-base grandstands is an active rail line along which chugged freight trains about every forty-five minutes. While river barges ferried grain south towards the port of New Orleans, railcars hauled imported goods north toward Minneapolis. Although Clinton is the corporate home to Nestle-Purina and International Paper, its commercial district near the ballpark appeared twisted and conflicted by these opposing transportation currents, strangled to the point of economic suffocation.

A few minutes after I had entered the ballpark and had begun to photograph its historic markers, a fan approached me and asked leading questions about the history and location of the ballpark. I confessed that since I had been in Clinton for only a couple of hours, the only information that I knew was on the plaque toward which I pointed.

As our conversation expanded, I learned that Bill Messenger was from Omaha and hadn't known that there was a team in Clinton until he had seen a notice about the game while driving through town. Expressing delight in the quaint character of the ballpark, he reflected on his love for his hometown's old Rosenblatt Stadium, where the minor league team had played until months ago. Earlier this season new fields had opened for the Triple-A Omaha Storm Chasers—Werner Ballpark in adjoining Sarpy County—and for the NCAA World Series, which shifted sites in the city to the TD Ameritrade Park.

Even upgraded in recent years, the Clinton ballpark featured no luxury boxes—perhaps a reflection of the populist ethos of Iowa and the public funds used for the stadium's construction and renovation. And unlike many ballparks where burgers, fries, and a brew might cost almost twenty dollars, populist concession prices prevailed. It was possible to lunch on a hotdog and soda for less than five bucks, and other drinks and foods were priced at about half what they had cost at most other minor league parks: taffy for a quarter, sunflower seeds for seventy-five cents, and cotton candy for two bucks.

Missing the historic character of Rosenblatt, Bill was delighted by the no-frills intimacy of Clinton's riverfront stadium and the city's century-old legacy of professional baseball. Established as the Owls when the ballpark had opened during the Great Depression, Clinton's league championship team that year eventually sent more than a half-dozen of its players to The Show, most to the parent Brooklyn Dodgers. More recently, Clinton's baseball alumni had grown to include former major league all-stars Orel Hershiser and Steve Sax, as well as World Series managers Jim Leyland, Tom Kelly, and Mike Scioscia. As the only remaining charter member of the Midwest League founded in the mid-1950s, the team became known as the

LumberKings in recognition of Clinton's former designation as the Lumber Capital of America.

Having coordinated my appearance at Alliant Energy Field, Mitch Butz greeted me as I entered the ballpark and told me that he wanted to convene a small Iowa caucus of Clinton's anthem performers. In preparation for my arrival, he had let David Wubbena from a neighboring farm community in Illinois know about my project and scheduled appearance in Clinton since David had occasionally sung the national anthem for the LumberKings in recent years.

More than thirty years earlier, David had requested the chance to sing the national anthem for a local civic celebration, but had been told that he needed to practice more. So he did, rehearsing the anthem hundreds of times to improve his pitch, tone, and tempo. Self-taught as a singer—in fact, he had been dismissed from the volunteer choir at his Baptist church about a decade before—David practiced again and again, often singing in the silo at his farm where the resonance was better than in a shower stall. He persisted in his efforts and eventually got the chance to perform the anthem for a public event in 2003.

Since then, David had performed the anthem for multiple games in several Midwest League ballparks, other sporting events, and various civic gatherings. In addition, after learning "O Canada" by playing it repeatedly on his cell phone, he sang it and "The Star-Spangled Banner" before a hockey game for the Rockford IceHogs, a minor league affiliate of the Chicago Black Hawks. Simply, David loves to sing the national anthem, proudly showing that almost anyone who persists in practicing not only can learn to sing it, but can sing it joyfully for others.

On this sweltering, sunny Sunday, my rendition was among my best, with several of the LumberKings calling out as I passed the dugout: "Nice job." "Way to go." "You scored!" And hitting coach Terry Pollreisz chimed in, "Thanks. That's the way it's supposed to be." Moments later from the box seats behind the dugout, one woman yelled, "Great job!" Intimate and friendly—that's Clinton.

During the early innings of the game, the bats of both teams seemed to wilt on the sun-seared field, neither team scoring off the starting pitchers. Still I hoped that there might be some offensive energy derived from the seventh-inning stretch. Yet when the P.A. announcer invited the fans "to take time now to stretch and sing America's favorite song," not even the crowd could rouse a motivating rendition of "Take Me Out to the Ballgame." While I understood how fans might consider the song a favorite, I thought that it should certainly be belted out. Even more, I wondered, shouldn't "America's favorite song" be the national anthem?

Immediately following the recording of the organ accompaniment to the traditional seventh-inning refrain, the speakers blared a medley of other rollicking tunes, including "Roll Out the Barrel" and "Hail, Hail, the Gang's All Here." Still, the crowd's disposition seemed to be muted by the heat and humidity. Or perhaps its lackadaisical participation resulted from the absence of an impromptu choir of kids to lead the singing. Or maybe the crowd would have celebrated more if Louie, the LumberKings mascot who was a fan favorite throughout the league, had not taken that afternoon off.

As one might expect, the feeble singing during the seventh inning failed to enliven either team; and through all nine innings and then a tenth, the line scores for both teams read the same: no runs on five hits and two errors. Perhaps the eleventh inning would prove luckier than the seventh, especially with new relievers anticipated for both teams. With two outs and none on in the top of the inning, Peoria strung together three singles to take a one-zip lead. But not to be out-dramatized, with two outs and none on the bottom half of the inning, the LumberKings spliced a hit batter between two singles before the game-winning hit by Carlos Ramirez.

A River Bandit Rescue: Game 80 in Quad Cities

Bonnie and I had experienced oppressive heat at a number of games: most notably at the sun-drenched, pre-noon start in San Antonio; at the midday, broiling ballpark in Columbus; and at the blistering afternoon in Clinton the day before, only to name a few of the most unbearable. In earlier years I had sung for two oppressively hot games, the one in Palm Springs when the official temperature at game time had been 116 and another in Cincinnati's Riverfront Stadium when the temperature on the artificial turf registered almost 130 degrees. But I had never been as uncomfortable at a game as I was at dusk in Davenport's Modern Woodmen Park, where the combination of ninety-degree temperature, still air, and humidity reaching at least 118 percent, or so it felt, created suffocating conditions. According to the local radio station, the heat index had climbed above 110.

"Is that all?" I thought.

Urban redevelopment projects in minor league cities have often selected riverfronts—like Louisville and Little Rock, Trenton and Charleston—as ballpark sites because of their scenic beauty as well as their potential for reviving nearby enterprises and area economies. An impressive aspect of the ballpark in Davenport is that its location was set long before redevelopment initiatives spurred cities to make riverfront properties into viable entertainment sites.

However, one disadvantage of riverfront ballparks is that the moisture from the river can make the air feel as gooey as its bottom mud. This adhesive quality of the soggy air was certainly our experience at the picturesque ballpark in Davenport, Iowa, home to the Quad Cities River Bandits.

Over the years, the ballpark's proximity to the Mississippi River has also allowed a different weather-related problem to affect games: high waters on the river. In 2001 when future American League MVP Justin Morneau was tearing up the Midwest League during his partial season with Quad Cities, the Mississippi River flooded and the River Bandits had to flee, playing many of their scheduled home games on the road.

A decade later, as new ownership and management assumed operations of the team, Modern Woodmen of America, a fraternal benefit society and financial management organization, purchased the naming rights to the ballpark. Therein lies a fundamental irony. Originally the Modern Woodmen society restricted membership to white men in non-urban areas in the twelve healthiest states, all of which were deemed to be in the upper Midwest (including Iowa) and Great Plains. The irony is this: Excluded from possible membership were men engaged in unhealthful and dangerous occupations, including professional baseball.

Back in the early part of the last century, Davenport's Municipal Stadium was erected on the riverfront site. Occasionally throughout its history modest improvements had been made to the ballpark, but it did not enjoy a thorough renovation until months following the 2003 season. While the ballpark's site and façade remained the same during the reconstruction, the field itself was rotated slightly to provide fans with a prime view of the river and Centennial Bridge. Fans' experience was also improved by the addition of luxury suites, picnic areas, new clubhouses, and a video scoreboard. And like ballparks in Richmond and Huntsville that displayed children's paintings and promotions of the team mascot, the Davenport ballpark featured winning entries by schoolchildren.

Before the game, a man in the front row behind home plate called out to me about the previous day's game in Clinton, expressing appreciation for my straightforward anthem rendition. Len McMorrow and his sons Quinn (age twelve, a catcher) and Parker (age nine, an outfielder) had attended the game as part of their weeklong tour through the Midwest League. On this day, they had already heard one anthem performance at a Kernels game in Cedar Rapids seventy-five miles away; following that game, they had driven to Davenport in time to catch the second half of what he called "a McMorrow double-header." When Len indicated that he especially appreciated anthem performers who avoid embellishments, I strongly encouraged him and his sons to sing along with me.

Thankfully, I had been made aware that the audio transmission was out of sync with the video display on the scoreboard. The staff member who assisted me on the field described the delay as being "about three seconds" and warned me not to look at the scoreboard, which was adjacent to the flag. "You don't want to see yourself singing what you're not singing," she added. The misalignment was not as severe as her three-second description, even though the sound delay created a kind of self-dissonance. In addition to the distractions caused by the mismatch between the melody and my apparent lip movement, a metallic reverberation persisted throughout the audio transmission. Even so, the anthem went well, at least as well as possible: the words were right, the notes on pitch, and the pace brisk.

Since the video display had lacked coordination with the sound production, I wondered whether it was experiencing a meltdown from the heat when its player introductions started featuring unusual photographs. When Geulin Beltre, Kane County's second hitter, came to the plate, the image of an alluring woman flashed on the screen. Behind Beltre's name and number appeared a picture of a seductively clad brunette framed by ads for Modern Woodmen and a collision repair center. Moments later, Beltre struck out "looking." The only question I had then was whether he was looking at the called third strike or at the scantily covered figure on the videoboard.

When River Bandits center fielder Oscar Tavares stepped into the batter's box in the home-half of the inning, the jocular approach to player profiles continued. Behind his name and number was the photograph of a hunk, a bodybuilder flexing biceps the size of most guys' thighs. But Tavares did not flex his hitting muscles and promptly grounded into a double play.

While these playful displays certainly added a bit of levity to the sluggish pace of a three-run shutout that would run almost three hours, Bonnie and I were more enticed by the prospects of dinner in air-conditioned Arbie rather than munching ballpark fare in the sweltering conditions. With the River Bandits leading 2-0 after three innings, we retreated from the game much earlier than usual.

Disoriented by the discomfort of the weather, I didn't realize that I had lost my little black book of game notes until we returned to the comfort of Arbie. After searching high and low in and around Toad, I called the ballpark shortly before the game ended with Quad Cities winning 3-0, and left a message with anthem coordinator Shelley Heyward that I had lost my little black book, perhaps near my seat in section 8, row N. Although I had transcribed most of my notes about ballparks and games, I had not yet transferred the information from the last ten days, nor had I transferred detailed notes about days-off excursions that Bonnie and I had enjoyed.

Needless to say, I slept poorly during the night, awoke at 6 A.M., slipped out of Arbie quietly, and returned to the ballpark. I retraced steps through the parking lot and to the locked entry to the stadium. *Nada.* Frustrated, I drove back to the county park where Arbie was anchored, stopping along the way at a front-yard tomato stand to buy a few ripe heirloom varieties. Something about my early-morning venture needed to be worthwhile—and it was: the tomatoes, which we sliced for lunch a couple of hours later, were among the most flavorful that I had ever eaten.

Within an hour after rejoining Bonnie in Arbie, I received a call from Shelley, indicating that she had found my book, which I retrieved before noon. Who would have thought that a bandit would find and return a lost item? Not even Robin Hood was keen on restoring stolen goods to the proper owners—much less on finding booty and not keeping it, to boot! Yet in Davenport, a River Bandit rescued my sanity, at least temporarily, by finding and returning my little black Moleskine book.

Serendipity at the Snappers Park: Game 81 in Beloit

Following the scare about losing my little black book of game notes in Davenport, I wanted to transfer my daily scribbles to computer files as quickly as possible. So Bonnie took control of Toad and drove much of the way to Beloit for the evening game there, allowing me to type and expand notes from five games on my small netbook, which routinely accompanied me in my camera bag to the ballparks. Heading into Illinois, we followed freeways and tollways to Dixon, where we exited and skirted Ronald Reagan's boyhood home. Coursing upstream beside the scenic Rock River, Bonnie shared her adventures of the previous weekend with a group of women whose retreat site had been one of the river homes that we passed between Dixon and Byron, a town emblazoned in my memory from a college-search road trip with my son years earlier. Its gnarly feature had been a huge banner hanging from a bar at the center of town: "Home of the Turkey Testicle Festival."

Although Bonnie and I were backtracking much of a route that we had driven a few days earlier, the home schedules of several of the Midwest League teams required that we move first one way, then another, and finally reverse—twice. Consequently, we took advantage of the opportunity to berth Arbie for three days at the Scott County RV park just west of Davenport. From there we then bungeed out in Toad to home games for Quad Cities, Beloit, and Peoria.

Two hours before my scheduled arrival for the Snappers, we stopped at McDonald's for coffee, a snack, and easy Wi-Fi. Routinely as we targeted possible RV parks for our hookups, we looked for cleanliness, easy access, cable TV, and Wi-Fi. Often we found that the distance of our site from the Wi-Fi router prevented us from having dependable use. So McDonald's and Starbucks became favorite spots for coffee, snacks, and lunch, and Panera enticed us also with its promise of fresh bread in addition to its reliable, free Wi-Fi. Initially, we had planned simply to sip coffee and check e-mail at McDonald's before heading to the ballpark for batting practice and a visit with Dee Maxson, a friend from our church choir in Tustin, California. Dee had been vacationing at a summer home near Lake Geneva and had let us know that she would come to the game. But when a thunderstorm blitzed through the area with the suddenness of a blown save, we settled in for a long snack, and I continued to work on transcribing my notes and uploading an entry to my blog.

In Beloit, the municipal stadium blended into an established neighborhood like a cordial old boarding house. Contributing to its family-room feel, its simple architecture spread across open spaces that encouraged kids to play catch within the flight of foul balls; and in the grandstands field-level, front-row seats were exactly that—front row and field level, a kind of commoner's precursor to the dugout-level seats now popular at several major league stadia.

Beloit's ballpark design also locates the team clubhouses beyond an open concession area that divides the lockers from the diamond and dugouts. While fans in minor league parks regularly interacted with players along the fence between the bullpen and dugout, here the autograph hounds were able to intercept them, literally blocking the way between their sanctuaries on the field and in the clubhouse.

Standing in this liminal area before the game, I was greeted with smiles by several of the visiting Kane County players, some of whom seemed to recognize me as they passed the concession line. Within the past few days, they had heard me sing twice, once at their ballpark in Geneva, Illinois, where the introduction had identified me and the tour, and the previous night in Davenport, where the P.A. announcer had made no mention of my anthem efforts. Among the pride of passing Cougars was starting pitcher Jason Adam, who blinked at me with recognition.

"You guys will get tired of me," I suggested.

"Not at all," he responded with a smile. "You're good."

With that, I wished him good luck for the game and suggested that his teammates could help by doing more than they had done the previous night in Davenport, where they had been shut out.

He did. He pitched effectively and he got unexpected support from catcher Kevin David, whose lofty prayer to centerfield was answered by the ballpark's short dimension—380 feet to dead center, a distance deadly for fly-ball pitchers. The homer was David's first—and only—round-tripper of the season. Then to balance the directions of home runs a few innings later, Brett Eibner launched one to right before Jacob Kuebler belted one to left. Propelled by these drives to a six-run lead, Adam held the Snappers scoreless through his six strong innings and eventually got the win.

Also pausing to chat on his way to the dugout was injured pitcher Elisaul Pimentel. While other players continued to scratch across the concrete in their cleats, he beamed and said that tonight would be the sixth time that he had seen me this season. I did a double-take faster than his electric smile. What? How? Quickly, he rattled off the list of places: "In the Carolina League at Winston-Salem, Lynchburg, and Wilmington. Last night in Quad Cities, and last week at our place in Kane County, and tonight."

Pimentel had spent the first half of the season with Wilmington, the Kansas City affiliate in the Carolina League, before being shifted for a short time to Kane County. I teased him that he was logging as many minor league miles as I was, and I encouraged him to sing with me, perhaps as a duet. He smiled.

Moments before the pregame introductions, a father approached the Snappers staffer and asked if his son Dawson, who was turning ten that day, could throw out the first pitch. It happened. At most ballparks the selection process or the birthday request takes place in formal ways through competitions, applications, auctions, sponsorships, or even as a scratch-off prize, as a kid in Kane County had enjoyed a week earlier. Here, a simple familial request proved effective, and Dawson tossed a decent ceremonial pitch.

Now it was my turn to follow through on a series of applications and appeals that had begun more than a year earlier. Taking my position between home and the backstop, I scanned the crowd and did not see our friend Dee among the few fans in the stands. The official attendance of 414, the second-smallest crowd that I had encountered, certainly included all of the late arrivers, folks standing in line for burgers and fries, and kids playing behind the first-base concession booth. After finishing the anthem with gusto, I turned toward the visitors' dugout, where Pimentel signified "thumbs up."

Then turning to walk past the Snappers' bench, I heard more than congrats from their manager Nelson Prada. He must have remembered me from the previous weekend when I had sung for the Snappers' victory over the Timber Rattlers in Appleton since, moments earlier, I had been introduced by name only.

Prada stepped up to the track and started to ask me about my tour:

Prada: "You're the guy who's making the tour singing at ballparks. Where have you been?"
Me: "All over—Texas, the South, Florida, the East Coast, New England, Indiana, Ohio, here. Now I'm heading west for the rest of this month."
Prada: "How many games?" He glanced toward the mound where Manuel Soliman, his starting pitcher, was starting to warm up.
Me: "This was number eighty-one."
Prada: "Ever forget the words?"
Me: "Nope. I rehearse it at least once right before every performance."
Prada: "Did you sing for any games before this year?"
Me: "In twenty major league ballparks."
Prada: "Which ones?"
Me: "The White Sox, Cubs, Brewers, Twins, Royals…"
Prada: "The Twins? In the Metrodome or Target Field?"
Me: "The Humphrey Dome."

Prada sighed, perhaps recalling his dream to play there. More than a decade earlier, he had spent four years as catcher in the Twins organization, never advancing above their Hi-A affiliate.

Prada turned to watch Snappers catcher Toby Streich fire a throw to the shortstop covering second. "Thanks and good luck," he called out as I moved through the gate, and the first hitter stepped into the batter's box.

Moving toward Bonnie in our seats behind home plate, a woman approached and introduced herself as Cindy Schliem. "I've read your blog," she smiled.

How? Again I wondered. There had been no Beloit publicity, no P.A. recognition, merely an identification of me by name.

Cindy explained. Her lifelong friend Cheryl McClain had been the Keys staff member in Frederick, Maryland, who had handed me my tickets when I had sung there a month earlier. After Cheryl and I had talked about anthem performances, she had checked out the schedule on the AnthemTour website and had told Cindy about my blog and when I would appear in Beloit. I smiled then, as well as months later, about this encounter as one of the serendipitous connections that the anthem facilitates.

I love the support of friends who made significant effort to participate with me on the tour, either by joining me in singing or by celebrating its significance. In the second inning, Dee Maxson found us easily in the grandstands, introduced her daughter and her son-in-law Donna and Rob Grisham, and apologized for having missed the pregame ceremonies because of the rain, the heat, and automotive woes.

Since they had not heard me sing the anthem, I followed the model of Dawson's father's last-minute request and asked—for the only time on tour—the home team to let me lead "Take Me Out to the Ballgame" during the seventh-inning stretch, thereby giving Dee and the Grishams at least a chance to see and hear me sing at the ballpark. Graciously, they stayed for that quick refrain, then departed for their return toward Lake Geneva.

An inning later, Bonnie and I also bade the ballpark goodbye before the Snappers rallied in the bottom of the ninth, then scoring their only runs in their defeat, 6-2. Since we needed to get back to Arbie before the county park locked up at midnight, we returned to Davenport via the faster, more boring sequence of a quartet of interstate highways. Still, we missed the curfew and had to park Toad alone outside the RV lot's locked gates before walking around them and toward Arbie a few hundred moonlit yards beyond.

Babe Ruff, the Greensboro Grasshoppers bat dog,
retrieved a bat after a base hit.

The birthday party guests for Bowie's mascot Louie included mascots from other teams, universities, and corporations.

Across the street from the Frederick ballpark, the memorial to Francis Scott Key provided the focal point in the cemetery.

The widely tiered grandstand without seats
encouraged Pulaski Mariners fans to bring lawn chairs.

On a Wiffle ball field between the Salem Red Sox ballpark and its Hall of
Fame building, children tried to hit one over the miniature Green Monster.

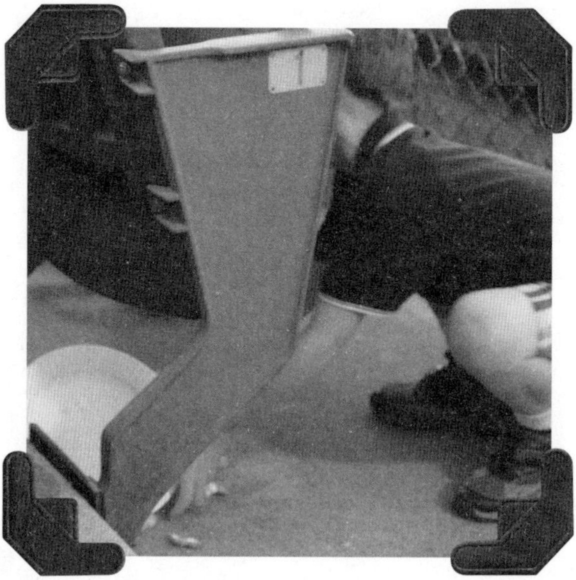

Undeterred by the added flavor of dirt, a boy in Wilmington retrieved his slice of pepperoni pizza before consuming it moments later.

Trenton usher Mike Nolan, a traveler to more than a hundred minor league baseball parks in recent years, and I discussed distinct venues.

David Smith, Sr., became the first "human home run" as he was launched over the right field wall at the Lowell ballpark.

At New Hampshire's ballpark, the pregame participants were restricted to the cordoned area in front of the Fisher Cats dugout.

The right-field wall in Lehigh Valley was so extensive that it seemed to serve as the local Yellow Pages.

A child enjoyed climbing and sliding
on the supersized ball glove in Pawtucket.

The ghosts of Yankees spirits (especially Babe Ruth and Bucky Dent)
seemed to be hovering above the Red Sox bullpen in Pawtucket.

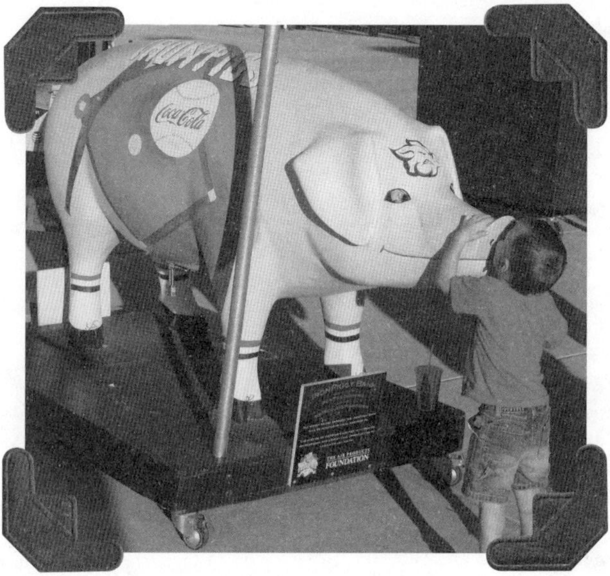

A child magnified the chance for good luck
by kissing the pig at Lehigh Valley.

Indy, the mascot of the Indianapolis Indians,
had a nose for interacting with happy fans.

For my birthday in 1961, my father drove us to Chicago for two Yankees games, during which enjoyed these box seats along the first-base line.

Like children at several ballparks, kids in Idaho Falls climbed the rails down the aisles like a jungle gym set at a park.

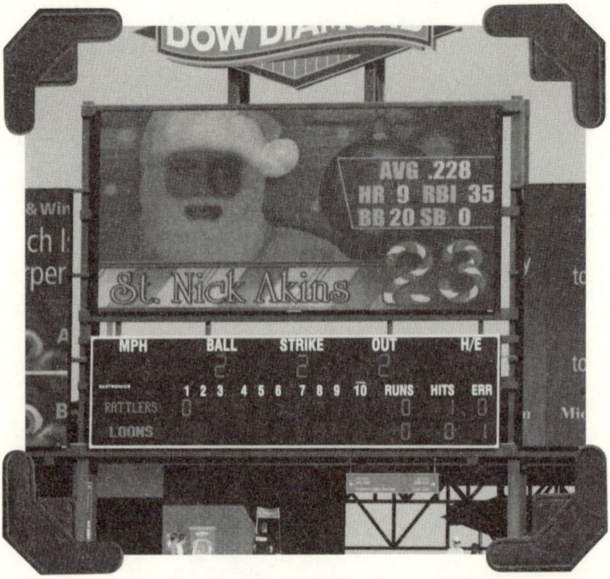

Great Lakes Loons outfielder Nick Akins was portrayed as St. Nick for the Christmas in July celebration at Midland, Michigan.

After a thunderstorm delayed the start of the game in Appleton, Wisconsin, infielder T. J. Mittelstaedt assisted the grounds crew by sweeping water out of the dugout.

From beyond the centerfield fence in Wisconsin,
children could simultaneously enjoy baseball and beach activities.

The panorama from Quad Cities box seats featured
the mighty Mississippi and the span of Centennial Bridge.

While we waited out the rain delay in Iowa,
Tony Oliva showed me his World Series ring.

Whittier alumnus Tom Vessella was San Jose's starting pitcher
on the night when I sang there and threw out the first pitch.

On the morning after the storm in Omaha,
Bonnie examined the damage to Arbie's awning.

After Bonnie had expressed homesickness for our Havanese Winston on our way to the ballpark, she enjoyed holding look-alike Riley for several innings during the Ghosts' "Bark at the Park" promotion.

The installation of painted tiles by Sacramento area children decorated multiple pillars on the concession concourse, including one that visually celebrated baseball as America's national pastime.

From beyond the right-field berm in Reno,
walkways curve through gardens above the Truckee River.

Former student Mihael Herrera and his daughter Cassidy
greeted Bonnie and me as we arrived for the final game
in San Bernardino for the Inland Empire 66ers.

Throughout the country we were joined by scores of friends and family.

With the temperature stretching toward 120 degrees, the stands were virtually empty when I sang the national anthem in Bakersfield.

10.

Faith at the Ballpark

Playing in Peoria: Game 82 in Peoria

After the wee-hour return to Davenport from Beloit, we whiplashed back into Illinois hours later, heading south this time to Peoria's O'Brien Field, as it then was known, where the Midwest League's Chiefs shared their home with the Bradley University Braves.

To say that there are competing or conflicting baseball alliances at the ballpark and in Peoria is to put things mildly. When Peoria joined the Midwest League in 1983, it played its home games in Bradley's ballpark, which was then named for its longtime athletic director John "Dutch" Meinen. A decade later, the stadium, which still served as the home to the university's baseball team, was renovated and renamed for the owner of the Chiefs, Pete Vonachen. The complex relation between the Chiefs and the Braves continued when both teams transferred their homes to the city's new ballpark in 2002.

While the stadium was built by the Chiefs, its display of retired numbers and tributes to area baseball heroes created some confusion about who actually controls the facility. On the concourse behind third base was a permanent display case featuring the numbers, photographs, and brief biographies of former Bradley Braves: outfielder Kirby Puckett (#14), a first-round draft pick by the Twins in 1982 and subsequently a perennial American League All-Star, Gold Glove award winner, and Silver Slugger recipient; pitcher Mike Dunne (#11), a seventh-round draft pick by the Cardinals in 1984 who ended his five-year, four-team major league career with a losing record (twenty-five wins and thirty losses); and coach Leo Schrall (# 2), an inductee into the Hall of Fame of the American Baseball Coaches Association for his twenty winning seasons, seven Missouri Conference Championships, and two College World Series appearances. Their numbers were also displayed at the top of the right-field wall adjacent to the foul pole. Typically, minor league ballparks feature a roster of former players who have made it to The Show, but the way it played in Peoria's ballpark was that the list featured former Bradley Braves who had been signed by major league teams to minor league contracts.

Even though I diligently looked for a list of former Chiefs who had made it to the majors, I couldn't locate one. But there were large action images of several former Peoria stars in Cubs and Cardinals uniforms, Joe Girardi and Albert Pujols. Two of the Chiefs-to-Cubs alumni had had their numbers retired: Greg Maddux (#31) had started twenty-seven games for Peoria at age nineteen before being promoted to Chicago; he later won almost 200 games while pitching for the Atlanta Braves and winning three Cy Young awards with them. And Mark Grace (#17), a "doubles machine" and lifetime .300 hitter, had played for the Chiefs in 1986. Replicas of their Cubs jerseys—featuring their names and numbers—were also found on a banner slung over the lower outfield wall in deep centerfield. Missing from the roster of retired numbers were the St. Louis stars and perhaps future Hall of Famers Albert Pujols and Yadier Molina.

All of this brings me to another confusing aspect of Peoria's baseball alignment: The city itself lies on the chalk line between upstate and downstate Illinois, the Cubs den and the Cardinals nest. Baseball fans in northern Illinois have long followed the Cubs on WGN while those in the southern part of the state have cheered for the Cardinals on KMOX. Memories of the Brock-for-Broglio trade—infamous for Cubs and divine for Cards—continue to slash the divide.

Now, to complicate these matters of baseball identity further, here's the Chiefs imbroglio: After a decade of functioning as the A-level affiliate of the Cubs during the late 1980s and early 1990s, the Chiefs aligned with the Cardinals system for almost a decade before resuming their formal connections with the Cubs. And during the season following my tour, Peoria's organizational vacillation continued with the Chiefs shift back to an alliance with the Cardinals! Does that portend that Pujols and Molina will also get their numbers retired? Is it any wonder, then, that Peoria might suffer from baseball schizophrenia?

Thinking about Peoria's muddled baseball identity as Bonnie and I approached O'Brien Field, I found a parking spot in front of the Rescue Mission on Walnut Street about a block from the front gates. Opening the car doors, I could hear a choir singing gospel hymns, the most robust being "Amazing Grace." I figured that the doors to the chapel must be open as an invitation for street sleepers to join the service before the soup supper. Yet as we walked away from the mission and toward the ballpark, the music got louder. It was coming from inside the ballpark! Did the Chiefs expect gospel music to inspire their batting practice? Did the ballpark play recordings of hymns as pregame entertainment for the crowd? Yet the blend of voices and the articulation of phrases suggested the performance had a local character.

At the Will Call window where I gave my name as the anthem singer, the agent looked startled when she could not find tickets filed under my name, nor could she locate my name on the list for complimentary admission. "What group are you with?" she asked.

"None," I replied, and she looked puzzled.

My anxiety soared, especially since the choral music, now sounding live, poured past our ears. Had I been replaced at an even "laster" minute than the unnatural, game-morning notification that I had received from the Naturals when I had been replaced by an enclave of grade-school choirs at Northwest Arkansas?

"Who set up your appearance?" she continued.

"Megan Miller," I said as I checked my notes. Thankfully, that name spelled relief. The tickets had been filed under her name; and the choir, from nearby Bethany Baptist Church in suburban Edwards, simply had provided live entertainment before the game, finishing their repertoire with a rendition of "God Bless America" immediately before I sang the anthem.

Also participating in the pregame ceremonies were two Goth-dressed guys whose costumes looked like a rejected wardrobe for archenemies in a failed superhero animation. Initially, it wasn't clear whether the garb of these first pitchers was meant to mimic the ugly, thistle-finned fish or whether the spikes on their helmets, shin guards, and breast plates were to protect prospective fishers from possible attack by the carp. When asked, one of the guys grinned, confirming that the jocular gear was designed to protect his jugular.

The satirical tribute, as I later learned from environmentalist advocates at information kiosks along the concourse, was to heighten awareness about the invasive piscine species in the Illinois River, which flows through Peoria at the base of the hill a half-mile below the ballpark. Information about the fish and methods to control and eradicate it were also featured in mid-inning fan activities and video clips throughout the game.

In recent years the spread of the fish throughout the river had begun to threaten Lake Michigan. In a protective move, the Illinois wildlife authorities had spent millions of dollars erecting an elaborate set of electrical gates to prevent the fish from migrating upstream toward Chicago. Yet that effort had not proven to be very effective.

One of the tragedies about the Asian carp invasion is that the fish's introduction into the Southeast had been intentional. Hoping to control various weeds and parasites, aquaculture industries in the Southeast had interjected the species into their operations, only to suffer worse destruction by their incursion into the Mississippi River watershed. Not only have the fish rapidly reproduced, they have also moved into the river's tributaries through their own aggressive behavior and through unintentional transportation of their roe by boaters moving from one body of water to another. Flooding has also facilitated the carp's spread into lakes and ponds normally separate from the free flow of streams. In fact, following expansive, high waters in central Illinois, one fisherman killed—rather than caught—a forty-pound carp in a cow pond by using a pitchfork to spear it. The dangers posed by the fish are not simply their encroachment into other species' habitats or their decimation of plant life; the fish also pose a safety hazard to humans since they are able to jump eight feet above the surface and potentially injure unsuspecting boaters or knock them into the water.

In the playful spirit so typical of minor league promotions, the Chiefs had floated a number of thematic ideas about the evening's opportunities, such as offering free admission to anyone escorting an Asian carp to the game. But fearing the possibility of fetid fish driving away fans, the Chiefs rejected that idea. Still, MiLB blogger Ben Hill facetiously had suggested that the Chiefs could transform Ladies Day—one of Bill Veeck's earliest promotions—by providing a discount for female fans wearing "fishnet stockings."

Such ideas lend credence to the cliché that if *it*—whatever it is—will play in Peoria, it will be well received throughout America. Yet while it's not clear whether the Asian carp tribute had positive educational and environmental effects on fans, it is certain that the Chiefs played well enough to win 5-2, with clean-up hitter Richard Jones leading the offense with two hits, including a home run, and two RBIs.

Kinsellas and Kernels: Game 83 in Cedar Rapids

Driving past Iowa cornfields on our way from one ballpark to another, I recalled the cornfield diamond in the magical film *Field of Dreams*. Perceived by some of the characters as heaven on earth, the field of dreams lured a crowd of baseball characters to fulfill their destinies: Shoeless Joe Jackson and his fellow banished teammates from the Black Sox scandal; deceased doctor and former baseball hopeful Archie "Moonlight" Graham; reclusive software designer, alienated fan, and former author Terrence Mann; Ray Kinsella's late father John, an ex-minor leaguer and worn-out factory worker; and Ray himself, the unfulfilled farmer who, years earlier as an emerging teenager, had refused to play catch with his dad.

While I knew that neither the riverfront field in Clinton nor the urban diamond in Davenport resembled the dream field on the movie set near Dyersville, I kept gazing beyond the passing crops as we rolled past the rising forests of corn. I somehow hoped to catch a glimpse of an ephemeral field that could transform long-passed promise into the karmic consummation that Kinsella's field of dreams had facilitated for so many of the film's characters. Yet instead of being wooed by such wonder on the route between Davenport and Cedar Rapids, I was brought back to earth by the sight of the world's largest truck stop along I-80, a place with spaces for 800 big rigs.

However, when we arrived at Perfect Game Field in Veteran's Stadium in Cedar Rapids, I did find a tribute to some of Iowa's historic players that resonated with Kinsella's fictional world. The Cedar Rapids Hall of Fame, which is located in the ballpark's souvenir store, recognizes more than fifty players—including Cooperstown luminaries John McGraw and Lou Boudreau—who had starred with the Cedar Rapids teams dating back to the city's first pro-team, the Canaries in the Illinois-Iowa League that began in the late nineteenth century.

Expanding on this celebration of notables in the city's Hall of Fame, a timeline display of posters, sample jerseys, and memorabilia lined the walls of the suite level of the ballpark. Additional Cedar Rapids standouts like Trevor Hoffman, Bengie Molina, Paul O'Neil, and John Lackey were recognized with stars embedded in the walkway of the concession concourse; and bygone greats Rocky Colavito, Allie Reynolds, and others were featured on directional placards to seat sections.

Even with all of the outstanding players who had played for the Kernels in their half-century history, only one former player was honored with his number retired on the outfield wall: Nick Adenhart, who had posted ten wins for the Kernels during a partial season, and who had been killed by a drunk driver around midnight following his first start in Anaheim for the parent Angels in 2009 after making their opening-day roster.

Meeting me to provide pregame orientation was Kernels staffer James Odegard. A first tenor who was studying biology at Luther College, James had subbed three or four times during the season for scheduled anthem performers who had cancelled. Since the Kernels, like most of the other teams, did not schedule a sound check for me, I asked James about what kind of delay and feedback I might encounter. "Don't listen to the sound system," he suggested. "When I heard myself, I slowed down and then thought I should speed up."

"What key did you sing it in?" I asked.

"B-flat," he said, adding that the low notes had seemed a bit low. When I countered that I sing it in F-sharp, he smiled and said that would be far too low for him to join me in a duet.

A short time later when I was introduced, I was pleased to hear the Cedar Rapids announcer read the brief introduction that I had sent to teams when I routinely confirmed arrival information. At the recent games in Davenport and Beloit where I had been introduced simply by name, few fans had interacted with me about the tour. But in Cedar Rapids, the fifteen-second introduction prompted numerous comments and fruitful discussions with fans throughout the game.

Stopping me on the concourse an inning or so later, Teresa Dvorak introduced me to her mother. A week earlier Teresa had attended the Kernels game at Kane County, and when she heard the brief introduction at Cedar Rapids, she had thought that my name sounded familiar. Then when she heard my voice, she knew that I had been the one whom she had heard days before. Having rooted for the Kernels since childhood, Teresa continued to follow the team into her late twenties, in part because of her mother's ongoing support of the young players.

The Dvoraks' sponsorship of players was a common practice in the lower levels of the minor leagues, especially for new immigrant players and late-adolescent rookies away from home for the first time. For most of the young players, the support of community families was necessary since their average starting salary was less than $2,000 a month. The challenges connected to that minimal amount were compounded by the fact that the players were paid only during season, which might run as short as three months. While many of the novices accepted the poor pay as a necessary means for keeping their major league dreams alive, the reality was that fewer than ten percent would eventually play in the majors, another fact that meant most of them were fodder on the field to provide competition for the few true prospects possessing the talent and fortune to make it to The Show, even for sipping a decaf cup of coffee.

Unlike many of the players' hosts connected with other teams, "Mother" Dvorak had persisted for more than two decades, providing room and board for the adolescent hopefuls in her five-bedroom house that stood within a home run's cheer of the ballpark. Without divulging the identities of players who might have needed such accommodations, she wryly added, "When they have had a bit too much to drink, they can safely walk to their rooms at my home."

While the Dvoraks enthusiastically talked about players who had become a part of their family, Kyle Swaney approached us and identified himself as a Whittier alumnus from a few years before my arrival at the college. Favorably recalling his advisor David Volckmann (a professor of psychology and a fellow bass in a community choir), Kyle discussed his current work with ACT, the college admissions and placement test organization whose home office was in Iowa City. As part of his work with the organization, he had co-authored research reports related to career groups and career counseling, studies that drew from and affirmed his undergraduate liberal-arts education with a major in psychology.

Our conversation was disrupted by a foul ball that took aim toward us, caroming off the façade above our heads and bouncing back toward the front-row seats. Retrieving the ball on the rebound, a man turned and handed it to a boy whose face exploded with delight. The response personified the inscription on the statue of Pete Vonachen that I had seen in Peoria the previous night: "There is nothing more rewarding than the look of joy when you give a kid a baseball."

Rob Thompson, the ball retriever, had returned to Cedar Rapids to attend his high-school reunion the following night. He had arranged his itinerary to include a Kernels game, a schedule that he tried to follow each time he had returned to the city to visit family. Self-described as an "inveterate baseball fan," he said that giving the ball to the boy was "really no big deal" since he already had major league balls from Rangers games near his Texas home, signed souvenir balls, and a minor league ball that had been given to him by the mascot at a game in Hickory, North Carolina. I wondered if "Mr. Shuck," the Kernels mascot, would similarly favor him. But a different chance presented itself a few innings after our conversation: He was selected to be the person interviewed for the trivia contest. Rather than needing the prompt or hint from the staffer, he knew already that the answer to the question was option "B," Eric Davis, a star for the Kernels in the early 1980s.

Near his seat, season ticket holders Greg and Maria Camburn summoned me to sit by them for a half-inning. "We're envious," they said. "We'd love to explore America through minor league ballparks." And most of their questions could be answered by the complete account of my tour: "When did you start planning? Where did you begin? How many miles have you traveled? Where have you stayed? What ballparks have been your favorites? Why? What surprises have you found? Which places were the most exciting? What unusual baseball plays and players have you seen?"

In the section behind the Camburns, Jim Hutton sat in a wheelchair, confined to that means of mobility after having suffered multiple injuries in a biking accident years earlier. A former lead tenor in a barbershop quartet, Jim was most complimentary about my anthem performance, especially since, as he put it, "you didn't add any stuff or do something personal." Following his accident, the damage to his jaw had required that it be wired shut, a treatment that necessitated a tracheotomy, which then caused damage to his larynx and, regrettably, ended his singing with the group. Now, he said, he enjoys evenings at the Kernels games, often humming harmony with the anthem singer.

For several innings I enjoyed engaging fans in various baseball, musical, and academic conversations, all of which were prompted by the brief introduction for my performance of the anthem. I had expected to spend more time talking with Whittier College expats Gerry Adams and his wife Sara, who reconnoitered with us that evening. Two decades earlier they had immigrated to Iowa and had become immersed in its corn culture. Having taught chemistry before moving to Grinnell to become the registrar of the college there, Gerry regaled me throughout the late innings about the advantages and challenges of the genetically engineered corn that had increased the productivity of the Iowa crops, which now were primarily destined for cattle consumption or use as bio-fuels.

While I enjoyed stimulating conversations with old friends and new acquaintances, the Kernels reached new levels of support from corporate sponsors for local charities because of their strong performances on the field. The ten strikeouts of River Bandits batters by a quartet of Kernels hurlers earned $250 for Kids First, the first American law center with a mission to mitigate divorce's negative effects on children. Additional support for better-known charities was generated by the Kernels six runs (for Meals on Wheels), Travis Witherspoon's two stolen bases (for Camp Courageous), and Randal Grichuk's home run (for Veterans Group).

Throughout the game the whole cob of Kernels enjoyed clutch-hitting, going five for eleven with runners in scoring position. And the game itself finished with a flourish. After the Kernels had cut the River Bandits lead to a single run on a solo shot with two outs in the bottom of the eighth, the ninth inning was filled with bases-loaded drama. With two outs Quad Cities mounted a final threat to increase its lead, filling the bases with an error and two walks before Geoffrey Klein, who had homered earlier in the game, fanned to end the inning. In the bottom half of the frame, the Kernels scored the tying run on a pinch-hit triple before loading the bases with only one out. But an unassisted double play on a line drive to the River Bandits third baseman sent the game into extra innings. Then in the tenth, Cedar Rapids rallied to win 6-5 after a hit batter was followed by a couple of singles.

Gene Kelly and Me: Game 84 in Des Moines

One of my favorite musicals—other than my own troubadouring of "The Star-Spangled Banner"—is *Singing in the Rain*, especially its title song. Even though I certainly cannot soft-shoe along the third-baseline while twirling an umbrella to imitate Gene Kelly's stroll down the street, I joined his joyful way of singing in the rain when the Iowa Cubs hosted the Fresno Grizzlies in Des Moines.

Hours before the game, I feared that my Friday baptismal jinx might prevail and that rain might prevent me from singing again. Already during the tour, the two rainouts had been on Fridays three weeks apart. Since it had been four weeks since the Connecticut cancellation in New Britain, I hoped that I had broken the kind of baseball pattern that generates superstitions. And the most intense deluge that I had encountered had been on Good Friday in Charleston, the nearest lightning strike had been on a Friday in Winston-Salem, and the cancellation of the game in Northwest Arkansas and its rainout had occurred (you guessed it) on a Friday. Not that I'm superstitious. Still, I tried to figure out if there were a baseball talisman that I could manipulate to ward off the rain or if there were some juju dance that I could perform. Instead, I simply pleaded and prayed that the downpour would pass over Principal Stadium in downtown Des Moines and permit the game to proceed.

At about four o'clock, as I had sat typing in Arbie in the Yellow Banks County Park ten miles east of the ballpark, it had started to rain, lightly but persistently. An hour or so later when I began the drive to the ballpark, I maneuvered Toad around dips and deep puddles, finding that the rain had fallen quite heavily between the RV park and the stadium.

There also must be some connection between rain and commando parking attendants. At ballparks everywhere, parking-lot attendants had granted me free access with one exception and one close call, both on the rainy nights when games had gotten postponed. This time, the situation was like that in New Britain, Connecticut. My name was not in the Book of Life, at least for baseball games. And since my name did not appear on the pass list, I had to fork over seven rain-drenched dollars to park near the entry.

Nonetheless, the parking fee seemed worth the gamble of getting the chance to sing the anthem in Des Moines. The rain continued steadily, even while I parked the car, picked up my ticket, and checked in at the front desk, where I heard the receptionist repeatedly begin her telephone response saying, "At this point the game is still on...." I was relieved. At least, I kept telling myself that I was relieved. Perhaps this evening could be like the ones in Durham and Richmond where, despite heavy showers leading up to the scheduled game time, the game would go on.

Waiting for the storm to stop, I wandered through the concourses photographing fans and displays before I ran into a hosted party for employees, clients, and friends of DeWaay, a corporate supporter for the evening's game. Permitted to join the gathering, I heard former all-star Tony Oliva being interviewed about his baseball career and friendships. When attendees were invited to get his autograph and take a photograph, a few moved toward the table where he sat, and I followed.

Once the short line had dispersed and he sat alone, I approached and asked him about memorable anthem performances from his days as a player. He paused to recall pregame performances of "The Star-Spangled Banner," which, of course, is not the national anthem of his native Cuba. He cited multiple performances by former Twins teammate Mudcat Grant as memorable. "Mudcat did a wonderful job," he added. "He's a good singer." While most of the DeWaay partygoers talked with their friends and clients, I chatted with Oliva about baseball matters and cherished the fact that, yes, the undesirable rain had actually permitted me the chance to spend time with him.

Before the Cuban missile crisis and its subsequent embargoes and emigration restrictions, Oliva had signed a contract with the Minnesota Twins, whose scout had recognized his quick bat and powerful swing. After hitting over .400 in his first season in the minor leagues, Oliva progressed through the Twins' system, tasting a cup of coffee with the big-league team during September call-ups in 1962.

After spending the next season back in the minor leagues, he became the first major league player to win the American League batting title and Rookie of the Year award in the same year, 1964. Building on this exceptional start, he was selected as an all-star in his first eight seasons, breaking Joe DiMaggio's record streak of six. Before being hampered by knee injuries, Oliva went on to win three batting titles and ended his fifteen-year career with a .304 average. Despite this outstanding record, he has not been elected into the Hall of Fame.

While sitting with Oliva, who was scheduled to throw out the final first pitch, I heard an announcement over the P.A. system alerting fans to the fact that, while rain was still falling and the field's cover was being removed by the grounds crew, the game would not start on schedule at 7:05. No new start time was then projected. Even so, at 6:40 we watched the grounds crew turn back the tarp, surely a hopeful sign.

Yet within minutes the crew reversed its action and re-covered the diamond. There it remained in place until a half-hour later when, with applause from fans following an announcement that the game would start at 8:05, the crew returned to take it off the field yet one more time.

"Home free," I thought—as if I were scoring from second on a ground-rule double. Instead, there was a series of fourteen first pitches, the first of which was tossed by a Special Olympics participant who had taken the mound early, toed the rubber, and pantomined repeated virtual warm-up pitches. Following his actual lead-off toss that bounced, he didn't want to leave his mound position until he had thrown a strike.

Before the pregame ceremony ended with Oliva's toss, each of the other first pitchers was introduced before walking from the baseline to the rubber, each basking in the moment like a reliever taking the mound accompanied by his walk-on music. To say the least, the ritual was protracted. With first pitches finally finished, Iowa's starting pitcher and catcher moved into position for warm-ups while drizzle continued.

Alas, the rest of team remained in the dugout while the home-plate umpire convened with the grounds crew supervisor. In the meantime, my name appeared on the scoreboard as the designated anthem singer for the evening. The pace of the rain increased. Nate Teut, the Cubs staffer who assisted anthem performers and with whom I had talked about my project, wryly smiled: "Eighty-three and counting…and counting." This game would be my eighty-fourth, if ever sung.

The home-plate umpire held out his hand like the pose in Norman Rockwell's classic painting, and, catching raindrops, he summoned the Cubs manager out from the dugout. He let him know that he thought the conditions at that time were playable, but he was concerned by the report that "a yellow spot" had appeared moments earlier on the radar. While they stood talking and while I stood waiting, the intensity of the rain increased. The first pitches had been thrown; the anthem was yet unsung.

Since the Iowa players would be taking the field first, the home-plate umpire wanted the consent of Iowa manager Bill Dancy, who said simply, "Let's play." Relieved while rain fell on me, I turned toward the flag, heard the cue of my introduction (which, by my name only, was briefer than the intros for first-pitch participants), and waited for the crowd to quieten (which it didn't). So I started amidst the sounds of fans chattering.

Although my performance in Des Moines was not one of my better renditions, I was still pleased that I got to sing while rain dappled my shirt and splashed my glasses. I didn't mind. I was singing in the rain; and number "84" was in the books, not that anyone other than me and Nate was aware of my anthem box score.

Wet, but not soaked like the children who had played in the right-field fountain during the pregame rains, I stayed to see Justin Christian lead off at 8:06 for Fresno, San Francisco's Triple-A team in the Pacific Coast League. Christian, of course, was the fleet-footed Giants outfield prospect who had scored from second on a deep fly to centerfield when he had been playing for Richmond when I had sung there six weeks earlier. That play certainly made my list of top-ten plays during my minor league summer. Not to be completely outdone by his earlier performance in Double-A, Christian doubled in the last of the Grizzlies runs, providing the margin for the Grizzlies 3-2 win over Iowa's Cubs.

Storm Chased Near Omaha: Game 85 in Omaha

No team's moniker applied to my tour experience more ironically, unexpectedly, and personally than the one in Omaha.

In preparation for moving into a new ballpark after forty years of having called Rosenblatt Stadium its shared home with the NCAA World Series, the Omaha Royals Triple-A team sought a new identity. A public competition was held to create a new name for the team's first season in Werner

Ballpark, and the nickname "Storm Chasers" was chosen. Little did I anticipate how fitting—even in a twisted way—that name might be for my experience in the Omaha area. Although I had not chased active storms on the tour, I had retraced routes of recent tornado wreckage through northern Alabama, across central North Carolina, and near Wales, Massachusetts, and I had narrowly preceded the devastating storm in southern Missouri, the "category-4" twister that ripped through Joplin.

Even though clear skies had prevailed throughout the morning and afternoon, an unpleasant feeling had hung over the day. I had woken with a ruptured blood vessel in my right eye, causing it to look more inflamed than if I had had an allergic reaction, a drunken splay, or even pinkeye. Although my ocular condition did not affect my vision or cause discomfort (other than to others who might look me in the eye), it seemed to color the entire day with difficulties.

Heading west from Des Moines, Arbie had struggled with the unyielding undulations in the terrain of western Iowa. Down a slope on I-80 we would rumble as fast as possible, reaching about seventy miles per hour, clinging to the right-hand lane and still moving as the slowest vehicle on the road while eighteen-wheelers easily passed us. Then we would huff and puff our way up the opposite grade at forty-five to fifty miles per hour. Throughout the alternation of these speedy descents and arduous climbs, Arbie's temperature needle consistently hovered at a millimeter or two below the red zone.

Construction on Omaha's freeways continued Arbie's challenges—and mine—until we reached the sun-drenched hilltop site in the Walnut Creek recreation area by mid-afternoon. While the outside temperature crested at ninety-two degrees in the shade, Arbie's thermometer registered 104 on the site's slab. I placed sunshields in the front and side windows facing west, plugged in the cord for air conditioning, and extended the awning—the last, and fatal, extension of that marvelous, twenty-four-foot retractable sunshade. Even so, the air conditioner struggled to provide a cooling effect but enough comfort to enable Bonnie to fall asleep before I slipped out to the game alone.

About a half-hour ahead of schedule, I arrived at the ballpark and stopped at a couple of tailgate parties to sample fan enthusiasm and appreciation for the new stadium. Approaching the Will Call window, I was a bit concerned when I saw that sixteen or seventeen people were already in the line, but I reasoned that at 6:15 I still had ample time to make it to the field in time to meet the contact person as scheduled at 6:30. But seven minutes later when I identified myself as the anthem singer, a waiting staffer whisked me through the gates without a ticket since the game time had been advanced by a half-hour to accommodate a Faith Night, postgame musical performance. Incredible! With less time to warm up than a middle-innings reliever, I was handed the microphone, oriented toward the flag, and told that my cue would be my name. I should have sensed the unexpected, swift pursuit of the subsequent storm!

A few of my anthem renditions are ones that I'd like to forget. This was one that I could easily put in a storm cellar. Nothing was really wrong: it was simply that I didn't feel comfortable since I hadn't been able to complete my warm-up routine. Even so, while walking toward my position behind home plate, I hurriedly sang through the song in my mind to make sure that the words wouldn't burst out of order.

A bit harried after my performance, I neglected to find out the name of the pregame staffer who escorted me to the field. Even so, I asked her about what happened when an anthem performer canceled or failed to show up on time: "Do the Storm Chasers play a recording?"

"No," she responded. "Usually we draft one of the staff or get a season ticket holder to lead everyone in the anthem."

Hmmm, I wondered: "Who would have 'pinch-sung' for me this night and how much advance warning would he or she have received?" Only thirteen minutes had elapsed between my arrival at the ticket window and my singing the anthem's opening phrase.

Thus began my game in Papillion, Nebraska, the new home of the newly named Omaha Storm Chasers.

Although my pregame routines had been disrupted, I left the Storm Chasers staff member and began my usual ballpark maneuvers by checking out the concession stands, locating walls of recognition and banners featuring former players, scoping out the children's play spaces and entertainment options, exploring artistic displays and architectural features, and reading notices of ballpark rules and other signs posted throughout the concourse.

Right away, I scanned the nineteen Werner Park rules bilingually displayed at the entry gate. While many of the directions for ballpark behavior duplicated standard codes of conduct, several of the instructions were distinct, if not unique, to the Storm Chasers:

Tailgating is allowed only in designated areas of the parking lot.
Only one parking space per vehicle is allowed.
Umbrellas are permitted. Lawn chairs are not allowed.
In the event of an evacuation, all guests are to abide by the directions of authorized personnel.

Naïvely when I had read this last regulation, I did not immediately associate the need for possible evacuation with stormy weather. I had thought that the instructions might apply to an accident, a fire, a terrorist act, or a different human-generated catastrophe. About an hour later, the distant lightning, roping wind, and impending rain chased me from the ballpark before I could learn whether this storm would command an evacuation.

Innings later, rain began to fall, driving the crowd to the covered areas of the concourses. Yet their movement seemed, at best, ironic by reversing the course of action designated by the team's new name: The fans were being shoved by the storm rather than chasing it. That cloudburst, thankfully, was short-lived. Not even the grounds crew had time to roll out the tarp; and the Storm Chasers whirled around the bases, scoring four runs to take the lead from the wetter Sacramento River Cats who had stayed on the field throughout the downpour, after which I resumed my survey of the stands.

Other signs, art, and player recognitions throughout the ballpark also reflected the particular character of the community. Most prominent among the local baseball heroes honored at ballpark was Bob Gibson, a native of Omaha, a graduate of Creighton, and a pitcher for Omaha's Triple-A team then affiliated with St. Louis. A perennial major league all-star with the Cardinals, Gibson simultaneously won the Cy Young and MVP awards in 1968 while hurling thirteen shutouts, compiling a miniscule 1.12 ERA, and leading the league with 268 strikeouts. His season set the modern standard for pitching untouchability.

In simpler ways other former major league all-stars—Nebraskans Wade Boggs and Richie Ashburn—were recognized by having VIP suites named after them. Like Gibson, Boggs had been born in Omaha, and neighboring Tilden claimed to be the birthplace of Ashburn, a Phillies star from the Whiz Kids era. Others players who had enjoyed successful seasons in Omaha before becoming accomplished Royals in Kansas City were also "suitely" celebrated: catcher John Wathan, pitcher Paul Splittorff, and slick fielding second-baseman Frank White. Yet without having been identified specifically with Omaha, Dick Howser and Frank Robinson also had VIP quarters named in their honor. Howser's baseball career had been shaped by the parent Royals in Kansas City who had signed him after graduating from Florida State, started him at shortstop in his rookie year in 1961, and finally played under his management for six years in the 1980s.

What I never figured out, however, is why the "Nut-Free Suite" was named for Frank Robinson, an all-star with Cincinnati before winning a Triple Crown with Baltimore. Why would he be so extoled in Omaha where, even during his few minor league seasons, he never played a game? Certainly, his role as the color-breaking player for the Redlegs merited commendation, even as his baseball exploits had secured his first-ballot election into the Hall of Fame. But what I never learned was his connection to Nebraska.

What wasn't a mystery was the cause of the chorus of laughter and squeals of delight from children playing in the areas known as the Family Fun Zone and Borsheims Diamond. Their joyful sounds erupted when they slid through corkscrew tubes or hit Wiffle-ball home runs. Joining the kids in laughter were several adults, including me, at the Wiffle-ball game when one preschool batter finally hit the plastic ball. At the pitcher's mound a Storm Chasers staffer purposely dropped the boy's pop fly and intentionally continued to fumble the ball while the batter ran and ran and ran, never hesitating in his flip-flops until after he had circled the bases and slid into home.

In additional ways, too, the formal spaces and informal activities provided at the ballpark for children, the family and faith culture of Omaha—the theme for the night's promotion—was evident. On the family front, baseball-loving kinfolk gathered for tailgate barbecues in the parking lot before watching the game from their picnic blankets spread on the ramparts beyond left field. On the faith front, Lutherans, in particular, congregated to enjoy the game and to participate in the public celebration of faith. And for the faithful fans who, unlike me, had not been chased away by the immersing rain, a postgame Christian concert capped off the evening of the Storm Chasers 7-5 victory over the River Cats.

In the fourth inning clouds began to roil and hurtle toward the ballpark, and lightning accelerated its slicing through the horizon. I considered options and decided to leave the game early, to return to Arbie where I had left Bonnie after a hot and strenuous day of travel.

Although the RV site in the Walnut Creek recreation area was less than five miles from the ballpark, I didn't make it back to Arbie in time to prevent major damage from the gustado that charged through the area. That's right, a "gustado." Although the term hadn't made it into an official meteorological lexicon, it was used by an Omaha newscaster that night to describe the squall with tornadic force that sheers directly downward at the front end of a fast-moving T-cell.

With winds whipping wildly on, above, around, and seemingly through Arbie, Bonnie had difficulty retracting the long awning. Phoning me moments after I left the ballpark, she asked what to do to minimize the turbulent rocking caused by the invading storm. Abruptly stopping, she cried, "There it goes." A torrid burst had ripped the awning off Arbie's ribs, tossing it up onto his roof. I heard the crash and worried about her safety. "Just get here soon," she implored. There was little that could be done when, three minutes later, I drove up and saw the compound fracture of the awning.

While the storm raged about us and rocked Arbie as though we were in a rowboat crossing the wake of a Jet Ski, we considered abandoning RV life for the night and checking into a hotel, and we began to think about what to do to prepare for the next day's scheduled journey westward toward Wyoming.

By midnight, the storm cells had passed into Iowa, and we slept—or at least tried to sleep. Rising at dawn under clear skies, we quickly surmised that the awning was a complete loss: the support arms were twisted, the canvas torn, and the roller bar bent. The entire setup would need to be removed. As I began to disengage the roller bar, the hydraulic spring in the arm released, thwacking my right thumb, which throbbed with pain as it began to swell despite the immediate and repeated application of icepacks throughout the day. I was lucky that the injury was merely a crushed nail, severe bruise, and possible hairline fracture—not a sudden amputation.

Thankfully, minutes after my injury two RVers who had been residing at the park for several weeks offered to help with the removal and disposal of the awning. Both brought tools, expertise, and energy that were indispensable. Vern Bridgewater, who spent winters in Alabama and summers in Walnut Creek Park, had been a metalworker and tool specialist before his retirement a few years earlier. While I unbolted the arm supports and drilled off the heads of rivets securing the sidebars to Arbie, he used his reciprocating saw to cut through the final portion of the support whose complete release had been prevented by the hinges on a storage bay.

Meanwhile, Mike Meehan, whose retracted awning had also been slightly damaged by the storm, began to cut the canvas from the roller bar. Since he was sporting a Red Sox cap, I turned some of our conversation to baseball and the national anthem and learned that, although he had spent most of his career in San Diego, he had never shifted his allegiance from Boston to the Padres. Whether wintering in Georgia or summering in Nebraska in his rolling home, he was permanently a citizen of Red Sox Nation.

For an hour the three of us toiled together, Vern sawing the pieces into six-foot lengths, me loading them into Mike's van, and Mike hauling them away to the dumpster. I bid them farewell knowing that their assistance was the reason that I might be able to keep the next engagement in Casper, Wyoming.

After a quick breakfast, Bonnie and I attached Toad to the tow bar and headed west across the recurring sameness of Nebraska's prairie, a flat terrain across which Arbie sighed in relief.

A Different Kind of Prairie Fever

The day-plus trek across Nebraska was fraught with frustration, pain, and fatigue. While Arbie persevered for more than ten hours en route from Papillion to Scottsbluff, my thumb throbbed with the rhythms and resonance of bongo drums. Double doses of Advil made driving possible while I tried throughout the day to steer left-handed, holding my right arm across my chest and resting my fingers on my left shoulder. I had severely injured my right thumb at dawn when I had begun to remove the ruptured awning from Arbie. (It would eventually take a year for the nail to thicken and regrow.) When I had started to separate the shade's roller from its attached points, the tension in the automatic arm had released, causing the metal wing to retract with rifle suddenness and catch the last inch of my thumb in its explosion. Although I iced the wound immediately, the sudden swelling and discoloration could not be thwarted. I now know that I could have reduced the swelling and the pain by heating a needle and pressing a hole through my thumbnail to allow the pooling blood to escape. But then, all that I knew was the throbbing pain and the necessity to make significant progress toward Caspar, more than 600 miles away.

Somehow, I still hoped that I would be able to sing the following evening for a game in Wyoming. Not that I expected that my voice would be affected by my thumb pounding in its own rhythmic pattern. Rather, my repeated attempts to reconfirm my assigned date with the Caspar Ghosts had not prompted replies.

Somewhere along the eternal stretch of I-80, we stopped to eat an early lunch and to gas up Arbie; he would require almost two refueling stops between the Omaha area and our Wyoming destination. There, in a nondescript truck stop while Bonnie and I ate sandwiches, I received a wild affirmation from the person who had originally scheduled my apparently haunted appearance. He indicated that—yes!—the *West Virginia Power* would be happy for me to sing the following evening. Since his Casper e-mail was being forwarded to his new address and position with the Rookie League team in the Appalachian League, he was not aware that I was aiming toward and nearing Wyoming, not West Virginia.

With the speed and frustration of protesting a called third strike high and outside, I responded, letting him know that I was trying to reconfirm the date with the Ghosts, not his new employer. Right away, he sent me the contact information for Tim Ray, the Ghosts executive director. And before we resumed the tedious pace of I-80, I e-mailed Tim with the update on my tour and the information that Monday's date had been confirmed months earlier.

Throughout the afternoon, I kept Arbie in the right lane of the interstate highway while eighteen-wheelers created draft tunnels, sucking us one way and shoving us another as they roared past. The infinite reach of the prairie stretched past the horizon, teasing us on toward an imprecise destiny. In previous years when I had driven back and forth from California to Wisconsin to see my son when he was in college, I had begun to think of the perpetual prairie of Nebraska as America's purgatory: the expanse between home and hope. Meanwhile, my thumb throbbed with kettledrum strikes, and my spirits sank with the prospect of losing Caspar, my only possible appearance in Wyoming. Indeed, I felt like I was in a limbic state where pain persists and desire forms as a figment of imagination.

To my surprise when we exited I-80 at Ogallala and turned northwest on US 26, we climbed through a scenic stretch of hills overlooking Lake McConaughy that had been created by the Kingsley Dam on the North Platte River. The remote ascent of the roadway without the incessant whirr of semis soothed my still-pulsing spirit—and thumb. Coursing upstream adjacent to the river, we slipped through small settlements and towns, starting with Lewellyn, notable because of its variant spelling of my given middle name. On we aimed toward Chimney Rock, which had guided pioneers centuries earlier in their pursuit of dreams along the Oregon Trail. On one side of the highway, the North Platte River flowed to the southeast; on the other, the train tracks connected the Dakotas with the Southwest. Incessantly, heavily-laden coal trains—more than a dozen passing us in our single afternoon—trafficked south, each with 100 cars and more pouring toward Texas and its yawning power plants.

A few degrees north of Chimney Rock, we reached Scottsbluff and settled Arbie into a lovely pre-dusk site at the Robidoux RV Park. While the brilliance of the afternoon sun slid into the liminal western colors before stars could splash their radiance across the gaping night sky, we moored Arbie, ate dinner, and strolled through the sparsely occupied campground, down its access road, and on toward town. The sunset spawned a sense of calm after Omaha's storm, Arbie's amputation, and the revelation of the schedule glitch in Caspar.

The following morning we rose early in the soft northern dawns of August, disconnected Arbie's multiple lifelines—electrical and cable, water and sewage—and pressed Northwest. Before we reached the Wyoming state line, my phone rang, and Bonnie pressed the speaker button, allowing me to hear the Ghosts Tim Ray indicate that a local performer was set to sing the anthem for the game that evening. I pleaded my case, pointing out the national scope of my tour and imploring that the other assigned singer be offered the chance to perform at one of the games later in the season. Tim said that he would see what he could do.

Within an hour we crossed into Wyoming, and before we reached its first town, Torrington, Tim's assistant called with good news that I could sing as originally scheduled. Relieved and reassured by the Ghosts schedule adjustments, we ambled easily along in Arbie and continued straight through Lingle where Highway 26 had made an abrupt, minimally-marked left turn. Its companion route—US 85, which had blended with our roadway miles earlier near the Nebraska-Wyoming border—continued north toward Lusk, the next town, population less than 1,500, almost fifty miles away. And just as US 85 continued north, so, mistakenly, did we.

I discovered our failure to follow US 26 when I saw two signs several miles north of Lingle, one identifying Highway 85 and the other warning of the nothingness before Lusk. I dreaded that our errant route might cause such a delay that we might not get to the Ghosts game in time for me to sing. With Toad in tow, there appeared to be no place to turn around.

Immediately I asked Bonnie for help. Using our location, she quickly Googled possible side roads back to Lingle. The only alternate way appeared to lie across a small canal, a dirt road that apparently reconnected with our highway several miles behind us. The most pressing problem seemed to be that the few small bridges over the culvert did not look like they could support Arbie's weight. Gulp. I drove on, making matters worse by taking us farther from our desired route while Bonnie continued to point out feeble ties to the road beyond the wide irrigation gulley.

For one of very few times on the tour, we argued. I had asked for her help with navigation and now I was ignoring her advice. "Aren't we a team?" she asked.

She was right. Even so, I tried to explain my concern about the viability of the culvert crossings. I feared that even if a rudimentary bridge would provide us with safe passage, we might then be marooned on the other side of the deep ditch, a worse predicament than going more miles out of our way.

Having slowed Arbie to survey our possibilities more effectively, I noticed that ahead to our left was an open gate to a ranch house with a large, flat, dry-caked area adjacent to a barn. I pulled Arbie into the driveway and across the cattle guard, swirling Arbie as tightly and as quickly as possible before exiting back onto the highway before a rancher might appear with Wild West shotguns, ready to fire at our intruding modern Conestoga.

Back in Lingle a dozen miles later, we turned correctly toward Fort Laramie and resumed our anticipated course toward Caspar. By the time we reached Douglas, where we enjoyed a picnic lunch, the grasses of the high prairie had provided a pacific panorama that soothed our earlier distress.

Barking at Ghosts: Game 86 in Casper

During the fifteen-minute drive from Arbie's berth at the River's Edge RV Park to the ballpark in Casper, Wyoming, Bonnie sighed that she missed Winston, our lovable three-year-old Havanese that we had left in Whittier in the care of our older son. To our surprise when we arrived at the game, the evening's promotion was a "Bark in the Park" celebration, my third on the tour following ones in State College and Trenton. Unlike the two earlier events where dog food and pet supplies were promoted, the one in Wyoming was designed to raise awareness about the local Paws2Help Fund, a resource to provide medical care for pets in animal shelters and foster homes. The occasion also served as a fundraiser for the organization by offering at silent auction several custom ceramic serving pieces—ghost-themed party platters for human festivities and player-autographed water or chow bowls for humans' reputed best friends.

Dogs of all sizes and breeds were everywhere in the ballpark: waiting in line at the concession stands for treats, panting at the entry to the grandstand, or lounging along the grassy median between the left-field foul-line fence and the walkway to the seats. The only restriction was that the dogs were not allowed on the field or in the grandstand. I loved having the chance to approach the dogs, offer them the back of my hand to sniff, and wait for their approval before scratching behind their ears or stroking the backs of their necks. Yet I kept hoping that some foul fly would bound past me so that I could see whether the retrievers might revert to primal instincts, lunging to run and fetch.

When raindrops started to fall shortly before the scheduled start of the game, I chuckled, imagining that cats might start falling from the sky since the dogs in that proverbial, stormy pair were already around me. My good humor quickly morphed into anxiety when I noticed that there was no tarp for a grounds crew to unroll over the diamond. Even in Williamsport there had been half tarps used to overlap the diamond during the downpour. Yet I needn't have fretted because the shower passed quickly, and I later learned of the uselessness of a tarp in Casper since the region's average rainfall throughout July and August is less than two inches. With only thirty-eight home games scheduled during the summer season, the expense of a tarp for use during rain showers and between games proved unnecessary.

A second distinct feature of the ballpark was something present, not something absent, like an infield tarp. Beyond the right-field fence, a tantalizing billboard featured a portrait of local real estate agent Jim Edgeworth standing with legs crossed, left hand hidden in his pocket, and right hand extended in a friendly greeting. Emblazoned across his photo was his name in foot-high letters with a large, red arrow swooping toward an open-hole "O" just below the crook of his right elbow. Baiting the arrow was a somewhat familiar, outfield sign plea: "Hit it here." But unlike other ballparks' home-run targets for a free suit or dinner or used car, this sign's appeal was its promise of $20,000 for hitting a ball through the open "O." To certify the flight of a home run through the hole, a net extended behind the opening to catch a ball worth twenty grand. Now with fewer than a dozen games remaining in the season, Edgeworth's escrow seemed secure. But during the third game of the season, Edgeworth himself had probably gotten a scare when Ghosts third baseman Sam Mende had hit Edgeworth's portrait's right wrist, missing the reward by less than a foot.

In addition to an actual, post-shower rainbow whose end almost placed its supposed pot of gold behind Edgeworth's "O," several routine activities during Ghosts games enlivened the evening. Like a few other ballparks, Casper identified one of the opposing hitters as the designated "beer batter" for the game. If that hitter struck out during the game, draft beers would be sold for ten minutes for only two dollars. So When Darian Sandford struck out in the fifth inning, he created a rush past the dogs to the concession stand for cheap suds. An inning earlier, a similar soda promotion had spotlighted two-dollar Pepsis during a ten-minute hubbub following an around-the-horn double play turned by the Ghosts.

At other ballparks I had occasionally heard and sometimes had sung "God Bless America" during the seventh-inning stretch. In Casper a different—and perhaps more regionally fitting—patriotic song preceded the customary chorus of "Take Me Out to the Ballgame." While the "purple mountains' majesty" could still be discerned in the dusky distance above "the fruited plains," a local student sang "America the Beautiful." Fans stood at reverential attention, and players came out of the dugouts and bullpens, faced the flag, and placed their caps over their hearts. If only "The Star-Spangled Banner" regularly evoked similar sentiments!

Another new feature that I encountered at Casper was management's recognition of a "Sweetheart of the Game" by providing a lucky female fan with a bouquet of flowers presented by the team mascot. According to some of the staff, the bouquet encouraged wives and girlfriends to attend the game. Even when a sweetheart didn't win the bouquet, she often referred to the gesture in such a way that her baseball-blinded beau could get the idea about the effectiveness of flowers. Flowers for female fans at the ballpark? Did that mean that tears of happiness would follow and that crying would soon be allowed in baseball?

Earlier on my way to our seats after singing the anthem, Ghosts executive director Tim Ray grinned broadly and high-fived my rendition. Before he had begun to talk with me, Tim had been approached by two wide-eyed, season ticket holders who had exclaimed in response to the anthem, "Wow! Who was that guy?" To a certain extent, they already knew since they had heard the brief intro that I had provided to the Ghosts.

"I told them, a professor who loves baseball," he said.

So simple and so true.

From the seats where Bonnie and I sat below the press box, I spied a small dog discreetly held in the lap of its owner who sat in the fourth row behind the backstop. It looked exactly like Winston—black with a white mustache, white eyebrows, and white paws. After I pointed to the Winston "imdogerator," Bonnie and I quickly moved to a row adjacent to Terry and Phyllis Letz and her mother Evelyn McClure, owner of Riley, a ShiDoodle. The Shih Tzu line of Riley's mixed breed is cousin to Wintson's Havanese pedigree. Although dogs were restricted from the grandstand area, Ghosts management seemed to extend a therapeutic exception to Bonnie and me since she ended up holding Riley for several innings in a seat directly behind home plate.

In adjacent seats two sisters joined our fun time of talking about dogs and baseball. From the Yellowstone area, Kathy Moline was visiting her sister Sharon Sullivan for several days. When they would get together, they would try to fill part of their itinerary with baseball. On several occasions they had coordinated shopping and adventure trips to Denver to coincide with games at Coors Field so they could watch the Rockies in person. And Kathy had made sure that her visits to her sister in Casper would coincide with Ghosts home games. For them, baseball resonated with childhood and family. As young girls in South Dakota, each week they had gone to their grandmother's house for Sunday dinner. There the telecast of a Minnesota Twins game was always on, no question. Enthusiastically, then, I shared my fortunate encounter and conversations with Tony Oliva several days earlier at the ballpark in Des Moines. Although as Wyoming residents they had begun to root for the Rockies (when it had been the only major league team in the Mountain time zone) and its Rookie League affiliate Casper, they seemed to have been transported to their grandmother's house by my story about my encounter with the Twins not-yet, but deserving Hall-of-Famer whom they had adored.

They regaled me with Oliva's accomplishments. A perennial all-star, he had won the Rookie of the Year Award and multiple batting titles, led the Twins to their first World Series, and retired as a career .300 hitter. A native of Cuba, Oliva had signed his professional contract only two months before the failed Bay of Pigs invasion in 1961.

While we talked baseball, Sharon also lauded the local National Historic Trails Interpretive Center. The interactive museum pays tribute to the pioneers along the Oregon, Mormon, and California trails, all of which had followed the North Platte River past Chimney Rock, Scotts Bluff, and Ft. Laramie, the route that we had traversed during previous days.

Since I was not scheduled to sing the evening after the game in Casper, Bonnie and I delayed our departure the next morning so that we could explore the trails center. I wish that I had taken a picture of Arbie in the parking lot there as a modern counterpoint to the Conestoga wagons of the pioneers' era. Equipped with its own sanitary system, Arbie stood in stark contrast to the covered wagons displayed throughout the exhibit, and we, unlike the trailblazers of yesteryear, were not exposed to cholera, which had killed so many during the height of trail traffic around 1850.

During our traversing the trail across Nebraska in previous days, Bonnie had read aloud several chapters of Bill Bryson's *At Home*, a fascinating history of the stuff and fixtures in the rooms of a Victorian manse. The coincidental relevance of Bryson's book was this: In its intentional digressions about the development of toilets and plumbing systems, the chapter on the bathroom included a brief medical history about the discovery of the cause of cholera, the fecal contamination of water supply. And in the National Historic Trails Interpretive Center we learned about the decreasing frequency of deaths from cholera as pioneers had moved up the Platte. Because the river had served as their constant water supply, the people followed it closely—all too closely, in fact, often infecting its adjacent watershed with their waste. Consequently, folks further downstream had been increasingly exposed to the deadly disease borne through the water that often served as the source of their hope and sustenance, now contaminated.

Displaying personal accounts of some who had trekked along the trails, the museum's exhibits brought to life the threats of death that they routinely had faced. As I reflected on the incredible difficulties that the pioneers had confronted in their westward journey—painfully jettisoning furnishings and goods and, more traumatically, experiencing accidents, illness, and death—I felt fortunate that our only real loss had been Arbie's awning near Omaha.

In an extended metaphorical way, the label of pioneers applied well to Casper's baseball team. At an obvious level, the Ghosts competed in the Pioneer League. But more than that, like the other novices in the Rookie League classification, the players were on a quest upstream through the minor leagues, a journey so challenging that fewer than ten percent would reach the desired destination of the majors. And in Casper on the night when we were there, the Ghosts and visiting Chukars from Idaho Falls played as roughly as pioneers, amassing seventeen runs on eighteen hits, while committing seven errors. But as the dark deepened, the Ghosts could bark at the moon all night long because they won 11-6.

Memories and Memorials in Montana: Game 87 in Billings

It's that simple and certain. I love Montana—its rivers that laugh their way toward human delight, its mountains that outreach imagination, and its sky that stretches all the way from memory to hope.

For two summers prior to our anthem tour, Bonnie and I had vacationed in the western part of the state, staying with friends in Anaconda and taking daily and overnight outings throughout the region. We had coursed beside the Clark Fork and Blackfoot Rivers before picking a picnic spot at one of the frequent places for public access to the ever-flowing streams. We had watched the antelope gambol across the valleys and slopes north of Ennis as we meandered away from Yellowstone, and farther north, we had seen a grizzly bear paw its way across a meadow as we neared St. Mary's Lake. We had seemed to soar toward earthly orbit on the historic Highway to the Sun in Glacier National Park. We had mourned the tragic massacre of Native Americans commemorated at the Big Hole National Battlefield near Wisdom, where Chief Joseph and the Nez Perce had engaged the pursuing U.S. Army in the bloodiest battle of their five-state flight toward possible freedom in Canada. We had visited the local historic museum in Dillon where we saw on display an early map of Beaverhead County surveyed by Bonnie's paternal grandfather, whose engineering firm had also been the first to publish a detailed topographic map of the entire state. We had explored the ghost mining town near Philipsburg days after reading a long-saved letter from Bonnie's maternal grandmother about her friends and families departing from the community following the silver-market collapse caused by the government's shift to the single monetary standard of gold at the turn of the twentieth century.

Fifty summers before Bonnie's and my recent forays into Big Sky country, I had first experienced the grandeur of the state when my family had stopped in Butte to purchase hoodies to warm our nights during tent camping in Yellowstone. When we had left our Mississippi home weeks earlier for a vacation featuring western national parks, we had not packed winter wear, not fathoming the summer need for warm clothing. As stunning as I recall Old Faithful, I was awed even more by the expanse and heights of Montana's landscape, especially its glorious, grand mountains that punctured the wide night ceiling pixelated with a fireworks spray of stars.

It shouldn't come as a surprise that I made sure to design our route to coincide with the Pioneer League's short-season schedule and to coordinate dates with most of Montana's teams—the Mustangs in Billings, the Brewers in Helena, and the Osprey in Missoula. The state's fourth team, the Great Falls Voyagers, had agreed to let me sing if dates could be coordinated, but they were on a road trip throughout our trek through the state. Unlike my previous ventures to the region, this time our schedule restricted sightseeing to ballpark vistas and interstate panoramas, spectacular nonetheless.

Although I had no personal memories of Billings, my introduction to the three-year-old ballpark there was filled with memories of a different kind—impressive memorials to local baseball heroes and passionate fans. Nearest the main entry gate stood a life-size, bronze replica of former Baltimore all-star lefty Dave McNally, mid-delivery to the plate. A local baseball product, McNally had achieved stardom in the Billings Little League, but had been unable to play in high school since Central Catholic High, where he had attended, couldn't field a team because of the short spring and lack of schools with whom Central could easily compete. Even so, he excelled on the city's renowned American Legion team, which played a summer schedule sometimes of eighty games, longer even than the Mustangs Rookie League season. During his American Legion career, McNally once struck out twenty-seven batters in a single game (including five in one inning), he had posted a nearly perfect 18-1 record one season, and he had led his team to the American Legion World Series title game before signing with the Orioles. Outside his professional baseball career, McNally lived his entire life in Billings. The narrative tribute accompanying his statue also featured his role, with "Andy Messermith" (a regrettable typographical error omitting an "s" between the "r" and "m" in "Messersmith"), in winning the suit against Major League Baseball to end the "reserve clause."

Opposite the statue of McNally was an equally active, bronze tribute to his former American Legion coach Ed Bayne, who had taught fundamental baseball skills to young players for more than a quarter century. During his coaching career Bayne's teams had won twenty state championships and had advanced to World Series play on four occasions. Celebrated for these accomplishments in baseball, Bayne was even more respected by the Billings community for coaching kids about life, summed up in this way by one of his former players in his 2003 obituary in the *Billings Gazette*: "He taught me right from wrong, he was tough, and...he challenged you to reach the level your ability would allow....He showed respect for you whether you were the last guy in the dugout or one of the best players. We learned the fundamentals of baseball but we learned also how to be successful in life."

At the ballpark in Billings, the American Legion tradition appears to rank more highly than professional baseball. While many minor league ballparks feature players and sometimes managers who set franchise records or later achieved stardom in the major leagues, only a handful of walls at other minor league ballparks displayed the names or photos of stellar collegiate players who had shared the facility. By contrast, the dugoutlength Wall of Fame in Billings—by far the biggest bronze tribute that I had seen at any ballpark—honors local American Legion coaches and players. In the first two years of its existence, the organization inducted more coaches than players. Of course, leading the roster were Ed Bayne, whose name now graces the award given to inductees, and Dave McNally, whose name is associated with the award given to supporters of American Legion ball.

Others also were recognized in less formal ways. Between the two statues, the walkway to the main gate featured bricks inscribed with tributes to fans and former Billings baseball personnel. The children and grandchildren of Alvin Schlenker remembered his love of the Mustangs, "especially when they were winning." One inscription honored coach Dennis Sahli, who inspired players to love the game, and another recognized Andy Andrews, the "fantastic" concessions manager from a half-century earlier. Noteworthy was the message describing his work, indicating that he gave many kids their first job.

While the sculptures, memorials, and tributes summoned our appreciation, my experience was dampened by several unexpected difficulties. At the Will Call window, I was dismayed to find a single ticket for me in the envelope, none for Bonnie. And since the game was sold out except for picnic and berm seating, the staff member couldn't locate available adjacent seats. Recalling the distress that we had experienced in Durham when separate seats had finally been offered, I insisted that our inclusion of Billings on the tour merited appropriate seats. After making several offers of disconnected seats, the staffer finally departed to secure authorization for us to sit in a reserved section.

The second challenge was unique. As I moved to the area behind home plate about ten minutes before singing the anthem, Matt, the staff member who coordinated pregame presentations, pointed above the bluff behind the trees beyond the left-field wall and said that the end of the runway at the Billings airport was less than a mile away. "Every night between 7 and 7:05," he said, "a FedEx flight takes off and comes over the field. Some nights, it's during the anthem."

If that happens, I immediately reminded myself, whatever you do, don't stop. Although it was certainly possible that my rendition might get blasted by the roar of the jet's engines, I also thought that it might be fun for the timing to work out to make the departure a fly-over as the anthem ended. Thankfully, the take-off occurred before I heard the full introduction about the anthem tour.

A different distraction briefly occurred during the pregame ceremonies. Selected to throw out the first pitch was a star softball pitcher who was dressed in running shorts and a tank top. When she learned that I was a professor at a California college, she indicated keen interest in possibly playing for a long-season West Coast school. I enthusiastically responded by describing Whittier's academic distinctions and the success of its softball team, then handed her my business card. Having no pockets, she pinched her tank top with one hand while slipping the card into her bra with the other. Yes, that move distracted my attention from normal pregame routines.

As I walked toward the dugout gate following my rendition, Billings pitching coach Bob Forsch asked, "How many games?"

"Tonight was number eighty-seven," I replied.

"Where've you been?"

"All over: Texas, Florida, North Carolina, New England, the Midwest, and now Wyoming and Montana for the Pioneer League." And I added that several years ago I had sung for a game that his brother Ken had pitched at Anaheim.

"Did he win?"

"Yes."

"Too bad!" he countered with typical sibling rivalry.

After encountering so many late-afternoon and early-evening thunderstorms in the Midwest and even dry Wyoming, we could anticipate the almost daily difficulty of a rain delay. In the third inning lightning struck so close by that players fled from the field. Not bothering to see whether the grounds crew would hazard covering the diamond, Bonnie and I left the ballpark as raindrops started to splash quarter-size spots on our shirts. Although the size of the raindrops summoned my mother's theory that "the larger the raindrops, the shorter the storm," we found refuge in Toad, and rather than waiting out the shower, we returned to Arbie before play resumed. We missed Billings third-baseman Sean Buckley slugging a home run to lead the Mustangs to a 4-1 win over visiting Great Falls.

An Unexpected Helenic Hello: Game 88 in Helena

Since childhood, I've been fond of Helena simply because of the possible pronunciation of its name. In the fifth grade when my classmates and I had learned the states and their capital cities, my friends Bubba and Bobby and I laughed and laughed about the name of Montana's capital. We concocted a joke that would delight us time and again: "Who wants to go to Helena Cadillac?" We needn't reply, only cackle "Har, har, har," thinking that we had cursed by saying "Hell" while not getting caught, punching and slapping each other, as preadolescent boys are wont to do.

More than a few decades after our childhood sparring, I finally made it to Helena, not in our boyhood dream of a Deville, but in Toad, a 1994 Saturn sedan that was almost small enough to fit into the back seat of the big Cadillac from the early 1960s that Bubba, Bobby, and I had conjured. I doubted that either of my buddies had beaten me to the city in a newer Escalade or, more likely, a beat-up pickup truck, especially since it was almost 2,000 miles and several decades from our boyhood playgrounds. Even so, as I approached the Brewers ballpark, I knew that the old automotive joke that we had retold now seemed as rusty as the junkyard of cars that mounded adjacent to the ballpark.

Still on my initial visit to Helena, I experienced a sense of déjà vu shortly before I moved to the spot behind home plate to sing the anthem at Kindrick Legion Field. When I walked through the gate from the grandstand to the dugout area in the historic ballpark, I was dumbfounded when I heard a friendly voice call out, "I wondered when you'd get here." Certainly not Bubba or Bobby, I knew, since they wouldn't recognize me after all these years. The voice came from Ned Yost, the first-base coach for the hometown Brewers. Immediately I wondered, "How did he know me?"

Almost three months earlier Yost had seen and heard me sing in Huntsville, Alabama, then home of the Brewers Southern League affiliate. Once the short season had begun in the Pioneer League, Yost had shifted to his primary duties to the Rookie League team. Yost and I chatted about the route that I had pursued, the ballparks that I had seen, the anthems that I had sung. Specifically, he wondered if I had been rained out or missed a game or two.

"By the way," he asked, "what game is this for you?"

When I indicated "number eighty-eight," he nodded knowingly, figuring that, as much as I loved the game and the anthem, I was growing season-weary and road-worn. I bobbed my head in agreement, understanding—at least in part—the long-season fatigue that affects players. While my gigs on the field lasted less than ninety seconds five times during a week, I had increasingly begun to identify with the rigors of travel and daily game preparation that swallow players and coaches. I told him that I admire those who make it through the grind of August, night after night, city after city, evening compounded by the next morning's bus ride, dittoed by the same sequence every three or four days. Overhearing our conversation, pitching coach Elvin Nina gestured two thumbs up as he chewed sunflower seeds and spit their shells a few feet away.

Before talking with Yost I had checked in with Richard, the Brewers game-day staffer. Serving as a summer intern while on break from his university studies in sports management, he oriented me to the typical pregame routines. Since he had assisted most of the anthem performers during the season, I inquired about soloists who had presented distinct performances.

"Up to now," he twisted and tilted his head as if trying to put faces on the singers whom he had heard in previous weeks, "there was the fifteen-year-old girl from Townsend," a town of 2,000 or so about thirty miles southeast of Helena.

"Why was she memorable?" I asked.

"Well," he paused again, "she wins all kinds of contests around here." Then, he added, almost apologetically, "Of course, you."

Hearing Richard and me comparing his university and Whittier College, broadcaster Steve Wendt, who had attended UC Santa Barbara, asked Richard if he knew Whittier's most famous graduate. Furrowing his brow differently and squinting like Bubba and Bobby when our fifth-grade teacher called on them to identify Idaho or South Dakota's capital, Richard shook his head and gave both of us a blank look—also like Bubba and Bobby. When Steve hinted that Helena had a player from Yorba Linda, the birthplace of Whittier's most famous alumnus, Richard still looked perplexed. And when Steve specified "Nixon," Richard's expression suggested that Nixon seemed as remote to him as the Civil War.

Turning from that historic tease, Steve pointed out the ballpark's renovation plaque as a means of appealing to my interest in the quirks and distinctions of the ballparks where I had been. Built in 1932, the grandstands had burned twice before their most recent renovation in 1973. Even through the fires and restorations, one of the ballpark's original anomalies persisted: the playing surface dips toward the middle of the field. With a wide conical effect, it slopes from the foul poles toward second base, creating a wide-brimmed funnel toward the infield. Unlike the rising warning track at old Crosley Field in Cincinnati or the initial, centerfield moraine in Houston's Minute Maid Park, Helena's slope affects the entire prairie between the foul lines.

In addition to the ballpark's conflagrant history and outfield contour, a few routine ballpark practices took a screwball turn at Helena. For starters, the first-pitch ceremony, which elsewhere often seemed more celebrated, if not longer, than my seventy-five-second rendition of the anthem, here appeared secondary, if not perfunctory. Not having scheduled a first-pitch promotion, one of the game-day interns approached Luke, a five- or six-year-old kid who had just walked through the turnstiles with his parents and two older brothers at 6:50, and offered him a chance to toss out the first pitch. What a contrast Helena provided to the double-digit waiting line of pregame tossers in Richmond, Lehigh Valley, and Des Moines! Smiling as though he had won Powerball, minutes later Luke strode to the designated spot between the mound and home, assumed the posture of a baseball evangelist, and proceeded to enjoy every instant of the wind-up, delivery, and follow-through.

Even before Luke had charmed the fans, who understood the fundamental pleasure that his fingering the seams of a baseball had brought, the P.A. announcer had bellowed the name and position of the evening's strikeout batter. In place of other ballparks' routine announcement of cheap beer sales for ten minutes or so following a strikeout by a designated hitter, the promotion for the strikeout of a specific opponent featured ice cream: If the identified opposing player should strike out in his first at-bat, fans could buy a dairy treat for a dollar at the grandstand concessions thanks to the association of Montana Dairy farmers.

I appreciated that Helena's P.A. announcer provided the brief introduction that I had suggested; in response, fans applauded *before* I sang. An inning or two after I had finished, an octogenarian season ticket holder wearing a pearl necklace expressed particular appreciation for my tempo and diction, as well as for my including Helena in my tour. While remarking on the anthem, she looked suspiciously at the ballpark grilled hamburger—corrugated and cold—that I was squeezing. Her expression was one of "Oh, my! I should have warned you." Most often, I had tried to avoid ballpark concessions. But this night I was particularly hungry, and the drive back to Bonnie and Arbie in Anaconda loomed long and late. Although it was really as tasteless as cardboard except for its mustard slather, the hamburger at least slaked my hunger for a while.

My anthem rendition prompted speculation about my profession by usher Duke Hudson, who concluded that I must be a professor because of my crisp articulation of the star-spangled phrases. Saying that he wished I would sing most nights, I quipped, "I am, but in a different ballpark each time!" He indicated that if he had earlier known of my trip, he would have invited me to sing and speak at his Kiwanis Club that noon, which, of course, would have been infeasible given my constricted schedule.

Like many, Duke asked about where I had been and which ballpark had been my favorite. Usually, I retorted, "Favorite in what way? Architecture or history or something else?" This time, I simply replied that the ballpark in Pulaski, Virginia, had been a favorite. Reference to that Appalachian League team brought a quick Mariner smile from Hannah Estes, who overheard our exchange.

The daughter of Helena's clubhouse manager Hannah was moving around, photographing players, fans, and the dusky lighting of the ballpark from multiple angles, but especially the players. We started to talk and talk and talk baseball. She asked about whether I'd sung for the Wisconsin Timber Rattlers, whose shirt she was wearing, and other Midwest League teams—especially Clinton, where her friend pitched. Simply, she missed the Midwest. A few years earlier her family had moved to Helena to be with her grandfather during his last battle with cancer. Now she photographed players, often sending shots to their families and girlfriends.

When she had lived in Wisconsin, the team in Appleton had been aligned with Seattle, and she had enjoyed seeing several of the team's former players advance to the parent Mariners. Even so, at heart she had rooted for the Brewers ever since her first game in childhood at County Stadium in Milwaukee. Mention of that ballpark immediately brought a home-run smile to my face because, years earlier, I had there met and talked briefly with Warren Spahn and Hank Aaron on the field prior to the final game in the ballpark. And talk turned to heroes past rather than prospects on the field.

At a few ballparks there seemed to be no end to stimulating conversations with fans about baseball, the anthem, and my travels. Helena was certainly among the most gregarious despite the small crowd at the game. Seated within bunting distance from Hannah and me, Rick Phillips joined our discussion about baseball. The athletic director for a nearby high school, he boasted that his school's athletic facilities were among the best in the state even though his town had fewer than 10,000 residents. Then typical questions resumed about what minor league levels I had included on the tour, where I had been, where I would go next. And like so many others along my trek who had little conception about the preparation required to set up the tour, he also asked if I drive to a city, find a ballpark, and ask to sing.

I wished it were that easy.

While we talked, Max Walla came to plate for Helena, and Rick indicated that Max was the son of one of his former high-school classmates who had brought him to Helena from New Mexico. This visit to the ballpark was the first time he had seen her in almost thirty years, and Walla, wearing "#30," promptly homered.

Comfortable in our baseball-oriented conversation, Rick reached around the back of my neck and peeled the "Inspected by 7" sticker off the collar of my white AnthemTour shirt, which I think I had also worn the previous night in Billings. Oops. Bonnie must have mishandled me before that game—and even this night before leaving Anaconda where we had rested Arbie. Handing the sticky tag to me, Rick looked somewhere between apologetic and enlightened. "Number 7," I mused looking at the number on the tag. "I was honoring Mantle!"

In the eighth inning, Missoula's second-baseman Eric Groff lofted a fly ball into short left centerfield. Simultaneously, the Brewers' left fielder, center fielder, and shortstop lost sight of it; and Helena's broadcaster justified their miscue by saying that the lavender sky at dusk makes it the hardest time to see a ball that goes through the lights. Only in the Big Sky of Northern Montana could an eighth-inning pop fly get lost in the twilight after a 7 o'clock start.

For the record, Missoula won 5-2, scoring three runs in the final two, dusky innings approaching ten o'clock.

Double City Doubleheader: Game 89 in Missoula

Twice before—once in Florida and again in Texas—I had seen teams seek revenge for losses against their previous victors within a week or so. After losing to Dunedin in the first week of the season, Lakeland claimed the advantage of home field a week later and won. A few weeks thereafter the reverse occurred when the visiting team proved victorious in the separated games between Corpus Christi and Midland. And thrice I had seen a particular team play on successive nights. But until Montana in August, I had not seen two teams flip-flop home fields on consecutive nights for what might be called—stretching things a little—a night-night doubleheader in ballparks a hundred miles apart.

After the game in Helena, the Osprey had headed home to Missoula for a midnight arrival while the Brewers followed them the next morning. In contrast to the direct westward route that both teams took, I had triangulated my route between the state's capital and the university's city, initially driving south to Anaconda where I had left Bonnie and Arbie at the home of Fay and Jack Weber, friends with whom we had vacationed during previous summers. Although the Webers were in Europe at that time, they had offered us the use of their historic house, which had been built by the superintendent of the copper smelter at the edge of town. Not only did we appreciate the elegance and spaciousness of their home, we especially enjoyed the use of their full kitchen and laundry room.

In Anaconda, we also took advantage of other services. Bonnie followed Fay's recommendations for a salon where she made appointments for a haircut and a manicure, during which I stopped by the city's public library to see if *Sports Illustrated* had published a brief piece about the anthem tour. When the librarian asked if he could help me with the search for an article, I indicated that I wanted to check on a story that would feature an interview I had given a couple of weeks earlier.

"Interview?" he questioned by inflecting the single word. "Did you need some information for an interview?"

"No," I replied. "I was interviewed for an *SI* blurb that is forthcoming."

"Are you famous?" he continued.

"Hardly," I chuckled, "but I am doing something no one has done before. I'm singing the national anthem at more than a hundred Minor League Baseball parks this summer."

Then, the stunner: "Do you drive an RV with a tow car?"

I nodded.

"We passed you three times the other day between Sheridan and Billings."

So the signage on Arbie had made an impression, at least for reference-oriented folk. A few days earlier when librarian Mitch Grady and his wife had been returning to Anaconda from Denver along I-25, they had passed us several times, once before stopping for lunch, then passing us again before pulling over during a brief hailstorm, and finally passing us a third time before ending our automotive game of leapfrogging.

Although the signage on Arbie had been of no help en route to Missoula since we had left it parked on the street in front of the Webers' house, the same AnthemTour logo on my shirt drew attention in Missoula. While Bonnie and I sat on a bench outside the ballpark waiting for the gates to open, Bill Clapham approached me and asked if I were singing "again" tonight. Like a few of the players' fiancées and friends, Bill had seen the teams play on the previous night in Helena's aged facility, then followed the Brewers to the Ospreys newly constructed home at Ogren Park. Bill and I struck up a baseball-tour conversation while the ballpark's gates remained closed less than an hour before game time.

Clapham was taking a baseball road trip of his own, and this one was not his first baseball vacation. A lifelong lover of the game, he and his wife years earlier had undertaken a baseball road trip that rivalled the significance of the one on which Bonnie and I were nearing completion. For their honeymoon the Claphams had traveled to games in a dozen ballparks. Between then and now, Bill had served as one of the owners of Calgary's minor league teams that initially had played in the Pioneer League before securing a Triple-A league affiliation. Now, while Calgary had no team, Vancouver enjoyed the status of being the only affiliated minor league team still located in Canada. For this brief road tour, Bill had lined up seeing games in three of the Pioneer League cities against whom his first Calgary team had competed. Although baseball had provided a bridge between his bachelorhood and marriage, on this ballpark trip his wife had remained at home to play in a bridge tournament.

Like the previous night in a ballpark hours away, Brewers coach Ned Yost seemed pleased to see me again. I prompted this night's conversation by asking about the ride from Helena. Raising a side of his mouth, squinting one eye, and ever so slightly dropping his shoulders, he conceded that with the players he had bused over from Missoula earlier in the day. I recognized those reluctant gestures. Now having exceeded 20,000 miles on the road during the season, I commented on my difficulties with travel woes and weariness, and I expressed special admiration for the durability of the coaches, even more than the players, since the coaches are frequently about my age, no longer dreaming to stand in the batter's box or peer from the mound toward home plate. I asked a couple of the coaches and roving instructors how they recharge their batteries. "Sleep," one replied. When I suggested that my travel, as exhausting as I might think it was, might be less draining because my wife was traveling with me, another replied, with a laugh while kicking his head back, "I probably get more sleep because my wife *isn't* with me."

From the Brewers coaches, I moved toward the home-team side of the field to chat with several of the players who were sitting between the on-deck circle and the dugout. Two players on the DL smiled as I approached. Several games earlier one had been hit flush in his face just below his left eye. The pitch had broken three cheekbones—on an 0-2 count, an up-an-in fastball that had taken off. He expected to be out for several more games, perhaps until the short-season playoffs. I asked, "Which pitcher?" meaning who had hit him and what would he do next time. I assumed that he had noted and filed that significant datum. He shook his head, not knowing.

His fellow DL teammate said, "He's going to be a pastor." Did that mean that he had forgiven the pitcher who hit him? Or did it suggest that without keen attention to the details—knowing exactly who, when, where, and what the pitch was—he wouldn't have the drive or skills to make it to The Show, so he might as well pursue a different calling soon?

"What put you on the DL?" I inquired of the other, who commiserated with his friend's separation from the game. "I strained my oblique muscle"—he didn't indicate how—"and now I'm having back spasms." Walking by us, one of the Osprey administrators asked both players if they would be ready for the playoff push. Both nodded, saying that they hoped to be ready within a week. Their playoff participation had already been secured by having won the first half of the season. "Besides rest," I asked the second player, "what kind of therapy do you receive for the back spasms?"

"The trainer manipulates the muscles and then massages the area until it hurts," he responded, tagging his reply with a coda: "hurts in a good kind of way."

Adjacent to them, Missoula's manager Hector de la Cruz leaned forward with an elbow on his knee and started chewing Bing cherries, spitting the pits toward the backstop as though they were sunflower seeds. He offered some of the fruit to both guys, a gesture to which the prospective pastor responded, "I don't pop cherries. I'm waiting until I'm married."

I tried not to acknowledge his typical locker-room humor while de la Cruz ignored the comment, even though both players elbowed each other and broke into teenage, tooth-splashing smiles.

Reacting to their laughter, second-baseman Eric Groff, a forty-fourth-round draft pick a year earlier, sidled over. He had put together a solid season, hitting well over .300 and ranking in the top ten hitters in the league. Hearing about my project and musing about his future, Eric asked about where I had been and what ballparks had been best. I profiled a few and described the route of the tour. "Sounds like a great tour," he added, then he wondered aloud, "Only minor league ballparks?"

"Yes," I acknowledged. "But after the minor league season is over, I'll sing for the Dodgers in mid-September. I guess that will make me a September call-up."

He laughed knowingly, perhaps because he had been called up in September the season before, not to the Diamondbacks, but to their Triple-A team, where he had singled in thirteen plate appearances.

Like the Missoula players who engaged in a bit of typical sexual and scatological humor, the concessions at the ballpark also played with sexual innuendo in naming the most unusual menu item that I encountered. Even as I had avoided the deep-fried Moon Pie in Asheville and the Ultimate Love Burger in State College, in Missoula I failed to fork over six dollars for their serving of "Bats and Balls." When I inquired about their popularity, the concessionaire said that they served about two orders a night, adding that first-time fans at the ballpark sometimes ask, "What are bats and balls?" When told that they are French fries and Rocky Mountain oysters, a few naïve fans express surprise, responding, "I didn't know you served oysters," before ordering them. Indeed! Surprise, surprise, surprise!

The ballpark at Missoula was also distinguished by the presence of their mascot. Like multiple teams whose mascots appeared as cartoonish representations of the team's moniker, Missoula's Ollie Osprey mimicked an overgrown bird. Adding to Ollie's presence and enlivening the Osprey sobriquet was the nest of an osprey atop the centerfield light stanchion. The ballpark also featured a different approach to its posted Hall of Fame. Instead of identifying former record-setters and current major league stars with posters or plaques, the stadium's display recognized ballpark donors and team supporters, while the list of notable Osprey alumni was sequestered on the website, which distinguished them as an "all-time" roster.

The Osprey's website also flocked to the scatological motif by identifying the team's blog as "Bird Droppings," a crappy name that described how Missoula played. Committing three official miscues, they allowed three unearned runs and dropped the game to Helena 6-4.

The Spiritual Significance of Baseball: Game 90 in Salt Lake City

The distance from Anaconda, Montana, where we had spent the night following the game in Missoula, to Salt Lake City far exceeded Arbie's daily quota of miles. It would have been ideal if a game had been scheduled in Idaho Falls for the evening between my singing for the Osprey and the Bees, but the home schedules for teams required that we descend two hundred miles beyond Idaho Falls into Salt Lake City for a Sunday-night game before resurfacing in Idaho for a Chukars game the following night.

That meant that we would need to leave an open date on Saturday, enabling us to break the stretch of the drive from Anaconda to Salt Lake into two manageable legs for Arbie. So heading south from Butte on I-15, we enjoyed a more leisurely day of travel, taking a long refueling break and rest stop at Dillon (where Bonnie's grandfather had worked before enlisting in the Army during World War I), viewing the scenic landscape along the Red Rock River and Clark Canyon Reservoir (where we mused about billboard ads for an "Ice Bowl" competition, which apparently required predicting the day and hour for the first solid freeze of the lake), and stopping for lunch in Dell at the Yesterdays Calf-A (where the "must-stop," home-cooking restaurant was the only enterprise at the freeway). There I ordered a hot roast-beef sandwich and mashed potatoes, and Bonnie selected pies. She lucked into the last piece of chicken pot pie before shifting to the sweet lemon-chiffon pie for dessert. And for takeout we picked up a couple of hand-shaped cinnamon buns for her breakfast the following morning.

Since the route from Butte to Salt Lake took us through Idaho Falls, we docked Arbie there in an RV park adjacent to the Snake River, and the following morning we unhitched Toad and hopped on down to Salt Lake City where we met Bob and Sarah Shaw, friends from grad school who had moved to Utah a couple of years earlier. Joining them as our guests for the Sunday late-afternoon game was one of Bob's colleagues, Tom Cronin, who had sung the anthem at several Bees games in recent years.

I always find it fun to share anthem stories with others who love to sing at ballgames, and I was delighted to hear about Tom's pursuit of anthem opportunities. Following his audition several years earlier, he had been told that the staff would call him to schedule a date for him to perform. They didn't. He persisted. And finally he got his chance. Now he served as their utility singer, often coming off the bench to perform for Sunday games when the Bees crowds tend to be smaller because of Mormon proscriptions regarding work and entertainment on their Sabbath. To be sure, that's why I had targeted my schedule to feature a Sunday in Salt Lake City, projecting that there wouldn't be a line of aspiring anthem performers waiting for the chance to sing on such a day.

While Mormons dutifully adhere to Sabbath observance and avoid attending games on Sunday, they nonetheless embrace baseball. At the beginning of the twentieth century, Mormon players in Salt Lake City collaborated with others to form the independent Inter-Mountain League with teams in four Utah cities. Initially, the teams had sought the recreational pleasure of playing baseball, but by 1903 the "Salt Lake City Mormons, Elders and Bishops," which joined the Pacific Northern League, had been organized to compete with gentile communities in neighboring non-Mormon states. The team effectively used baseball as a means to assert the American character of Mormons during their state's first decade in the Union.

Tom Cronin's own patriotic fervor was genetic. His father had been in the 101st Airborne, and his mother had served as a Navy nurse. Tom's love of baseball also ran deep in his blood. As a child he had learned of his grandfather's exploits on the Red Sox' Triple-A team, and he had watched his father play for a semi-pro team in an industrial league. But his passion for the game had come alive when he had attended his first game at Fenway Park.

While I often talked with game-day staffers about distinct anthem renditions that they had heard during the season, I got to hear from Tom about his memorable performances. Foremost among them was the pregame ceremony on July 4, 2008. To celebrate that Independence Day, the Bees had arranged for dramatic accompaniment to "The Star-Spangled Banner" by securing the services of two different birders, a raptor handler and a breeder of homing pigeons. Beside Tom at home plate the raptor handler stood with Liberty, a trained bald eagle, perched on his gloved hand. When Tom completed a couple of ornamental turns before reaching "o'er the land of the free," Liberty followed his free cue and started flapping its wings. Moments later as Tom resolved the melody and held the final word of the stanza, the other birder released pigeons to animate the peaceful symbol of a dove in flight. "For a while," Tom smiled, "the video of that performance was posted on YouTube."

Another riveting memory was of his performance the night after former Bees pitcher Nick Adenhart had been killed by a drunk driver following his first major league start in Anaheim. In the previous season, Adenhart had starred for the Bees, winning nine games before logging his single major league win during a September call-up by the Angels.

Tom then turned the questions to me, asking if I were going for the record for ballpark performances. *The Guinness Book of World Records* certifies that Mark Reiman was the fastest to complete the singing of the national anthem at all major league parks; and that is the single record that the publication recognizes for anthem performances associated with baseball games: "Reiman of Everett, Washington, USA, sang 'The Star-Spangled Banner' in all thirty major league baseball parks in one season between 6 April and 24 September 1998." Remarkably, Reimer had accomplished his feat while suffering from ALS, and his major league anthem campaign—"A Season of Hope"—had been set up to raise awareness about amyotrophic lateral sclerosis and ongoing research about its cause and its treatments. For Tom, Reiman's record took on a personal dimension since his brother-in-law suffered from the disease.

When I moved to home plate to begin this night's anthem, two of the umpires looked knowingly at me. "Haven't I seen you guys before?" I teased home-plate ump Quinn Wolcott. Even as I had seen teams on repeated occasions, I had sung for PCL games with this crew weeks earlier at New Orleans and Memphis. Like those occasions in the South, my performance in Salt Lake City was rather routine. With little distraction from the sound delay generated by the outfield speakers, I finished my unembellished rendition in less than seventy-five seconds. As I left the field, the umps subtly gestured "safe," and Bees manager Keith Johnson tipped his cap as he returned it to his head and said, "Good job. Travel safe."

For several innings I had agreed to engage in an interview with Matt LaPlante, a journalist working on a feature story for the *Salt Lake City Tribune*. Throughout the tour I had spoken to newspaper columnists and magazine writers, broadcasters and bloggers, all of whom had contacted me about my journey with an appreciation for "The Star Spangled Banner." While Matt wanted to talk about baseball, he wasn't really interested in my tour. Instead, he wondered about the deep meaning of the game, and he had sought me out because of my book on baseball and religion. Particularly, he was interested in understanding the transcendent experience of Ron Polk, a baseball coach who coincidentally was a Whittier College alumnus.

So as dusk descended on the Sabbath within eyesight of the Mormon Temple, Matt and I discussed the spiritual significance of baseball. Matt began by recounting Polk's story, whose love affair with baseball had begun in the mid-twentieth century.

When he had been five years old, Polk's father had taken him to Wrigley Field where the view of the diamond and the ivy, the smells of newly mown grass and cotton candy, and the sounds of bats cracking and the crowd cheering bonded him forever to the game. After his own amateur playing days were over, he started to coach the game—and that's when Polk's story took an unusual turn. Because the Scottish National team confused him with the famous coach at Mississippi State who shared the same name, Polk was invited to become one of Scotland's coaches, and he soon managed Edinburgh's team in Europe's 2003 Confederation Baseball Cup.

By 2010, baseball's half-century of wear and tear on his shoulder caught up with Polk, and he consented to undergo standard surgery to repair his rotator cuff. Although the procedure should have been routine, for inexplicable reasons his heart stopped while he was under anesthesia. While the clinical analysis of his cardiac arrest could not be medically explained, his six-and-a-half-minute death experience absolutely defies description. Polk had told Matt that "it's like trying to explain a sunset to a blind person when you don't even speak the same language." The experience was so vivid, so peaceful, so ethereal that he didn't want "to come back" to life.

Now that he had returned to life, however, he felt discontented and displaced. Even after what he interpreted as a conversation with God, Polk didn't find that worship services in churches could provide the spiritual connection and comfort that he yearned for. Instead, the only place that he now felt at home—where he could sense a peace that passes all understanding—is at a ballpark.

While Matt and I discussed the deep spiritual lure of baseball, the second-base umpire needed to make a much more mundane adjustment to a heavenly phenomenon: The angle of the descending sun behind the ballpark roof required him to stop play and send the clubhouse guy to fetch his sunglasses.

The game that Matt and I were watching featured only a couple of highlights or distinct plays, both of which paled in comparison to our heady discussion about the spiritual dimensions of the sport. In the bottom of the sixth with the score tied, Bees center fielder Jeremy Moore doubled to lead off the inning and was promptly picked off second by the Storm Chasers starter Vin Mazarro. Then with the score still knotted at one in the bottom of the ninth, Freddy Sandoval led off with his first home run of the season for the Bees, who stung Omaha 2-1.

11.

Road Weary

"Fowl" Balls in Idaho Falls: Game 91 in Idaho Falls

Until I visited the Idaho Falls Chukars website when I was preparing to contact teams in the Pioneer League about my project and tour, I didn't know what a chukar was—or is. It's a bird that looks a little like a quail. Yet even when I found out that it was kin to fowls, I mispronounced its name until my Whittier colleague—biologist, birder, and baseball fan Warren Hansen—corrected me: chuck-KAR, not CHOO-kar. I had run afoul.

Like my normal follow-through with teams, I had contacted the Chukars within a week of my scheduled appearance to confirm arrival time and pregame instructions; so I was surprised when I received a call four hours before game time asking if I were still singing. "Indeed," I replied with a bit of alarm in my voice. "I'm already in town at an RV park a few miles away." A couple of hours earlier, Bonnie and I had returned to Arbie after our dip down into Salt Lake City. While Bonnie napped, I had started to transcribe my notes about the game in Utah and about the list of things that Doug Karr, an RVer in our adjacent site, had commended and recommended about Arbie two nights earlier after we had arrived. On the phone, the Chukars staffer also seemed surprised that I really had made the trip to Idaho Falls. While a few other teams had sought to verify my singing by contacting me several days or a few weeks in advance of my scheduled appearance, including one that had mis-recorded the date for my performance, this inquiry within a few hours of the pregame ceremonies certainly took first place for being the latest.

Shortly after our initial arrival at the Snake River RV Park in Idaho Falls two days earlier, Karr had pulled his new Artic Fox cab-over camper into the space adjacent to ours. Within minutes after hooking up his electrical and plumbing systems, Doug introduced himself and inquired about Arbie's signage and what it meant. Even though he expressed some appreciation for the venture as we described my project, we quickly discerned that he wasn't primarily interested in the sign on Arbie's side, our RV trek of more than ten thousand miles in recent weeks, or the national anthem.

Doug was the regional sales manager for a major RV enterprise in the Northwest, and he was curious about our well-kept and finely appointed 1994 Fleetwood Flair. Initially, he eyed its sides, standing at the rear and squinting down their length as though he were a surveyor aligning coordinates for a bridge. He saw no swerves in the panels, nor flaws in their plumb. Obviously impressed, he said that the roof must be incredible since there was no warping from seepage, and he asked to climb the ladder. When he saw the new roof topped off by premiere vent covers and a solar drip charger for the battery, he wahooed. Minutes later he continued to admire Arbie's interior: its special "party feature" of a separate shower/tub that could serve as a beer bin during tailgate parties; its new refrigerator/freezer that automatically shifted between alternating current and propane for its power; its custom twin beds that accommodated a seventy-five-gallon, fresh-water tank and covered additional storage; its new regulators to protect against electrical surges and explosive water pressure; its new sound system and video components; and its updated décor featuring room-darkening, honeycomb shades whose cornices matched the duvets.

When he started the engine and lifted its cover, he finally detected something wrong with Arbie. The RV needed a new manifold or a re-bored one, which Doug offered to arrange if we would drive it on to the Seattle area when I was scheduled to sing in Everett during the following week. He assured us that the engine's increased efficiency would significantly improve Arbie's average of 6.5 miles per gallon on recent fill-ups. He sweetened the invitation by offering us the chance to park Arbie at his house and hook up to his water and electrical systems. But he assured us that if we needed to wait until we returned to Whittier, there would be no danger—only louder engine noise and poorer gas mileage—in delaying the repair until we had a more extended period of time. Alas, as things would work out, other more demanding repairs would intercept our route and deter us from driving Arbie over Snoqualmie Pass between Yakima and Seattle.

Although Melaleuca Field in Idaho Falls was only four years old, the tradition of the city hosting a team dates back a century to a team originally known as the Spuds. Shortly after World War I, an amateur team carved out a diamond in the tilled fields nearby, and the fledgling city built a grandstand in 1926 that stood for a half-century until it burned. Remarkably, a new facility was then designed and erected in a matter of months, enabling Idaho Falls to continue its record run for continuous seasons in the Pioneer League.

Along the tour I had met ballpark staffers who had lived in Southern California or had visited Whittier. But in Idaho Falls, game-day staffer Emily was the first to mention a connection with SCIAC, the athletic conference to which Whittier belongs. Having graduated from conference rival Claremont-McKenna College three months earlier, Emily was serving as the Chukars game-day coordinator while also getting marketing experience in sports operations. We talked about challenges that she faced in moving from the Los Angeles area with its diverse cultures and multiple entertainment possibilities to Idaho Falls, a city with one percent of LA's population and an ethos dominated by the Mormon temple within eyesight of the ballpark. She also acknowledged that a more challenging adjustment had actually been her shift from the distinct freedoms and rhythms of daily college life to those of the working world, even as much as she loved her job.

In that respect, she noted, my summer's sabbatical work resembled hers since making a patriotic road trip to ballparks must be fun. I heartily agreed but indicated that, since the game in Idaho Falls would be my ninety-first of the season, my work was also exhausting, simply to stay on schedule. "Wow!" she exclaimed. "That's more games than we play." As one of the teams in the short-season Rookie League, Idaho Falls was scheduled to play seventy-two games between late June and the beginning of September.

Hearing our discussion, visiting manager Pat Kelly and pitching coach Bob Forsch jovially greeted me and congratulated me on making it all the way across and out of Montana. They recognized me from their home game several days earlier, and we chatted about the long drive from Billings.

"Was it seven hours or eight?" I posed.

"Seemed longer," Forsch replied.

"At least you weren't in my RV that trudged up one mountain rise at eighteen miles an hour," I countered.

Forsch then turned to Emily and continued his repartee from our conversation the week before. "Don't let this guy sing tonight. When he sings, the home team wins. Like us last week."

Before the game in Billings, I had assured Forsch of a Mustangs victory that night, pointing out that the home team had won almost two-thirds of the time when I had sung. And they did.

While he enjoyed blaming me for the likelihood that the Chukars would peck the Mustangs that night, he probably knew that his team would play flat following their prolonged trek to Idaho Falls. And he was right.

Although Billings lefty Tony Cingrani threw crazy stuff in the first four innings, striking out nine Chukars in getting the twelve outs, he reached his pitch-count limit and left the game with the Mustangs down 2-1. His relief corps went crazy in a different way, introducing a distinct bout of diamond dyspepsia. In the next three innings, two relievers allowed eleven runs by issuing six walks, tossing two wild pitches, and dulling the pace of the game to such a degree that the Mustangs committed five errors and a passed ball during their stints in the field.

In the end the Chukars feasted on the Mustangs by a lopsided score of 13-2.

While I had been sparring with Forsch during pregame preparations, Bonnie cruised the general admission section where our tickets had directed us. The Chukars were one of a small handful of teams that did not offer us preferred seating. In her usual way, she turned their relative indifference to our advantage, finding two seats in the shade next to members of the Jensen family. Sporting red Billings tee-shirts, the enclave of cousins from Idaho, aunts from Ohio, and uncles from Arizona joined Ness and Jennifer Jensen, parents of a Mustangs pitcher who had journeyed from Suffolk, Virginia. All were there to cheer for Dan Jensen, who had been drafted a couple of months earlier by the Reds and who was scheduled to start for Billings the following day. Their incredible devotion epitomized the way that extended families often embrace the pursuit of baseball dreams by sons and nephews and cousins.

Healing and Ministry in Boise: Game 92 in Boise

Some ballparks were distinct because of their architecture, history, concessions, or even their sounds: the cacophony of fans heckling opponents, the blare of heavy-metal music between innings, or for me, the repercussions of the P.A. system during my anthem rendition. Others became most memorable because of the difficulty of getting to the ballpark itself, often because of traffic clogs, street closures, or automotive failures.

This last reason applied to Memorial Stadium in Boise where the Hawks played host to the Tri-City Dust Devils on the night of my appearance. Even having allowed an extra day for driving from Idaho Falls, getting to the ballpark required more dedication than giving up an at-bat for the team by advancing a runner with a productive out.

When we had left Idaho Falls, we had heeded Doug Karr's diagnosis of Arbie's engine sluggishness and shifted our anticipated route. Initially, we had planned to take the most direct highway from there to Boise, following Highway 20, stopping at the Craters of the Moon National Monument, and perhaps finding a spot for Arbie there on the infrequent night without a game. But thinking that we might need road assistance if Arbie's manifold issues caused him to cough too violently, we opted for the truck-friendly, crescent approach to Boise along interstate highways.

Yet we shouldn't have worried that day about Arbie. Throughout the 325-mile drive, he had chugged along rather routinely on the freeway, even edging up past his comfortable pace of fifty-five miles per hour a few times before we pulled into the Country Corners RV Park a few miles west of Caldwell. There we found wide sky, clean air, and a natural wind symphony: The melodies from nearby chirping birds found counterpoint in the mellow bellows of distant cattle. Their music was joined by the jovial voices of the park's owners, who pointed us toward an easily accessible space and offered us corn, tomatoes, green beans, and cucumbers freshly picked from their garden.

Salivating in anticipation of dinner with homegrown vegetables, I disconnected Toad, climbed into Arbie's cockpit, and glided him into his evening slot. Quickly, then, I returned to Toad and turned the ignition key to silence. Dead silence. Toad had croaked or was playing possum.

The problem was that Toad couldn't croak. His battery had flat-lined, not even retaining enough of a blip to jumpstart the engine, which we tried to do. Dismayed, I called AAA—the auto club, not the office of the senior minor leagues—to schedule assistance for the following morning.

Thankfully, Bonnie soothed my spirit and my hunger an hour later with the sweet corn and succulent tomatoes.

At dawn the next day, AAA's battery technician was unable to wake up Toad and finally called a tow truck to tote the little Saturn to the auto club's only authorized repair shop in the vicinity, about twenty miles back toward Boise. There the mechanic's diagnosis was discouraging: Toad would require more than pacemaker replacement. Necessary repairs, he said, should start with the expected installation of a new battery. Effectively, an MRI of Toad had also revealed malfunctions in his neural system and blood circulation, as well as lung congestion and calloused feet. Literally, the car suffered from a faulty electrical system, abraded brake rotors, sludgy transmission fluid, and a cracked radiator. Even though we had recognized that Arbie might require immediate therapy, we had not anticipated Toad's woes that now required emergency surgery.

While Bonnie was confined to Arbie miles away at the RV park, I left Toad at the repair shop for his transfusions and radiator transplant and walked a mile to McDonalds, comforting myself there with burgers, fries, and free Wi-Fi. Discouraged by the prospect that the repairs could not be completed in a timely way, I started to make tentative plans to rent a car to get to the game that night in Boise.

Thankfully, the contingent plans went unneeded because Toad was released from his intensive care barely in time for me to drive back to the RV park to change clothes and pick up Bonnie before retracing the repair route on our way to Memorial Stadium. While the ballpark's site adjacent to the Western Idaho Fairgrounds added to its distinct features, it became most memorable because of the difficulties that Toad had posed in getting there.

The ballpark itself exuded a simplicity and charm that belied its construction twenty years earlier. A single, quaint skybox perched above steeply pitched, narrow rows in the uncovered stands between the bases. On the concourse near the main gates, a non-descript souvenir store nested in a portable trailer where Hawks paraphernalia could be purchased. And adjacent concession stands tempted appetites with a surprising array of international fare and regionally inspired specialties. Appealing to tastes and thirsts from afar were the Basque chorizo, Greek gyros, German bratwurst, Polish kielbasa, Italian sausage, Philly cheesesteak, and a slushy drink called Siberian Ice, while more local dishes included buffalo wraps and Idaho nachos made with potato chips rather than tortilla strips.

In Boise's thirty home games that had preceded my appearance, fans had heard some remarkable anthem performances. According to Stephanie, the on-field pregame coordinator, the most memorable were two really bad performances. One singer had completely lost the melody, ricocheting from one note to another like a ground ball glancing off two infielders' gloves; and another man had lost the words like a fly ball in the sun: no clue.

In contrast to these vocal bombs, there had been several star-spangled performances, including a few by Keith, a local fan and professional musician with a reputation for elegant anthem renditions at Boise sporting events. Bearded like a Mennonite with no mustache and whiskers trimmed on his cheeks, Keith had completed his collegiate degree in vocal performance before setting aside his passion for singing while serving as an innkeeper for almost two decades. In recent years, he had returned to the musical stage, performing locally in scores of dramatic roles. Occasionally, he sang the anthem for the Hawks and often for Boise's minor league hockey games.

Although Keith had missed my rendition, a Hawks staffer had told him that it was so good that he should find out more about my project. Locating Keith near the first-base ramp, the staffer introduced us and let him know that I had already sung in more than ninety ballparks during the season. Wide-eyed, Keith immediately asked how I had set up so many gigs. "Planning and persistence," I briefly replied, adding that I had begun to set up the project a year earlier and had spent about 300 hours contacting teams, configuring schedules, and designing possible routes. For more than half an inning, we compared our experiences of deep joy in singing, as well as sharing the challenging conditions that we occasionally encountered with audio feedback.

While the Hawks were falling behind in the third inning, I sought out the staffer to find out Keith's surname. Shrugging his shoulders and flipping his palms, he then turned to another regular fan who often talked with Keith during games. The man also shook his head from side to side, admitting that he also didn't know. But then, smiling with a nod, he said, "You know, the anthem was so good tonight I thought it might have been Keith singing."

Quickly pointing to me, the staffer affirmed, "This was the guy who sang."

"Wow!" the man responded. "Your project is spectacular. Are you in a ministry?"

Before I could respond, Bonnie interjected, "He is ordained."

Right away the man acknowledged that he had pursued ministerial studies for a year and had sung in evangelistic services before shifting his attention to another field.

As I listened I realized that, in a patriotic way, I was in a ministry of sorts—evangelistically sharing the anthem with others by celebrating the freedoms that American forces had maintained in the inspirational defense of Fort McHenry against the British frigates and in hundreds of battles and initiatives in centuries since.

Boise was my first game for teams in the Northwest League, a short-season Rookie League like the Pioneer and Appalachian Leagues where I had frequently seen more walks than strikeouts in a game and as many errors as hits: The Hawks and Dust Devils routinely displayed the rough skills of recent draftees, many of whom were younger than my undergraduate students. During Tri-City's second turn at bat, the Hawks exposed the range of their raw play within the infield. The pitcher issued a walk and tossed a wild pitch; the shortstop committed a throwing error; and the third-baseman booted a ground ball. By contrast, the catcher threw out an attempted base-stealer and the second-baseman backhanded a staccato hop, pirouetted on the bag, and threw to first for a double play. Within the next few innings, the Hawks clawed their way back into the game, taking a tie into the bottom of the ninth when Reggie Golden led off the inning with a single and scored on a double by the next batter, Ryan Cuneo. Final score: Boise Hawks 7, Tri-City Dust Devils 6.

Alas, I held a useless winning ticket at the end of the game. One of the season-long promotions at the ballpark was a Jiffy Lube "Mega Run Rule" that offered an eight-dollar discount for Jiffy Lube's signature-service oil change when the Hawks would score six or more runs. Now six hours too late, the discount coupon served only as an ironic souvenir of the game and Toad's roster of repairs that had included an oil change.

An Angelic Evening with the Dust Devils: Game 93 in Tri-City

Since Arbie had performed admirably en route from Idaho Falls to Boise where Toad had been restored to good health, we optimistically set out on the five- to six-hour drive for the Tri-City area of eastern Washington, a tri-rivers area where the Snake, Yakima, and Columbia Rivers converge. Yet in the first hour of Arbie's climb to the top of the mesas beyond the Snake River boundary between Idaho and eastern Oregon, he began to wheeze persistently before suffering coughing spasms so severe that, despite the searing outside temperature, we turned off the air conditioner to prevent overheating. Yet our sweaty efforts only delayed Arbie's furious fever during the highway climb beyond the Columbia River bridge. Although I implored him to emulate "the little engine that could" while he trudged up the low, long range leading to the Tri-City area, he couldn't make it to the crest without stopping to catch his breath—three or four times. Simply, Arbie would need a tune-up, if not a transplant of his manifold as diagnosed by Doug days earlier in Idaho Falls.

Hours after securing AAA's help for Toad, Bonnie Googled an approved automotive shop where Arbie's issues could be treated the following morning, and arriving in Tri-Cities, we left the RV in the repair line at the auto shop in Kennewick. Although we had expected to moor the RV at the Sacajawea State Park, we checked into another friendly Hampton Inn that serenely overlooked the Columbia River, and our room was one of the most pleasant all summer.

Retaining Tri-City in the tour's itinerary and actually arriving there represented at least two significant accomplishments. Not only had we overcome Arbie's bout of bronchial distress, we reached the area in time to get to the ballpark. Five weeks before my scheduled appearance on August 18, I had received a call from a Dust Devils staffer asking if I would confirm my appearance for July 18. Incredulously, I replied that I was scheduled for August 18, not the 18th of July. Politely, she replied that someone else was on the docket for August 18, a date that I had verified months earlier. And since July 18 was only a day or two away when I received the call in Ohio, I indicated that I certainly could not drive to south central Washington in time for a game in mid-July.

"But…," she started, and I cut her off, protesting vigorously that the Dust Devils had confirmed *August* 18. Both of us sounded flummoxed if not bedeviled. I pleaded for her to respect the earlier commitment and suggested that she shift the other performer to July 18.

Minutes after hanging up, I retrieved the e-mail confirmations from the team's general manager and forwarded them to her, adding an appeal to retain my scheduled appearance since that was the only Tri-City game that would work in my tightly drafted itinerary. A day or two later I received a reconfirmation of the August date for the Tri-City team.

The day-long difficulties with Arbie's emphysema seemed like a second strike against my possible performance for the Dust Devils. All that I needed to be called out was a third strike of rain!

Fortunately, when I pulled into the parking lot at Gesa Stadium an hour before the first pitch, the sky was Montana big, the temperature had begun to slide into the mid-eighties, and the late afternoon soon got even better. As usual, after warming up I made grand rounds of the ballpark, identifying unusual architectural features, locating the souvenir shop to survey its stock, and stopping at concession stands to scan their menus. Unlike most ballparks, the field at Gesa Stadium was oriented toward the South in order to capture a panoramic view from the grandstands. This unusual direction of the field also meant that the setting sun each evening could blind players in hazardous ways for multiple innings. To prevent them from losing fly balls or even "Baltimore chops" in the sun, the ballpark architects had designed an enormous sun-screen to stretch almost ten stories high behind the first-base stands, making the edifice the most impressive structure in Pasco.

On the opposite side of the concourse at the souvenir kiosk, Lauren Davies, the young staffer attending the display, looked at my shirt and asked about the AnthemTour logo. When she learned that my rendition for Tri-City would be my ninety-third performance since opening day, she offered me a tee-shirt of my choice. At first, I thought she was kidding, especially since no other team had extended such a concession-souvenir offer. Without requiring further encouragement, I selected the newest design in dark blue that celebrated the Dust Devils first half-season Eastern Division Northwest League Championship.

As always, I scoped out the concessions even more carefully than I surveyed the souvenirs, and I hoped that the menus would feature distinct regional fare or at least cleverly conceived burgers, fries, or dogs. Sometimes these unusually dressed ballpark staples prompted inspiring names associated with the team's mascot or its general manager. In Pasco, the dusty character of the ballpark and team was well applied to their signature wiener, the "Dusty Dog." An apparent fan favorite, it was powdered with dry mustard before being smothered by mounds of relish and onions and a sludge of catsup.

During the game a mid-inning activity lured participants with a stunt that I had not seen. A selected fan was given five large dice with letters on their faces rather than numbers. If the contestant rolled consecutive letters to spell out "Dusty," the moniker for Tri-City's mascot, the activity's sponsor Wild Horse Casino would award a prize of fifty thousand dollars to the lucky roller. Not the same kind of wagering that had proven thorny for Rose, the sanction of Wild Horse nonetheless was akin to the endorsement of the Atlantic City casino decades earlier by Willie Mays that had jeopardized his relationship with Major League Baseball. Had baseball changed its restrictions about consorting with casinos, or did MiLB operate with a "Get Out of Jail Free" card from the commissioner?

Architecture, souvenirs, concessions, promotions—the Dust Devils found a distinct angle for each. Even so, the most memorable part of my ballpark experience in Tri-City emerged from my encounters and conversations with the fans. Frequently at ballparks in every region of the country, I had observed the fascination with baseball by persons with limited mental and physical abilities. I especially enjoyed their squeals of delight as the ball soared over the fence or as an umpire would gesture "safe" for a close play at the plate. There must be something deeply good about a game that makes cheering or crying possible for persons of all abilities—from gifted athletes to crippled persons confined to wheelchairs, and from Mensa members intent on analyzing esoteric statistical relations to fans with limited verbal and cognitive skills. These varied baseball enthusiasts simultaneously experience intense emotional responses to the game: applauding the performance of their favorite players; or cursing an opponent's seeing-eye, game-winning blooper; or simply lamenting a playoff loss.

In so many ways baseball encourages ongoing conversation and building a participant community. Baseball's pace allows for plays to be savored and digested and remarked before the next batter faces off against a glaring pitcher. Its rhythms encourage ruminations among seatmates about the previous half-inning's highlights and lowlights. Foul balls frequently fly into the stands, occasionally falling near fans who, by sheer proximity to the bounding souvenir, become participating fielders on alert. And pregame ceremonies present opportunities for ordinary fans, including those with various abilities, to appear on the field to shout, "Play ball!" or to toss out a first pitch like the exuberant, disabled enthusiasts in Erie and Des Moines.

At Pasco the love affair between baseball and fans limited by their physical condition rose to angelic heights. During the second or third inning, I met Mailia Goforth and her father Max in their season box seats behind home plate. With a heart and lung condition known as Eisenmenger's Syndrome, Mailia had to rely on an oxygen apparatus to assist her breathing even when living in a warm climate at low altitude. In winter months when the cold and snow would sweep through the Northwest, Mailia would be restricted in her movement; so the onset of warm summer and baseball season released her to attend the Tri-City home games. As a family the Goforths annually sponsored and hosted one of the Dust Devils players, certainly an irony since Mailia herself appeared so angelic. Emphasizing her love of baseball, particularly the minor leagues, Max talked with me about his daughter's desire to make a tour of small-town ballparks, much like my own trek through the Pioneer and Northwest leagues.

While Mailia prayed for the chance to begin a trip to various cities and their ballparks, other fans at the game were completing minor league jaunts of their own. Tom Loveday and his companion Peggy from Corvallis, Oregon, had heard me the previous night in Boise, and like Bonnie and me, they had driven 300 miles that day from Idaho, their journey much smoother than ours. We talked about the Northwest League, their love of the minor leagues, and their support of players by sponsoring one—like the Goforths—during the short season for their team in Salem. Their love of baseball extended beyond their attraction to professional teams. Tom was an experienced high-school umpire, and his shirt identified him with an umpiring school. Regrettably, Tom said, he and Peggy would not be in Salem several days later when I would sing for the Volcanoes.

The Dust Devils' full introduction of my anthem performance prompted other conversations about my tour. The parents of the choral director from Washington and Lee University expressed appreciation for my rendition and the expanse of the tour. In passing, another fan specifically complimented my pronunciation of "land" in "land of the free." Invoking yet another musical leader, he said that his choral director had always stopped the choir to make sure that the singers would approach the word with a long, soft vowel, reducing the nasality so often prompted by the "nd."

Overhearing us talking about the anthem, a peanuts hawker named Eric paused to ask about my anthem journey. With a smile as wide as the press box, he shared a few stories about his trips to forty minor league ballparks where he purchased souvenir hats. Now his wall was covered with them. He confessed that he couldn't carry a tune but that he'd love to participate in pregame ceremonies or in-game activities. For several minutes we had fun imagining how he might be able to get into the act in some of the ballparks remaining on his bucket list: dancing atop the home-team dugout, launching tee-shirts to the crowd, or racing a six-year-old kid down a baseline. We laughed the good laughs of a minor league night.

As for the game itself, unlike most that I had seen in Rookie League play, this one was a pitchers' duel that featured flawless fielding and few walks. In fact, the game was the shortest of my season: two hours and twelve minutes. After the Yakima Bears scored on two singles, a stolen base, and a ground out in the first inning, they mustered only three harmless hits during the rest of the game while the Dust Devils scored in each of their last three at-bats to win 3-1.

Coincidences and Connections: Game 94 in Everett

Several of the ballparks on the tour had been initially constructed as municipal recreational facilities, and a few others had been erected in collaboration with local universities to maximize use. But none that I had seen had been originally built specifically for high-school teams—that is, until I reached Everett, Washington, home of the AquaSox. At the center of the scoreboard, that history and identity were writ large: Everett Memorial Stadium, Everett School District.

After members of the Elks Lodge in Everett had donated the property for the construction of a baseball diamond in memory of Everett residents who had served in the Armed Forces in World War II, the first high-school game was played on the field in the year of my birth: 1949. During the next three decades the school district, city, and volunteers installed lights and fences for the field, dugouts for the players, and grandstands for the fans in an effort to improve the facilities for all participants and to prepare for the return of professional baseball to Everett.

Finally, in 1984 the San Francisco Giants agreed to an affiliation with a newly formed Short Season A-level farm team in Everett, the first time since 1905 that professional baseball had called the city home. A decade after the Giants arrival, the ballpark was redesigned and remodeled with funds provided from a hotel/motel tax approved by voters. Even so, by 2011 the facilities appeared modest even in comparison to the municipal ballpark in Pasco where I had sung a couple of nights earlier. Not only were Everett's concession and souvenir stands minimal, the teams' clubhouses also were uncommon. They were located in a classroom-style building adjacent to the ballpark and separated from it by the stadium's outer fence. Not even in Beloit or Jamestown where players had to walk across the entry concourse to get to their dugouts did the team find their lockers beyond the ballpark.

Although Everett's stadium was spare, the afternoon seemed full, perhaps because several Whittier friends joined me for the game. Leslie and Howard Fisher, with whom I had worked in various community events in Whittier, had retired a few years earlier to Port Angeles, a ferry's ride away across the Puget Sound. Having kept up with Bonnie's Facebook "check-ins" throughout the tour, they had planned their first Washington baseball excursion to coincide with my appearance there. While I was pleased with the pitch and pace of my anthem rendition, I wondered how Leslie and Howard might have cringed in response to the quality of the amplification of my performance. As superb deejays and sound engineers, they had always made me sound better than usual when I had sung for Whittier events.

The sound system at Everett, however, was on par with that at most of the ballparks where I had sung, including most major league stadia. Even so, the AquaSox game-day intern Dan told me about how the sound delay had caused a botched anthem performance earlier in the season. The man had taken a breath after every couple of words, allowing the "amplified echo" to fade before resuming the song. Consequently, Dan said, "the anthem dragged on longer than an extra-inning doubleheader."

The Whittier connections also included my colleague Charles Adams. For three decades, we had collaborated on various scholarly projects related to American culture. In several semesters we had teamed up to teach a course on American history oriented toward literature and religion rather than politics and wars. Often we had developed presentations on the cultural significance of sports, mostly baseball, and after the completion of the anthem tour, we anchored the team of founders of the Institute for Baseball Studies at Whittier College.

While I had expected to reconnect at the game with Leslie, Howard, and Charles, I had not anticipated running into other folks from Whittier. When I moved into box seats along the first-baseline to take a few photographs of the players, the person in the adjacent seat asked if I were the one who had sung the anthem. I nodded and he introduced himself and his wife as Dave and Linda Carson. He was interested in my identification with Whittier College because they had graduated from there in 1971 with majors in sociology and math. We spent several minutes musing about their professors, including sociology professor Charles Browning and my predecessor in religious studies, Milo Connick. Both of the legendary Whittier faculty had been formative in the Carsons' liberal-arts education and both of them had been influential for me in my early years of teaching.

A few months before the Everett game, Charles Adams had already seen me perform in Rancho Cucamonga, an hour's drive from our Whittier homes. Now he was spending several weeks in Seattle with his aging parents Hazard and Diana. Following the game, they hosted Bonnie and me for a fabulous sunset dinner overlooking Puget Sound. Throughout his career, Hazard, a renowned literary critic and avid baseball fan, had inspired numerous imaginative works connecting baseball and literature. And sure enough, during our dinner conversation, he stimulated yet another project.

As we talked about my routine examination of each ballpark's architecture, art, signage, concessions, souvenirs, and such, he suggested that I was treating each ballpark as a text and that I should write a guide on "how to read a ballpark." While he sipped a martini and I a single-malt Scotch, we began to outline a text about ballparks as texts: How does the ballpark blend or impose upon the landscape? What baseball cues direct attention toward the main gate? How is the ballpark entry defined? Where do ballpark rules appear, and how are they expressed? In what languages? Where is the fan-assistance booth located? Is it before or beyond the souvenir shop and concession stands? What kinds of businesses dominate the ads on the outfield walls? How are successful ballplayers honored and remembered? Where are their tributes located? On and on we mused about baseball and its parks.

Another symbol that contributes to a ballpark's interpretation is the team's logo. Particularly for the AquaSox, Charles pointed out that their logo was directly related to the former emblem of the parent Seattle Mariners. Initially, the Mariners had adopted an inverted trident as the logo for their caps and clothing, and by turning that symbol on its side, the resulting figure could be read as both an "E" for Everett and as a connection with the Mariners. But embracing baseball superstitions, the Mariners adopted a new logo since they suspected that the trident's inversion drained energy from the team, thus contributing to their failure to advance to the World Series.

While Hazard, Charles, and I began to talk specifically about reading Everett's ballpark, I pointed out that the scoreboard and outfield fences featured the typical tempting invitation "hit this sign and win"—this time promising not a car or cash, but a suit. While the outfield walls at other parks were dominated by advertisements for banks and hotels, insurance and real estate agents, plumbing and legal services, Everett's array included gambling operations and labor unions, perhaps growing out of the area's shipbuilding industry that had a long history with collective bargaining. The Washington State lottery's sign appeared center-stage beneath the scoreboard, and the red ad for the Tulalip Casino stretched from centerfield to the foul pole in right. Adding to the casino's allure, it sponsored the mid-inning fan-participant promotion of rolling the dice: six dice were tossed for a chance to win a fifty-thousand-dollar prize if five of the six dice should land with the casino's logo face up.

In addition to the distinct array of outfield billboards in Everett, the game with the visiting Eugene Emeralds featured noteworthy players and weird plays. A unique baseball legacy distinguished the roster of the Emeralds. Their center fielder Kyle Gaedele was the great-great nephew of Eddie Gaedel, the 3' 7" actor whom Bill Veeck had signed to pinch hit in a game for the St. Louis Browns in 1951. Unlike Kyle's diminutive relative, who never saw a strike in his one plate appearance, the 6' 4" Emeralds outfielder struck out twice in four hitless at-bats. Drafted by the Padres two months earlier, Kyle was prone to strike out in this, his initial pro season during which he whiffed once in every three at-bats. And unlike his "Uncle Eddie," who walked in "all" of his plate appearances, Kyle managed to take ball four in one-eighth of his plate appearances, which is, coincidentally, the fractional number that Eddie had worn on his tiny uniform in his single plate appearance for the St. Louis Browns.

There had also been unusual plays in the afternoon's game, if an unplayable foul ball and an errantly tossed bullpen pitch can legitimately be considered plays. In the third inning a fierce foul tip glanced off the crest of the catcher's helmet whose angle deflected the ball back, not only catapulting it over the backstop but all the way over the press box! In the same inning a baseball got loose in the Emeralds' bullpen along the right-field foul line, and the bullpen catcher walked twenty-five feet onto the field to retrieve the ball while the pitcher on the mound went into his stretch. With the base umpire watching a runner on first and the home-plate umpire peering over the catcher's shoulder anticipating the pitch, neither saw the additional ball and tenth-man on the field. There was no stoppage of play.

Another distinct play occurred in the sixth inning when AquaSox catcher Larry Gonzalez tried to pick Emeralds baserunner Larry Miller off first. His strong throw hit the seam of grass and dirt in front of the bag, danced a fandango high and quick, and hit first-baseman Ethan Paquette in the face. While the ball glanced to the fence by the dugout, Miller dashed to second, and AquaSox pitcher Jordan Pries ran to retrieve it while Paquette crumpled and bled. Felled by the pickoff throw, Paquette was led on wobbly legs from the field.

While ballparks everywhere routinely provided promotions and activities for children, none that I had seen had engaged them in an environmentally supportive and economically productive exercise like that at Everett. Rather than offering kids the chance to dash across the outfield between innings or to run the bases after the game, the AquaSox developed an activity known as Garbage Gremlins. During the eighth inning, kids were encouraged to grab a yellow garbage bag from a staff member and roam the stands while collecting trash from fans. After retrieving wrappers and cups and programs and such, they could return the bags to a staff member in exchange for "Gremlin Bucks" that could be used for prizes in the team store or for a turn at the ballpark's inflatable Fun Zone.

Meanwhile, I found a virtual fun zone with a coincidence in the game's box score. AquaSox pitcher J. Pries (a variant spelling of "Price," or vice-versa) had recorded his fourth win of the season while I notched my ninety-fourth anthem performance. Dual wins by the "Pryce" kin! Final score: the AquaSox 8, the Emeralds 2.

Homecoming in a New Place: Game 95 in Yakima

If it's possible to experience a return to a place where I had never been, then Yakima was one such place. There I reconnected with a former student who had taken one of my early-morning classes, and there I remembered and revered someone whom I had never met or whose name I then did not know. In this odd way Yakima provided a semblance of homecoming, not because I had ever lived or visited there, but because of catching up with the former student and because of visualizing a close friend's memories of his father's playing days there.

When I had contacted Yakima a year earlier about the prospect of singing for the Bears, the general manager had responded that one of his staff had attended Whittier. Then I didn't know that Luke Moedritzer, one of my former students and a former Poets baseball player, was on the Bears staff at Yakima. When Luke had been a first-year student, he had taken my large, team-taught course in American Intellectual and Cultural History. Now as the director of group sales for the Bears, he had sought me out a few nights earlier in the Tri-City ballpark when he and other Yakima staffers had taken a brief road trip to scope out the new Dust Devils stadium and to see how other ballparks operated, especially gauging the effectiveness of their promotions. That night, the Bears had been bedeviled by the Tri-City Dust Devils.

On this night in the familiar confines of their home ballpark, his fellow staffers repeatedly approached me and requested scoops about his performance in my class. I realized that the teasing and heckling spirit of baseball extends all the way from the dugout to the front office. All that I would reveal to them about Luke's performance was that he had been a first-year student who had passed the course, which had met at the earliest class hour twice a week, a schedule that—at the time—had proved quite challenging for him. They grinned, understanding.

Thanks to Luke, the Bears hosted me in a way that I had enjoyed at few ballparks throughout the summer. He issued me a gold pass, which provided access to the VIP lounge where I could sip free drinks and crack roasted peanuts. For much of my time in the lounge, I was the only fan being served by Denise, the hostess for the evening. Like other Bears staffers, she asked about the tour and my experience with Luke as one of his professors. In turn, I inquired about Yakima and her work with the ballpark. Smiling, she said that she enjoyed baseball and her work so much that she had not requested the night off in order to celebrate her thirtieth wedding anniversary that day. In return, I shared with her my April experience of Bonnie's baseball gift to me for our thirty-eighth anniversary, letting me start the wild adventure of the anthem tour alone in Florida before she could join me a month later in the RV.

In contrast to the new Tri-City facility, the public stadium in Yakima seemed to be about as old as the city's professional baseball teams. The Yakima Indians, the city's first team, had competed during the 1920 season in the Northwest International League. During that team's brief history, the father of my good friend Warren Hanson had excelled as a star player. Having traced some of the childhood routes that Warren had coursed as a kid, I was keenly aware of his vicarious presence with me in Yakima. In an e-mail that I had received from him a few days before singing for the Bears, Warren had urged Bonnie and me to stop by the Cle Elum Bakery as we made our way through the Snoqualmie Pass on our drive to Yakima from Seattle, and he had identified the depth of his family's affinity with Yakima.

"Mom was born in Italy," Warren had written,

> but raised in Cle Elum, and her family knew the bakery people in her childhood (from 1903 when she arrived at age three) to age eighteen or so when she moved to the big town of Yakima. When you sing for the Bears in Yakima, give a thought to my Dad, who played for Yakima in the twenties. My folks moved to Tacoma in 1928 but, for the years after the First War until 1928, Dad played for the Bears (and, on occasion, for the Indians since in those days Yakima had two teams). I remember many summer trips to Yakima (with stops in Cle Elum at the bakery) after the Second War and into the fifties when we would go to the old ballpark in Yakima for Old Timers' Games.

Indeed, while I sang the anthem I thought about Warren's connections with Yakima baseball, and I realized that when his father Al had played, "The Star-Spangled Banner" had not yet been designated as the national anthem—the Federal legislation would be signed in 1933—nor were pregame rituals then routine.

When Al had retired from the Yakima Indians in 1928 after fifteen years of playing baseball in the region, he had been recognized as the most popular player in recent memory. Although he had played all positions, he had primarily caught until he was called upon to pitch, which he did for five or six years, posting an impressive record until an arm injury forced him back behind the plate. I had never met Al, I had never seen his picture, nor had I even heard Warren refer to him by his given name. But I understood Warren's reverential references to his father's baseball exploits, especially his having competed against the House of David barnstorming team. As I sang the anthem and looked at the rise of the expansive, twilit hills in the distance, I derived a full sense of baseball joy in knowing that Warren's father had seen the same scene at the same time of day when he had played eighty years earlier.

After finishing the anthem, I walked past the home-team dugout. Often when I returned to the box seats following my anthem performance, players would flash me a thumbs-up sign, shake my hand, or simply say, "Good job." This night, Yakima hitting coach Jacob Cruz, who had spent the previous three years as a player in the Mexican League, greeted me: "Wow," he said, and instead of extending his hand in congratulations, he thrust his stopwatch toward me. It read 1:09.4. He had timed my performance, and he commented that anything below 1:20 is celebrated by the players and coaches. "Below 1:10," he beamed. "Gold medal!"

Like the old ballpark in Boise, Yakima County Stadium was a civic facility adjacent to the county fairgrounds complex. Although the Yakima ballpark had been built relatively recently in 1993, it no longer met the desired specifications for minor league facilities. At the time of my appearance the Bears recognized that the county's declining economy could not support the construction of a new stadium, and consequently, they were pursuing an invitation to move to Vancouver, Washington. When that possibility collapsed a few months later, the team negotiated the franchise's relocation to Hillsboro, Oregon, to start a season later. There, a dozen miles west of Portland, a new ballpark awaited the team to be renamed as the Hillsboro Hops.

Yakima County Stadium's architecture featured no concourses or covered grandstands for possible retreat during inclement weather or shade from blistering sun. Yet the simple design was enhanced by grassy areas with plenty of picnic tables with wide and long benches. While the diamond and dugouts appeared standard, the outfield dimensions distinguished the field. The foul poles stood closer to home than any professional ballpark, even those in right field in New York, Boston, and Asheville, where minor league hitters were challenged not by the distance but by the size of the Blue Ridge Monster that stretches twenty-five feet high. And among major league ballparks, the short porch in right at Yankee Stadium is famous for its cheap home runs, and in Boston the waist-high wall at Pesky's Pole slides quickly back in the power alley to make homers more difficult. Not solely favoring left-handed pull hitters, as other ballparks often did, Yakima's distance from home plate to each foul pole was the same short stretch: 293 feet. Yet in both left and right fields, the wall angled obliquely and deeply to 340 feet before reaching the power alleys, thus legitimizing most home runs in the ballpark.

Functioning like the architectural sunshield at the new stadium at Pasco, three tiers of advertisement banners hung above Yakima's third-base grandstand to screen the setting sun. Torn and sagging, the middle bottom banner, which featured the Bears' URL, unintentionally signified the hopelessness of Yakima's baseball future as it drooped in the dusk.

Outside the main gate the stadium also displayed an unusual conduct code that itemized the ballpark's rules regarding unacceptable behavior. In addition to the typical prohibition of intoxication and use of foul or abusive language, the list specifically forbad wearing obscene or indecent clothing, displaying affection inappropriate for a public setting, and sitting in a seat other than the one ticketed. Failure to adhere to this fan's code of conduct could result in expulsion from the ballpark. On this Monday evening, however, the ballpark staff had little cause to worry about rowdy crowd behavior since nothing was happening in the fairgrounds and since most of the Bears fans appeared to be on family outings.

As for the game itself, the Bears pounced on Willengton Cruz, Boise's starting pitcher who lasted only one-third of an inning, even though the short fences down each line had nothing to do with the shortest outing that I had seen by a starter. Alternating walks with singles, the Bears put five of their first six batters on base and scored three runs before Cruz's removal. Two innings later Boise rebounded with five runs to take a 6-4 lead aided by three doubles and a home run by Ryan Cuneo. But Yakima came back to tie 8-8 in the eighth by piecing together two singles, a walk, an error, and a triple. In the tenth the Bears worked their eighth base on balls, literally walking away with the win by scoring the final run on a walk-off walk issued by wild lefty Andrew McKirahan, who failed to retire any of the four batters that he faced. Final score: In 10: Yakima 9, Boise 8.

More Western Travel Woes

After retrieving Arbie from his engine massage at the automotive shop, we headed to Sunnyside where we anchored him for a couple of days while shuttling in Toad toward Seattle before completing the Washington sweep in Yakima. En route from Tri-Cities to the RV park an hour's drive away, Arbie hiccupped two or three times, and I should have been wary about his condition. Instead, I ignored the slight disruptions in his breathing. Three days later, when we departed for Salem, his ails continued. Although he seemed to climb confidently across the Yakima Reservation, over the Toppenish Ridge, and through Satus Pass, his prior hiccups on the way to Sunnyside had developed into coughing spasms during our descent toward the Columbia River. At The Dalles, then, we paused to refuel, both Arbie and us. I faintly and futilely hoped that Arbie's congestion had been caused by bad gas.

While we scored a delectable Thai lunch featuring lemongrass soup, we pondered what to do if Arbie's symptoms worsened. And when we resumed our drive, I prayed that the gradual westward descent of the freeway along the river gorge would ease Arbie's discomfort and that we could make it to the Salem ballpark in time for me to sing two national anthems, my only chance all summer to perform both "The Star-Spangled Banner" and "O Canada." But Arbie's coughing yielded to constant wheezing so severe that I had to downshift while going downhill when our speed slowed below thirty-five miles per hour. Yet on toward Portland we chugged.

As we reached the outskirts of the city, I realized that our sluggish pace coupled with Portland's thickening, afternoon traffic would likely prevent us from making it to Salem in time for the game. Bonnie came to the rescue yet again. With her facile fingers, she worked her iPhone magic with a search for an approved auto shop in the East Portland area. The search hit on Honest-1 Auto Care, a name that I suspiciously considered before realizing its appropriateness. Immediately she called and heard the manager assure her that the mechanics could work on Arbie's Chevy 454 engine.

Luckily, the next exit for Fairview Parkway provided the most direct route to Honest-1. With some relief, we exited, only to discover that the first half-mile climb up Fairview required Arbie's most arduous effort all summer. With no running start, Arbie chugged and chugged in the right-hand lane while I turned on his hazard lights. Steep, steep, steep. Cough, cough, cough. Gasp, gasp, gasp. Pleading with my posture, I rocked forward over the steering wheel, ever urging Arbie forward. Still in first gear, I fully depressed the accelerator pedal, and I prayed for the slope to ease. Arbie's speed slowed from twelve to nine to seven miles per hour, while the road ahead curved right, around our line of sight. Instead of hoping like "the little engine that could," I worried that another children's story might apply to our predicament—that some days were like this one, "even in Australia."

Mercifully, Arbie made it to the top of the incline, and a mile or so beyond its crest we located the repair shop. While I negotiated about Arbie's possible diagnosis and the duration of his contingent treatment, Bonnie secured a reservation in a nearby hotel where, minutes later, we checked in. Before we finished freshening up for the hour-plus drive to Salem, we received honest news from Honest-1. Arbie's only problem was that his timing was "way out of whack." Days later as we claimed a refund from the Kennewick repair shop where Arbie had received a tune-up days earlier, we learned that the mechanic there had assumed that Arbie had computerized timing, certainly an impractical inference related to an RV almost twenty years old. Encouraged by the report that we would be able to retrieve Arbie the following morning, we made our way down to Salem in time for the start of the game.

The following morning, with Arbie's engine throbbing evenly as we headed south out of Portland, we believed that our road woes were over; but our confidence was premature. When we stopped for a sandwich lunch at a rest stop near Ashland, Arbie's six-month-old water pump failed. Although we were able to hook up the plumbing systems when we stopped for the night at an RV park in Corning, we were without the customary convenience throughout the day for tap water and toilet flushing.

And the following day, about a hundred miles before we reached my in-laws' home, we encountered Arbie's final problem of the tour. For half an hour or more, we had followed a cement truck down I-5, hugging the right lane and cruising at fifty-five miles per hour. But shortly before our anticipated turn toward the Bay area, the truck blew one of its rear tires, hurling its carcass back towards Arbie's nose. Although it fell short of the windshield by a few feet, Arbie couldn't hurdle the dense carapace, running over it and thrusting it beneath his own torso, thump-thumping before sliding under Toad's tummy. Since Arbie's gauges didn't change and there appeared to be no trail of fluids that I could see in the rearview mirrors, we kept going to the next exit. Pulling off the freeway, I discovered that the bounding hulk had severed the electrical leash between Arbie and Toad.

For four months we had stowed emergency repair tools and replacement supplies—fuses, oils, and various cords. Now within days of completing the tour, I dug through Arbie's storage bins, located the original cord (worn and frayed) that had come with Arbie's purchase, and attached it effectively before resuming our way toward Bonnie's sister's house in the Bay Area. While we boon-docked in their driveway for the evening, her neighbor removed the cabin water pump, dismantled it, and found that it had an uneven spot on its flywheel—or at least that's how I saw and understood the problem. Within an hour he had found the tools to fix it, reinstall it, and make sure that it functioned properly.

A Volcanic Eruption: Game 96 in Salem-Keizer

Back to the game in Salem: Throughout the progress of the tour, I was fascinated by team names, especially their ties to local or regional culture. Intentionally disrupting that connection, I occasionally whiled away my driving hours by playing an imaginary game in which I could ignore geography and cluster teams into "species leagues" based on their names. In that mental game, I aligned the Salem-Keizer Volcanoes (Oregon) team and their explosive name with their seismic cousin, the Rancho Cucamonga Quakes (California), as well as their meteorological kin: the Lake Elsinore Storm (also in Southern California), the New Orleans Zephyrs (Louisiana), and the Brooklyn Cyclones (for whom I was invited to sing, but could not work out the scheduling). To round out this geological league, I added the Huntsville Stars (Alabama) and the Jacksonville Suns (Florida).

In terms of my topological itinerary, Salem-Keizer was the final short-season team on my list, and its stadium proved to be the most accessible and commodious of those in its league. Virtually adjacent to I-5 a few miles north of Salem, the ballpark, while simple in its design and construction, featured a dozen skyboxes with mezzanine seating, an extensive array of box seats, and picnic space above a berm area for blanket seating along the third-baseline. Before the Volcanoes season begins in mid-June each year, the ballpark, which has been lauded by the American Institute of Architects, hosts the Oregon High School baseball championship games.

While the Volcanoes had initially hooked my attention with their seismic signature, my primary attraction to this game was their opponent, the Vancouver Canadians, the only affiliated minor league team north of the border. What that meant for my season of anthem performances was my lone opportunity to double-dip, not by adding the fourth stanza of "The Star-Spangled Banner," which I offered to deliver time and again, but by also singing "O Canada."

Habitually, I sang through the national anthem at least once during my vocal warm-ups prior to each evening's performance. But I had no routine for the Canadian anthem. For days, I had recited its words and hummed its rich tune. I didn't want to deliver an inverted Robert Goulet by forgetting the words to the anthem of his native land. Having rehearsed "O Canada" flawlessly several times on the way to the ballpark, I was still a bit worried about beginning the phrase "the True North strong and free," perhaps because the words seemed heretical to my Mississippi roots.

Focusing more on the words as I took my anthem position behind home plate, I errantly fingered my pitch pipe and began the Canadian anthem a third lower than I had wanted. Although I was distracted by the lower range, I was disappointed only by the fact that the resonance of the final invocation of "O Canada" was not as brilliant as its melodic line highlights. Even so, the words flowed easily.

To make sure that I would start "The Star-Spangled Banner" on a C-sharp, I re-fingered its opening on the pitch pipe and blew softly. As I began to hear the slight delay from outfield speakers, I made a concerted effort not to pause following breaths or to elongate phrase endings, and by the time that I reached the final cadence, I was quite pleased. Nightly, I graded myself on pitch, pace, resonance, and expressiveness, not on audio quality. After experiencing some frustration about the Canadian anthem, I judged my performance of "The Star-Spangled Banner" as at least a "95," one of my best renditions all season.

When I turned from home plate after accenting "the home of the brave," Volcanoes manager Tom Trebelhorn blurted out, "Great job!" Then grinning, he added, "106.8." I must have furrowed my brow with a quizzical look because he beckoned me to follow him into the dugout and pointed to a chart on the wall where the team kept score of the length of anthem performances. I asked how I had fared. While giving me thumbs up, he identified the briefest rendition of the season at fifty-one seconds—a trumpeter's flourish—and the longest drawn out almost twice as long as mine, which made it seem, he said, "longer than a losing streak."

Rarely had I gotten a chance to talk with a manager or player after singing, much less been invited into the dugout for a chance to ask about distinct anthem performances that he had heard. Knowing that Trebelhorn had spent decades in the dugout—in fact, having managed more than 3,000 games in the minors and majors—I asked him if there were memorable anthems that he had heard over the years. Quickly, he identified another drawn-out rendition. At a game in Anaheim some years earlier on postal-service night, he recalled, one of the uniformed letter carriers had sung the anthem, dragging it out so long and pausing between half-phrases in such a way that players turned to each other and started giggling when a fan yelled during one long caesura: "No wonder the mail is so slow!"

By contrast, the comment that I heard from a fan that night had nothing to do with the anthem's pace, simply my diction. "Thanks," the woman said, "for pronouncing the words so that I could understand them."

Like Trebelhorn's career, the life of Volcanoes senior marketing executive Jerry Howard had been circumscribed by baseball. Initially a player and then a coach, Jerry finally shifted to a position behind the plate to umpire in the Pacific Coast League and eventually the Olympics. He had followed up these varied perspectives on the game by serving as a major league scout before accepting the offer to spearhead the Volcanoes small full-time staff, challenging each—including himself—to perform multiple functions in ballpark operations. Following his coordination of pregame activities, he assumed a different role in the middle innings, taking the P.A. microphone and conducting a brief interview with me about the tour, minor league ballparks, and my love of singing the national anthem.

Jerry also took delight in the number of former Volcanoes players who had made it to The Show. In the team's fourteen-year history in Salem-Keizer, sixty-three alumni had made it to the majors, including seven on San Francisco's World Championship team the previous year. Evaluating the players on the field that night, he suggested that a few would likely join the stream of successful former Volcanoes. The most promising were San Francisco's first-round draft pick from St. John's, shortstop Joseph Panik, who collected two hits and two RBIs, worked a walk, and scored a run while raising his league leading average to .349; leadoff hitter and center fielder Jesus Gallindo, who walked twice, stole three bases (increasing his season total to forty), and scored three runs; and catcher Mike Murray, who doubled, walked twice, knocked in two runs (his forty-sixth and forty-seventh), and continued to hit at a .333 clip.

Continuing our practice of trying to connect with family and friends at ballparks, Bonnie and I invited her cousin Stephanie, husband Dan, and their two-year-old son Wesley to drive down from Portland to share the evening with us. Not only was this ballpark the first one visited by Wesley, but it was also Stephanie's first baseball game—ever. Also joining us for the game was David Wheeler, a friend from college days who had in recent years also taught courses in my department at Whittier. Now a pastor in Portland, David had brought with him Earl White, one of his elderly church members who lived in a retirement community near Salem. Convinced that baseball had revitalized him throughout his ninety-five years, Earl tried to attend at least a couple of Volcanoes games each year. I was fortunate that he had chosen this evening since we talked baseball inning after inning.

One of the stories that Earl told was about his baseball relationship with Tom Trebelhorn, both of whom were Portland natives. Although Earl was thirty years Trebelhorn's senior, they had opposed each other on the diamond. When Trebelhorn had been catching for Portland's Cleveland High School team, Earl had coached third base for the visiting Babe Ruth all-star team. "Trebelhorn was so sharp," Earl said, "that he had stolen all my signs by the end of the first inning."

By contrast, in our game the Canadians catcher didn't have a clue about the steal sign being flashed by the Volcanoes third-base coach. By the time that Salem-Keizer had taken a commanding lead and called off its running game, the Volcanoes had stolen five bases and had another nullified by batter's interference without the runner being caught.

Throughout the night, the active mountains in the Cascade Range remained silent during our conversations while the Volcanoes on the field erupted for fifteen hits, bunching them together in four- and five-run scoring outbursts while coasting to a 12-0 shutout of the Canadians.

12.

Final Pitches

Knowing the Way to San Jose: Game 97 in San Jose

One of the final lines in Dionne Warwick's hit song by Burt Bacharach in 1968 asserts that "I've got lots of friends in San Jose." That phrase approximated my experience for the game there. Although few of my friends live in San Jose, I met a score of them and family and alumni there, each certifying by their presence their affirmative response to the song's title: "Do you know the way to San Jose?"

Even though Bonnie and I had rendezvoused with friends in almost half of the ballparks where I had sung, no place proved more magnetic than San Jose. To a certain extent, that could be expected since Bonnie had grown up not far away and since many of her family lived within an hour's drive of the city: brothers and nephews, aunts and nieces, cousins and cousins and cousins. Congregating with them were four of Bonnie's high-school friends, one of my former colleagues, and two good friends who had traveled with us in Arbie for two games in the Northeast. All told, three rows of family and friends found their way to sit with us in the grandstands. I felt overwhelmingly welcomed back to California after trekking through more than forty states.

While San Jose's Municipal Stadium was the oldest California League ballpark that we visited and among the least upgraded facilities that we encountered, it was a favorite, not simply because of the family and friends attending, but because of its charisma. It joined several of the historic public ballparks that made indelible impressions because of design features. The one in Williamsport, Pennsylvania, was particularly nostalgic because of its wobbly wall and its proximity to the primeval Little League site. The setting of the field in Pulaski, Virginia, appeared Edenic in its nestle among the hills of Appalachia; and its stone entry and wide, seat-less tiers along third base invited fans to bring their own chairs for comfort. In Burlington, Vermont, Centennial Field manifest its antique character with head-ducking clearance in the gangway to the grandstand, and with the steep slope of its reserved-seat section accenting the narrow foot space between its rows.

Unlike the aged ballparks that had made charming impressions with quaint, architectural features, San Jose's municipal stadium captivated my interest at almost every turn other than its design. Although the stadium in San Jose lacked the idiosyncratic architectural features of Salem's structure, it visually celebrated baseball's history and culture by integrating art and artifacts throughout the stands. Approaches to the main gate were splashed with Giants insignia and announcements about playoff dates. Inside the ballpark, walls of the undercroft and gangways to the grandstands presented murals of players as well as a rendering of San Jose's popular mascot Gigante, a gorilla created after the San Francisco Giants' first World Series appearance in four decades. I wondered whether there was a relation between Gigante's genus and the fact that Anaheim's "Rally Monkey" had undone San Francisco in Game 6 of the World Series in 2004.

Adjacent to Gigante's likeness, a list of essential data included his birth stats, his current weight at "5,000 bananas," and his history. Gigante's brief bio indicated that his baseball talents had been displayed at an early age when he had played catch with coconuts and batted with bananas. Known for his adroit athleticism, he had been "scouted by the San Francisco Giants organization during the World Baseball Classic and signed to a contract," according to the team's website, before making his professional debut in San Jose.

Like most of the mascots at other ballparks, Gigante could be easily tamed for photographs with young fans, including my great-nieces Maya and Madelyn. Not only had they come to the game with their father, they had tracked our route throughout the summer, marking each stop on a U.S. wall map in their kitchen as we had coursed across the country in Arbie.

Also appealing to children and other lighthearted fans was the game's giveaway that night, a copy of *Captain Underpants and the Wicked Wedgie Woman*, a graphic novel for young readers. And for the youngest fans, on the diaper-changing table in the restroom, a mural of the Flintstones playing baseball enlivened their view.

Fascinating fans of all ages, a wall near the concession stand identified the retired numbers and names of players for the major league Giants, whether in New York or San Francisco. As would be expected, the Willies (Mays and McCovey) along with Juan Marichal and Orlando Cepeda led the West Coast entourage, while the New York era included the numbers of Mel Ott, Bill Terry, Cark Hubbell, and Monte Irvin, as well as the prenumeric names of Christy Mathewson and John McGraw.

Another corridor display recognized favorite Giants broadcasters and symbolically celebrated Bobby Thompson's "shot heard 'round the world" with the simple invocation to "Remember '51," accompanied by a graphic of a ball in flight, rising high and fast to prompt Russ Hodges's ecstatic cry: "The Giants win the pennant! The Giants win the pennant!"

Along vertical surfaces throughout the ballpark, including the restroom walls, murals of players were interspersed with witty baseball quotations and historical data about the California League and baseball in the region. Even Bonnie's hometown of Watsonville near Monterey Bay had temporarily fielded a professional team in the league in the late nineteenth century. In 1898, the final standings of the California State League showed the Sacramento Gilt Edge Brewers winning the title, with the San Jose Prunepickers in sixth place, while the Watsonville Babies had barely crept out of the crib with a woeful 6-13 record.

Further evidence of Watsonville's team was presented on one of the entertaining signs along the looping line to pick up "Turkey Mike" Donlin's barbecue, which Bonnie and I enjoyed thanks to the hospitality of the San Jose Giants. "Turkey Mike" had earned his nickname because of the waddle in his walk and had achieved stardom for the New York Giants during the dead-ball era of the early twentieth century. But prior to his major league days, he had played for San Jose, Santa Cruz, and Watsonville during the 1890s.

The names of other players who had appeared in Municipal Stadium also were listed on a timeline that honored the various teams in San Jose's history: the Owls, Josox, Pirates, Bees, Missions, and Giants. More recent tributes to players in the California League identified all of its former players who had been inducted into the Hall of Fame. Two were unusual because of their multiple years in the league since the pattern for promising players was to move up to Double-A after a single year. The two were elected to Cooperstown for different reasons. A Bay Area native who began his pro career immediately after high school, Dennis Eckersley spent his first two seasons pitching for Reno's Silver Sox before excelling as a starter for Boston, then closer for Oakland; and Sparky Anderson had two stints in the league, initially as an infielder for the Santa Barbara Dodgers in 1953 and then as the manager of the Modesto Reds more than a decade later.

As interesting as the historical representations and charts were, the folk art paintings on the stadium's walls proved to be more alluring. Two framed the main gate. On the left side of the entry, a painting featured a generic nineteenth-century ballplayer within patriotic graphics promoting "The National Pastime," and somewhat oddly, on the right another spotlighted a left-handed Orioles player signing a ball for a front-row fan. The unusual element of the latter portrait was that, in its seventy years of professional baseball, San Jose had been affiliated with the Angels, Red Sox, Royals, Indians, Pirates, A's, Expos, and most recently the Giants, but never the Orioles.

Elsewhere, various paintings depicted famous plays and players. On one surface Willie Mays could be seen making his catch of Vic Wertz's 460-foot drive to deep centerfield in the Polo Grounds during the 1954 World Series. At a different spot was a large painting of Juan Marichal on the cover of a 1962 issue of *Sports Illustrated* celebrating the "Latin conquest of the Major Leagues." Similarly, near the locker-room entry a baseball-card likeness of Roberto Clemente accompanied the table of his stats year by year. Another mural—this one with the title "Welcome to Our Field of Dreams"—revised the fictional history of Shoeless Joe Jackson's return to Iowa by portraying the team of dead old-timers wearing San Jose uniforms. And although the major leagues weren't integrated until Jackie Robinson's debut in 1947, one of the old-timers emerging from the corn rows in the painted scene was African American.

Even in the men's restroom, the wall above the urinals featured a mural of the backs of two ordinary uniformed ballplayers peeing. Between them, a beer ad cleverly promoted its brew with the simple phrase: "Expose yourself to another Lagunitas IPA." And above the captioned mural, one of Harry Caray's quips prompted further laughter: "What does a mama bear on the pill have in common with the World Series? No cubs."

By contrast, in the women's restroom (according to a photo taken by Bonnie at my request), a seductive Humphrey Bogart claimed aphoristic prominence with his statement, "A hotdog at the ballgame beats roast beef at the Ritz." The murals and tributes there were also gender- and space-appropriate. Artwork portrayed players in the All American Girls Professional Baseball League, the lockers of stars Dottie and Sophie, and the names of teams in the former league.

The witticisms of ballplayers and commentators were also inscribed on other passageways throughout the stadium. The multiple adages of Yogi are so oft repeated that they needn't be relisted, while a comical statement by Graig Nettles, now almost a classic, prompted chuckles by several passersby:

"When I was a little boy I wanted to be a baseball player and also join the circus. With the Yankees, I've accomplished both."

Others also provoked smiles and laugher. Tommy Lasorda's comment about the speed of his former catcher: "If Mike Scioscia raced his pregnant wife, he'd finish third." Billy Martin's maxim: "Everything looks nicer when you win. The girls are prettier. The cigars taste better. The trees are greener." And Bob Uecker's wisecrack: "Baseball hasn't forgotten me. I go to a lot of old-timers games and I haven't lost a thing. I sit in the bullpen and I let them throw things at me. Just like old times."

While humor seemed to be the norm for the quotations pitched on the ballpark's walls, several other statements were more inspirational than comical. Gaylord Perry is credited with such devotion to baseball that he bemoaned its "trouble…is that it's not played the year round." And Joe DiMaggio, hardly one to inspire others with his words rather than his bat and glove, is commended for his comment, "There is always some kid who may be seeing me for the first or last time. I owe him my best."

So, too, did I owe the crowd of family and friends my best efforts with the anthem, which ranked as one of my best, not only by my evaluation but also in the estimation of others. One fan called out, "Good job! We grade anthem singers in this section. You get an A+++." Later another man in the concession area congratulated me: "Great job," he said, then added, "The echo was marvelous. When you can hear the echo, too, it's a great job." Did he mean that the resonance of my voice was rich or that, having stood nearby, he actually enjoyed hearing me as well as the rebounding rendition from the outfield speakers?

For part of the pregame ceremonies, Giants marketing manager Juliana Paoli invited me to throw out the first pitch, only the second time that I had been offered such an opportunity. On my previous "first pitch" for the Great Lakes Loons, I had bounced my excited throw over the plate. This time, I followed my friend Don's advice and aimed high. Generally on target, my toss was a bit inside, perhaps foreshadowing the walks that the Giants pitchers would issue. Although not embarrassing, it did not match the stellar quality of my anthem rendition.

When I had seen the starting lineups posted near the ballpark entry, I was pleased to learn that the starting pitcher for the Giants would be Tom Vessella, a Whittier College graduate who had majored in philosophy. When he had completed his degree five years earlier, he had been drafted in the eleventh round by the Astros. In 2011, he had begun the season with the

Richmond Flying Squirrels, the Giants' Double-A affiliate in the Eastern League, and I had looked forward to greeting him there, only to learn in June that he had already been sent to San Jose.

Accompanying Tom and me onto the field for the pregame ceremonies was my former colleague Karen Mendonca. A decade earlier, she had heard me sing in Camden Yards while we and a dozen other academic administrators were attending a conference. On that occasion one of our other friends had accompanied me to the home-plate area to take photographs during my performance. Tonight, however, she enjoyed being the designated shooter. As a token of her appreciation for the game in Baltimore, she had sent me a commemorative piece of folk art—a regulation-size baseball, including seams, carved out of solid walnut. Now part of my collection of baseballs that I have caught, tossed, or had signed, it enjoys prominent placement atop my desk.

Once the game started, Vessella suffered from an inconsistently called strike zone by repeatedly nibbling at the corner of the plate that I had missed during my first pitch and yielding seven "free passes." With men frequently on base, he pitched out of jams in several innings, once picking a runner off second base and twice coaxing ground-ball double plays. Tom's breaking pitch worked well, and his fastball was clocked in the low nineties by the scouts who sat directly in front of us. However, after issuing back-to-back walks to start the fifth inning, he yielded a couple of singles and left the game holding a four-run lead, but needing one more out to qualify for the win.

With former major league all-star Pat Burrell in the Giants lineup while rehabbing before his return to the parent club, I had hoped that the team would provide sufficient support for Tom's outing. Although Burrell collected a single in his four trips to the plate, the hitting star for the evening was Giants center fielder Gary Brown, who led off the game with a home run, followed by two doubles, another home run, and a single while knocking in four—collecting a lucky thirteen total bases.

As outstanding as his performance was, an equally memorable play distinguished the game. In the seventh inning, Stockton's designated hitter Michael Choice lined a ball within a breath of the pitcher's glove and then within a frayed seam of the leaping second-baseman. From behind me, I heard a voice provide one of the best descriptions of the season: "I've heard of a seeing-eye single that escapes a couple of lunging infielders as it bounces between them, but this was a seeing-eye line drive." Still, it wasn't enough offense for the Ports, who fell to the Giants by a final score of 11-5.

Rooting for the Rawhide: Game 98 in Visalia

On the first afternoon that I had begun to contact teams about the prospect of the anthem tour, I developed a kinship with Crash Davis—not by focusing on a year in the minor leagues, but by anticipating the next year's possibilities in Visalia.

In the penultimate scene of *Bull Durham*, Crash Davis returns to Annie's house after swatting a late-season home run in Asheville to set the minor league career record for round-trippers. Worn out by the grueling pace of the season, Crash muses with her about his future—and theirs, he hopes—understanding that baseball, which had brought them together, should be a part of their future. Turning to teary-eyed Annie, he suggests, "Next year, there may be an opening for a player-manager in Visalia."

And so it had been for me. Not the tears, but the anticipation of good possibilities "next year" in Visalia.

In July 2010, I had begun to project the anthem tour by e-mailing teams with a request that they preapprove my online audition and allow me to sing the anthem for one of their games the following season if a date could be worked out. I had projected working on a book on the national anthem and the national pastime, a book that I then conceived quite differently than this one. Within hours after sending the request to Visalia's general manager, he enthusiastically responded, the first team to validate my efforts.

A year later when I finally arrived in the Central Valley's city in the searing heat of August, I found another anomalous connection with Crash, whose supposed career home-run record was 247. Historically, that tally had been superseded by Visalia Hall of Famer Bud Heslet, who initially had signed a minor league contract with the Yankees as an outfielder. After spending fourteen years in the minors, he ended his career as a catcher, like Crash, but with the Visalia Cubs in 1956. That season, he had slugged fifty-one home runs, bringing his career total for round-trippers to 314. His single-season achievement still stands as the record in the California League, along with another season's standard of 172 RBIs that he collected in the same summer. But unlike Crash, Bud never enjoyed tasting a cup of coffee in the major leagues.

Even Heslet's career mark falls short of the minor league record for home runs. Through the years few minor leaguers have clubbed more than

400 homers, with two players in the Mexican League outdistancing others: Hector Espino hit 484 and Andres Mora 444. Stateside, Buzz Arlett, who played most of his career with the Oakland Oaks in the Pacific Coast League and whose single season high was fifty-four with the Baltimore Orioles in the International League, led the way with 432 in the two decades between the World Wars. In 1931, his single year in the major leagues with the Philadelphia Athletics, Arlett added eighteen more home runs to his lifetime total.

Visalia's Recreation Ballpark, which had been built in 1946, effectively blends history and contemporary comfort, thanks in large part to the complete reconstruction and expansion of the facility in 2009. Playing with the team's western identity, the grounds-keeping shed is designed as a barn, and its large doors serve as part of the right-centerfield wall. The western motif also extends to the names of distinct areas of the ballpark. A covered picnic section called the Bullpen Family Deck adjoins the barn, and an open-air pub, located along the third-baseline and protected by a screen from foul balls, is familiarly known as the Snakebite Saloon. Situated below the saloon and the warning track in foul territory is a unique carrel, a "fan dugout" that features a players' bench and a built-in water mister along its upper lip to cool the applauding benchwarmers on scorching days.

The ballpark's sense of history is displayed in various areas with timelines marking team accomplishments, lists of players making it to the major leagues, and bronze plaques honoring inductees into the Visalia Professional Baseball Hall of Fame, which had been founded a few months before my arrival. Among the six former baseball stars initially recognized were Heslet and former major league umpire Doug Harvey, lauded as the first Tulare County resident to have been inducted into Cooperstown.

While many of the team's baseball achievements could be strikingly exhibited, one of the ballpark's great stories eluded visual representation. When the ballpark had opened in 1946, a portion of the grandstands had remained unfinished since the construction crew had run out of paint. Yet a more significant problem that day was presented by the clubhouses. The players from Bakersfield had to dress in their hotel since the Visalia players were actually living in the visiting team clubhouse because of a housing shortage in the community.

By contrast, Bonnie and I faced no housing shortage. A few miles away we had parked Arbie at the childhood home of Andrew Gus, one of my former students whose parents also offered us their air-conditioned guest room to escape the triple-digit heat. Andrew and his wife Atsuko, whose wedding I had officiated a year earlier, were able to join us for the first game of the doubleheader.

Although the ballpark enjoyed multiple upgrades, I couldn't locate its family restroom, a private space where I often did my vocal exercises and practice of the anthem. Few ballparks had provided a private warm-up room for anthem performers, and even fewer had arranged for a rehearsal on the ballpark's sound system, which often meant that the first phrase during the performance would require adjustments with the position of the microphone and increased focus on tempo to block out the echo.

When I failed to find my preferred warm-up space, I typically sought out the most remote men's room where I might avoid much exposure, especially for the dramatic facial exercises that once had prompted a fan to ask me if I were having a heart attack. Although I enjoyed the seclusion of the outlying restroom at Visalia, I almost had a heart attack when a scorpion with tail up-curled charged across the floor toward me! Immediately, I decided that a more public warm-up would work fine, especially since few fans were arriving early on a scorching afternoon, even if it was fan appreciation day, which featured 100 prizes for attendees.

At several ballparks, I had seen the doors to the umpires' room on my way from the undercroft to the field, but in Visalia I noticed that their room took on all the more spiritual character of their diamond omnipotence since their room was labeled in Spanish with quasi-ecclesiastical language: the "Vestuario de los Arbitros," a designation that resembled the vestment quarters for priests, "Vestuario de los Padres." Above these words affixed to the door with athletic tape was the official notice of the duties of the umpires' attendant, who, between games on doubleheader days like this one, would provide a light meal of cold cuts, fruit, or similar fare.

Leading off the fifth inning, Modesto designated hitter Jared Clarke lifted a pop fly behind second base. While Visalia's shortstop and second baseman went back for the ball, center fielder Keon Broxton ran in yelling loudly, "I got it! It got it!" At the last minute, however, he could be heard pleading, "You take it! You take it!" a split second before it glanced off his glove for an error.

Despite the enthusiastic efforts of fans clanging cowbells—like the loud efforts of quintessential Brooklyn fan Hilda Chester who persistently rang her bell in support of the Dodgers—the Rawhide got corralled by two late-inning Nuts rallies and lost 6-5. Even so, Visalia's first-baseman and clean-up hitter Matthew Davidson slugged his seventeenth home run to lead the team (a far cry from Heslet's record a half-century earlier) and collected his 101st RBI with an accompanying double.

Between games, the Rawhide attempted to set a world record of more than fifty simultaneous first pitches between pairs of pitchers and catchers. Despite the raw heat, which shrunk to ninety-three degrees for the start of game two, fifty-four batteries signed up to validate the effort. I thought that I had already seen the record set in consecutive first pitches in Des Moines and Lehigh Valley, where more than a dozen tossed the ceremonial offering. I let the staffers know that even if they failed to set that record that afternoon, they had already set a record by hosting me for the ninety-eighth single-season anthem performance, each in a different ballpark. "That would mean we could come in late to work tomorrow," one beamed.

No Bluffing: Game 99 in Reno

When I finally began the anthem tour in early April, I wouldn't have placed a bet on my chances to sing in Reno. Although I had received initial approval to work with the Aces to set up a date, I had sent unanswered messages to the team in November, January, and February requesting the chance to sing on August 29, an open evening on my itinerary between confirmed appearances in Visalia and Sacramento. Having secured more than 100 commitments from teams as I prepared to leave for the opening anthem swing through Florida, I still wanted to add Reno to my itinerary since my older son, who had lived there for five years, could easily attend the game with some of his friends.

Three days before my season's debut in Florida, I still hoped to play my cards right and sent yet another follow-up e-mail to the Aces.

Again, I received no response.

Until the end of the month. Until I had returned to California to pick up Bonnie and the RV. Until Chris Erskine's feature story about me had run in the *LA Times*. Then I received a message from the Aces asking if I were still available on August 29. Since I hadn't been bluffing about the date, Reno got added late to my route, as well as the major league Dodgers who, also reacting to the piece in the *Times*, offered me a chance to sing following the conclusion of the tour.

On previous trips to "the biggest little city in the world" to visit our son Jared, I had seen Reno's new ballpark, which was within an easy walk of the downtown hotel and casino on the river where Bonnie and I frequently stayed. But each time that we had sauntered past or driven by the ballpark, I had failed to notice the impressive baseball sculpture apparently floating above its main entry, and I had been unaware of the inviting landscaping beyond the outfield fence.

Regularly I looked for artworks incorporated in or adjacent to the ballparks. Sometimes, the area at the main gate had featured statues of local baseball heroes like Judy Johnson in Wilmington or Dave McNally in Billings. Occasionally, steel silhouettes of pitchers and batters graced the grounds as in Albuquerque and Mobile. And rarely, a team's icon was represented in the ballpark's artwork, especially since cities often changed their name or logo when shifting their affiliation with major league teams. Nonetheless, in Lakeland, Florida, where the ballpark had provided the spring-training site for Detroit for more than a half-century, tiger stripes were incorporated into the permanent tilework of the stadium itself. Still, I had not encountered a work of such simplicity and charm as the suspended, open-air baseball with red stitches under which fans could enter Reno's ballpark. And it took on an even more ethereal aura as night descended and its up-lighting intensified its magnetism.

Unlike almost every other team, the Aces required a sound check at 5:30, well before they would open the gates for fans. To minimize the sound delay that I would perceive during the performance, the Aces offered ear-buds that would transmit "real-time" sound. I certainly appreciated the attempts to reduce the echo effect that had typified the transmission at so many ballparks. I began; and the sound check lasted for two phrases before the staffer said, "That's enough." I qualified.

My early scheduled rehearsal on the ballpark's audio system gave me a chance to interact, however briefly, with several of the players who were taking batting practice. One of the Fresno players did a double take when he saw me hand the microphone back to the audio specialist. "The last time I sang for you guys in Iowa," I teased, "you won."

"I remember you," Brandon Crawford nodded, perhaps because the Grizzlies 3-2 victory had come after a pregame deluge in Des Moines, or perhaps because I had sung the anthem in less time than the series of first pitches there.

"Play well," I added, "although I'll be rooting for the home team to win."

When Justin Christian, the Grizzlies starting center fielder, walked by moments later, I mentioned that in the two games where I had seen him play, I had been impressed with his power and speed. In the Grizzlies win at Iowa, he had walked, stolen a base, and eventually doubled in the winning run. Several weeks earlier when he had been playing for the Giants affiliate in Richmond, he had scored four runs, leading off the first inning by reaching on an error and then racing home from second on a sacrifice fly to the centerfield wall. He followed that fleet feat by slamming a home run, collecting a single, and getting a walk, each time scoring another run.

Sure enough, Christian led off the Reno game by working a base on balls, advancing to second on a balk, and then scoring the game's first run on a two-out single, which was followed by another run-scoring single by Crawford. It's too bad that those two players wouldn't superstitiously consider my singing as an omen for their productive games. For the first time for both Crawford and Christian, however, my singing didn't portend their team's win.

Before the game, I also found the Aces hitting coach Rick Burleson, whose son Tyler had attended Whittier for a year before transferring to San Diego State to pursue a major not offered at Whittier. Burleson expressed appreciation for the college, not only for having helped his son to figure out what he wanted to study, but also for its prominent role in the lives of his wife, mother-in-law, and grandmother-in-law, all of whom had graduated from Whittier.

With the long season entering its final two weeks, Burleson began to muse about what might be in store for the next season. After more than forty years on the diamond and in the dugout as player, coach, and manager, he suggested that he might be ready to hang up his spikes. "The weariness of travel mounts," he bemoaned. In a typical way, that morning he had gotten up at four to leave for the Tucson airport for a seven o'clock flight that had backed out of the gate on time. But a mechanical problem had caused a delay in departure, just long enough to disrupt the scheduled connection in Las Vegas. The result: The team had finally arrived in Reno almost eight hours later, barely giving Burleson time to drop off his luggage at his Reno home, grab a sandwich, and drive to the ballpark.

As often as possible in ballparks, I walked the circuit of areas accessible to fans, primarily to experience the sightlines from all of the ballpark's perspectives—like upper decks or skyboxes, grandstand seats obstructed by foul poles, outfield lounge areas with Adirondack chairs, and grassy berms for blanket picnics. Occasionally, I'd discover unusual spaces like the amphitheater beyond centerfield in Fort Wayne, or the centerfield sandbox in Appleton, or the fire pit behind left field in Midland, Michigan.

Behind the knoll beyond the centerfield fence in Reno, a landscaped trail bends through a garden of native plants and river rocks. The path offers fans a chance to stroll beyond the din of the crowd and to sit on a remote bench honoring Clarence "C.J." Jones, who was credited with having brought Triple-A baseball to northern Nevada. There was a tranquil quality about the space: from the bench amid the tall grasses and boulders, it was possible to enjoy the serenity of the deep sky, to hear the burbling of the Truckee River behind the ballpark, to see the colorful lights along the city skyline, and to view the ballgame at a buffered distance, seemingly even more distant than Cubs fans viewing a game from rooftop seats across Waveland Avenue.

As Reno luck might have it, while returning to my seat from my stroll through the outfield path, Candace Jones stopped me to express appreciation for my respectful rendition of the anthem. Her friend—John Masquelier—identified Candace's late husband as the one responsible for having brought the Aces to Reno. When I asked if he were the one honored in the park-like path beyond centerfield, she brightened. And I immediately experienced the joy of sharing the digital picture that I had taken minutes earlier of the memorial plaque on the bench.

Like Candace Jones, Jim Polka, a security officer for the Aces, also commented on the anthem and protocol, indicating that the security staff stops fans from entering the ballpark during the singing of the anthem but that, once they have passed through the turnstiles, it's not possible to enforce patriotic respect. I had perceived as much, particularly when I had heard some jeering during my rise to "the land of the free." Bonnie was also miffed by the disrespect that several fans around her had displayed by continuing to walk and talk during the anthem, certainly a sign of their indifference if not disrespect. Regrettably, we had witnessed similar insensitivity at various ballparks throughout the country. Most memorable were the ballgames in Durham, where young scouts had jostled and mumbled throughout the song on Boy Scout Night, and in Louisville, where a sequence of photos showed fans on blankets beyond the outfield fences continuing to sit and gesture throughout the anthem.

Even with the boisterous disregard that some fans exhibited during "The Star-Spangled Banner," more people in Reno commented favorably on my rendition than at any other ballpark, typified by a security officer along the first-baseline who commented, "What a great job! I'm jealous of your tour."

Although I performed really well for the game in Reno, I didn't trump the Aces, who dealt the Grizzlies a 5-2 defeat behind Cody Ransom's twenty-seventh home run of the year.

Performance Questions: Game 100 in Sacramento

It took my hundredth game to realize one of the projections that Don Musser had voiced during the first days of the tour. While we were driving to the game in Dunedin from his house in DeLand, Don recommended that I prepare a polite statement to decline invitations to sing the anthem or to talk about the tour while en route. He then predicted that assertive fathers in box seats would ask me to sing at their child's Little League game the following day or that various community leaders would ask me to speak at their service club meetings about the anthem or the tour.

The former never happened. The latter had almost occurred in Helena, Montana, when the program chair of a local service club indicated that he wished he had known that I would be in Helena that evening because he would have asked me to speak at noon earlier that day. While he affirmed my performance and admired the tour, he was not really inviting me to sing or speak since the impossibility of his offer had already passed. Around noon that day while his club had listened to their lunchtime speaker, Arbie had been trudging up one of the long mountain grades between Bozeman and Butte.

To receive a request to sing or speak at a civic event in one of the ballpark towns, I waited until my hundredth appearance. Even then, the invitation came from one of Bonnie's college friends, Jim Putnam, who had recently assumed the presidency of his local Kiwanis Club. The only problem with his request was that his club meeting would convene at seven o'clock for breakfast the morning following my appearance in Sacramento.

Unlike the Rogers-and-Hart Broadway musical number "Sing for Your Supper," I wouldn't get breakfast unless I also sang for that meal at "dawn's early light," a phrase with which I was now all too familiar. Despite the long evening and anticipated early rising, I agreed, especially since Jim and his wife Laura, who had been one of Bonnie's suitemates during undergraduate years at UCSB, had invited us to sleep in their comfortable guest room that evening. Also joining us for the game to expand the Gaucho reunion was another of Bonnie's close college friends, Pat Keegan and his wife Gloria, both of whom had entertained us a few nights earlier on our way from Visalia to Reno.

For the second consecutive night—and for only the fourth or fifth time on the tour—the home team required that I arrive at the ballpark early for a sound check. Yet for this trial run, I oddly couldn't gauge the volume or the sound delay. Simply, the sound check was not for my benefit, but for the audio engineers. Since the ballpark gates had opened early and fans had already begun to cluster behind the dugouts seeking autographs and conversations with players, I stood uneasily behind home plate and sang into the microphone, whose transmission could be heard only in the control booth, not on the field through the loudspeakers. But somewhat like the quick response and cutoff that I had gotten the previous night in Reno, the controllers signaled "thumbs up" after only a couple of lines.

At most ballparks moments before I would sing, I had been challenged to make a quick, mental musical shift from hearing heavy metal blare or hip hop wail through a ballpark's sound system. Not only did I need to focus on my starting pitch, I needed to hum and hear the opening triad turn "Oh, say can you see" to make sure that I would establish the right key. During this rehearsal, however, I heard the hard-rock selections blasting throughout the ballpark sound system while I sang a different song in a different key to a microphone whose amplification I could not hear. Now I knew how modern American composer Charles Ives must have felt when his father tuned his musical ear by playing patriotic songs in one key while having Charles sing them in another.

Frequently, the persons who expressed greatest appreciation for my renditions were ushers, perhaps because they heard the anthem every night. In Sacramento, I interacted with them in a different way than I had done when they had commended my diction or had coveted my tour of ballparks. Instead of wearing badges identifying themselves with their given names, the ushers wore pins with the names of favorite famous players: I saw Ken Griffey, Jr., Jackie Robinson, Yogi Berra, and Roger Clemens assist fans to their seats. When I asked the woman wearing Clemens's nametag about her identity, she said that the previous night she had been Mark Maguire. Raising my eyebrows then, I sarcastically inquired if she might have also impersonated Sammy Sosa in pursuit of filling out an all-steroid roster.

When the man wearing the Yogi tag learned that I was to sing the anthem, he asked, "How long?" Then he added, "Last night, a woman butchered it. She stretched it out for more than two minutes, and she messed up the words." I assured him that I'd come in under 1:15 since I had been clocked twice during the month under 1:10 and, for ninety-nine times this season, I had pronounced the words correctly. I succeeded again in Sacramento.

The ballpark's distinct ambiance was colored by its integration of children's art on pillars throughout the concourse. I had enjoyed similar displays of children's art in Huntsville and Richmond, where a few murals had decorated the ramps to reserved seats and the walls on the concourse. More permanent and prominent in their placement in Sacramento, the children's art had been created by hundreds of youngsters who had hand-painted tiles with happy faces of fans, baseball objects or themes, or patriotic symbols.

The feature of so many youthful artistic expressions evinced the River Cats' commitment to arts education in the Sacramento area. Among the works on display was the team's annual promotional calendar, "The Art of Baseball," which featured students' art and which identified the River Cats ballpark gallery with its goal of supporting students' artistic creativity.

In addition to these multiple pieces, one wall also featured a major mural installation by Stephanie Taylor, a work that captures the complex enthusiasm of River Cats fans, young and old. More than mere relief, the mural brings a father and son forward from the crowd by adding ceramic elements to the flat portrayal of the cheering fans and, thus, inviting viewers of the mural to join in the joy of applauding the Sacramento team's success.

The aesthetic experience at the ballpark was further enriched by its grandstand view of the grassy picnic knoll that slopes up beyond the outfield toward a levee of trees along the American River. As dusk sifted the lambent light of August into the cumin glow of sunset, the view of Sacramento's Tower Bridge and the downtown skyline beyond the shaded field fittingly added a serene quality to the sunset of the tour.

Although Sacramento's ballpark excelled with its display of young fans' art and its architectural orientation to the city's dramatic skyline, it missed the strike zone with its placement of the team's "Wall of Fame." Unlike most other ballparks that celebrated their former stars with a *hall* of fame near the main gate or along a well-traveled concourse, Sacramento's tribute to its popular alumni appeared in a peripheral area, in the restricted stairwell leading to the skyboxes for VIP ticketholders.

On the roster of honorees two names jumped out, not those of Barry Zito or Nick Swisher, both of whom eventually became prominent major-leaguers. The two players who aroused my keenest interest were Graham

Koonce and Jose Ortiz because I was unfamiliar with both of them. Ortiz, I learned, had starred at second base and shortstop in the team's initial seasons in the city, one year pacing the team with a .351 batting average and leading the league in hits. During his eighteen professional seasons in the minors, Mexico, and Japan, he compiled a career average of almost .300. Koonce, who lead the River Cats in home runs and RBIs in its first two PCL championship seasons in 2003 and 2004, played in only six major league games, getting a double and striking out a half-dozen times in his few plate appearances before spending his final year in Omaha in 2007.

After the third or fourth inning, I walked through the concourses once again to view the children's art and to talk with fans, many of whom had heard the introduction celebrating my hundredth ballpark anthem performance of the season. For the first time on the tour, someone asked a question about the text of "The Star-Spangled Banner." Rich Bricker posed a grammatical question about the final phrase: "Does a question mark follow 'the brave'?" he asked.

"Which stanza?" I should have retorted, since each of the four stanzas ends with the same full phrase: "O'er the land of the free and the home of the brave."

Rich was curious that the scoreboard had displayed the final lines of the first verse as the end of a question: "o'er the land of the free and the home of the brave?"

While his interest had been roused by punctuation, Rich's question raised deeper issues about the meaning of the text. For Key, who had been detained aboard a British ship during the bombardment of Fort McHenry on the night of September 13, 1814, there was a troublesome question that had lingered throughout the onslaught of the shelling: Would the stars and stripes, which had distinguished the Chesapeake skyline at dusk, still be flying over the fort when morning's light should break? With the first stanza's final interrogative sentence, the anxiety about whether the fort might have fallen during the night remains unresolved.

The second stanza, which recounts Key's view of the flag blowing surely through the morning mist, shifts from the worry of the previous night, to a glorious experience of seeing the flag standing tall as the sun's full rays shone upon it. The syntax of the introduction to this stanza's final line assumes the tone of a plea for "the star-spangled banner—O long may it wave o'er the land of the free and the home of the brave."

The turn of the third stanza is to the reality that "the star-spangled banner in triumph doth wave/O'er the land of the free and the home of the brave." And the climax of the anthem occurs in the repeated line of the fourth stanza. Not only had the flag survived the British attack, but it served as an emblem of assurance that the nation would continue to triumph while the flag "shall wave/O'er the land of the free and the home of the brave."

The genius of Key's poem is its tonal progression through the repetition of the final line in each of the four stanzas, moving from an expression of doubt about the survival of the fort, signified through the position of its flag, to an assertion of hope that the flag shall wave in the triumph of and for freedom because of the brave.

Yet since the anthem's sequence of stanzas is rarely heard with their increasing confidence in the triumph of freedom, I sing the first verse's final line in an affirming way rather than with an air of uncertainty, which is actually how the first stanza ends—with a question mark.

While Rich had questioned the accuracy of the punctuation following "the brave" in the first stanza, I observed an apparent inconsistency in his family's "sartorial punctuation." The attire of his bright-eyed infant boy, who was snuggly strapped to his chest, seemed about as out of place as the British in the Chesapeake Bay. Andrea and Rich were rooting for the Oakland A's Triple-A team while their smiling son sported a San Francisco Giants shirt. When I asked about that contrast, the parents smiled and said that, while they love baseball and support their hometown team in Sacramento, they love the Giants so much that they had honored San Francisco's first World Series Championship by naming their boy Cody after the previous year's World Series star Cody Ross.

In several respects, the Sacramento River Cats were enjoying a season like the Brickers' favorite Giants the year before. With more than two weeks left in the season, Sacramento had already sewn up the PCL South Division championship. And the team featured soon-to-be major league slugger and all-star Josh Donaldson and up-and-coming prospect Jermaine Mitchell, who had clobbered Texas League pitching for more than half a season before being promoted to Triple-A.

This night the River Cats continued their winning ways behind the hitting and base-running of Mitchell, who extended his hitting streak to sixteen games by collecting a bunt single and a double while raising his batting average within a few hits of .300, a mark that he would achieve during the final games of the year. And this night he also stole a base and scored two runs in Sacramento's 5-2 win over Las Vegas.

Baked Before the Blaze: Game 101 in Bakersfield

Because Bonnie and I anticipated driving to Whittier after dark, we arrived for the game in Arbie, only his third appearance at a ballpark all tour, and parked at the far edge of the lot. The empty asphalt field radiated the dry heat and the temperature registered 116 degrees shortly before four o'clock.

When I had begun to design possible routes for the tour, one of the parameters that I had established was to limit driving on game days to 300 miles. This day would be an exception since we desperately wanted to get home, to see our loveable dogs Winston and Tucker, whom we had left fourteen weeks earlier, and to sleep in our own bed. The route from Sacramento to Bakersfield had narrowly remained within the guidelines—296 miles. From Bakersfield to our home following our departure, we faced a three-hour drive, up the steep incline of "the Grapevine" on I-5 before descending to the Los Angeles basin and Whittier.

Although we had connected Sacramento with Bakersfield on a single day for games on consecutive nights, the contrasts between the ballpark experiences in the two cities were more dramatic than the different vocal ranges of a coloratura soprano and a basso profundo in an operatic act.

In Sacramento, Raley Park, whose naming rights had been purchased by the grocery chain, had been built a decade earlier, and it featured scores of luxury suites and fan amenities, including multiple restrooms. Down in Bakersfield, Sam Lynn Ballpark, named after a local supporter of youth baseball who had been instrumental in bringing professional baseball to the city, had been completed seventy years earlier when the California League had been founded, and it had no VIP seating or section, no auxiliary attractions, and single restrooms for men and women. When the ballpark's most recent renovation had taken place a few years earlier, the dugouts had been expanded and the batter's backdrop in centerfield had been improved; but for the most part the stands and concession areas remained austere.

In Sacramento, wide concourses were decorated with various artistic pieces while the Bakersfield ballpark's lone artistic display was a single banner of the team's insignia on the wall beyond the entry gate. In some previous seasons during Bakersfield's affiliation with the Dodgers, banners honoring star alumni had hung behind the grandstand. But after beginning the partnership with the Cincinnati Reds, the ballpark removed the tributes to former major league all-stars Don Drysdale, Pedro Martinez, and Mike Piazza, along with Alex Karros who had won the National League Rookie of the Year award. By contrast, although it was located in a peripheral stairwell, Sacramento's Wall of Fame honored several popular River Cats alumni, including two who were journeyman minor leaguers.

In Sacramento, multiple concession stands presented a full menu of mouth-watering treats, including one station where a chef carved freshly roasted beef for gourmet sandwiches. To make food purchases easier, the ballpark accepted credit cards for payment although the parking fee required cash. In Bakersfield, by contrast, the open-air, sun-seared concession area presented a single transaction window that was open for standard ballpark fare that required cash, although Bakersfield's parking lot was free.

Even though the dimensions of the diamonds were standard in Sacramento and Bakersfield, the distances of their outfield fences varied greatly. In California's capital city, centerfield stretched a respectable 403 feet from home plate. In California's country music capital, however, the depth of centerfield was the shortest in professional baseball, merely 354 feet from the batter's box and only thirty feet farther than the distance down the foul lines.

In Sacramento, the perspective from behind home plate spanned the city's skyline, highlighted by the reflected twilight glow on the twin pillars of Tower Bridge. In Bakersfield, the view from the backstop toward left centerfield was directly toward the setting sun, making Sam Lynn field the only affiliated minor league park to have batters and catchers look directly into the sun. Even with a screen of trees and a mini-monster wall in centerfield, the mitigations for sunset glare proved insufficient. Consequently, games in Bakersfield routinely began later than anywhere else—at eight o'clock on summer evenings—to minimize sun glare and game-time heat.

In Sacramento, an evening breeze across the adjacent American River slaked the heat of the long afternoon, and fans were shielded from the sun under the canopy of the grandstands. Although Bakersfield's ballpark was a similar distance from the Kern River, the still air enveloping the area accentuated the heat while the slumping sun baked the withered seats in every section of the fully exposed stands.

In Sacramento, the lineups featured players who had seasons' experience in the majors and others who were only a phone call and two-hour car ride away from donning a major league uniform, but in Bakersfield few players on the rosters realistically would make it to The Show even for a game or two, although two of the visiting team's players—both of whom figured prominently in their win this evening—would celebrate a September call-up a week or so later.

In Sacramento, the stands had been filled with 10,638 fans, while Bakersfield's crowd was the smallest that I encountered. As I returned to my seat following the anthem, I counted seventy-four fans in the stands, thirteen of whom were connected to Whittier; and by the end of the game—or at the time when the ticket-taker got too bored to stand sentry at the gate—the official attendance had risen to 301.

Yet despite the dramatic differences in ballpark ambiance in Sacramento and Bakersfield, both fields featured a baseball game. That was enough. And at both we enjoyed the company of longtime friends. In Sacramento, we appreciated the chance to reconnect with several of Bonnie's college friends with whom we had visited occasionally since their collegiate years. And in Bakersfield, we celebrated with several members of the Dezember family: Sherrie, who was my former student, and her son Carson; Katie, her sister, with whom I had worked during her days as a Poet; and their parents Joanie and Ray, himself a longtime trustee of the college. More importantly to me, I could call each of them a genuine friend.

Expanding the Whittier contingent was another of my former students, Sherrie Hill, and her daughter Jillian, who a few years earlier had sung the anthem for a Blaze game. Sherrie herself was a longtime supporter of the Bakersfield team, having served as Juan Castro's "Mom" when he had played for the Dodgers' farm team there, in addition to becoming close friends with Pedro Martinez and Mike Piazza. When I asked Jillian what she remembered most about her experience of singing the anthem in front of the baseball crowd, she smiled with relief and said, "Overcoming nervousness!"

An unexpected Whittier reunion also took place when I photographed the visiting team's bullpen. Turning to greet me was Tom Vessella, the Whittier grad who had pitched for the San Jose Giants when I had sung there during the previous week. Having started the night before against Bakersfield, Tom joined the bullpen staff during the early part of the game and told me about the friendly contest that the players have about predicting the length of the anthem rendition and the prospect of flaws by its performers.

After the fourth inning, with the Blaze behind 8-1, our friends had lost interest in the game and we were anxious to get on the road. For the first time following an evening game, we drove Arbie and towed Toad a significant distance—132 miles. At least, we towed the car for most of the way. When we reached the base of the Grapevine ascent from the San Joaquin Valley floor to the Tejon Pass at 4,100 feet, I feared that Arbie might overheat on his last leg. To minimize his temperature, Bonnie and I disconnected Toad and drove up the mountain separately, safely, and more speedily than I had anticipated. Arbie climbed the mountains in second gear at about thirty miles per hour, even passing four trucks trudging up the steep grade in their lowest gears in the slow lane; and when we reached the crest at Frazier Park, we refueled, coffeed, and reattached Toad for the home stretch.

Once we had begun the final descent from Gorman toward the Los Angeles basin, Bonnie said, "You did it. You really did it."

"I never doubted that I could." I don't think that I was arrogant in my immediate response. It's simply that, once it had begun, I never doubted that I could and would do it.

Although now reflecting on the magnitude of the project, I'm amazed that so many people worked in so many ways—scheduling, hosting, repairing, befriending—and in such time-constrained efforts to make the tour not only possible for me, but successful. With Arbie's portion of the tour merely miles from completion, I still faced three more games on the schedule, each requiring afternoon commutes from Whittier in our family car, not Toad.

When we reached home shortly after midnight, we unharnessed Toad, and I parked Arbie while Bonnie preceded me into the house to greet the dogs. I wish that I had a video of her smothering them with affection, and they, in turn, licking her with joy upon arrival. And I wish that I had an audio of the sounds that Winston made when he twirled and twirled and twirled at my prodigalian return, begging me to pick him up while he literally whimpered with delight. Really. He cried—as, probably, did I. Returning home was spectacular, made all the more poignant not because of a greeting crowd with well-wishers but with the deep affection of our two dogs and the batter-long bear hug from Jared, who had cared for our home during our four-month venture.

But a final word about Arbie's final game in Bakersfield: The Blaze barely flickered before falling to the San Jose Giants 10-1. Led by two players who would enjoy September call-ups to the parent Giants a week or so later, San Jose scored a half-dozen runs in the first. After walking to lead off the game, center fielder Gary Brown stole second, his fiftieth of the season, and scored on catcher Hector Sanchez's home run. Both players would defy the Class-A odds, join San Francisco's expanded season-ending roster, and see their first major league experience before the summer's end.

While they perhaps celebrated their lopsided win, I slept in my own bed for the first time in eighteen weeks.

Storm Sounds without a Cloud in the Sky: Game 102 in Lake Elsinore

Arbie retired to the long driveway at our house in Whittier, and I regained the immediate comfort of my own home, especially my bed and the kitchen. I celebrated the freedom to control the expanse of my domestic space and the freedom to forget about RV issues. I gave myself a morning off to walk the dogs, drink coffee on the deck, pore over major league box scores, puzzle through the crossword challenge in the *LA Times*, and catch up on local news before leaving mid-afternoon for Lake Elsinore's ballpark, which was less than a two-hour drive away. After five months on the tour, it was more than refreshing to wake up in my own bed, even if my lovable dogs did jump up to lick me alert earlier than I would have liked.

I luxuriated in the ease and routines of home that naturally seemed to resume, and Bonnie expanded her delight by also taking the afternoon and evening off, staying at home, playing with the dogs, and talking with friends and neighbors about the adventure that we had completed.

Rather than driving to the game alone, I persuaded Jared to go with me. Although I had never sung for the Storm on the field at Lake Elsinore, the tour's game would mark my second time for soloing the anthem in its ballpark. In 1996, the Los Angeles chapter of the Society for American Baseball Research had held one of its meetings in the then-new ballpark, and I had sung the anthem to open the meeting in its Diamond Club, a vaulted, glass-front restaurant near the third-base foul pole.

Frankly, I do not recall the quality of my performance that afternoon, but I do recall two significant things related to the ballpark. One was the tour of the innards of the stadium, during which I learned that the umpire's dressing room and shower area had been required to comply, like the rest of the ballpark, with local, state, and federal building codes. What that meant, in part, was that the showers in the umpires' room had to be constructed in a way that would make them wheelchair accessible. Despite arguments by baseball experts that wheelchair umpires would never be able to perform minimal umpiring duties, the strictures of the building code remained in place and the umpires' shower stall had to be made wheelchair accessible.

More significant was a presentation by Cece Carlucci, "Mr. Ump," a retired PCL umpire who had never missed a game in more than thirty seasons—more than 5,000 consecutive games, top and bottom halves of the frames—never missing a single pitch or play. He reminisced about his consecutive game achievement, which had been the first to beat the streak of the Iron Horse, and far eclipsed even Cal Ripken's remarkable record for consecutive games played that included a few appearances as DH. By contrast, Carlucci had endured the exhaustion of each inning after inning in every one of his games. In 2003, he had been inducted as the first umpire in the Pacific Coast League Hall of Fame. Following our interactions at that Lake Elsinore program, Carlucci agreed to come to Whittier to talk with students about his life and love of the game.

When Jared and I arrived at the ballpark an hour or so before the pregame ceremonies, we circled through the drop-off drive at the main gate where contrasting sculptures signaled the purpose of the stadium. Large concrete baseballs with raised stitches separated the driveway loop from the pedestrian promenade and protected entering fans from the passing cars. Providing an ephemeral, living contrast to the solid cement balls, a new topiary of a left-handed pitcher appeared at the center of the circular drive, striding as though he were on the mound. And at the other end of the walkway another rudimentary topiary stood poised to swing at the lefty's pitch. While the vines had climbed to the waistline of the pitcher, the form of the hitter remained naked since nothing had been planted around it.

Inside the ballpark I made my typical rounds through the grandstands, noting the team's ways to honor previous players and civic leaders, identifying distinct concessions, and observing the placement of advertisements. A single bronze relief recognized the contribution of Pete Lehr, who had donated the property for the field in the early 1990s. Although the ballpark itself was known as The Diamond, the field was officially named for Lehr. In addition to the acclaim accorded to him, the Storm also distinctly honored its alumni who had made it to The Show by framing a twenty-foot-long roster of the names and years when alumni had made their major league debuts. Entitled "Stormin' the Big Leagues," the display also featured action photos of its most prominent former pitcher and hitter, Jake Peavy and Chase Headley.

Like other ballparks, The Diamond also displayed the names and retired numbers of three former players: a major league all-star, pitcher Peavy (#22); a career minor-leaguer, infielder Joe Urso (#7), who spent three seasons with the Storm; and one who never suited up for Lake Elsinore but starred in *Major League*: Charlie Sheen (#99), the actor who played the fictional Ricky "Wild Thing" Vaughn in the film.

Although Sheen had never appeared in person at The Diamond, a bobble-head likeness of him wearing a Storm jersey had been given away for a ballpark promotion almost four months earlier. The publicity stunt, which garnered one of the season's largest crowds of 5,499, featured a controversial "Sheen-co de Mayo" celebration that included the retiring of Sheen/Wild Thing's number "99."

The Storm was innovative in other ways, too. It offered a "Baseball Nut" ice cream, which was simply vanilla ice cream with raspberry swirls (like a baseball's seams) and cashew nuts. The ballpark also scored with an engaging routine when the staff member known as the "in-game entertainer" threw pregame pitches from the mound that were timed on the radar gun and displayed on the scoreboard. Seeing the staffer's fastball, Storm manager Phil Plantier quipped, "With another twenty-four miles per hour on the pitch, you can play."

The Storm stimulated the "Thirsty-Thursday," cheap-beer crowd with entertainment by "live DJs," as they were announced during their introduction. I wondered if it were possible to have dead or comatose DJs? As they played various selections, I figured that "live" was a euphemism for "loud" since their amplified sound could probably have been heard all the way to Temecula a dozen miles away. Their throbbing bass and pounding volume seemed to appeal to the arriving fans but made my preparation for the anthem quite difficult. Where's my starting pitch? Are my first few notes in tune or are they slipping into the key of the song still ringing in my ears?

Adding to the difficulty and frustration of starting the anthem was the briefest of introductions, simply, "Tonight's anthem by Joseph Price." Nothing about the tour, nothing about Whittier College, only the wailing of the last Led Zeppelin number that had ended seconds earlier. Also complicating the start was the sound that rebounded through the ballpark speakers, an echo that was a full beat behind my production—a distracting, dissonant self-canon. Thankfully, my distress was not apparent in the photographs taken by Jared and by my former student Paul Gallagher, a professional photographer on assignment to capture the pregame ceremonies.

Throughout the game, the DJs continued to blast bits and pieces. To provide walk-on music for batters, the DJs often excerpted lines from different songs whose lyrics included the name or personality of the player coming to the plate. And between innings they repeated one song several times, each time as it had been recorded by a different artist. The volume of the DJs' music was so loud that putting my fingers in my ears hardly dulled the decibels. Since I wanted to finish the season without losing my hearing and to preserve whatever sanity I had left, we left during the middle innings with the Inland Empire 66ers leading 3-zip.

Before departing, we were tantalized by one of the in-game promotions, in part because we hadn't eaten dinner. Regrettably, its benefit was restricted to fans in section 102: If a Storm player should hit a double during the game, fans with tickets in section 102 would win a Double Double hamburger from In-and-Out, a popular Southern California burger chain. But if a Storm batter's double would generate a Double Double, wouldn't that really make the promotion a Double Burger cubed? Before getting on the freeway to return home, Jared and I stopped at an In-and-Out near the ballpark—not to order the Double Double, but simply juicy burgers with grilled onions. Munching the burgers and fries while we drove back toward Whittier, we shifted the radio to AM frequency, located the Storm's broadcast, and heard the final innings of the game. What an inverted way to complete the game: In the ballpark we could see but couldn't hear; and now in the car we couldn't see but could hear.

Although the Storm clamored in almost every inning, the hitters took sterile swings with runners in scoring position, going one for thirteen and leaving fourteen men on base. The lone bright spot came in the bottom of the eighth when Eddy Rodriguez and Danny Payne hit back-to-back home runs. For the record, the 66ers prevailed, scoring six runs while limiting the Storm to half that number.

Flying High: Game 103 in Lancaster

It was fitting that Lancaster should be scheduled at the culmination of the tour since it had played such a positive role when preparations for the trip had begun.

Several weeks after I had started to receive preapproval from teams to schedule me during the 2011 season, Bonnie had still been wary about spending more than four months on the road going to ballparks five nights a week. Her local teaching colleagues and her online group of friends had expressed a bit of envy about the opportunity to see so many cities and states, not to mention the impressive landscape between. Yet she remained unconvinced by her friends and uncommitted to the tour.

That is, until she read a witty piece in the *LA Times* about the entertaining atmosphere at a minor league game in Lancaster. As one of his occasional sports fan's columns, Chris Erskine profiled a JetHawks game that featured affordable tickets and cheap concessions, fans' proximity to the field and possible interactions with players, and crowd participation in middle-of-the-inning contests—all shaping an entertaining atmosphere. Charmed, then, by the notion that the ballparks could also be fun, Bonnie agreed to join me on the trek, especially if we could make the journey in an RV that wouldn't require nightly lifting of luggage and shifting from one hotel to another.

Recognizing the tangential, personal significance that Lancaster had played in getting Bonnie to join me for the tour, I had targeted Lancaster as one of the last games while hoping to complete the tour with the 66ers as a symbolic gesture to the great American highway and its historic and iconic significance for road trips. It would also be fitting to fly high at the end of the trip: How better might that be signified than with a game in the high desert, and for a team known for its aerospace name as a tribute to the Air Force base nearby?

Now in our home with two games remaining, we spent the morning relaxing before beginning the hundred-mile drive to the JetHawks ballpark on the Friday afternoon of Labor Day weekend. When we arrived at Clear Channel Stadium, as "the Hangar" was formally known, we found for the first time a parking lot shaded by awnings to support rows and rows of solar panels angled toward the south and west. The only other ballpark where we had seen any solar panels positioned had been in Midland, Michigan, where the Loons had installed a plot of panels beyond the south-facing outfield wall.

Inside Lancaster's ballpark we also discovered an unusual sports promotion, not for youth baseball or softball teams, but for a semi-pro football game a few days later. Wearing their unmistakable football jerseys, players from both teams passed out invitations and tickets to their games. At adjacent tables members of the JetHawks Flight Crew Boosters Club hawked treats and sold restored bats to support the baseball players, and they offered autographed baseballs to help sponsor the Antelope Valley Little League.

The JetHawks Hall of Fame also manifested a couple of distinguishing features: Not only were four of the original team owners in the first class of inductees, but also Jim Gilley, who had been Lancaster's city manager at the time that the team had formed. Altogether, thirty honorees had been selected for the honor in less than a decade, by far the largest and most inclusive group of any ballpark for such a short period of time. In addition to these local Hall of Famers, Lancaster's roster of former players who had made it to the major leagues included nine alumni who had made their initial big-league appearances during the previous year.

Elsewhere in the ballpark, signage about fan behavior and attentiveness revealed a keen wit. Warning fans about the hazards of balls hit into the stands, one read, "Watch for foul balls...they don't compliment ketchup and mustard very well on top of your hot dog"—never mind the confusion between the homophones "compliment" (meaning praise) and "complement" (suggesting supplement). Another sign similarly urged fans to "watch for foul balls [since] they can create a mess if they hit your soda."

Before moving to home plate for the anthem, I stood adjacent to the dugout and saw JetHawks manager Tom Spencer flip the elastic band around a couple of pages of a little black book like mine. I asked about his and, from my hip pocket, pulled out my little Moleskine. In his book, he kept game notes about players, matchups, and tactics. In mine, I recorded game notes, information about connections with friends and fans, and the statistics related to—if not the tactical results of—the games and travel.

Following my rendition, I made notes about my performance. For the second night in a row I was introduced by name only and faced the fans, not the flag waving beyond the centerfield fence. As frustrating as the lack of mention of the tour or Whittier College had been at most of the ballparks where that omission had occurred, it was even more frustrating when I was within the easy recruiting range for prospective Whittier students or, more likely, encounters with Poet alumni. Although I was flying high as I reached the final games of the tour, I felt a bit low because of the frequent indifference shown to national anthem performers. Often more recognition and enthusiasm had been accorded to the multiple participants in first-pitch ceremonies.

Not all of anthem performances rated at the top. I graded myself on every one, and the lowest grade had been B+/A-. This one, which I sang in G rather than a half step lower in F-sharp, suffered as usual from moderate delay in amplification. And I scored this one with one of my lowest marks because I took a couple of catch breaths, nothing that might distract most fans, but also nothing like the longer phrases that I normally executed to emphasize the continuity and meaning of the poetic lines. On only one other occasion had I failed to make it through the uninterrupted power of "the bombs bursting in air, gave proof through the night that our flag was still there." The meaning is not merely the spectacle of fireworks, of bombs bursting in air, but that their explosion illuminated the flag, evincing the survival of the young nation.

After I sang, I again walked past the JetHawks dugout where hitting coach Darryl Robinson stepped up said, "That was real good," and handed me a ball, the fifth one that I had been offered during the season. But like the others in the ballpark, he didn't know that this game had been my 103rd, almost as many renditions as he had heard all season.

While singing, I had seen two uniformed EMT staffers standing behind home plate, saluting, and singing along. In the second inning I sought them out and thanked them for joining in. One asked the other if he really had sung. Both claimed that they did—because, as they put it, "they felt it." When they expressed appreciation, a woman in the row behind them supplemented their enthusiastic response with the kind of compliment that I heard most often: "It's lovely to hear it sung the way it's written, without all that warbling."

For the most part, the pace of the game proved antithetical to the speed of either jets or hawks. While the Storm committed three errors, both teams combined for ten walks and twenty-one strikeouts. After seven innings Lancaster had scored the game's lone run on a middle-inning double play. Finally in the eighth the Storm stirred things up. After Lancaster's pitcher Jose Cisnero turned in his season-best performance, yielding no runs and striking out ten in seven innings, his pitching coach Travis Driscoll was suddenly ejected from the game by the home-plate umpire amid Lake Elsinore's skinny rally that produced the tying run on a sacrifice fly following a questionable walk that had loaded the bases. Apparently, Driscoll complained too often or too loudly about the ump's strike zone or his inconsistent vision of it.

Finally, in the ninth, a little action took place on the field. The Storm's second-baseman Jake Blackwood led off with a home run to nudge Lake Elsinore to a 2-1 victory.

Ending on a High Note: Game 104 in Inland Empire

Known simply and famously as Route 66, the highway angling from Chicago to Los Angeles was completed shortly before Ruth's record-making season in 1927. During the following decade it would wend its way into American hope by directing Okies from the opaque swirls of the Dust Bowl toward the fruitful fields of California. A few years later the road would secure a more playful place in the nation's lore by providing the central image for Nat King Cole's hit recording of "(Get Your Kicks on) Route 66." And the highway would continue to provide romantic images of adventure well into the 1960s with the television series featuring Buzz, Tod, and his new Corvette in their cross-country road trip. Had the highway been completed, or even surveyed, a century earlier, I imagine that Horace Greeley would have recommended tattooing its emblem on the biceps of newsboys in New York: "Go west, young man. Go west—on Route 66."

Now forsaken by freeway travelers quickly pursuing distant destinations, Route 66 serves mostly as a nostalgic image or a relic of crumbled concrete. Almost a year before I had set out on the series of anthem performances, I had projected possible routes for the anthem venture, targeting the Inland Empire 66ers as the ideal final stop for the road trip since their name captures the spirit of the asphalt rope of hope. The 66ers make their home in San Bernardino, where the ballpark sits a home run's distance away from the historic route.

Although most of the road trip guides, historical reviews, and coffee-table picture books about cafes, motels, and tourist attractions along Route 66 envision a journey beginning in Chicago and ending in Los Angeles, Bonnie and I reversed this flow on our only intersections with the highway. We began our cross-country drive in Arbie in late April by tracing the route from Los Angeles through Rancho Cucamonga, Victorville, and Barstow, before leaving its path to head to Las Vegas. Picking up the highway's course again near Flagstaff, we generally followed its channel upstream through Albuquerque and Amarillo, before turning south and abandoning it. Even when we later left Chicago and headed west, we missed its origin by taking a more northerly route than its initial southwesterly direction.

Again at our journey's end, we headed east along the highway. While tired Arbie and Toad recuperated in our driveway in Whittier, I guided our SUV along a short segment of Route 66 from Pasadena to San Bernardino, again reversing the normal flow, paying tribute to the route's symbolic significance before turning toward Arrowhead Ballpark to complete the summer's singing and driving. Certainly, I was getting my kicks by ending with Route 66.

Through a coincidence of scheduling, it was also fitting that on this night the 66ers featured an end-the-season promotion providing the first thousand entrants with a bobble-head Angel-gnome. After bouncing in Arbie across pocked and furrowed highways for thousands and thousands of miles, I easily identified with the jiggle-necked figure offered by the 66ers. While to most fans he mimicked an angelic, mythic elf, he not only resembled my road-jostled frame, but his smiling face looked like my own elated expression after coaxing Arbie to finish the twice-crossed continental journey.

More than an hour before the start of the 66ers game on the next-to-last day of their season, fans extended the line to enter the ballpark for more than a block. Standing among the faithful 66er fans were several of my friends, family, and former students. Having arrived before us, my sister Liz and her husband Pat eased back in line to join Bonnie, me, and our two sons Jared and David.

Minutes later as the line began to move when the gates opened, Whittier colleagues Charles Adams and Mike McBride also stepped into the queue. They had been supportive throughout the planning stages of the tour; they had regularly read my blog entries about the ballparks, games, and travel; and they had personalized their participation even more by joining Bonnie and me for out-of-state games along the way: Mike in Fishkill, New York, and Charles in Everett, Washington. Now, in the final stretch of the marathon, they came to bat for me once again. Being able to share the love and lore of baseball with good friends was one of the immediate and enduring joys of the venture.

While most of the fans who entered the ballpark received the bobble-head gnome, one special young fan named Kyle, who had been cognitively disabled by a stroke at birth, received a baseball-bat lamp for his devotion throughout the season. Kyle's love of baseball and the lamp-maker's gift provided a fitting emblem for the completion of the tour. Transformed from a broken bat into a source of light, the homemade souvenir provided an exemplary tribute to the health and hope that baseball can bring to its fans.

After passing through the turnstiles and getting the bobble-head figurine, I found friend and fellow traveler Missy Alden in the concession area. In fact, she scored the most states and games where she had joined us along the way. After she and her husband Jerry had hosted Bonnie and me for games in two states during our East Coast swing, they had also attended a couple of games near their home in Northern California during the final fortnight of the tour—games in San Jose and Sacramento. Now she had flown to Southern California to celebrate the last anthem game with us.

Not only had Missy been an enthusiastic supporter of the tour, she certainly exhibited the fervor of a zealous baseball fan. In recent years she had watched her two sons compete on their high-school teams, and she had attended hundreds of Oakland A's games near her home. Whatever the league or level of play, she routinely keeps score of the games she attends. She understands: She roots for her team, the home team, or the team with some personal allure. And thankfully, she cheers for me singing the anthem.

The concession area where we encountered Missy certainly seemed to be a prime gathering spot. There I also ran into former student and blog-subscriber Miheal Herrera, who, with his teenage daughter Cassidy, had lettered signs to welcome us home. Earlier in the summer he had let me know that he and his family had secured front-row box-seat tickets for the game. Now prepared with other signs to hold up as though the game would be featured on ESPN's "Baseball Tonight," he challenged me to end the anthem tour on a high note by starting my rendition on an E-flat—a full tone higher than my most frequent key of F-sharp. Although I later disappointed Miheal by singing the anthem in my most comfortable key, he did record my performance and post it on YouTube.

With so many friends and family joining us for the game, I was tempted to forego my routine warm-up exercises to enjoy spending more time with them on the glorious late-summer evening. Yet I also wanted to make sure that I could shine for my final minor league performance. As usual, I sought out the quietest, most private place in the ballpark—the family restroom. Throughout the summer, I typically found that the best place to warm up in the ballparks was in the family or handicapped restroom, a space usually without speakers blaring the pregame music and announcements. With sounds muffled in the sequestered room, I could do the physical and vocal exercises that might prove distressing or alarming to casual passersby, as had happened in a couple of ballparks where secluded spaces had been inaccessible.

Near the corridor from the concourse to the third-base seats, I entered the family restroom, locked the door, faced the mirror, and began the odd contortions and tongue-wagging that loosen facial muscles. Moments later, I started to vocalize braying sounds, focusing on my naso-pharynx resonance. Suddenly, the restroom door opened while I was making ugly sounds. A startled young woman looked at me and started to shut the door. Both of us were flustered. Thinking that she might need the privacy afforded by the single-toilet room, I explained my efforts in preparation for singing the anthem, and I let her know that, apparently, the lock on the door didn't work.

Since she looked somewhat desperate, I offered to leave the room and stand guard by the door with its malfunctioning lock.

Meanwhile, on the field batting practice concluded, the batters' boxes and foul lines got limed, and the infield got dragged and wetted to settle the dust. The pregame ceremonies were ready to begin. Lineups were read with a sense of excitement, first pitches were tossed as though they had meaning, and I stepped to the area between home plate and the backstop. Silhouetted against the dusky sky, the San Gabriel Mountains glowed at sunset as though they knew that I was completing the journey.

With an elaborate identification of my project and its conclusion, I was introduced to sing the anthem. I stood ready, hummed the C-sharp that I had blown a second earlier on my pitch pipe, and began to sing with an unusual sense of fulfillment and release. When I got to the line "o'er the land of the free," I smiled wider than the length of Route 66, I think, all the while thinking to myself, "I am, I am, I am. I am free from the travel on the road."

As I had requested, the 66ers P.A. announcer had featured my affiliation with Whittier College in the introduction. In response to the mention of Whittier, Chuck Perkins approached me and proudly said that his mother had gone to the college and that he had pictures and memorabilia from the 1940s related to her work in Broadoaks, Whittier's "lab school" for early childhood education. Shortly after he spoke with me, former student Marcie Holmer brought me a batch of double-fudge nut brownies. By providing these treats at the end of the project, Marcie effectively sanctioned the journey as sweet since she had also given me a box of baseball-iced cookies at my first game of the season in the L.A. area.

Finally, I moved to the row where my family was seated. Incredibly, in the seats immediately in front of Bonnie sat Jim Henderson, the dean of arts and sciences at Cal State L.A. Years earlier we had been colleagues as Fellows for the American Council on Education. Then he had joined several other ACE Fellows (including Karen Mendonca who had attended my game in San Jose) to accompany me when I had sung for the Baltimore Orioles in Camden Yards in 1998. Now with thousands fewer in these stands, he sat smiling as we reminisced about baseball, education, and life.

While I moved from one set of friends and family to another in the stands behind home plate, the game slipped past uneventfully, neither team scoring off the starting pitchers or middle relievers. Even so, the game featured an amazingly high moment. In the third inning, my older son Jared chased down a foul ball that had flown into the concession area.

During my trek across the diamonds of America, I had been almost hit by foul balls in several stadiums. I had retrieved one in New Orleans and handed it to a young boy. I had tossed out first pitches in Midland and San Jose. And I had been given balls by the managers and coaches. But no ball from the summer brought me more joy than this scuffed ball, which my son had scrambled to retrieve as a journey-ending gift.

After eight innings of shutout ball, the visiting Ports started the ninth with a single, a sacrifice, and an intentional base on balls. Then center fielder Michael Choice greeted the new relief pitcher with his thirtieth home run of the year, swinging Stockton to a 3-0 win.

Although the home team lost the last game on my tour, the 66ers made the postseason playoffs, which began a few days later. And me? I finished the tour on Route 66, fulfilling my dream of seeing and singing for more than 100 ballgames in ballparks throughout America. While I might not have sung my final anthem in the higher key as Mihael had urged, I ended the tour on the highest note with family, friends, and a foul ball.

13.

The Box Score and Post Games Report

The 28,712-mile journey ended, but its experience continues daily.

The season of memories—of ballparks everywhere, of riveting plays and energetic players almost every night, of rendezvous with current colleagues and former classmates each week, of serendipitous encounters with Whittier alumni and ex-patriot Southern Californians in unexpected places, and of enthusiastic encounters with devoted and vocal fans in almost every park—regularly refreshes my loves for baseball, America, and friends.

Friends were so crucial for the success of the tour: two gave us a great deal on Arbie and Toad; others encouraged us during formative stages; some donated funds; and many hosted us along the way. Yet during and following the tour, friends often appeared flummoxed as they fumbled to start a conversation about the magnum opus of road trips. Usually, they would begin by asking the seemingly easy question, "What was your favorite ballpark?"

Typically, I countered with a question: "Favorite in what way? Location, architecture, food, fans, acoustics, the game?"

The truth is that *none* was a "favorite." The entirety of the trip—all 104 ballparks and the travel in between—constituted my favorite experience.

Like most significant pilgrimages, the anthem tour became most meaningful not simply because I reached my goal of successfully singing in so many ballparks, but because of the complications—weather disruptions, audio difficulties, scheduling changes, indifferent introductions, traffic clogs, automotive failures, RV-park deficiencies—that I had to deal with along the way.

There were rain delays in Durham and Appleton and elsewhere—almost everywhere throughout July and August—and even a shower with a residual rainbow in otherwise arid Casper. There were floods along the Mississippi caused by its breached levees that we bypassed, and there were floods on the baseball fields in Charleston, State College, Appleton, and Des Moines that could not drown delayed evenings of baseball. There were rain postponements of games—and thereby anthem cancellations for me—for games in Potomac and New Britain. There were tornadoes that we escaped around Tulsa, near Joplin, and in northern Kentucky, while we followed the paths of their springtime destruction in Alabama, North Carolina, and Massachusetts. And seemingly everywhere, record heat beat upon us and adhesive humidity clung to us.

There were acoustical problems in Dunedin, Music City, and a score of other places where my voice rebounded through outmoded amplification systems as distinctly as a double off the wall. And at Williamsport, where the mike had accidentally been muted, I sang easily and joyfully without amplification.

There were schedule glitches and conflicts that I encountered with the late notification of my cancellation in Northwest Arkansas and contested schedules in Casper and Tri-Cities, Washington. And without warning, in Omaha, where I had re-contacted the team the day before my appearance, the start of the game had been moved forward.

There were traffic snarls that extended for miles in San Antonio, Birmingham, and Gwinnett, each threatening to prevent my arrival for pregame festivities. There were mechanical problems with Arbie in Texas (the generator); Virginia (the alternator); Massachusetts (the levelers); Chicago (the bushings); Omaha (the awning); Idaho (the manifold); Tri-Cities, Washington (the timing); and California (the water pump). And there were all sorts of automotive problems with Toad: a bumpy ride for hundreds of miles from beveled tires that resulted from having dragged the car in tow for almost a quarter-mile in Mississippi; overheating because of a faulty coolant fan in Massachusetts; and failure to start because of a dead battery, electrical shorts, and a cracked radiator in Idaho.

Adding to these transportation difficulties were several other bizarre problems. After encountering so many delays in the excessive heat in the gridlock on the backroads to reach Gwinnett, Bonnie and I checked into a Hampton Inn a few miles from the ballpark. The Friday-night stay was so comfortable that we opted to stay on Saturday, wash clothes, get the car washed, and celebrate a free day since we could complete the short drive to Asheville on Sunday in time for the game's late-afternoon start. The problem arose on Sunday morning after breakfast. When we returned to our room to retrieve our luggage and check out, we discovered that we were locked out of our own room by a malfunction of the security bar that had slipped to a closed position when I had shut the door. Even the special hasp key that the hotel manager used in such rare circumstances proved ineffective. After a half-hour of struggling to try to get the tool to work, the manager handed me bolt cutters to clip the iron latch. Freed to enter our room, we retrieved our belongings, boarded Arbie, and headed northeast on I-85 for Asheville, where we encamped for the night at a tranquil RV site adjacent to the French Broad River.

Like the peaceful RV park in Asheville, we found serene sites with excellent hookups in several other private parks—notably in Poplar Bluff, Missouri; Lynchburg, Virginia; Woodbridge, Pennsylvania; Randolph, New York; Lansing, Michigan; Scotts Bluff, Nebraska; and Caldwell, Idaho—and in county parks in Charlotte, North Carolina, and throughout the state of Iowa. Even so, we often found it difficult to locate available space in parks with desirable facilities, like adequate Wi-Fi access and laundry equipment. And in Springdale, Arkansas, and Hubbard, Ohio, the accommodations proved to be pathetic. In Springdale, I had needed to remove four dead birds from our gravel site before we could anchor Arbie. There, too, the park's single-stall restroom required purchase of a key for use, only to find that there was no toilet paper provided. The manager insisted that its absence prevented its likely theft. There, too, a sign on the inside door read: "Do not use corn cobs. They clog the toilet." And in Hubbard, the men's bathroom was so disgusting that I waited to get to the ballpark in Niles to use the restroom. Who would have imagined that a ballpark's facilities would be cleaner than those in a private RV camp?!

An unexpected, more natural problem bugged me in the Southeast. At Savannah, where the Sand Gnats host their home games, gnats had pestered me during pregame warm-ups and even buzzed near my open mouth during longer phrases of the anthem. Although I cringed while watching a couple of the bugs buzz near my face, I swallowed none. And in Visalia, a scorpion had run across the floor toward me while I had been warming up in one of the remote men's restrooms.

Yet more frustrating than any of these temporary occasions of annoying pests, uncomfortable weather, scheduling conflicts, and automotive ails was the recurrent apathy to the national anthem by fans who ignored protocol and chattered during its rendition, and by various ballpark staffers who often celebrated and honored persons throwing out the first pitch while perfunctorily dealing with the anthem and its performer.

Despite all of these passing difficulties, the joyful memories of the journey—of America, of baseball, and of friends—far outweigh the disappointing situations.

Routinely I recall my discoveries of natural beauty while driving along a stretch of the Susquehanna River between Williamsport and Harrisburg, or slaloming adjacent to the Willimantic River north of Norwich, or sitting on a deck above the Flint River in Huntsville, or following the flow of the North Platte River while angling upstream beside its course toward Chimney Rock. The sight of free-flowing waterways, cool and uncluttered by boats and barges, repeatedly soothed my soul after hours and hours of turgid traffic atop broiling asphalt highways.

The inviting crossings of the Appalachian Trail that we intersected several times called to mind the wondrous experience of Bill Bryson in his wilderness account *A Walk in the Woods*. While the verticality of the Rockies and the Cascade Range certainly challenged Arbie, their raw height fed my spirit, and the dense brilliance of the night sky in Montana seemed to stretch beyond desire. From sea to shining sea, America's natural splendor enchanted and enriched our travel.

Almost daily, I continue to think about the minor league ballparks—their impressive settings, their historic significance, their energizing architecture, and their embrace of art, especially the unscripted dramas of their play. Whether open to expansive pastures in remote locations or held closely among tall buildings in the hearts of cities, the sites of ballparks often reflected the temper of the communities where they were situated. The Smoky Mountains cradled Asheville's cozy field, and a stretch of Blue Ridge Mountains in southwestern Virginia framed the ballparks in Salem and Pulaski with unrivaled beauty and simplicity. The orientation of centerfield in Albuquerque and Corpus Christi seamlessly blended the ballpark structure with the landscape. The sunsets in Lynchburg and Fort Wayne were challenged by the rainbows' ends beyond right-field fences in Casper and Billings, where their dreamy fields suggested that their baseball parks might hide the proverbial pot of gold. The city skyscapes in Memphis and Sacramento lent an urban energy to their ballparks' spacious outfields. And the crown of stadium lights in the deep dark of night in Midland, Texas, and Scranton/Wilkes-Barre created auras for stark stadia whose reverential character evoked a requiem's serene coda.

While I continue to visualize the vivid settings of dozens and more stadiums, I also marvel at the architectural innovations and historical significance of others. Among the older ballparks, I recall the rich resonance of Daytona's facility with Jackie Robinson, whose recognition was immediate and memorable because of the various interactive displays featuring his athleticism. Savannah's huge veranda fans rotated slowly to cool the air and dispel the nasty gnats. Williamsport's wobbly old wall behind the third-base seats was as charming as the low viaduct in the gangway to the stands in Burlington, Vermont. There, too, the steep pitch and narrowness of the rows were unlike any other park's section of seats, as were the wide tiers for lawn chairs in Pulaski's grandstand. And San Jose's municipal ballpark celebrated its quaint character with murals of bygone players, lists of league standings throughout the century, and quotes related to the great game itself.

In light of the success of Camden Yards as a retro ballpark, a number of the newer minor league parks throughout the country have tried to capture the distinct character of their communities by introducing quirky elements related to local history and style. In Durham, the giant bull that had branded its legendary stadium was replicated at the new Durham Bulls Athletic Park, where it entertained fans as well as diners in the Tobacco Road Sports Café whose patio above the left-field fence provided bleacher views of the game. Similarly, in Manchester, New Hampshire, the terrace of the Hilton Garden Inn beyond the outfield fence enabled outdoor diners to see the Fisher Cats games. Even though these ballparks adjoin facilities whose perch invites views of the field, the new ballparks in Columbus and Fort Wayne incorporated mixed-use pavilions into their design to provide fans with rooftop views above outfield restaurants. And in Frisco, Texas, separate edifices stood tall behind the stands to provide large private parties with luxurious hosting accommodations and balcony views.

Also lending to the definition of almost every ballpark were memorials and halls and walls of fame. Especially noteworthy was the row of plaques honoring major league scouts in Fort Myers and Hudson Valley and Hall of Fame umpire Doug Harvey in Visalia. I also appreciated the tributes to otherwise unsung players, staffers, fans, and civic leaders: to slugger Brian Dopirak in Lansing, where the inaugural class of hall of famers included a former first-baseman with no major league appearances; to beer man David Cheatham in Nashville, where the grandstands displayed a brief paean to his decades of gregarious service; to longtime season ticket holder Fred Ziegler in Hagerstown, where his customary Section C was renamed as "Section Z"; and to local businessman Calvin Falwell in Lynchburg, whose team designed a bobble-head to commemorate his leadership in saving Minor League Baseball for the city.

Whether or not architectural elements or historical references distinguished ballparks, the integration of artistic works into the baseball campuses—the parking lots, the approaches to the entries, the concourses beneath grandstands and along walkway walls leading to seating sections—often enhanced fans' baseball experience. In Albuquerque, dynamic sculptures of batters and pitchers achieved their energetic character by the artist's circular positioning of multiple plates of the same image to create the illusion of motion in a swing or a pitch. A dynamic effect was also realized in Clearwater by the lasso swirls of a sculpted left-hander's delivery. In simpler ways, but provoking equal aesthetic and baseball engagement, the representation of balls, bats, and gloves demarcated old and new ballpark spaces. In Asheville an oversized Louisville Slugger stretched from the concourse to the roof above the grandstands. In Lehigh Valley, a bat the size that Paul Bunyan might have swung leaned near the doorway to the executive offices, and at the entry to Coca-Cola Park, an image of a baseball—almost as large as an infield—was displayed in the white-and-red cement. Similarly, in New Hampshire an inlay of contrasting bricks provided a baseball apse in the garden between an outfield gate and the parking lot. Oversized sculptures of baseballs also greeted fans along the walkways to the ballparks in Albuquerque and Lexington, where its piece invited autographs by fans. And in Reno, an open-air sculpture of a baseball, seams intact, graced the ballpark entry where its lighting at night lent it an ethereal glow.

Embracing baseball sculpture in a slightly different way, the ballparks in Pawtucket and Louisville featured colossal gloves that enticed children to climb up the thumb and slide down into the pocket for a PawSox putout, or in Louisville, to invite fans of any age to sit and rest.

A different piece of baseball equipment inspired interactive sculptures at the ballparks in Missoula and in Midland, Texas. There, huge replicas of home plate helped to direct fans from the parking lots toward the parks' main gates and, eventually, home plate.

While sculptures of players and paraphernalia were featured in many stadiums, Frontier Field in Rochester exhibited three works that were noteworthy. One that might be expected was a gigantic sculpture of a red-winged bird—the team's emblem—wearing a Rochester batting helmet. To a certain extent, the representation of the logo echoed the appropriateness of mascot art displayed in Lakeland, Florida. There, mosaic tiger stripes along the walls surrounding the ticket windows reflected the identity of the team in the Florida State League and its longstanding affiliation with the Detroit Tigers, who conduct spring training at the facility.

Another of Rochester's pieces could be appreciated for its simplicity and history, a stone boulder with the number "8" cleanly carved in its face.

The piece honors Cal Ripken, who—wearing #8—had starred for Rochester during his final minor league season in 1981, and who became a rock in setting the major league record for consecutive games played. Inside the main gate, the third sculpture—"Horsehide"—invited strokes from fans as they entered the ballpark. The unique nag looked well-loved because of its medium: hundreds of game-used baseball gloves.

Some of the most stimulating artworks in ballparks were paintings and murals oriented to or contributed by young fans. Attracting the attention of children in Huntsville, a playful mural of a frog playing ball promoted the Autism Society of Alabama. For babies and tots, the walls above the diaper-changing station in the family restroom in Hudson Valley captured their attention with a team of raccoons in the infield. Art created by children was featured in Richmond where multiple banners depicted Nutzy, the Flying Squirrels mascot. A more permanent exhibit of children's art appeared on pillars along Sacramento stadium's concourse, where a gallery of hand-painted tiles by youthful artists fused baseball images and patriotic themes.

In many respects, art became a significant secondary theme for the tour. Since Bonnie is not really a baseball fan, we targeted extended breaks for her in areas near art museums where, in years past, she had spent inspiring afternoons on repeated occasions: the National Gallery of Art in Washington, D.C., and the Art Institute of Chicago. What we had not anticipated was the fortuitous timing of our stay in Philadelphia, where we were able to tour the Impressionist exhibits at the Barnes Foundation two days before its permanent closure in its original location. Nor had we expected to enjoy spontaneous visits to the National Quilt Museum in Paducah, Kentucky, where we were stunned by the range of stitchery and design in historic and contemporary quilts on display; or to the Huntsville Museum of Art, where the collection of photographs by Weston evoked the earthy character of *Leaves of Grass*.

Even though tours through art museums provided us with a change of pace from the more permanent exhibits at ballparks, we enjoyed true baseball art again and again, night after night, when we witnessed live theater on the fields—not only with the unpredictable play of the games, but also with choreographed activities, ludic entertainments, and varied promotional appearances.

In the ballparks, several promotions and entertainments were outlandish. In Tulsa, the natural feature of an armadillo race between innings couldn't be topped. In Lowell, Massachusetts, between the games of a doubleheader, David Smith, "The Human Cannonball," became the first human home run when he was shot out of a cannon, over the right-field wall, and into a trapeze net. In Louisville and Fort Wayne, BirdZerk thrilled the crowd with dancing antics and a little butt of scatological humor. In Jacksonville, the game itself was sandwiched between an Easter egg hunt that enticed hundreds of children to search for the golden egg, not a golden baseball, and the animal theater provided by Whiplash, the Cowboy Monkey, that saddled a border collie to herd goats toward the visitors' dugout. In State College, Trenton, and Casper, "Bark in the Park" festivities encouraged fans to bring their dogs—on leashes—to the games.

And so many ballparks offered unusual concessions, some as regional specialties like the boiled peanuts in Charleston, Rocky Mountain oysters in Missoula, and Idaho nachos in Boise, where potato chips pinch hit for tortilla strips. Other places sweetened downhome favorites like Savannah's chicken and waffles with syrup, State College's cheeseburger served on a glazed donut bun, and Lansing's presentation of a fried bologna sandwich on a buttered waffle bun. With a different twist in Louisville, the deli featured a gluten-free, fried bologna sandwich by using the greasy sausage slices to enwrap grilled onions. By contrast, the gluten-heavy fried calamari with a side of arancini in Rochester could slow down a base-stealer faster than a throw from the Red Wings catcher. And among desserts, few could challenge the sweetness of the biscuits and jelly in Montgomery, the deep-fried Oreos in Gwinnett, or the larger and sweeter fried moon pies in Asheville.

While most ballparks appealed to fans' quirky tastes with distinct entrees and treats, local and ethnic restaurants often lured Bonnie and me for a postgame meal. Since she did not enjoy spending a full evening at a ballpark, we occasionally sought the shared fun of dining in more intimate and savory restaurants after leaving the game. We also scouted out quaint delis and gourmet bistros for lunches and dinners on days off. For many of these Yelp-aided ventures, she kept detailed notes to share with her friends on Facebook, and I regularly e-mailed reports of my entrées to Don. The restaurants and their regional fare often provided windows into local culture that, otherwise, we could not have sampled in so few hours. Among our favorite meals and restaurants during our eighteen weeks on the road were these: omelets made with Hatch chilies at the Owl Café in Albuquerque; the Slavic offerings including skunk pies at the Czech Café in West, Texas; an incredibly rich and dark gumbo at the Pujo St. Café in St. Charles, Louisiana; shrimp and grits at the Flying Fish in Memphis; the hickory-smoked barbecue at Starnes in Paducah; the chowder at Iggy's Doughboy and Chowdah House in Warwick, Rhode Island; the fresh pies and cinnamon rolls at the Yesterday Calf-A in Dell, Montana; and the varied curries with eggplant at Montiras Thai in The Dalles, Oregon. Restaurant ambiance also often reflected quirks of local history, like the uneven, loose floorboards in Josephine St. Café in San Antonio where the dining room was built around a huge tree, and the historic fireplace with a view of the harbor at the Captain Dan Packer Inne in Mystic, Connecticut.

As much as I enjoyed the foods that distinguished each place, the nightly promotions and mid-inning entertainments, the multifarious new ballparks in big cities and the quainter historic facilities in small towns, and the landscapes all across America, it was the people that made the journey so enjoyable, so meaningful: family, friends, alumni, fans, ballpark staff, players, and managers—the people of baseball.

When I had begun to project the route of the tour, we had planned scores of visits with family and friends in multiple places: family in Nashville, Gwinnett, Indianapolis, and San Jose; college friends in Lexington, Louisville, San Jose, and Sacramento; current and former colleagues in Clearwater, Daytona, Frisco, Mahoning Valley, Kane County, Cedar Rapids, and San Bernardino; former students in Las Vegas, Albuquerque, New Orleans, Lexington, and Pawtucket. In addition to those arranged encounters with alumni, relatives, and friends, we serendipitously met college alumni and former Whittier residents in Victorville, Asheville, Rochester, Wilmington, Cedar Rapids, Boise, and Everett. Most often, our unexpected encounters were stimulated by the mention of Whittier College during my introduction.

In several ballparks, I enjoyed interacting with players, coaches, and managers. In Pulaski, most of the Mariners rookie team mingled with fans and me near the grandstands before the start of the game. Other players occasionally engaged me in conversation from their seats in the bullpen, like visiting reliever Dan Jenkins in Mississippi who talked about Whittier College, its academic programs, its athletic mascot, and my challenges for scholarly publications; or from the dugout where, most notably, Bryce Harper congratulated me for my respectful, crisp rendition with a home-run handshake; or in a concession area where visiting starting pitcher Jason Adam razzed me in Beloit; or, incredibly, after the anthem on the pitcher's mound itself where Cole Cook in Eastlake shook hands with me and expressed delight about his Whittier connections through his brother, a Poet alumnus.

Pregame conversations with coaches in Corpus Christi, Billings, and Idaho Falls—and with managers in Mississippi, Midland, and Salem-Kaiser—were certainly stimulating and reassuring.

However brief and perfunctory, my opportunities for engaging them were occasioned by my singing of the national anthem, which I nightly loved to perform. Despite my frustrations about slights during introductions, I thrilled to sing "The Star-Spangled Banner" as Americans' anthem of freedom.

At a number of ballparks I also enjoyed speaking with first-pitchers, whether one among a score and more at Richmond, Lehigh Valley, and Des Moines, or more personally with Alisa Smith (a distant relative of Francis Scott Key) in Mobile, Governor Peter Shumlin in Vermont, and former all-stars Chipper Jones in DeLand and Tony Oliva in Des Moines.

Yet while I was gratified by the affirming comments and conversations with baseball's insiders who sit in the dugout, I derived even more sustained delight from fans, hearing a single loud follower of the Tigers cheer repeatedly in Lakeland or listening to the gaggle of rooters in Lynchburg heckle the umpires. They represented the heart of baseball. I also appreciated watching children fall in love with their evenings at ballparks while they played Wiffle ball in Salem and Omaha, tossed hardballs in Kannapolis and Beloit, climbed rock walls in Fort Wayne and Round Rock, rolled down outfield berms in Victorville and Bowling Green and elsewhere, dug in the centerfield sandbox in Wisconsin, or simply adapted handrails to use as sliding bars or jungle gyms in Tennessee and Idaho Falls.

Even though a number of ballpark staff members had not been made aware of or seemed to care about my project or the anthem itself, several general managers and game-day staffers in Tampa, Jacksonville, Huntsville, State College, Norwich, Great Lakes, and Tri-Cities, Washington, provided enthusiastic, informed support of me personally, featuring my performance on their websites, as well as expressing appreciation for the magnitude of the project. And twice they invited me to toss out a first pitch and twice to sing "God Bless America" about the "land that I love" during the seventh-inning stretch.

Now when folks ask, "What was your favorite ballpark?" I think about the possible expanse of fair territory stretching from sea to shining sea between the foul poles on every outfield fence.

So I reply, "My favorite field was America."

Acknowledgments

Without the support of Whittier College, family, and dozens of friends, the anthem tour would not have been possible. By approving my sabbatical leave for the anthem project, Whittier College provided me with the opportunity to undertake the venture. Because the endeavor required the extensive use of family resources, Bonnie's expansive support from the beginning was essential. Her daily assistance and encouragement were vital: her tolerance of my demanding schedule, her ongoing expressions of appreciation for my singing throughout the tour, and her facile work on her iPad and iPhone for troubleshooting alternate routes, locating repair shops for Arbie and Toad, and finding delectable places for us to eat. And during long rides in Arbie and Toad, her own voice softened the difficulties of travel when she read aloud various books by Bill Bryson, Charles Kuralt, Mark Schweizer, and Spencer Quinn, among others. Also essential was the care of our house and dogs, Winston and Tucker, by our older son, Jared, who relieved any worries that we might have about how things were on the home front while we were gone.

In addition to the numerous friends and colleagues who hosted us in various ways throughout the journey, several benefactors contributed financial support: Don and Ruth Musser, Jerry Fiddler and Missy Alden, Larry Blakeslee, and Ellen and Aaron Hathaway. For their confidence and camaraderie, I am incredibly grateful. Many of the names of friends and alumni who entertained us along the way appear throughout the narrative, and several of their pictures appear in the collage in the section of photographs.

Musically, I am indebted to the coaching preparation provided by Mike Stevens, member of the LA Opera and department chair of the vocal faculty at the Colburn School. I also appreciate the friendship with Helen and Jeanette Kelly, who sold us Arbie and Toad, and for the creative work of Heather Lybarger, who designed the anthem tour logo that repeatedly helped to generate stimulating interactions with fans, ballpark staff, travelers, and RV dwellers.

Without the assistance of more than a hundred general managers who preapproved my video audition, the project would never have moved beyond the stage of being a wacky idea. And for many of their staff, who subsequently worked to schedule dates that would accommodate my travel needs and to make most of the ballpark encounters so engaging, I express my deep appreciation.

Finally, I am grateful for the creative vision and efforts of the editorial team at Mercer University Press, whose director, Marc Jolley, provided cogent counsel during the final phases of the project, and whose own baseball memoir, *Safe at Home*, presents a model for blending the fascination with baseball, the devotion to family, and the exercise of faith.

Supplemental Sources and Recommended Reading

In preparation for my journey through the minor leagues and during my writing about the adventure, I read several league histories, journalistic accounts about players and games, and travel narratives, a few of which specifically featured ballparks and the minor leagues. Among the league histories that proved most engaging were two by Bill O'Neal, *The Pacific Coast League 1903–1988* and *The Texas League 1888–1987: A Century of Baseball*; and Jim L. Sumner, *Separating the Men from the Boys: The First Half-Century of the Carolina League.*

For profiles of players and analyses of teams and games, I found several works to be stimulating: Dirk Hayhurst, *The Bullpen Gospels: Major League Dreams of a Minor League Veteran*; S. L. Price, *Heart of the Game: Life, Death, and Mercy in Minor League America*; Dan Barry, *Bottom of the 33rd: Hope, Redemption, and Baseball's Longest Game*; Paul Hemphill, *The Heart of the Game: The Education of a Minor-League Ballplayer*; and Neil J. Sullivan, *The Minors: The Struggles and the Triumph of Baseball's Poor Relation from 1876 to the Present* (published in 1990).

Baseball travel narratives and vacation guides also intensified my anticipation about the tour: Tom Stanton, *The Road to Cooperstown: A Father, Two Sons, and the Journey of a Lifetime*; David Lamb, *Stolen Season: A Journey through America and Baseball's Minor Leagues*; Ernest J. Green, *Diamonds of Dixie: Travels through the Southern Minor Leagues*; Chris Epting, *Roadside Baseball: Uncovering Hidden Treasures from Our National Pastime*; and Bruce Adams and Margaret Engel, *Ballpark Vacations: Great Family Trips to Minor League and Classic Major League Baseball Parks Across America.* And among creative travel narratives unrelated to baseball, I found inspiration in John Steinbeck, *Travels with Charley*; William Least Heat Moon, *Blue Highways*; Charles Kuralt, *A Life on the Road*; and Bill Bryson, *A Walk in the Woods.*

Among reference works, a few books fetched my attention time and again. Especially on occasions when access to Wi-Fi was limited, I repeatedly consulted the *Baseball America Directory 2011* for information about ballpark locations and team staff. For introductions to older ballparks and for background information about earlier fields in cities with newer stadia, I often turned to Michael Benson's *Ballparks of North America: A Comprehen-*

sive Historical Reference to Baseball Grounds, Yards and Stadiums, 1945 to Present (published in 1989) and Michael Gershman's *Diamonds: The Evolution of the Ballpark*. And for clarification of and background about baseball terms and figures of speech, I found the third edition of *The Dickson Baseball Dictionary* by Paul Dickson to be indispensable.

In addition to these books, several online sources have been invaluable. On team websites linked to www.MiLB.com, extensive information was available about rosters, ballparks, and game reports. Players' statistics and brief biographical profiles were retrieved on www.baseball-reference.com. Articles about ballpark cities, team histories, regional cultures, and eclectic topics were often accessed on Wikipedia, which then lead to multiple works and sites for elaboration. And throughout my journey and the years of writing and revising this book since the completion of the anthem tour, Ben Hill's blog "Ben's Biz" on the MiLB website kept me informed and smiling about minor-league life and play.

Ballparks and Games